DEFENSE SENSE

DEFENSE SENSE:
The Search
For A Rational
Military Policy

Congressman Ronald V. Dellums
with
R.H. (Max) Miller and H. Lee Halterman

Edited by Patrick O'Heffernan

BALLINGER PUBLISHING COMPANY
Cambridge, Massachusetts
A Subsidiary of Harper & Row, Publishers, Inc.

Copyright © 1983 by Ballinger Publishing Company. All rights reserved. No part of this publication may be reproduced, stored in a retrieval system, or transmitted in any form or by any means, electronic, mechanical, photocopy, recording or otherwise, without the prior written consent of the publisher.

International Standard Book Number: 0-88410-942-9 (c)
0-88410-957-7 (p)

Library of Congress Catalog Card Number: 83-11796

Printed in the United States of America

Library of Congress Cataloging in Publication Data

Dellums, Ronald V., 1935-
   Defense sense, the search for a rational military policy.

   Testimony from Congressional hearings conducted by Rep. Ronald V. Dellums.
   Bibliography: p.
   Includes index.
   1. United States—Military policy—Addresses, essays, lectures. I. Miller, R. H. II. Halterman, H. Lee III. Heffernan, Patrick. IV. Title.
UA23.D444   1983   355′.0355′73   83-11796
ISBN 0-88410-942-9
ISBN 0-88410-957-7 (pbk.)

DEDICATED TO THE MEMORY
OF THE LATE
REV. DR. MARTIN LUTHER KING, JR.
AND TO
ALL OUR CHILDREN—

IN THE EFFORT
TO FULFILL HIS DREAMS
AND
TO GIVE THEM
A BETTER
AND
MORE PEACEFUL
WORLD

CONTENTS

EDITOR'S PREFACE

THE BOOK YOU are holding is unique in its scope, approach, the vision it presents, and its usefulness to readers. As a comprehensive examination of all aspects of American military policy and power it provides a thorough examination of the impact of defense programs and budgets on international relations and America's domestic well-being. But it goes beyond analysis to explore the moral issues inextricably intertwined with the use of force in international relations, a challenge untouched by other authors. Moreover, the diversity of writers, viewpoints, and descriptions it offers allows the reader to mine its pages for a variety of uses.

DEFENSE SENSE presents a sensible alternative to the present uncontrolled and dangerous pattern of American military spending by offering a coherent and consistent view of America's adequate defense needs and the impact military spending has on the domestic economy and employment. But it has also been organized to serve other needs and uses. It is a flow of logic and history based on Representative Dellums's thirteen years as a Member of Congress and over a decade on the Armed Services Committee. Readers can follow this flow by reading the volume from beginning to end to trace the progression of thinking presented by Dellums and the book's contributors to build an alternative vision of American defense policy.

Readers are also able to skip to particular sections of the book, since each of its five parts asks a direct question of American defense policy.

The contributions in each section approach the question from a different prespective but form a self-contained unit—allowing each part to be read alone and used by itself independent of other parts of the book.

Readers may also find that the variety of contributors allows them to pick and choose topics within each section. In this way, DEFENSE SENSE can be used as a reference on U.S. military policy and budgeting. The index can be a useful tool for this, as will the organization of the Table of Contents. Scholars who use the book this way can also take the question posed at the begining of each section as an hypothesis and skip to particular writers for different approaches to its answer. Advocates of change in U.S. military policy can do the same, posing a question and then choosing those writers who best suit their speaking or writing needs for factual information, quotes, and arguments.

However, two sections of the book are indispensible, the *Prologue* and the final chapter, *Peace is More Than The Absence of War.* In the *Prologue,* Representative Dellums develops the historical understanding of what led America to rely on military power to such an extent that it risks war internationally and economic collapse domestically to perpetuate its power. In the final chapter, Dellums presents an alternative budget and structure of the U.S. military establishment that serves America's legitimate defense, while defining a more humane and moral role for America in the world and for military power as part of the domestic fabric of our society. These two sections of the book can be used as a tight argument for drastic change in American military policy and power.

However you use this book, you will find that it can help accomplish the goal set out before us by Einstein as he reflected on his creation, the atomic bomb, the need to change the way we think.

Patrick O'Heffernan
June, 1983
Washington D.C.

ACKNOWLEDGMENTS

EVERY BOOK PROJECT, from inception to completion, is a collaborative effort, something that has been especially true in this instance. The collegial nature of my relationship to my district and Washington staff reflects their intelligence, creativity, and commitment. Their efforts to contribute to the development of a just and peaceful society are enhanced by the rigorous, informed analysis and judgment they bring to complex foreign and domestic issues in the contemporary world. Their individual and collective contribution to this book cannot be measured.

These hearings and a book format were first proposed by Max Miller in an extended series of discussions. The perceived goal was to educate a broader spectrum of the Congress and American society to the alternative ways of viewing the world, which can then lead to more constructive policies and legislation to implement these policy changes. Various staff members in Washington and the 8th Congressional District played key roles in the in-house policy debates and the final drafting of an alternative military budget. In alphabetical order, they include Bob Brauer, Marilyn Elrod, Dan Lindheim, Max Miller, Brian Mitchell, Carlottia Scott, and George Withers. Leslie Webb spent long hours typing an earlier, and much longer, draft of the manuscript.

I especially appreciate the courage and tenacity of those congressional colleagues who joined me during those six days of hearings. Their participation made the hearings—and this book—better in every respect. I extend my thanks to Anthony Beilenson of California, Jonathan Bingham of New York, John Conyers and George Crockett of Michigan, Mervyn Dymally of California, William Gray of Pennsylvania, Robert Kastenmeier of Wisconsin, Patricia Schroeder of Colorado, and Jim Weaver of Oregon. My dear friend and colleague, the late Phil Burton, also lent his presence and insight to these proceedings. Even though he was suffering painfully from the cancer that finally killed him, Ben Rosenthal of New York made a special effort to attend. I will always remember with appreciation his courage, humor, and intellectual integrity during that time.

Although he was unable to attend the hearings because of the press of congressional business, I also want to thank George Miller of California, who took the Floor of the House in a much appreciated effort to support the alternative budget that was the product of these hearings.

A special word of thanks is also due to those witnesses whose time, effort, commitment, and intellectual rigor contributed so much to the breadth and depth of these hearings but whose testimony, solely for reasons of space, was unable to be included in this book. They included: Professor Norman Birnbaum of the Georgetown University Law Center; Willie Brown, Speaker of the California State Assembly; Professor Owen Chamberlain, Nobel Laureate in Physics at the University of California, Berkeley; Professors Bogdan Denitch, Frances Fox Piven and A.W. Singham of the City University of New York; Ms. Randy Forsberg, executive director of the Institute For Disarmament; Professor John Lewis Gaddis of Ohio University; Jerome Grossman of the Council for a Livable World; Reverend Alan McCoy, O.F.M., Superior of the Religious Orders of Catholic Men; William D. Strong of the World Peace Tax Fund; Professors Frank Von Hippel and Barbara Levi of Princeton University; Andrew Young, Mayor of the City of Atlanta, Georgia; and Professor Howard Zinn of Boston University.

Special thanks is also due to the Pacifica Radio Network, which broadcast the entire six days of hearings. Helen Kennedy in the Los Angeles bureau of Pacifica made every effort to maximize network and affiliate coverage, while reporter Askia Muhammad and engineer Ken Mason went far beyond the call of duty in putting the hearings on the air. I also thank National Public Radio for making their satellite distribution facilities available to us, thereby making the hearings available to many millions more listeners. I also want to express my personal appreciation to Arthur Jones and *The National Catholic Reporter*. His extended coverage of all the hearings gave us a reading audience in this country, Latin America, and Europe that would otherwise have been denied because of the repeated failure of the national media in this country to cover the hearings.

Max Miller and Lee Halterman are largely responsible for the work of putting the book together. Through diligence, creativity, and knowledge of the subject matter they conceived and organized this book. Special recognition must be paid to Patrick O'Heffernan, whose editorial advice and judgment made this a better book than it might otherwise have been. Jennae Wallach, Roberta Brooks-Halterman, and Barry Hyams also gave portions of the manuscript a careful review at a critical juncture and made valuable suggestions. I also want to thank Carol Franco and Steven Cramer at Ballinger Publishing Company in Cambridge for their encouragement, patience, and constructive cooperation.

Finally, a special word of thanks to the people of the 8th Congressional District. You first sent me to the Congress in 1971 to fight for peace and justice, and you have renewed your confidence in me six times over. I hope this book is a reflection of your faith in me—and of my love and concern for you and the beliefs that you sent me to Washington to uphold.

Ronald V. Dellums
Washington, D.C.
April 1983

INTRODUCTION

SINCE 1945, AMERICAN foreign and military policies have been predicated on the central theme of preserving the "national security" of the United States. With the passage of time, the purported "national security" interests of the United States have assumed global dimensions. Both Democratic and Republican administrations have repeatedly sought, through covert or overt intervention, military solutions to international problems that are essentially political, economic, social, or cultural in origin.

This "national security" phobia has fueled the evolution of a permanent war economy that has made the United States, because of its superior technology, the principal force in global arms escalation, both nuclear and conventional. In fiscal year 1984, the Reagan administration has asked for an arms budget of some $280 billion, as part of a five-year (fiscal years 1982-86) military spending projection of $1.6 trillion, which, because of cost overruns and expected supplemental appropriations, has already been projected to reach $2.3 trillion. A recent study by the Congressional Budget Office indicates that, at present growth/inflation rates, we may well be spending $422 billion a year on the military by 1987.

When he was Secretary of Defense in the Kennedy administration, Robert S. McNamara defined deterrence as the capacity to destroy 30 percent of the Soviet society's population and 70 percent of its economic infrastructure. He felt this objective could be achieved through the use of approximately 400 strategic nuclear warheads. In January 1983, when the 98th Congress convened, the United States possessed more than 10,000 strategic warheads in its nuclear arsenal, plus 15,000 more of intermediate range for theater nuclear use. Given that there are fewer than 900 cities and towns in the U.S.S.R. with a population of 25,000 or more people, America's nuclear arsenal is the embodiment of "overkill," with enough nuclear warheads to destroy each city ten times.

The dimensions of disaster being plotted by the Reagan administration almost defy any rational analysis, as Robert Scheer discovered while interviewing President Reagan and his staff for the book *With Enough Shovels: Reagan, Bush and Nuclear War.* The Reagan administration has consciously and deliberately moved beyond the strategy of deterrence to one that proposes to fight, survive, and "win" a nuclear war. The latest example of this strategy, occurring just before we submitted the manuscript to the publisher, was President Reagan's March 23, 1983 speech formally and aggressively ushering in a public quest for space-warfare technology.

The Reagan administration is committed to developing nuclear weapons that go beyond our capacity to verify or control. In past years the necessity for verifiability and control has been an integral element of *all* arms control agreements and negotiations. The development of first-strike nuclear weapons such as the MX missile, the Pershing II missile, the Trident II (D-5) missile, and ground-, sea-, and air-launched Cruise missiles ushers us into a new era of the nuclear arms race, one that drastically reduces the prospects for a meaningful nuclear arms freeze and subsequent mutual, balanced force reductions of both nuclear and conventional weapons.

It was in this context that in January of 1982 I mounted a comprehensive legislative challenge to the policy assumptions and spending priorities of the Pentagon and the White House. Two days after the President's State of the Union message, I formally petitioned the Chair of the House Armed Services Committee to expand the committee's hearings on the military budget, in order to examine a broader spectrum of policy issues and economic factors relating to the military budget. The committee informed me that it had deadlines to meet and could not afford the time.

In response, I decided to convene the Special Congressional Ad Hoc Hearings on the Full Implications of the Military Budget. After raising the necessary funds from various peace groups, which also ensured the broadcast of the hearings on the Pacifica Radio Network, my staff and I invited more than forty expert witnesses to testify.

For six days, a number of concerned congressional colleagues and I conducted an in-depth examination of the military budget from the perspectives of its foreign policy and national security implications, escalation versus disarmament, its economic implications, its moral implications, citizen responsibilities in challenging the military budget, and the impact of global arms sales.

After studying more than 1,800 pages of transcript testimony, my staff and I then met with defense analysts and budget experts to draft a comprehensive alternative military budget. After Congressional Budget Office verification of the accuracy of our dollar figures and program projections, the budget was introduced in Congress. The peace community, in and out of the Congress, was surprised when, in an unprecedented ruling, the House Rules Committee designated our bill as the official substitute for the House Armed Services Committee bill.

Thus, on Tuesday, July 20, 1982, for the first time in the history of the Cold War, the U.S. Congress debated a comprehensive legislative alternative to the Pentagon's budget request. During the course of the extended debate, I argued for a military budget based on the policies of nonintervention, nuclear and conventional arms reductions, a mutual reduction of forces by both superpowers and their NATO and Warsaw Pact allies, and a rejection of the doctrine of nuclear superiority in favor of nuclear sufficiency. I proposed the total elimination of all crisis-destabilizing nuclear weapons systems, such as the MX missile, the Pershing II missile, all sea- and ground-launched Cruise missiles, the Trident II (D-5) missile, and neutron weapons. I also proposed the elimination of chemical warfare weapons, and such obsolete or useless conventional weapons systems as the B-1B Bomber, the M-1 tank, the two nuclear carriers proposed in the fiscal year 1983 Defense Department authorization bill, the Aegis missile cruiser program, and the retrofitted battleships.

Few people are aware that the research, development, production, and deployment of our current and proposed nuclear arsenal comprise less than 25 percent of the overall military budget. The remainder is for conventional forces, maintenance, overhead, and personnel costs. Accordingly, I proposed an initial 5 percent reduction in all U.S. military personnel as a first step toward mutual troop reductions. To reduce further the possibility of U.S. intervention in the Third World, I also proposed the total elimination of the Rapid Deployment Force and the incremental reduction of the U.S. Navy fleet to approximately 400 vessels (the Reagan administration has proposed that the surface fleet be increased to 640 vessels).

This alternative proposal would have reduced the Pentagon's budget authority by more than $50 billion in the first year alone. More important, it set the stage for continued cuts in nuclear and conventional weapon systems and in personnel, while establishing stringent over-sight controls for waste, fraud, and abuse. Within three years, such cuts and controls could reduce the annual federal deficit by more than 60 percent, without any lessening of America's national security.

Even though it was defeated, its opponents treated it as a serious challenge to the status quo. Many of those who opposed it did so in statements of rebuttal drafted with the direct assistance of the Penta-gon and the Armed Services Committee staff. They know that they have not seen the last of it because I have vowed to continue introduc-ing updated versions of this proposal every year until the madness of the arms race is halted and then reversed.

This book is the product of those hearings. The witnesses who tes-tified ranged from eminent foreign policy and arms control experts and retired military officers to doctors, economists, and other professional, church, and union leaders. Together, their testimony documents and dramatizes with scholarly and professional authority three important messages. First, the United States is endangering the planet by moving to a nuclear war-fighting posture. Second, our nation's foreign policy is archaic and dangerous and in critical need of constructive reassessment to meet the real challenges of the modern world. Third, the United States needs to reorder its national priorities to eliminate the causes of war and bring an end to our current economic dislocation. It is my hope that this book, and the alternatives it poses for the Congress, can lead us to that goal.

Understandably, we have had to condense the original 1,800 pages of testimony. The witness list has also been rearranged so that the book may present a more coherent picture for readers. Eliminating or edit-ing witness statements and testimony was fraught with difficult choices. We have endeavored, though, to capture the spirit, the intensity, the integrity, and the power of the entire six days of hearings.

The book is composed of a prologue and six parts. The first five parts are taken from witness presentations and colloquies. For each of these parts, I have composed a brief introduction as a "road-map" for the reader. The concluding part is my own analysis of where we have been, where we are, and where we must go if we are to build a just, peaceful, and secure world for our children, their children, and countless genera-tions to come.

Prologue

SANITY AND SURVIVAL IN THE NUCLEAR AGE

I

IN ACCEPTING THE Nobel Peace Prize in Oslo, Norway, in December of 1964, Dr. Martin Luther King, Jr. spoke of the "need to overcome oppression and violence without resorting to violence and oppression." He went on to say: "I refuse to accept the notion that nation after nation must spiral down a militaristic stairway into the Hell of thermonuclear destruction. I believe that unarmed truth and unconditional love will have the final word in reality. That is why right temporarily defeated is stronger than evil triumphant."

Were he alive today, Dr. King would still be using the unarmed truth to warn that we stand at the very precipice of the Hell of thermonuclear self-immolation. Why? Because we have spent the last four decades developing weapons of ever-greater destructive capability, while simultaneously institutionalizing the Cold War rationale that masquerades as U.S. foreign policy. This combination of belligerent diplomacy and destructive weaponry now threatens the very survival of the planet.

In the United States, this crisis has been caused in large measure by the deliberate unwillingness of too many of our so-called political leaders to analyze or debate, with either intelligence or integrity, the historical origins, fundamental premises, and contemporary needs of American foreign and military policy. Instead, for the past thirty-eight years, politicians from both major political parties have sustained and ad-

vanced themselves in office by following Senator Arthur H. Vanden-
berg's advice to President Harry S. Truman to "scare hell out of the
country" when it comes to any public discussion of dealing with Soviet
threats, real or imagined, to the "American way of life" at home and
U.S. multinational interests abroad.

Since 1945, American foreign and military policies have been predicated on a series of hypotheses, all revolving around the basic theme of
preserving the "national security interests" of the United States. With
minimal deviations, eight successive presidents have contended that
the cornerstone of this policy is, and must be, a sustained, unrelenting
response at all levels to the ongoing confrontation between the alleged
Communist crusade for "global hegemony" and the defense and maintenance of the "Free World"—as defined by Washington at periodic
intervals.

All too often, the U.S. response to changes in the world has been one
of political and military overreaction and subsequent alliance with corrupt dictatorships, more often of the Right than the Left, so long as they
professed the proper rhetorical anti-Communist sentiments. The perpetuation of this rhetoric and faulty policy analysis over the decades has
resulted in an expanding, bipartisan militarization of American foreign
policy. Both Democratic and Republican administrations have *repeatedly* sought, through overt or covert intervention, military solutions to
international problems that are essentially political, economic, social, or
cultural in origin—problems that demand constructive policy solutions
within those parameters.

In my judgment, the realities of recent history are at variance with
the assumptions on which these policies have been predicated. The
world of the 1980s is, and will continue to be, one of rapid change—one
in which the legitimate aspirations of Third World peoples must have
consideration in American planning equal to that accorded our obses-
sive concern with overreactive responses to the real or imagined menace of Soviet expansionism.

The world in the 1980s is significantly different from what it was in
1945, when the United States emerged supreme from the struggle
against fascism. In the process of helping to defeat the Axis powers we
became, by default, the defenders of, and the profiteers from, a European colonial system that should have been terminated in the wake of
the Great War of 1914-18.

Even worse, the United States, as both a society and a government,
failed to learn, much less understand, the reality and dimensions of
human suffering engendered by World War II. The havoc wrought was
almost immeasurable. Some estimates place the human toll at more
than 60 million dead, more than half of them noncombatants. More

than 20 million Russians were killed. The dead in Poland numbered more than 15 percent of the prewar population. European Jewry was decimated; the prewar estimate of approximately 10 million was reduced to less than 3.8 million at war's end. The Jews in Poland were virtually exterminated. Between 1939 and 1947 an additional 18 million Europeans were permanently removed from their homelands to other parts of the continent or to nations around the world.

The devastation of physical property was of similar proportions. In the Soviet Union, some 2,000 cities and towns and more than 70,000 villages were wholly or substantially destroyed. In the areas invaded by the Nazis and their collaborators, more than two-thirds of the industrial installations were in ruins and more than 40,000 miles of rail tracks destroyed. Russian agricultural production in 1945 was less than half the 1940 yield.

In contrast, the war scarcely touched the United States. The number of killed and missing was approximately 315,000. Physically, the war had left untouched the forty-eight continental states, save for a few shells lobbed ashore near Santa Barbara, California, by a Japanese submarine in early 1942.

Fiscally, the war effected an economic revolution because it ended the Great Depression that had afflicted American society for more than a decade. The index of industrial production doubled, while the Gross National Product (based on the 1939 dollar valuation) increased from $91 to $166 billion. The American share of the world's merchant marine in 1939 had been 17 percent, as opposed to Europe's 63 percent. By 1945, the United States had more ships afloat than the rest of the world combined. And the United States had sole possession of the atomic bomb.

The triumph against fascism in Europe and the Pacific spawned a series of myths that have been nurtured, hyperbolized, and perpetuated by the government, schools, and community pressure groups in the years since World War II. Foremost has been the concept, fostered by John Wayne type war films, that war is something that happens in other people's countries. Enemies are stereotyped and dehumanized, while human suffering is confined to newsreels or television screens—except when the remains in the body bag from Korea or Vietnam belong to one's immediate family. Thus the public has been conditioned to endorse too easily government plans for war, both nuclear and conventional.

Similarly, the myth that the United States virtually "won" World War II singlehandedly has grown despite the documented suffering of the Soviet peoples in the years 1941-45. It has become a self-sustaining myth that Soviet manpower—and casualties—counted for less than

American technology, especially since *we* had the atomic bomb at war's end. Indeed, there are still those in America who argue that the United States should have waged "preventive" war against our former Soviet ally in 1945 because *we* had "the bomb" and *they* didn't—at least until 1949.

Viewed in the context of historical reality and not mythology, the evolution, expansion and globalization of the Cold War can perhaps better be understood by a non-American. As a consequence of its post-war efforts to preserve its economic hegemony over friend and foe alike, the United States became, too often by design, the inheritor of colonial wars in which the nonwhite peoples of the Third World were struggling for national independence.

Successive interventions in the Third World—from Korea to Iran, Guatemala, Indochina, Chile, Angola and now possibly El Salvador, if not all of Central America—have been rationalized on the grounds of responding in kind to alleged Communist aggression or subversion of one sort or another. In addition, as a justification for the deliberate distortion of what constitutes proper "collective security," military alliances were conceived, maintained, and subsidized around the world by the United States. From NATO to SEATO to CENTO to ANZUS and beyond, the common denominator of policy analysis has been the containment of Communist expansionism, real or imagined.

The Soviet contribution to the evolution and escalation of Cold War confrontation has also been considerable. Notwithstanding the oppressive methods used to expand their "sphere of influence" throughout much of eastern and central Europe as a result of their military conquests in World War II, this was accepted as political reality in the Yalta and Potsdam Agreements of 1945 and confirmed as historical reality by the Helsinki Accords of 1975. Their serious efforts to put the nuclear genie back in the bottle, through real restraints on all nuclear production and use, were not matched by good faith efforts at conventional force reductions and the implementation of civil and political rights in the Soviet Union and its satellites.

Like their counterparts in the West, the Soviets became the victims of their own fear, leading to military coercion against foes real and imagined, foreign and domestic, and to repression of nations in their sphere of influence. So the Cold War confrontation was escalated, institutionalized, and rigidified. In the United States the proclamation and implementation of the containment doctrine led almost inexorably to the Marshall Plan, the NATO alliance, and globe-girdling regional military alliances. The Soviets matched it with the Molotov Plan, the Warsaw Pact, and other regional alliances. The United States "had" Iran and Guatemala; the Soviets "had" Czechoslovakia and Hungary. The

Monroe Doctrine, the Rio Pact, and the Organization of American States have their Soviet counterpart in the formalization and implementation of the Brezhnev Doctrine. The United States has the blood-stained infamy of Indochina, and the Soviets the blood-stained infamy of Afghanistan—truly a mutually miserable record of moral malfeasance on the part of the greatest powers that history has yet seen.

In the United States, the inevitable consequence of this increasing militarization of U.S. foreign policy has been the formation and growth of a national security/warfare state. Abroad, it has led to the institutionalization of illegal, covert actions around the world by American agents, including government-initiated and sponsored blackmail, bribes, coups d'état, and even political assassination.

This "national security" psychosis has also made possible the evolution of a permanent war economy that has made the United States, because of its superior technology, the principal force in both nuclear and conventional global arms escalation. Relying on the demonstrably faulty analysis and hysterical assumptions of a Report to the National Security Council (NSC-68, April 1950; a principal author was Paul Nitze, now America's disarmament negotiator at Geneva) President Harry S. Truman's Democratic administration *tripled* the military budget in 1950 as a consequence of the commitment to the globalization of the containment policy. It was a Democratic administration, headed by John F. Kennedy, that first proclaimed a missile gap with the Soviet Union when it knew the opposite was true and then brought the planet to the verge of a nuclear holocaust during the Cuban Missile Crisis in 1962.

It was a Democratic administration, headed by Jimmy Carter, that prepared and began to implement Presidential Directive 59 (PD 59, July 25, 1980), which committed the United States to a nuclear first-strike capability. The *only* two U.S. presidents in the entire Cold War era who *reduced* military spending were Dwight D. Eisenhower and Richard M. Nixon. The latter did so in four out of five years that he was in office.

Since then, and despite the termination of American military involvement in Indochina, there has been a rapid, substantial, and sustained increase in the military budget during the last decade. In the past six years alone, the United States has spent more on the military than was spent during the first thirty years of the Cold War. Again, contrary to popular mythology, this rapid increase did not begin the day Ronald Reagan was inaugurated. He simply accelerated a process that had been initiated with Truman and fueled by Jimmy Carter and his Secretary of Defense, Harold Brown.

In 1977, when the Carter administration assumed office with a pledge to reduce military spending by \$5-\$7 billion in its first year, the total military budget was slightly less than \$100 billion. Four years later it was \$173 billion, but Carter left office asking for an increase to \$194 billion. The Reagan administration immediately raised that figure to \$226.3 billion, as part of a five-year military spending projection of \$1.6 *trillion*. Because of cost overruns and projected supplementals, that figure has already been raised to *\$2.3 trillion* for the same period. This is more than twice what we spent during the entire decade of the 1970s, or nearly five times the rate of expenditure during that time period.

II

A nuclear weapon is an equal opportunity destroyer. It is blind to sex, race, creed, national origin, economic condition, political position, or geographic location. As citizens of humanity and the global community of conscience we have a moral obligation to address, challenge, and eliminate the insanity and immorality of nuclear war and preparations for nuclear war.

What is needed in America in 1983 is a systematic and sustained challenge to the policies of past administrations, both Democratic and Republican, that have brought us too often to the brink of nuclear confrontation. What is needed is a fundamental reassessment of American foreign policy goals and objectives—goals that redefine our legitimate national security interests as the proper defense of the United States.

A constructive transformation of present policies requires a conscious change in two institutionalized policy assumptions that have characterized Cold War decision making in this country. Both are rooted decades-deep in Soviet-American relations, but both have become increasingly irrelevant to the realities of the contemporary world.

The first assumption is, to borrow Ronald Reagan's own words of June 1980, that we should "not delude ourselves, the Soviet Union underlies all the unrest that is going on." Or, as he particularized this fantasy with regard to El Salvador in his Caribbean Basin Initiative speech of February 24, 1982: "Very simply, the guerrillas armed and supported by and through Cuba are attempting to impose a Marxist-Leninist dictatorship on the people of El Salvador as part of a larger imperialist plan."

The historical complexities and contradictions of the contemporary world are such that no truly informed person can provide evidence demonstrating that the Soviet Union was responsible for the rise of Fidel Castro to power in 1959, the tidal wave of nationalism that swept over Africa, both north and south of the Sahara, in the 1960s, the thousand-year struggle for nationhood in Indochina, or the continuing "unrest" in Central America, which antedates Lenin's seizure of power in 1917.

The "unrest" in the contemporary world has not been "caused" by Soviet power but by conditions of injustice and human degradation. What must be recognized is the Soviet government's ability to act as a political scavenger among the Third World's neocolonial remains. Thus, there is an absolute need to transform U.S. foreign policy by terminating a second basic Cold War policy assumption; *viz.*, that military force is more than the ultimate arbiter, that it is often *the* preferred method for "resolving" confrontations between the nuclear superpowers or their surrogates. Given the reality that both the later Carter administration and the Reagan administration have shared the view that Third World problems are virtually East-West crises by proxy, there is increasing support for the proposition, however flawed, that increased U.S. military capability can resolve such crises by military force rather than through diplomatic negotiation.

The falsity of this second assumption, that military power can be used to resolve East-West confrontations or to control indigenous revolutions in the newly emerging nations, actually works to the advantage of the Soviet Union, although many Americans seem reluctant to analyze or appreciate this advantage. The Soviet system *can compete militarily,* although in its present form it is structurally incapable of competing economically or of acting successfully as an ideological or cultural model in these newly emerging nations and societies. The ultimate paradox is that the Reagan administration, like many of its predecessors, has persistently pursued a policy that plays to that single Soviet strength, military power, at the same time that it escalates the prospect of a nuclear confrontation to an incalculable degree. In pursuing this policy the Reagan administration is transforming Soviet propagandists into prophets by making a reality of the oft-repeated Marxist assertion that the "military-industrial complex" is the main prop of a decadent capitalist system.

The United States must reject a foreign policy predicated on the false and dangerous assumption that it can intimidate and shape Kremlin policies into a form "acceptable" to the United States. The legacy of global military containment and confrontation must be rejected in favor of the search for constructive, positive alternatives, not negative, destructive reactions.

It is absolutely necessary for the United States to respond to the challenges and opportunities of the late twentieth century rather than to try to restore the mythology of an earlier era of American history. Such a program of constructive change demands arms limitation and reduction, not a further escalation of the arms race. Peaceful change also means the constructive transfer of resources—fiscal, technological, intellectual, and human—away from the military to the human needs sector of American and global society. The challenge is there. How we respond will determine our place in history and whether or not our children will have a future in which to write our history.

III

In 1970 I was first elected to the Congress as the collective expression of a constituency strongly opposed to the military adventurism of U.S. government intervention in Indochina and vitally concerned with the escalation of the arms race, both nuclear and conventional.

During my twelve years of service in the U.S. House of Representatives, I have consistently challenged the policy assumptions and spending priorities of the military budget and foreign asssistance programs that include arms sales and transfers. I initially thought that I could best oppose the increasing militarization of our foreign policy through service on the Foreign Affairs Committee, but I quickly learned that the Pentagon tail was wagging the State Department dog, so to speak. Immediately following my reelection in 1972, I secured a transfer to the Armed Services Committee in order to challenge directly the weapons programs and force structures that were determining, rather than implementing, our foreign policy.

I soon discovered that the Nixon administration's reaction to the SALT I and ABM treaties of 1972 was to push for a new generation of weapons systems, which made inexorable a further escalation of the nuclear arms race by both superpowers and which would necessitate another SALT treaty, just to curb the excesses wrought in the wake of SALT I. I therefore introduced a series of floor amendments in opposition to these new crisis-destabilizing weapons systems, whenever they were brought to the House Floor for congressional approval.

In all honesty, it was a rather lonely effort for many years. For example, on April 22, 1977, I was the first member of Congress ever to introduce an amendment against all funding for the development, production, and deployment of the MX missile. However, I could muster only eleven votes in support of this proposal, not enough even to secure a record vote on the issue. Five and a half years later the Congress was more aware of the danger and voted to withhold temporarily a portion of the funds for procurement. In the interim, though, billions of additional dollars had been wasted on a dangerous first-strike weapons program that brought us even closer to the brink of nuclear disaster.

An even more unsettling experience came in April of 1979 when I went to the Soviet Union as a member of a congressional delegation to discuss nuclear weapons issues with our counterparts in the Soviet government. On a personal level, I was moved by the constant reminders of the legacy of suffering that the Russian people had endured in resisting the Nazi aggression. The innumerable war memorials to the victims of the war against fascism and conversations with Soviet citizens in many walks of life, virtually every one of whom had lost several members of their immediate family in the conflict, reinforced my deepseated belief that the ordinary people in Soviet society have been seared and scarred forever by the carnage of World War II and have no wish to see it replicated in the total devastation that nuclear war would guarantee.

On a political level I became even more disturbed as the formal talks progressed because it became quite evident that both sides were talking past each other, literally and figuratively. The Soviet delegation was committed to a position that reaching arms control agreement was a matter of international necessity and utmost urgency because of the rapidly accelerating pace of nuclear weapons technology. On the U.S. side there was neither a consensus on arms control nor a willingness to abandon electoral expediency in order to reach a commitment to halt, and then reverse, an arms race that threatens the very survival of the planet.

I returned from the Soviet Union with the definite perception that the SALT II treaty would not be ratified by the U.S. Senate and that *both* sides would use this failure to ratify as an excuse for the further escalation of the nuclear arms race and the intensification of Cold War tensions. Within months the Carter administration had bartered away any chance for Senate ratification of the treaty by trying to buy off congressional "hawks" with renewed promises of "real growth" increases in defense spending. Within months the Soviets launched a massive invasion of Afghanistan, thus providing the Carter administration with the formal excuse for legitimizing a decision already made to undertake a massive increase in virtually all aspects of the military budget over the decade of the 1980s.

Perhaps most ominous of all was the formal embrace by the Carter administration, in Presidential Directive 59, signed on July 25, 1980, of a "counterforce," or nuclear war-fighting, strategy first proposed in the waning months of the Nixon Administration. The driving force behind the earlier proposal was then Secretary of Defense James M. Schlesinger, whose ideas substantially prevailed in the drafting and acceptance of National Security Decision Memorandum 242, the precursor to PD 59. In fact, Schlesinger was later to boast to a reporter from *Business Week* magazine that 80 percent of his views had been incorporated into

PD 59, the principal inspiration for which was Carter's Secretary of Defense, Harold Brown.

Although PD 59 is still classified "TOP SECRET," enough of its substance has appeared in the public press to warrant serious concern. Whereas NSC-68 was a blueprint for the globalization of the military containment of the Soviet Union and the establishment of a permanent war economy, PD 59 was unique in the dimensions of its Strangelovian audacity. While paying lip service to the doctrine of nuclear deterrence that had been operational since Bernard Brodie first broached the concept in his landmark essay "War in the Atomic Age" almost forty years ago, PD 59 proposed the full development of a nuclear first-strike strategy that would enable the United States to fight, survive, and "win" a nuclear war with the Soviet Union, regardless of the cost in human suffering.

The Reagan administration has simply expanded and accelerated PD 59's policy through an unrestrained growth of the military budget at the expense of the domestic welfare. That policy decision caused me to reassess the nature and dimensions of my opposition to the military budget in years past and future. After extended reflection and analysis, I concluded that for the future the most comprehensive, effective, and constructive manner in which to confront Pentagon planners and spenders had to be through a direct challenge to the policy assumptions that determined spending priorities.

I decided to use these hearings as a learning process for the Congress and the American public. It was a unique learning experience for me and my colleagues. The essence of what we learned and the legislative effort we undertook are set out in the pages that follow.

PART ONE

WEAPONS
FOR
WHAT PURPOSES?

■ ■ ■

As a military man who has given half a century of active service, I say in all sincerity that the nuclear arms race has no military purpose. Wars cannot be fought with nuclear weapons. Their existence only adds to our perils because of the illusions which they have generated.

Admiral Lord Louis Mountbatten, 1979

■ ■ ■

DURING THE CUBAN Missile Crisis of 1962, the world held its breath as the United States and the Soviet Union edged toward global thermonuclear war. In that moment of global brinkmanship, pride, ego, and the mutual failure of statesmanship nearly uncorked the nuclear genie.

Unfortunately for humanity, policymakers in Washington and Moscow chose to learn the wrong lessons from this crisis. Rather than undertaking to eliminate these heinous weapons, both sides commenced massive weapons building programs. Spasmodic efforts at arms control, such as the founding of the Arms Control and Disarmament Agency by President Kennedy in 1961, the Atmospheric Test Ban Treaty in 1963, and the Anti-Ballistic Missile Treaty (part of SALT I) in 1972 were among the few positive steps cutting against the grain of this massive nuclear arms build-up.

Fueled by the lingering paranoia generated by the so-called missile gap of the 1960 election campaign, the Kennedy administration committed the United States to a military strategy based on ever-increasing technological sophistication. New submarine and ground-based missile technology was developed, continuously improving accuracy and firepower.

For every new weapons program proposed by the Pentagon, developed by the defense industry, and bought by the U.S. government, there has been a corresponding Soviet response, reflecting a Soviet commitment to never again be inferior *vis-à-vis* U.S. strategic capability. Although the Soviets could not keep pace with U.S. developments in MIRV (multiple warhead) missiles, antisubmarine warfare, and electronic intelligence technology, they attained rough parity by developing weapons with larger "throw-weights," or destructive capability. As a result, instead of the once relatively small arsenals of bombers, missiles, and submarines, some 50,000 increasingly powerful and accurate nuclear warheads wait to annihilate the world—a number that increases daily.

These arsenals exceed any legitimate deterrent need. When

he was Secretary of Defense, Robert McNamara testified before Congress that scarcely 400 strategic warheads would ensure sufficient retaliatory capability to make fighting a war too costly for either side. Whether or not this policy of mutual assured destruction (MAD) ever made sense, it is clear that our current arsenals are far beyond any necessary threshold for adequate deterrence.

During the Carter administration, the United States formally shifted the policy grounds for nuclear arms planning. In the far-reaching, and still classified, Presidential Directive 59 of July 25, 1980, the United States committed itself to the development of a nuclear war-fighting capability. The key to this strategy remains the development of first-strike weapons with accuracy and fire-power sufficient to strike and "kill" hardened Soviet targets.

The 1980 election brought a new administration to Washington but left PD 59 intact. President Reagan embraced it as his own and then initiated an unprecedented nuclear weapons expansion program. A new generation of weapons systems is being designed, tested, and scheduled for deployment and is bringing us closer to nuclear conflagration. The MX missile, the Pershing II or Euromissile, the Trident II missile and the ground- and sea-launched Cruise missiles are visible examples of such weapons. In addition, the Pentagon planners are looking to space, thus far virtually unmilitarized, to expand the war fighting terrain.

We must quickly stop the design and production of these weapons. If we do not, we will put into place technology that either defies verification, the keystone to all arms treaties, or that creates a "use-them-or-lose-them" mind-set regarding deadly accurate, but vulnerable, weapons.

The witnesses presented in Part I examine and critique this new weapons acquisition program and the assumptions that underpin it. In Chapter 1, Robert C. Aldridge explores the components this administration is developing that are necessary to a first-strike capability: space detection and warfare systems; "hard-target" weapons like the MX, Trident II and Pershing missiles; antisubmarine warfare improvements; antibomber and antimissile programs; and the hardening of command and communication systems to withstand nuclear attack. He explains how this increasingly sophisticated technology is leading us to the point where computers, rather than people, may well make the decision to launch a nuclear attack.

In Chapter 2, Dr. Herbert Scoville, Jr., forcefully argues the need to pursue arms control rather than escalation, negating the administration's oft-repeated contention that there is a "window of vulnerability" endangering our strategic forces. Pointing out that technology has made land-based missiles obsolete, he outlines the character of an exclusively deterrent nuclear force. Pointing out the dangers to the arms control process of deploying Cruise missiles that defy verifiability, he castigates the adminstration's lack of good faith and confidence in the arms negotiation process.

In Chapter 3, Paul Warnke argues the case for the development of a rational nuclear weapons strategy, one based on survivable and unprovocative weapons. Also debunking the "window of vulnerability" scare, he argues for a bilateral nuclear weapons freeze and the abandonment of U.S. plans to deploy new-generation weapons such as the Pershing II missile. He points out the incredible danger in believing, as the administration argues, that the United States could survive, much less win, a nuclear war.

In Chapter 4, Richard J. Barnet notes the advantages of nuclear disarmament and bemoans our national leaders' constant harping on the risks. This blindness results in the development of ever more sophisticated weapons that may be beyond our social institutions' ability to control. His comments on the fears underpinning U.S. foreign policy presage the dilemma of U.S. military policy explained in Part II. □

1

AMERICA'S STRATEGIC ARSENAL

Robert C. Aldridge

■ ■ ■

Robert C. Aldridge studied aeronautical engineering at California Poly-technical University and then at San Jose State University. He was a design engineer for three generations of the Polaris submarine-launched ballistic missile program at Lockheed Missiles & Space Co. and the multi-ple individually-targeted reentry vehicles (MIRVs) for the Poseidon mis-sile. Before resigning in protest, because of the inherent first-strike po-tential of the program, he worked on the initial phase of the Trident missile program. His books include *The Counterforce Syndrome* and *First Strike*.

THE MILITARY-INDUSTRIAL COMPLEX is very strong in the United States today. It has infiltrated government at every level, and it has an inordinate influence on domestic and foreign policy. Industry is the controlling arm of that complex because businessmen occupy most of the decision making positions in the Department of Defense; therefore, decisions tend to have a business flavor.

The corporate community has found the arms race very profitable. Pentagon contracts to U.S. companies are now soaring—probably ex-ceeding $60 billion annually in 1982-83. Foreign arms sales are ex-pected to exceed $23 billion in 1982. Building sophisticated weaponry is a lucrative business because production is highly automated to reduce labor costs while investment is small. Many facilities and tools are fur-nished by the government.

On the global scale, large American multinational corporations need the strong military umbrella to protect their investments in smaller countries—what is euphemistically referred to as our national interests. Senator Alan Cranston of California a few years ago noted that the United States supports forty-six military dictatorships that repress their own people to provide a favorable climate for U.S. businesses to exploit the best land, the cheap labor, and the supply of natural resources in those countries; that number remains about the same today. Those dictatorships are the main recipients of foreign arms sales by the United States and it is because of this exploitative activity that the United States must be number one in military might.

This is the perspective needed for viewing the military technologies arms race and nuclear buildup I would like to now address. But keep this profit imperative in mind. Failure to do so may lull one into believing that we can change the picture by political, technical, and economic arguments regarding weapons production. Such naïveté will meet with the same defeat as in the past. It is only when viewed in the light of profiteering interests that nuclear brinkmanship presents that systematic pattern that led to first-strike technologies. That pattern must be clearly recognized before it can be altered.

There are five distinct first-strike technologies in the arsenals and on the drawing boards of the United States and the Soviet Union.

1. **SPACE WARFARE.** If the United States could continuously track and instantly destroy Soviet early warning and communications satellites, it would then be very difficult for the U.S.S.R. to get a launch command to its missile commanders before its weapons were destroyed. Two U.S. technologies are being developed to meet this goal.

Space Tracking. Existing space-tracking sensors are composed mainly of various types of radar located around the globe. Because radars are limited to about a 3,000 mile range, they are not effective for deep space. To help correct that deficiency there are special telescopic Baker-Nunn cameras stationed around the globe and operated by the U.S. Air Force and the Smithsonian Institution. These cameras are used to spot and classify satellites and determine their orbits. They cannot discover new satellites, however, and their use is limited to a few hours a day in good weather.

An interim improvement for detecting satellites in deep space called GEODSS (ground-based, electro-optical deep space surveillance) uses very sensitive television cameras in telescopes. Five GEODSS stations will eventually girdle the globe. The one at White Sands, New Mexico, is now operational. These sensors would still be limited to certain hours during the day in good weather, but they will also be able to detect new satellites in deep space.

Ultimately there will be space bases using arrays of tiny infrared detectors with integral charge-coupled devices (CCD) for instantaneous data processing. About 100,000 detectors will be placed in each square inch in the focal plane of a telescope. Each station will be in geosynchronous orbit, and each detector in the mosaic will stare at a given spot to achieve greater sensitivity. The entire array of millions of detectors will give a composite view of the area under surveillance and will note the slightest movement.

Space Weapons.   During the early 1960s each branch of the military was competing in various antisatellite tests in the Pacific. These predated the commencement of the well-publicized Soviet test series. The Air Force then had a force of Thor missiles equipped with Burner-2 upper stages for maneuverability and nuclear warheads for destroying satellites that was stationed at Johnston Island in the Pacific until 1975.

Now the Air Force is developing a small nonnuclear, nonexplosive satellite interceptor that can be boosted into space by a two-stage SRAM/ALTAIR-III rocket launched from an F-15 aircraft. The interceptor uses infrared sensors and maneuvering rockets to put itself on a collision course with the satellite to destroy it by impact at a relative speed of 27,000 miles per hour. The so-called air target defeat warhead may be used in conjunction with this interceptor for assuring a kill, even if there is a near miss. It uses the "advanced self-forging fragment technology" associated with antitank weapons, and has a dimpled case that is broken into high velocity fragments by an explosive charge.

Over the longer haul, with talk of being speeded up, are high energy "killer" lasers and the neutron subatomic particle beam (code-named White Horse) that, when mounted on laser battle stations in space and aimed with the Talon Gold technology, will instantaneously zap enemy satellites out of the sky.

2.   **STRATEGIC NUCLEAR WEAPONS.**   The destruction of Soviet silo-based missiles and other military targets in the U.S.S.R. would be accomplished by U.S. intercontinental ballistic missiles (ICBMs) and submarine-launched ballistic missiles (SLBMs). Besides Russian missile silos, the new generation of ICBMs/SLBMs (Improved Accuracy Trident I, Trident II, and MX) would also be able to destroy underground command posts, bomber fields, nuclear storage depots, communications facilities, and submarines in port. The tactical Pershing II missile based in Western Europe will also have pinpoint accuracy with its maneuvering warheads, which will give it strategic importance against Soviet targets west of the Ural Mountains. The various types of Cruise missiles and penetrating bombers would be too slow for the time-urgent targets but would be very effective in preventing Soviet missile silos from being reloaded.

Destroying the Soviet Union's silo-based missile force would do most of the disarming because three-quarters of its strategic warheads are in those silos. Furthermore, Soviet strategic bombers are land-based, and 85 percent of the U.S.S.R.'s submarine fleet are always in port, thus capable of being targeted.

NAVSTAR Global Positioning System. Receiving navigation corrections from NAVSTAR satellites while in flight will greatly improve the accuracy of ballistic missiles. During the last half of the 1980s there will be eighteen to twenty-four of these satellites in orbit and sending out continuous signals. The missiles will receive these signals from at least four satellites, solve four simultaneous equations with its onboard computer, and determine its exact position within thirty feet. By taking a series of fixes, the precise direction and speed can be determined. The attitude control system for the "bus" (warhead dispensing section of the missile) then makes the necessary course corrections before dropping off each of the MIRV warheads.

Maneuvering Warheads. A means of correcting the warhead's course during the last few seconds of flight can be used to make a fine tuning on accuracy and compensate for any deviations during reentry of the earth's atmosphere. Such zero-miss accuracy could be accomplished by target-sensing warheads that are being developed in the advanced strategic missile systems (ASMS—formerly ABRES) program. Arms control impact statements have also mentioned putting NAVSTAR receivers in the reentry vehicles themselves so that they can maneuver for a direct hit. Such a scheme would do away with target sensors and give a theoretical accuracy within thirty feet.

3. **ANTISUBMARINE WARFARE (ASW).** The U.S.S.R. has about nine or ten of its strategic missile-launching submarines at sea at any one time. A first-strike capability requires their destruction if that strike is to remain unanswered. In recent years military research into ASW has been at the $6 billion to $7 billion a year level. The general categories for ASW are sensors, weapons, and carrier vehicles.

ASW Sensors. Sound travels for thousands of miles under water. For that reason and because electromagnetic waves such as radar are virtually useless beneath the ocean, sonic sensing has been the primary means of detecting and tracking submarines. For almost thirty years the United States has had underwater sound receivers (called SOSUS, for sound surveillance system) planted in fixed positions on the continental shelves throughout the world. They have been constantly upgraded and improved. They are connected to land stations by underwater cables and are particularly prominent in narrow bodies of water through which Soviet submarines must pass.

One problem with fixed underwater sound sensors is that they have blind spots in the ocean. To correct that problem, Project Seaguard was commenced by the Defense Advanced Research Projects Agency (DARPA) and the Navy in 1975. It developed the surveillance-towed array sensor system (SURTASS), which can be towed around by slow-moving ocean surveillance ships named TAGOS. Also close to completion are the so-called rapidly deployable surveillance systems (RDSS), which are sensor arrays packed in special buoys that can be seeded in areas of interest by aircraft, ships, or submarines. These are not to be confused with sonobuoys that are dropped from P-3 and S-3 ASW aircraft and ASW helicopters. The latter are for local detection and RDSS is to complement oceanwide sensing.

Preliminary evidence indicates that there also seem to be nonsonic sensors in development to locate and track submarines. One that has been hinted at from time to time is the use of infrared sensors in aircraft or satellites to locate submarines by their wake. The temperature difference in the wake, due to micro-organisms killed by the submarine's passage, discharge of reactor cooling water, or churning up of the thermal layers with the submarine's propeller, would make a different infrared signature.

ASW Weapons. Numerous tactical nuclear and conventional antisubmarine weapons are available and are being improved. The Mark-48 submarine-launched torpedo and the lightweight Mark-46 for airplane and other use are now available. The Mark-46 Neartip (nearterm improvement) program is providing kits to modernize the Mark-46. An advanced lightweight torpedo (ALWT) is also in development. Mark-57 nuclear depth bombs can be dropped from aircraft and be delivered by ASROC (antisubmarine rockets) from ships and SUBROC (submarine rockets) from submarines. Mark-46 torpedoes can also be delivered by ASROC. Mines for various water depths that seek out and destroy hostile submarines are also being developed. CAPTOR (encapsulated torpedo) uses a Mark-46 torpedo. The Quickstrike family of underwater mines work at shallow and intermediate depths. The submarine-launched mobile mine (SLMM) is a converted Mark-37 torpedo that can be launched clandestinely from a submarine, and propel itself into shallow harbors and channels, and wait for an enemy sub.

ASW Carrier Vehicles for Sensors and Weapons. After the U.S. Navy's oceanwide surveillance system locates a submarine, it has to be pinpointed and tracked by some antisub vehicle. One very efficient submarine chaser is the "hunter-killer" attack submarine. It has powerful sensors and weapons and is very good for clandestine operations where surface ships and aircraft would not be safe.

Virtually every U.S. warship has sensors and antisubmarine weapons. Destroyers, frigates, and cruisers also carry ASW helicopters equipped with sensors and torpedoes. These copters are known as LAMPS (light airborne multipurpose system). Every aircraft carrier has a squadron of ten S-3A Viking antisubmarine patrol airplanes and six Sea King helicopters that are adapted to ASW work.

Some B-52 bombers have been converted to perform ocean surveillance. They are very effective for that purpose because of the long time they can remain aloft and the load of instruments and computers they can carry. Probably the most active of all subchasers are the land-based P-3 Orion airplanes. They have bases located throughout the world and can patrol virtually every ocean and sea.

4. **MISSILE AND BOMBER DEFENSE.** There are certain to be some missiles and bombers belonging to the Soviet Union that would survive a U.S. first strike if it ever were launched. It seems certain that they would be fired in retaliation. It is also possible that some missiles would be fired before they are destroyed. If a first strike is to remain unanswered, these weapons must be intercepted before they reach the United States. That would be the function of ballistic missile defense (BMD) and bomber defense.

Early Warning. Radar is currently the main system used to warn of attack by missiles and bombers. There are lines of radar along the upper North American continent and extending into Greenland and Britain. There are also radars along the U.S. coasts and in flying radar planes (AWACS). In addition, three earth-synchronous early-warning satellites using infrared sensors watch for ballistic missile launches from silos in the U.S.S.R. and from submarines at sea. Future warning systems will use the mosaic array of infrared detectors in a telescope on space platforms to detect bombers, Cruise missiles, ballistic missiles, and satellites.

Antiaircraft and Antimissile Weapons. At present the United States has no interceptors for ballistic missiles. It does have strategic and tactical fighter squadrons to defend against Cruise missiles and bombers, and the Patriot surface-to-air missile (SAM) is in production. The scant number of Soviet strategic bombers, however, does not call for a large antibomber defense.

The planned antiballistic missile system is called a layered defense.

The first layer, now under development, will directly protect the area to be defended. Called "endoatmospheric," or terminal, defense, it will be closest to potential U.S. targets and may consist of fast interceptors. It is a last-ditch stand to destroy remaining Soviet warheads as they reenter the earth's atmosphere. The idea is to use fast interceptor missiles equipped with nuclear warheads in an attempt to destroy incoming hostile warheads traveling at twenty times the speed of sound.

The second layer will use the nonnuclear, nonexplosive interceptor described under space warfare to destroy enemy warheads way out in space. Called "exoatmospheric" defense, this is like hitting a bullet with a bullet. But shooting down a missile flying in a ballistic arc is about the same as knocking a satellite out of orbit.

The third layer is a boost-phase intercept, shooting down missiles while the rocket motors are still burning. Killer lasers and particle beam weapons (directed energy) are being developed to catch the launch vehicle before it starts spewing MIRV warheads all over the sky and creating many targets—getting all the eggs in one basket, so to speak.

5. **COMMAND, CONTROL, COMMUNCIATION AND INTELLIGENCE (C³I).** The final criterion for a disarming first strike is to be able to coordinate and integrate all of the various weapons, carrier vehicles, and sensors needed to mount a disarming first strike. Communication with every frequency, from extreme-low to super-high, will be used, as well as lasers and sonar. Devices to overcome nuclear blackouts, eliminate jamming, and codify messages are other important aspects. Means of communication include satellites, submarines, aircraft trailing long antennae, and large underground antenna grids. Numerous underground and flying command posts are provided. Computers are critical for reducing and analyzing instantaneously the floods of data accumulated by a wide spectrum of sensors, and for coordinating the massive volume of events that take place. C³I is very complicated and very delicate, but there would be no first-strike capability without it.

A deterrence strategy is extremely dangerous, but, at least ostensibly, both countries are prepared only to fire nuclear weapons in a second strike after the opponent struck first. Under those circumstances it is not likely that either the United States or the U.S.S.R. would intentionally strike first. But when one, or both, superpowers are prepared to launch an unanswerable first strike, the situation becomes volatile. It becomes a case of trying to out-guess each other to be able to punch the button first. Part of the volatility comes from new accurate missiles and U.S. ASW initiatives that unbalance the nuclear standoff.

Missile Accuracy. Pentagon officials claim they are developing silo-killing missiles only to destroy remaining Soviet missiles if retaliation is necessary—these are the so-called counterforce weapons. They have developed an incredible scenario called "second-strike counterforce." This is a departure from being prepared only to launch a retaliatory second strike. It is a doctrine that generates a first-strike capability, moving this world much closer to nuclear war—very much closer. I can best explain the destabilizing nature of this by quoting from official government documents that were published as long as four years ago. The warning is not new. A Congressional Budget Office paper warns: "It would be virtually impossible to deploy a force of MX ICBMs large enough to provide a significant second-strike retaliatory capability, yet small enough to avoid posing a [first-strike] counterforce threat to the Soviet silo-based ICBM force." (*Planning U.S. Strategic Nuclear Forces for the 1980s*, June 1978, p. xv.) That same warning would apply to the Improved Accuracy Trident I and Trident II. In effect, these all become first-strike weapons.

The announcement by Pentagon spokesmen that U.S. missiles will not be used for a disarming first strike against the Soviet Union does not mitigate the perceived capability. Another Congressional Budget Office paper discusses the problems and danger of designing any counterforce capability—even for a second strike:

> Several objections have been raised to the development of U.S. counterforce capability. Perhaps the most serious problem with U.S. forces designed for second-strike counterforce stems from the possibility that they would be seen as first-strike weapons, and thus be destabilizing. Two types of nuclear stability might be threatened by the development of U.S. counterforce capability: crisis stability and arms control stability . . . .
> (*Counterforce Issues for the U.S. Strategic Nuclear Forces*, January 1978, p. 32.)

The report then goes on to discuss the effect of a perceived counterforce capability on stability during times of international crises and the incentives to strike first that each side would face:

> . . . There may be an inescapable dilemma involved in the procurement of second-strike counterforce capability: a U.S. arsenal large enough to attack Soviet ICBMs after having absorbed a Soviet first strike would be large enough to threaten the [entire] Soviet ICBM force in a U.S. first strike. Moreover, the Soviet Union looking at *capabilities* rather than *intentions*, might see a U.S. second-strike capability in this light. Faced with a threat to their ICBM force, Soviet leaders facing an international crisis might have an incentive to use their missiles in a pre-emptive strike before they could be destroyed by the United States.
> (*Ibid.* Emphasis added.)

The Soviets would be far more sensitive to a threat against their ICBM force than would be the United States because three-quarters of their strategic warheads are on silo-based missiles. The United States only has 25 percent in silos. Even the president's arms control impact statements, which he is required to furnish Congress each year, indicate the danger of building silo-killing missiles: "Still, under extreme crisis conditions, Soviet leaders, concerned that war was imminent, and fearing for the survivability of their ICBMs if the United States struck first, nonetheless might perceive pressures to strike first themselves." (*Fiscal Year 1979 Arms Control Impact Statements*, June 1978, p. 21.)

Another statement says that: "If MX were deployed in substantial numbers, the U.S. would have acquired, through both the Minuteman and MX programs, an apparent capability to destroy most of the Soviet silo-based ICBM force in a first strike. This could be of major concern to Soviet leaders . . . ." (*Fiscal Year 1980 Arms Control Impact Statements*, March 1979, p. 25.) In addition, that document states: "The additive effects of two potential advances, Trident II and MX, in U.S. counter-silo capabilities . . . could put a large portion of the Soviet fixed ICBM silos at risk." (*Ibid.*, p. 55)

There is a glaring paradox here that should not be ignored—it should be scrutinized with critical eyes. The Pentagon claims that its new generation of counter-silo missiles is needed to deter the Soviet Union from launching a first strike against the United States. On the other hand, official congressional studies and the president's own statements warn that these silo-killing weapons might actually provoke a Soviet first strike. This represents a political and, more important, moral dilemma of the highest order. It is criminal to build such weapons.

Additionally, the United States's vigorous effort in ASW and the capabilties being developed for oceanwide sensing magnify the instability caused by super-precise missiles. The Congressional Research Service of the Library of Congress has reported that the United States has a significant lead over the U.S.S.R. in ASW technology, that the Soviets have no effective oceanwide ASW capability, and that U.S. strides in ocean-wide surveillance are aggressive. One report concludes:

> . . . If the United States achieves a disarming first-strike capability against Soviet ICBMs, and also develops an ASW capability that together with attacks on naval facilities could practically negate the Soviet SSBNS (strategic missile-launching submarines), then the strategic balance as it has come to be broadly defined and accepted would no longer be stable. . . . Current trends in U.S. ASW programs should fall under close scrutiny. It is also important to recognize that sharp constraints on ASW programs

may be necessary, if and when confidence in either side's ICBM deterrent is lost.

(*Evaluation of Fiscal Year 1979 Arms Control Impact Statements: Toward More Informed Congressional Participation in National Security Policymaking*, 3 January 1979, pp. 103-19.)

American strategic and tactical programs fit together into a first-strike pattern. Significant U.S government studies and documents show how these programs and the pattern they form are dangerous and destabilizing—how, in fact, they are actually leading us toward nuclear war. There is no doubt in my mind that the evidence is compelling— a warning that has been sounded for some time.

Instead of heeding this warning to curtail aggressive and destabilizing weapons, the Congress has done little more than rubber-stamp Pentagon requests. Now the Reagan administration, apparently through the orchestration of large business interests, has disclosed a policy that escalates and accelerates development of the very military systems that have been identified as aggressive and destabilizing. This escalation is at the expense of other programs that help the old, the invalid, and the needy but that, by business standards, are not profitable.

Except for some staged in-house debate and some token adjustments, I see no indication that Congress will not continue to approve military plans. When the time comes, I will consider every representative and senator who does not vote to freeze first-strike weaponry as being derelict in his or her duty to the people of this nation. They have had warnings, but they have not listened.

One reason that legislators consistently vote for military plans is because they do not hear other testimony. When the Pentagon budget comes up for debate each year, the halls of Congress swarm with generals, admirals, and DOD officials to prod the fear of Russia and to champion weapons spending. I follow congressional hearings very closely, and there are volumes of transcripts telling why we need more arms. There is only a miniscule amount of a critical nature.

■　　■　　■

■ *CHAIRMAN DELLUMS:* Could you respond to what you perceive to be the efficacy of concepts such as "limited options" and "flexible response"?

■ *MR. ALDRIDGE:* I think it was significant that when then-Defense Secretary Schlesinger introduced the targeting doctrine of "selectivity and flexibility" in 1974, Congress had, for five years prior to that time, refused funding for improving the accuracy of existing U.S. weapons because having an accurate weapon is more aggressive. It means going after things like Soviet silos, things you would have to destroy in a first strike before they could serve their function. But when that concept of selectivity and flexibility—which is another term for "limited" nuclear war—was introduced, it allowed the development of the same type of accuracy that would be needed for a first strike. We have seen now that we have developed an improved accuracy for the Minuteman missile and are working now on the improved accuracy for the Trident I missile.

Again, looking at the computers, at the absence of control you can have over factors in a nuclear war environment, at all the commotion and confusion that would be going on at that time, I agree with former Defense Secretary Harold Brown. I don't think a "limited" nuclear war can be kept limited. I think that control would be lost on both sides, that the exchange would be unconstrained, and that it would escalate to a total thermonuclear disaster. These "options" are just scenarios to justify things, just like the second-strike counterforce is a scenario to justify the increased accuracy of missiles. I think it is all very dangerous, and I think that they should be curtailed.

■ *MR. BRAUER (staff):* We now have an R&D Trident II missile to be put into the Trident submarine, potentially with an SLBM (submarine launched ballistic missile) maneuverable warhead capacity. Have you had a chance to calculate how many Trident subs, so armed, it would take to destroy those 1,500 Soviet ICBMs?

■ *MR. ALDRIDGE:* Depending on the size of the warhead—I use quite often the seventy-five to one-hundred kiloton warhead—if you could hold about seventeen warheads on each submarine-carried missile, there would be about 408 on each submarine. Four submarines would put one warhead on each Soviet land-based missile.

■ *MR. BRAUER:* Using a 2-to-1 take-out ratio, eight Trident submarines so armed would endanger, in a first strike, with probably about 90 percent assurance, virtually all the Soviet land-based ICBMs?

■ *MR. ALDRIDGE:* Yes, excluding the effects of fratricide—of one nuclear missile destroying subsequent incoming missiles—and things like that that are not clearly understood.

■ *MR. BRAUER:* Just looking at the Trident subs alone, a Soviet planner would have to have a great deal to fear. Given those developments, isn't the nation that is facing the greater fear of vulnerability really the Soviet Union and not the United States?

■ *MR. ALDRIDGE:* I think they are probably very nervous about our capability. Actually, most of their strategic forces could be destroyed by the accurate missiles: 85 percent of their submarines, their bomber bases, and then three-quarters of their strategic nuclear warheads, which are in missile silos.

■ *CHAIRMAN DELLUMS:* Could you speak to the issue of verification? Do we have the technical capacity to bring ourselves back within the confines of an arms control environment through a sophisticated and effective verification system?

■ *MR. ALDRIDGE:* I think we have adequate verification capacity to verify quantities. I don't think, without the cooperative verification of on-site inspection, we can verify quality. There were many things in SALT II that I don't think could have been verified by national technical means, such as the range of Cruise missiles and the number of warheads on a Trident or a MX. But if you came to something like a nuclear freeze where you would not deploy any more weapons, you could not verify the completion of some of the quality improvements that are in work and developed—for example, putting the rest of the Mark 12-A warheads on Minutemen. But anything new would be able to be verified.

First of all, you would be able to verify that there was no increase in numbers of missiles. You would be able to verify there was no testing to develop new systems. You cannot develop new systems without testings—underground testing for the warheads and flight testing for the delivery vehicle. We have the adequate means for that type of verification now. Then, of course, the reduction could be verified. I have no real qualms about verification of a treaty of that sort. I did have qualms about verification of SALT II.

■ *CHAIRMAN DELLUMS:* Could you elaborate on some of the major problems concerning command, control, and communication functions at the present time?

■ *MR. ALDRIDGE:* I won't go into a lot of detail, but what frightens me most is the computerized automation—massive amounts of data are collected and assimilated and must be used to interconnect and coordinate all of these other first-strike capabilities. As former Ballistic Missile Defense Commander Dr. J.B. Gilstein pointed out, it would be impossible for any human being to enter the decision making loop. It all has to be preprogrammed with logic so that the computer can make the decision and run the game.

Recent GAO studies examine the deficiencies of military computers, particularly the NORAD computer system that gives the early warning. I think we are all familiar with the false alarms that have been generated by the NORAD system. The one that concerns me most was that of November 9th, 1979, when the system indicated a submarine-launched ballistic missile attack on the United States. A submarine-launched ballistic missile can get close enough to the United States so that the missile flight would be only ten minutes, or possibly even less. But that alert went six minutes before it was determined to be a false alarm. I imagine that there were many fingers getting very itchy on the nuclear button at that time because they were halfway into what would be the flight time of those submarine-launched missiles before they learned it was actually a false alarm.

No Department of Defense official has ever denied that we have a launch-on-warning strategy under certain conditions. When General Richard Ellis was commander of the Strategic Air Command, he indicated in testimony to Senator Henry Jackson that, under certain crisis management conditions, we may have to revert to launch-on-warning to save the Minuteman force. I think it is very scary when we have to depend on computers to make the decisions under these crisis conditions; they must decide very quickly, very accurately, with information that is gathered very quickly and assimilated very quickly. The number of false alarms that these computers have had—the failure of the computers during tests and military exercises—makes, I think, for a very touchy situation.

2

ASSUMPTIONS BEHIND U.S. STRATEGIC POLICY

Dr. Herbert Scoville, Jr.

■ ■ ■

Herbert Scoville, Jr., is a graduate of Yale University and holds a Ph.D. in chemistry from the University of Rochester. He was a senior scientist for the Atomic Energy Commission at the Los Alamos Project, worked as a special weapons analyst for the Department of Defense, worked for the Central Intelligence Agency as a specialist on scientific and technological issues, and from 1963 to 1969 was assistant director of the Arms Control and Disarmament Agency. Since then he has been affiliated with the Carnegie Endowment for International Peace and the Arms Control Association, which he heads. His books include *Missile Madness* and *MX: Prescription for Disaster.*

THE WHOLE SUBJECT of the military budget and tactical and strategic assumptions is of paramount importance these days, not only from a financial perspective but also from the perspective of the safety and security of our nation and the peoples of the world. The strategic weapons program in the current defense budget will not only cost prodigious sums of money and resources in the years ahead but will, in many cases, increase the risks of a devastating nuclear war breaking out. There has been a tendency by the Reagan administration to argue against cuts in weapons programs on the basis that such cuts will not seriously decrease the deficit until later years. While it is true that the actual expenditure of funds this year will be relatively low, but by no means inconsequential, approving them now will commit the United States government to these programs for many years into the future when the expenditures will be very much higher.

On October 2nd, 1981, President Reagan announced a five-point strategic weapons program calling for a major expansion in the development and procurement of new nuclear weapons systems. This program has been translated into specific weapons projects in Secretary of

Defense Weinberger's Annual Report to Congress for Fiscal Year 1983.

To date, there has been no parallel program for curbing the arms race and reducing the Soviet threat through arms control negotiations. Negotiations have been started on intermediate-range nuclear weapons in Europe. But negotiations on intercontinental range systems still remain in the indefinite future. The negotiations on intercontinental weapons have changed their acronym from SALT to START. That is about the only progress we seem to have had in the first fourteen months of the new administration.

We have repeatedly heard President Reagan decrying the so-called freeze proposal as being an inadequate arms control measure and affirming that he would be very much in favor of real arms control that involves reductions. That is great rhetoric, but we have not seen one single move to accomplish what he claims to be so interested in, which is reductions. We do not have any administration position. We do not have any negotiations. We do not even have people on board in their official capacities in the Arms Control and Disarmament Agency to staff out these programs. However, at this time, the administration is abiding by the provisions of the SALT II treaty, even though it condemned it very strongly, and has said that it is not prepared to abrogate the ABM treaty.

The primary justification for the greatly expanded weapons programs has been the desire to close the so-called window of vulnerability in the 1980s. This slogan was used with telling effect during the presidential and congressional campaigns. It is still cited as the justification for new weapons. Secretary Weinberger has repeatedly blamed an inferior U.S. strategic position on the U.S. government's reliance on arms control agreements.

Neither of these justifications can be supported by the facts. It is totally misleading to imply that, after SALT I, the United States stopped its strategic nuclear weapons program and relied on SALT for its security. The United States, actually five years ahead of the Soviets and before they even tested a MIRV, carried out a major MIRV deployment program for both ICBMs and SLBMs. Furthermore, the United States developed and started to procure advanced guidance systems and higher-yield warheads so that each warhead would have a high theoretical probability of destroying an ICBM silo. This was done in advance of the Soviet Union; the Soviets followed in our footsteps, not we following in their footsteps. These two developments are probably the two most dangerous of the past decade, since they markedly increase the risk that a nuclear war will break out.

The claim that our strategic forces have a "window of vulnerability" in the 1980s is also without foundation. The only element of our strategic deterrent triad that is even theoretically becoming vulnerable is the land-based ICBMs. I stress theoretical because, for the Soviets to be able to launch a surprise attack and destroy a thousand ICBMs in hardened silos is probably not possible and certainly would involve major risks to that nation, even if each of their warheads had a theoretical probability of being able to destroy one of these silos.

The overall strategic deterrent of the United States is not vulnerable. Secretary Weinberger does our security a great disservice when he makes statements to that effect in order to justify more money for new weapons. We have 3,000 or more warheads at sea at all times in submarines that are survivable for the indefinite future and certainly for this century.

We have several hundred bombers that will soon be equipped with several thousand air-launched Cruise missiles that can attack hard targets. At least 100 of these bombers are on fifteen-minute alert status, so they cannot be destroyed on the ground. For the Soviets to consider launching a first strike, knowing that retaliation by such a force, is possible is almost incomprehensible. There is no such thing as a "window of vulnerability" for our strategic deterrent in this century.

The second assumption that is driving President Reagan's strategic program is that the United States must have missile systems that can threaten the Soviet ICBM force, a policy that encourages the Soviets to launch a first strike. These so-called counterforce or hard-target weapons systems are ostensibly sought to match Soviet forces. However, the initial requirements for such weapons were established by then-Secretary of Defense James Schlesinger in the early 1970s in anticipation of the Soviets' having such a capability and even before they had tested any MIRV missiles.

This concept of matching the Soviet Union is misleading, since the United States has always been first in this area. Our Minuteman alone can destroy more of the Soviet deterrent than they can destroy of ours under any circumstances. Nevertheless, the Reagan administration's new program puts major emphasis on counter-ICBM missiles.

It is time for this administration and for all our military planners to recognize the facts of missile life—whereas land-based ICBMs served in the 1960s and 1970s as a very satisfactory leg of our deterrent triad, technology has out-paced them. No one will probably find any way in which you can make land-based ICBMs surely survivable into the long-range future. It is just too easy to destroy land-based ICBMs, at least by paper calculations. We have been looking for ways of protecting them for years, and none of these schemes works. It is time to stop pouring billions of dollars down this rat hole of "improving" land-based ICBMs and trying to make them survivable when technology has gone beyond that.

The Pershing II is an extremely dangerous weapons system because it will be deployed in West Germany with a capability of threatening destruction of Soviet command and control centers and missile silos without warning. It takes only six minutes from launch to arrival on the target. There is no feasible warning system that would permit people to take evasive action or to protect their command and control on this timescale. It would either mean that all the political leaders would have to stay in hardened shelters or be flying around in airplanes, or something like that, so that nobody would know where they are. One just cannot operate a government on that basis for a protracted period.

Furthermore, the Pershing II can almost certainly not be made assuredly survivable. This is a much more difficult job in densely populated Western Europe than it would be for the MX in the deserts of Nevada and Utah, which have no visible protection scheme. Thus, the Pershing II deployment provides a vulnerable target that is a direct threat to the survival of the Soviet command and control structure. This will provide them with a strong incentive to launch a preemptive strike, perhaps even in advance of any large-scale conflict in Europe. For example, if there were a real confrontation in East Germany similar to what we have recently seen in Poland and it looked as though a conflict might break out between West Germany and East Germany or would cross the borders, I do not see how the Soviet leaders could sit there with Pershing II missiles stationed in West Germany and not have to take some counteraction against them. In so doing, we are increasing the chances of nuclear war in Europe. Almost everybody agrees that no one knows how to prevent a nuclear war in Europe from escalating into an all-out nuclear war that would destroy us all.

Arms control is the other half of the nuclear weapons equation. To date, the Reagan administration has not demonstrated in any way that it is seriously seeking to enhance our security and protect our deterrence through arms control. The agreement, under European pressure, to start negotiations on intermediate range systems based in Europe is a useful move. So far, the administration's zero nuclear weapons proposal appears to be a "take it or leave it" political ploy rather than a first step toward constructively dealing with the dangers of these weapons systems.

The negotiations cannot be productive when both sides put out "take it or leave it" proposals. The Soviet proposal is equally unacceptable, but perhaps you could have said the two proposals were the basis for starting serious negotiations. Thus far, there is no evidence of that. Also, we do not have any firm indications of when the negotiations on the longer range systems are actually to begin.

In sum, the administration's program seems directed almost entirely toward the procurement of more new weapons, particularly those that can threaten the current mutual deterrent posture. Limiting the threat by arms control is not being given serious attention. Nuclear war does not seem to be a danger that influences the Reagan administration's strategic decisions. Instead, the American people are being asked to spend increasingly large sums of money for weapons that would decrease our safety and that will commit the United States to deficit spending for years to come.

■   ■   ■

■ *MS. SCHROEDER (D-Colo.):*   Is there any way to get the superpower leaders to negotiate? Is there any way to do it through intermediaries? Is there any way to do it in Geneva, or is it just all rhetoric?

■ *DR. SCOVILLE:*   The only way that you can get serious, meaningful negotiations going is by developing a very broad public understanding that then gets translated into political action. I think this administration recognizes political imperatives. At least, the intermediate-range weapons negotiations got started primarily from public pressure in Europe—first on their governments and then on our government—to actually start those talks. I think we are seeing the same thing here in this country. I am not all pessimistic, even though the outlook is not bright, because of what I see going on in this country.

■ *MR. BEILENSON (D-Calif.):*   What is your assessment of what our nuclear forces should consist?

■ *DR. SCOVILLE:*   In my view, the primary requirement for nuclear forces—in fact, the only legitimate requirement for nuclear forces—is to deter another nation from actually using nuclear weapons. The idea of using them for military purposes—having them knock out tanks, like the so-called neutron bomb—is just plain madness. Deterrence is the grim reality as long as nuclear weapons exist. The key element in having a deterrent force is to have it be survivable. Our submarines that are survivable—and I would not like to rely entirely at this juncture on submarines—backed up by a bomber force that can get off the ground in a relatively short period of time and that can continue to penetrate air defenses, constitute a very satisfactory deterrent.

It is essential that you do not turn the existing Minuteman force into a truly first-strike, counterforce system. It should not be given this new guidance system and the new warheads. We ought to cut back on those systems possessing counter-ICBM capabilities that can threaten their deterrent, thus giving the Soviets incentives for going to launch-on-warning. I hesitate to say we ought to strike a hard bargain and keep this capability as long as they have it because having it is not giving us security either.

■ *MR. BEILENSON:* Is it true that the Russian ICBMs are, or soon will be, as vulnerable to us as ours are, or will be, to them?

■ *DR. SCOVILLE:* Yes. Their vulnerability is much greater than ours. Even when the Minuteman program is finished, it will not threaten the entire Soviet ICBM force because it just does not have enough warheads. On the other hand, when you add on the MX and the Trident II, then the numbers get very scary. The Trident II supposedly is being designed with that in mind. It is still fairly early in the game, but the Trident II had originally one rather useful characteristic, although in my view unnecessary. It would have a 6,000 mile range instead of the 4,000 of the Trident I. This gives it more ocean and less vulnerability, although we've got so much already with the Trident I that I do not think this is necessary. But what has happened is that this characteristic of the Trident II has been sacrificed. As far as I know now, we are not going to give it that long range; instead, what we are doing is giving it this hard-silo capability.

■ *MR. BEILENSON:* Should we be concerned about the proliferation of Cruise missiles? Clearly these are weapons that, once we start putting out thousands of them, then I suppose the Russians will counter as usual within three or four or five years, and there will be thousands of these eighteen- or twenty-foot long, and one- or two-foot wide missiles that nobody is going to be able to verify, or know how many are in existence, or where they are, or who has got them. I take it that poses perhaps an insurmountable problem with respect to arms control limitations in the immediate future.

■ *DR. SCOVILLE:* We, unfortunately, could not put it into the SALT II treaty because of the opposition. Once the land-based and sea-based Cruise missiles are deployed, it will be very hard to verify the number that are deployed. That poses a threat not just to arms control, but it also means that, in the future, we will not know the size of the Soviet threat. Knowing the number of missiles the Soviets have is not only useful for arms control purposes, it is the basis of our intelligence on the Soviet strategic thrust. That information we will never have. I don't think you could verify a complete ban on land- and sea-based Cruise missiles because the chance of not finding one of them, if a significant number were deployed, is high. You have a good chance of finding one of them, but when you start to say you are allowed to have two or three thousand, or you want to know if they have five or ten thousand, there is just going to be no way you can do it.

■ *MR. BEILENSON:* Is it possible for some of us to argue logically that we should not go ahead with Cruise missiles because of what is going to happen on the Russian side?

■ *DR. SCOVILLE:* I do not believe we should go ahead with Cruise missiles on land or on sea.

■ *MR. BEILINSON:* Even air?

■ *DR. SCOVILLE:* We did work out a way in SALT II of verifying the numbers of air-launched Cruise missiles through the airplanes that were modified to deliver them.

■ *MR. BEILENSON:* But something similar could be produced that could be launched on land or on sea?

■ *DR. SCOVILLE:* That is possible, but it is much harder to visualize for a submarine or other ships or for land deployment. Perhaps numbers could be verified by observing test programs, if you have banned them completely on land or sea. But again, that is a total ban. If you find even one on land or on sea, then you have caught them in a violation, and I think the chances are that you could verify that.

Just from the military point of view, putting these Cruise missiles on attack submarines, which is what the Reagan administration proposes to do, is a very poor use of attack submarines. We want all the attack submarines we can get to protect our sea lanes. If they are to be given a strategic mission of attacking strategic targets in the Soviet Union, that means they have to be relatively close to shore. They have to be given that mission. That uses them up. They are no longer available to protect the sea lanes. If you are going to take a platform like a submarine, which is expensive, it is better to use ballistic missiles on them and dedicate them specifically for that mission. Instead of just a small number of very large Trident submarines, we should spread that portion to small submarines. One of the things that we should have a research program for is these so-called minisubmarines, which have been proposed by Sidney Drell, Richard Garwin, and myself, as an alternative to deploying the MX on land.

■ *MR. CONYERS (D-Mich.):* If you feel good about the growing opposition that the Reagan administration's military posture has caused to occur, how then do you feel about the imminent nuclear peril that has also grown proportionately more dangerous?

■ *DR. SCOVILLE:* I think that we are just at the beginning stages of this public opposition, which has been fueled by statements of the administration. But the real danger, and the reason I am so concerned, is the growing likelihood that a nuclear conflict actually will break out. We are far from getting these weapons under control, and every day we are coming closer to having a situation in which both sides will have strong incentives actually to use them. That is a very, very dangerous situation. In my view, the short-range tactical nuclear weapons in Europe are also madness. If the military cannot come up with a better solution of dealing with a Russian tank attack than committing suicide by using nuclear weapons to try to destroy them, then I do not think they should be defending us. What we have to face is the reality that you cannot actually use nuclear weapons to achieve some military objective. They are good only to deter somebody else from using nuclear weapons.

We have got to get on with the job of deterring conventional aggression without threatening the use of nuclear weapons. As long as we rely on the nuclear crutch in Europe, we are never going to face up to the problem of dealing with any possible aggression in Europe without having to resort to nuclear weapons. I am very worried about it. Even though I am gratified to see the change in public attitude, it is a long way from turning the political process around.

■ *MR. CONYERS:*   How do you respond to charges like these? "The Reds are coming, and you cannot sit around and talk this kind of nonsense. We may wake up dead tomorrow. The attack may start before the end of the year. These people are dedicated and totally committed to our destruction, and so it is folly to consider anything else." Or: "You can never trust them; to talk in terms of good-faith negotiation would be naïve."

How do you feel about these underlying misconceptions—misconceptions that some, including myself, feel are the deeper problems that must be solved before we can get to the incredibly technical discussions that are frequently engaged in by the federal government?

■ *DR. SCOVILLE:*   I fully agree that these points you have made are myths that drive the arms race and make arms control difficult to achieve. They have succeeded in destroying SALT II and preventing it from being ratified. They are the driving force behind the programs that you see in the current budgets. Many of us, including you up there and me down here, spent a great deal of time trying to explode those myths, but it is a lot easier to arouse the public about "the Russians are coming" than it is to arouse them about the fact that we are secure.

What we must do is try to build on that uneasiness on the part of the public by giving them the facts. I find it incomprehensible that Secretary of Defense Weinberger, who is the primary officer of the U.S. government responsible for our security, can go around publicly stating that we do not have a secure deterrent force, a survivable deterrent force, when he knows damn well that we have a survivable deterrent force—if you will excuse my language. What this does is to make our allies think we are weak and our enemies to take advantage of us. He is playing the Russian game. He is the best advocate for Soviet policy that exists in this country.

■ *MR. CONYERS:* Dr. Scoville, is there a mirror image problem in the relationships between the military establishments of the two superpowers—that is, are there "hawks" in each camp that continue to aggravate and spur their own governments forward so that we engage in this inevitable, upward spiral?

■ *DR. SCOVILLE:* I am sure there are. It is hard to say exactly how these pressures have been exerted within the Soviet Union, but there is no question that they have a military-industrial bureaucracy. It is different from ours, but it is there. In many ways, their bureaucratic stuffiness, or whatever you want to call it, is even worse than ours. They change things even more slowly than we do. We both get tied down with bureaucratic red tape. There are people who then realize the dangers. I basically think that the political people, and even the military people, in the Soviet Union recognize that a nuclear war would be a catastrophe for all concerned and that this is not the way in which they could gain or promote their political interests.

To put a number on what constitutes a survivable deterrent is very difficult. On the other hand, the submarine forces that we have today with about thirty submarines at sea all the time (actually about twenty-five now because we have taken some out) with about 3,000 warheads on them are virtually invulnerable. There is no way that they can be put out of action as a force, and they are always there for retaliation. That is a survivable deterrent and will continue to be a survivable deterrent for the foreseeable future.

If we cancel the ABM treaty so that the Soviets could build ABMs, then you might start questioning whether these are still a secure deterrent because you might worry about whether the warheads could get through. They are banned by the ABM treaty so this is not likely to happen. Even abandoning the treaty would not bring this into effect for quite a long while.

Also, you always like to have a few hedges in case you haven't calculated right. We have a very good hedge in the airborne force, which has a much better command and control system than does the submarine force. That is one advantage; you can always recall bombers. That provides a good second back-up, and I think that is a quite adequate deterrent. The ICBM served a very useful purpose in the 1960s and 1970s. Now they are, at least theoretically, vulnerable, so we ought to not spend a penny more trying to upgrade them in the future.

This idea that we have to match the Soviets weapon for weapon, and warhead for warhead, and in type of capability—even though it makes no sense in terms of our security—is, to me, a completely mindless policy. We are clearly not better off or safer by having both sides have more weapons. We haven't gained a single thing, and, unless you have some kind of an arms control agreement, there is no other way to keep the Soviet levels down.

A good example is this nonsense of what has been going on in Europe. Back in October of 1979, before NATO made the decision to procure and deploy the Pershing and Cruise missiles in Europe, Leonid Brezhnev made an offer in which he specifically stated the Soviet Union was prepared, unilaterally, to reduce the number of its medium-range weapons aimed at Europe if the United States would not make the decision to deploy Pershing II and Cruise missiles in Europe. President Carter, with Brzezinski at his elbow, did not even explore that offer. They cast it aside without even considering it.

We will be extraordinarily lucky if we ever get the Soviet Union's SS-20 force back to what it was in 1979. At that time, they had only eighty SS-20s. As many predicted, when we refused to even ask the Soviets what they meant by that offer and explore it, they went ahead and now have 300. Are we better off by their having 300? We still have zero. Our bargaining position is not better now than it was then. Our experience with the SS-20 only underscores that trying to buy or procure weapons as bargaining chips, or to match the Soviets, is a losing proposition.

3

THE NEED FOR ARMS CONTROL

Paul Warnke

■ ■ ■

Paul Warnke graduated from Yale University and attended Columbia Law School. He has held the positions of general counsel for the Department of Defense, assistant secretary of defense for International Security Affairs in the Johnson administration and director of the Arms Control and Disarmament Agency in the Carter administration. He currently practices law in Washington, D.C.

NUCLEAR ARMS IS one area in which arms control can work. The reason it is not working is because we are not trying hard enough. One of the reasons we are not trying hard enough is that we do not have any coherent strategic nuclear arms policy. There are conflicting signals from this administration. Most people who have studied the subject have come to the conclusion that nuclear arms can serve only one purpose—that is, to prevent the other side from using theirs, or making a plausible threat to use theirs, against us or against our friends.

Regrettably, there have always been voices that call for some more ambitious plans for strategic nuclear weapons. Some say that we ought to be able to use the threat of our nuclear force to free us to use our conventional military force as we see fit. These same voices also tell us that we need not tolerate the other side's using its conventional military force because we will be able to intimidate by our nuclear superiority. There is this constant drive to secure strategic nuclear superiority—but it cannot be obtained. There is no way in the world that either the United States or the Soviet Union is going to gain any meaningful strategic nuclear superiority unless the other side gives up.

We have no reason to expect that the Soviet Union is going to give up, no matter how many billions and trillions of dollars we spend. They can match us. They can match us because the nuclear balance almost intractably becomes a balance close to parity. It is not like battleships. At one point in history, if you had thirty battleships and the other side had twenty-five, you could claim superiority; you could afford to lose twenty-nine of your battleships to sink its twenty-five and you would be the battleship king.

Today, we have almost 10,000 strategic nuclear warheads. The Soviet Union has approximately 7,500. That is a great lead—2,500 strategic nuclear warheads—but it does not mean a thing. We cannot use any of ours without inviting, and in fact inevitably attracting, nuclear retaliation that would destroy us as a functioning modern society.

Under those circumstances it makes absolutely no sense to try to work out some refinements in our strategic nuclear weapons. It is futile to think that refinements would enable us to use these nuclear weapons to gain political and national security objectives. The current debate, unfortunately, is raging around an issue that should have been settled, and that I thought was settled, more than a decade ago. There are still today some people in the present administration who call for developing the kind of nuclear forces that will enable us to wage nuclear war rationally. That is a contradiction in terms.

The two sides of the debate have been characterized by somewhat colorful acronyms: "MAD" (mutual assured destruction) for those who believe in the theory of deterrence, and "NUTS" (nuclear utilization target selection), for those who feel that we need a war fighting capability for our nuclear arms. Unfortunately, it now appears that the NUTS are winning. We are going from bad to worse, and we have got to stop it.

There are also indications of an effort by some officials to downplay the horrors of nuclear war. You may have noticed an article in *Newsweek* last Summer (August 31, 1981, p. 13). That article referred to a film that was being prepared by the Federal Emergency Management Agency. According to the producer of the film, his objective was to paint *a rosier picture of nuclear war,* to point out that all was not doom and gloom and that the answer to nuclear attack was the same as the answer to floods or hurricanes—that is, to evacuate the stricken area. Trying to equate nuclear attack with floods and hurricanes would be, in my opinion, laughable, if it were not so deadly serious.

A Defense Department official (Mr. T.K. Jones) also was quoted in articles in *The Los Angeles Times* a few months ago (January 15-16, 1982) as saying that the United States could recover from an all-out nuclear war within two to four years. He called for a massive civil defense effort, telling the interviewer that everybody is going to make it if there are enough shovels to go around. His plan is for each American to dig a hole, put two wooden doors over it, and pile three feet of dirt on top of the doors. He does not explain how you get into that hole once you put three feet of dirt on top of the wooden doors, unless you are going to count on a self-sacrificing friendly neighbor to cover you over once you get in. The proposal might serve one purpose; it might help solve the problem of body disposal, provided there is anybody around to worry about that particular problem.

To delude ourselves that such a defense is possible is merely to add to our risks. No number of fallout shelters is going to do us any good other than to provide a choice between being fast-fried or dry-roasted. It does not really matter which way you die. At best, civil defense against nuclear attack is a waste of money. At worst, it may foster the illusion that we can fight, survive, and win a nuclear war.

There also have been statements to the effect that, after all, Japan recovered from two primitive atomic bombs, each one with the explosive power of 13,000 tons of TNT, an almost incredible power. But today we are dealing with, between the two sides, 17,000 strategic nuclear weapons, and some of those warheads have the explosive power of several million tons of TNT. Under these circumstances there is no credible scenario in which we and the Soviet Union could fight a nuclear war and have either one of us be declared the winner. Either one of us might come out somewhat better than the other, but each would be worse off than Uganda or Bangladesh. We would no longer be recognized as superpowers. In fact, there is a question whether we would be recognizable as a national entity.

I think that it is imperative that the American public understand the facts about nuclear weapons and nuclear war. Only then will we find our strategic nuclear plans substantially revised and cut back.

We must develop a coherent strategic nuclear policy. Step one should be to decide and state that we will never be the first to use strategic nuclear weapons. Regrettably, that option has still been kept open. Until we do decide that there is no objective for which initiating a nuclear war would be appropriate, we will have this uncertainty about which nuclear weapons we should develop.

If we state a policy of no first use, then it becomes clear to the Soviet leadership that their land and their people will be safe from our nuclear weapons as long as they do not use or threaten to use their nuclear weapons against us. Then both sides can begin to pull back from this nuclear abyss. I know the argument is made that we ought to keep the other side guessing. In some circumstances that might be appropriate. I do not want the other side to guess whether or not we might start a nuclear war, however, because then they would have to speculate about under what circumstances they should start a nuclear war.

Nuclear war is not going to start because we rationally decide that we can gain some kind of desirable national objective. It will start, if it starts at all, because of panic, because of desperation, because of fear that the other side has developed the ability to strike first and prevent retaliation—in other words, fear that our deterrent is gone. This is not the case at the present time, but it could become so if we have an unrestrained nuclear arms competition that goes on with both sides developing, or thinking that they have developed, a nuclear war fighting capability. It is under these circumstances that we may find ourselves pitched into a nuclear exchange. Each side may then feel that, unless it draws first, the other side is going to get the drop and the other side will prevail.

This sort of desperate action can be prevented. It can be prevented not only by a declaratory policy of no first use but also by redoubling our efforts to secure effective, genuine constraints on nuclear arms. We ought to be redoubling our efforts to bring about this kind of nuclear arms control and reduction. The only thing that is holding us back is the lack of sufficient political will to get the job done.

Let me point out just one of the items that evidences this. There is negotiated and signed a treaty that is known as SALT II. I had some part in that negotiation, but it certainly was not a treaty I negotiated by myself. It was negotiated under three presidents over a period of seven years, and two of those presidents were Republicans. Many of the major provisions had been worked out before I ever took over the responsibility as chief negotiator. That treaty remains unratified. At the same time, we have said that we will abide by the provisions of that treaty as long as the Soviet Union does the same and the Soviet Union has said that too; so that we have a treaty that is officially unratified but unofficially ratified.

There is only one major difference between this situation of tacit adherence to the treaty and the situation that would prevail if the treaty were ratified. If the treaty had been ratified, the Soviet Union would have been compelled to cut over 10 percent of its strategic nuclear systems by the end of last year. By not ratifying the treaty, we have spared them that inconvenience.

The administration says that it wants to start arms reduction. In fact, it has called for a change from SALT to START. It can get that 10 percent reduction simply by submitting the treaty to the Senate and having it ratified. That would not be the complete answer; there are several other steps that ought to be taken. But not taking these steps has brought about a very broad-based peace movement, the antinuclear weapons movement, in Europe.

In this country, it is impatience and fear on the part of the American public that has led to this grassroots movement calling for a freeze on the further development, production, and deployment of nuclear weapons. I hope that our politicians begin to respond to this popular movement. It is real and eventually they will pay a political price if they do not respond.

In addition to ratifying SALT II, we ought to negotiate with the Soviet Union for further reductions. I have been intimately enough involved in the negotiations to know that we could get agreement with the Soviet Union on a schedule of annual reductions—perhaps not a significant number initially, but enough to add up. Ten percent a year for ten years is a pretty substantial cut in the nuclear arsenal. We could do that.

We also could complete a comprehensive test ban, which is perhaps the most important single step in freezing the nuclear arms race. We have been negotiating about this with the Soviet Union and the United Kingdom since 1977. The major problems for a comprehensive test ban have been solved. Again, it is a lack of political will that blocks progress. The United States has not been pressured sufficiently to complete these negotiations.

We are told today, according to official American statements before the United Nations, that the U.S. government supports a test ban only as a long-term goal. We are told that a test ban is a goal for the future but not for today, "because international conditions are not now propitious" for immediate action on this worthy project. I submit that there will never be a better time and, unless we are lucky, that there will never be another time. Time is not on our side. We now have no binding legal restrictions on offensive nuclear arms. The SALT I interim agreement expired in October of 1977, and SALT II has never been ratified. There are certain steps that the Soviet Union could take that would totally destroy the negotiated provisions and put us back on square one. We cannot have that happen.

I know the administration has other ideas on arms control. Anything that it can do in addition to these steps is certainly very desirable, as is anything that it can do to limit the number of warheads and to improve verification. But at least let us start. Let us take the immediate steps that will spare the world the growing risk of nuclear devastation. I would agree that nuclear arms control is not an alternative to a strong defense, but just as clearly it is an essential part of a strong defense and an indispensible component of our genuine national security.

■   ■   ■

■ *CHAIRMAN DELLUMS:* I have heard some people suggest that in order to negotiate back from the brink of nuclear disaster in

Europe we must involve the Europeans in the negotiations. What are you thoughts about that?

■ *MR. WARNKE:* I think that the Europeans are a bit schizophrenic about participating in the negotiations. One of the most interested parties is the Federal Republic of Germany. Because of the bloody history of relations between Germany and the Soviet Union, I think the Germans feel some trepidation about being active negotiators on nuclear matters.

At the same time, we ought to recognize that Europeans should make the basic decision whether or not new American missiles that can strike Soviet targets will be deployed in Western Europe. We ought to make it clear to them that our only reason for proposing this deployment is to try to allay European fears about the deployment of the Soviet SS-20s. That is how all of this got started. What we should do is consult them at every point in the negotiations. When the Soviet Union agrees to a proposal that the West Europeans accept, we should say that this is plenty good enough for us because we gain nothing by having another 572 warheads in Europe. They can strike only Soviet targets that we can already hit with 10,000 strategic warheads.

■ *CHAIRMAN DELLUMS:* If we agree that there is no such thing as a "limited" nuclear war—that if war started in Europe, even as a conventional war, it would escalate inevitably to global strategic nuclear war—then counting medium-range missiles is an absurd exercise because, at some point, our entire nuclear arsenal becomes an aspect of that exchange. Thus the whole notion of European missile superiority becomes an absurd concept.

■ *MR. WARNKE:* I would agree. I think that any use of nuclear weapons has inherent risks of escalation to an all-out nuclear exchange. The entire concept of a "limited" nuclear war makes no sense at all. To contemplate a nuclear war limited to Europe would be adopting a policy analogous to the famous statement made during the Vietnam War—that we had to destroy Europe in order to save it.

We now have 7,000 tactical battlefield weapons in Europe. When any substantial fraction of those weapons begins to go off, we will find that we have lost what we are trying to protect. As far as a limited strategic exchange between the United States and the Soviet Union is concerned, that is a fatuous concept. The only scenario that I have heard is one in which the Soviet Union would launch a preemptive strike against our retaliatory forces.

What would that surgical, limited strike entail? We have 1,054 ICBM silos. Military planners calculate that an attacker would have to target each one of those silos with two warheads, one to burst in the air and one to burst at ground level—that is 2,108 Soviet warheads. In addition, if they try to prevent retaliation, they would try to strike all of our in-port ballistic missile submarines located in key populated areas of the East and West Coast, and also strike our Strategic Air Command bases to try to destroy our B-52s.

What you are talking about is not a surgical strike, but something like *4,000 to 5,000 strategic warheads,* which is most of the Soviets' strategic arsenal. That would make an awful mess of the United States. We would retaliate, and we would destroy them. So, the concept of a "limited" nuclear war is fundamentally an absurdity.

■ *CHAIRMAN DELLUMS:* What are your views on the current proposals for a nuclear freeze?

■ *MR. WARNKE:* I support the effort to bring about a mutual negotiated nuclear freeze. I think some of the critics talk as though the call were for an immediate unilateral American nuclear freeze. They say that, under those circumstances, we could not develop the kinds of weapons that perhaps would give us our greatest security.

Well, believe me, there is no risk that the negotiations are going to proceed too fast. We do not have to worry about getting too far along toward a freeze. I think that by the time a freeze has been negotiated we would have completed our deployment of the air-launched Cruise missiles on our strategic bomber force. We probably would have installed our Trident II missiles on our ballistic missile submarines. These are not bad weapons, as nuclear weapons go. They increase the survivability of the deterrent. But I would sacrifice even them if we could get an immediate negotiated nuclear freeze because at the present point we have a stable strategic balance.

The president has said that the freeze does not go far enough. I agree, but that is not a reason for being against it. It is a reason for being for it, because then you could go on from there, as the Kennedy-Hatfield Resolution proposes, to have selective reductions of the more dangerous and the more destabilizing systems, such as the land-based intercontinental ballistic missiles with the multiple independently targetable reentry vehicles.

■ *CHAIRMAN DELLUMS:* On a number of occasions, the president and other representatives of this administration have suggested to the American people that the Soviet Union has some kind of extraordinary nuclear superiority that serves as a justification for their incredibly escalated military budget. Would you comment on that?

■ *MR. WARNKE:* There is no basis in fact for the assertion that the Soviet Union has strategic nuclear superiority. We lead in strategic warheads. Again, it doesn't really matter, but we have a lead. We also lead when it comes to survivable forces. Look at what we have done in diversifying our strategic nuclear forces. I am totally against developing weapons with the idea that you can fight and win a nuclear war. But it is important to have survivable weapons, weapons that cannot be readily destroyed by a first strike. It is also important that we not have weapons that threaten the survivability of the Soviet deterrent.

Today we have the three parts of our strategic nuclear deterrent known as the triad. We have the land-based ICBMs, our submarine-launched ballistic missiles, and our strategic bomber force. We have over 50 percent of our strategic resources in the submarine-launched ballistic missiles. That is a force that is invulnerable for all practical purposes, and some 60 percent of our ballistic missile submarines is on station at all times. So we have a survivable deterrent. We are equipping our B-52s with long-range Cruise missiles that would be able to penetrate Soviet air defenses. We have approximately only 25 to 30 percent of our forces in the theoretically vulnerable land-based ICBMs.

The Soviet Union, regrettably, has something like 80 percent of its strategic resources in a vulnerable system. I would rather that they had a greater percentage in survivable forces because the survivability of the deterrent on both sides gives us the only security that we can have in the nuclear age.

But the concept that we somehow have let them get ahead is really a criticism of our having made certain decisions. We have made the right decisions and we ought to be proud of them rather than poor-mouth our capability.

■ *CHAIRMAN DELLUMS:* Are the concepts of mutual assured destruction and deterrence still viable, given the accelerating progress of our nuclear technology?

■ *MR. WARNKE:* They are viable at the present time. The troublesome element is that, if we insist on building more sophisticated and more accurate weapons, we can count on the Soviets to do the same thing. Thus, as time goes on, the weapons on both sides will become more deadly and more vulnerable. I have equated it to the "High Noon" situation, in which it is a question of which one is going to draw first, except that we are dealing not with guns, but with nuclear missiles. And that is a duel in which both sides would be destroyed.

■ *CHAIRMAN DELLUMS:* In the FY 1983 military budget, specifically in the research and development section of the budget, there is over $800 million for research in ballistic missile defense. Some people speculate that, if we attempted to build ballistic missile defenses, it would exceed $100 billion and that it would require that we abrogate our treaty. Could you comment on the implications of building a ballistic missile defense system?

■ *MR. WARNKE:* I was struck by the fact that, in the Department of Defense materials that accompanied the announcement of the Reagan strategic program on last October 2nd, reference was made to the fact that there is no known technology that would give us any sort of effective ballistic missile defense. Even though this is an option that is held open, perhaps for the basing decision on the MX, these same materials indicate that there is nothing in prospect that would give us an effective ballistic missile defense. As a consequence, if we were to spend additional billions of dollars on ballistic missile defense, it would produce nothing but bad effects. We would have to abrogate the ABM treaty, which is the most effective treaty that we have thus far been able to negotiate.

There is no way in which, with any known technology, ballistic missile defense can stay ahead of the offensive destructive capability. That is just a question of figures. How many antiballistic missiles would you need in order to strike down the thousands of Soviet missiles that could be directed against our own ICBM silos?

Let me give just one illustration. The Soviets have an SS-18 intercontinental ballistic missile. It is their largest ICBM. It presently has a maximum of ten warheads on each SS-18. That gives them something slightly in excess of 3,000 warheads on the SS-18s. Not all of them have ten at the present point, but potentially they could. Under SALT, they are limited to ten. If the SALT restrictions expire, existing technology permits them to add at least another ten or twenty warheads on each SS-18. If they add twenty, so that each SS-18 has a total of thirty warheads, that is another 6,000 warheads. They can do the same with their other missiles. They can also build additional missiles if the SALT restrictions are allowed to expire.

How could an ABM defense keep up with that? We decided to ban ABMs back in 1972 because there is no way that an ABM defense can do anything except encourage an offensive nuclear warhead race, and the offense will win.

■ *CHAIRMAN DELLUMS:* Would you also agree that pursuing ballistic missile defense also strikes at the very notion of deterrence and moves our entire nuclear armaments policy to a completely different realm?

■ *MR. WARNKE:* That is correct. The problem is that all of these things add to the illusion that somehow you can fight and win a nuclear war. It is very unsettling to think that our security rests only in our ability to destroy the other side. But struggling against a fact does not change it.

■ *CHAIRMAN DELLUMS:*   One of the major arguments for the MX missile is that our fixed-base ICBMs are becoming increasingly vulnerable to Soviet attack and that, if we placed our fixed-based missiles in a mobile mode, we would increase their survivability. We understand that the administration has rejected all of the various basing mode proposals thus far and is planning "in the interim" to deploy a number of these very powerful MX missiles with Mark 12-A warheads.

Some of my colleagues have voted against the various basing modes of the MX, but they accept the argument that we need the missile. My argument is: Why do we need the missile if we no longer need the mode? The MX missile has a very powerful warhead that, in my estimation, can be perceived only as a counterforce weapon. How do you perceive the Soviet planners' view of the deployment of these very powerful MX missile warheads in fixed silos, since we may be no longer talking about a mobile mode?

■ *MR. WARNKE:*   The criteria that any new strategic nuclear weapon should meet are two: that it be the most survivable and the least provocative to the other side's force. The MX flunks both of these criteria. It would still be vulnerable, theoretically, and it would represent a counterforce threat to the other side's deterrent. The answer to the MX is to forget about it. We do not need it. It does not do us any good. What we really ought to do is to concentrate on survivable weapons that do not threaten the other side's deterrent capabilities. The MX adds nothing that we can use, but it does add to the threat that the other side may feel so that they adopt a launch-on-warning policy. That is particularly true when taken together with the planned deployment of the Pershing II missiles in Western Europe.

■ *MR. BRAUER (staff):*   Looking at theater nuclear weapons and the expressed concerns of Chairman Brezhnev, is there any reason, given the significant decrease in warning time that the Soviets would face with the Pershing IIs, that they would not react with the same alarm as we did when the Soviets placed missiles in Cuba in 1962?

■ *MR. WARNKE:*   I think it is quite clear that they do view this prospect with a great deal of alarm. Regrettably, they brought the problem on themselves by deploying the SS-20s. We would not have contemplated stationing these new American missiles in Western Europe if it were not for the concerns of our Western European allies. That is why I favor a negotiated solution that will cut back substantially on the SS-20s. That will make it not only unnecessary but obviously impossible for us to deploy our new missiles in Europe.

■ *MR. BRAUER:* Can you see any military benefit in a new theater nuclear weapon in Europe?

■ *Mr. WARNKE:* I see no military benefit at all. Basically, talk of new weapons is politically symbolic rather than militarily useful. It is a way in which we send signals back and forth to one another. It is a ridiculous way to communicate. There are much better ways; for example, the bargaining table.

■ *MR. BRAUER:* You alluded earlier to the so-called vulnerability of our ICBMs. How do you see this translating into the likelihood of a Soviet attack or into greater U.S. vulnerability?

■ *MR. WARNKE:* I think that we have talked ourselves into a nonexistent problem. The vulnerability of the ICBMs is a theoretical vulnerability, not an actual vulnerability. First of all, what point does it make for the Soviet Union to try to destroy less than one-third of our nuclear retaliatory force? They would still be faced with the certainty of destruction from our remaining ICBMs because not all of them would be destroyed; neither our strategic bomber force nor our ballistic missile submarines would be destroyed.

Second, think of the problems involved in planning an attack that would have any chance of destroying even a majority of our 1,054 ICBMs. You would have to plan that at least two warheads would land on each ICBM silo at just about the same time because once the first silo blows up, we would empty the remaining silos in a retaliatory attack against the Soviet Union.

Third, you have to contend with the problem of nuclear fratricide, even assuming that you are able to time your attack with this sort of exquisite precision. How do you deal with the reality that preceding nuclear explosions would destroy later incoming warheads?

■ *MR. BEILENSON (D-Calif.):* Given the importance of both sides' present tacit adherence to the limitations in the SALT II treaty, do you think it might be useful to have some congressional efforts to formalize our remaining within those limits? Do you think it might be useful, since the president does not seem to want to go ahead with the SALT II treaty, for the Congress to try to pass an amendment to the defense appropriations bill that says, for example, nothing appropriated herein may be spent for any weapons systems that would violate the provisions of the SALT II treaty in the absence of the Russians violating the treaty?

■ *MR. WARNKE:* I think that would be an excellent idea. We are now in a situation in which, although both sides are tacitly adhering to the treaty, there has been no attempt at formalization at all. Obviously, the best way to formalize it would be to ratify it.

■ *MR. BEILENSON:* Is it still in our interest to ratify it?

■ *MR. WARNKE:* If we do ratify it, the Soviets have to destroy 10 percent of their nuclear systems immediately, which is certainly getting started on reductions. It is also very important that we formalize it so that the Soviet Union has some basis for feeling that they have an interest in sticking with the restrictions themselves. I would also call for some form of reciprocal formalization from them.

■ *MR. BEILENSON:* Would not ratifying the SALT II treaty speak to the problems of our going ahead with some of the destabilizing weapons systems?

■ *MR. WARNKE:* It is not enough. We, principally for tactical reasons, wanted to have permission to build the MX missile, so the SALT II treaty provided that each side could build one new ICBM. I would have preferred a total ban on any new ICBMs. That would have been a definite plus for us. I think it is beginning to be clear that the MX is not going to be built.

■ *MR. BEILENSON:* Could the Trident II missile be built under the SALT II treaty?

■ *MR. WARNKE:* Yes, it could because there would be no restrictions on new types of submarine-launched ballistic missiles. The only control would be the overall numerical limit. Of course, there would be a limit on the number of warheads.

■ *MR. BEILENSON:* Do you think we ought to go ahead with the Trident II missile program?

■ *MR. WARNKE:* I would prefer that we do not, provided that we can get similar restrictions on the Soviets—which is the advantage of a bilateral, mutually negotiated freeze. Again, our nuclear weapons ought to meet two criteria: One is survivability, and the other is the least provocative weapon, one that represents the least counterforce threat to the other side. The Trident II meets one test but not the other. It does increase the survivability because it has longer range—6,000 nautical miles, compared to the 4,000 nautical mile range of the Trident I. But it does have counterforce capability, as does almost any new ballistic missile we will have.

■ *CHAIRMAN DELLUMS:* For a number of years, you and Mr. Paul Nitze have been leading public figures in the debate over nuclear arms escalation versus arms control, freeze, and reduction proposals. Could you give us your assessment of how these respective positions evolved, and what you foresee as the possible outcome of the ongoing debate on these matters?

■ *MR. WARNKE:* Paul Nitze is negotiating for the United States in the intermediate range theater nuclear talks in Geneva. Having been in a similar position myself, I certainly do not want to say anything that in any way would undercut Mr. Nitze or interfere with his effectiveness. I think all Americans wish him well. Everybody hopes that his efforts succeed. We have had our differences of views in the past. I regard him as a serious man who does know the field. I think that, given the proper kind of support, he can achieve effective results.

■ *CHAIRMAN DELLUMS:* Does this proper kind of support include American public opinion in a very clear way?

■ *MR. WARNKE:* I think that is indispensable. I think that was lacking in 1979 when the hearings on SALT II were taking place. I am obviously not totally objective in this regard, but I thought all the arguments against the SALT II treaty were very effectively answered during the hearings. It really was just the absence of the necessary constituency that made it politically infeasible to get SALT II ratified.

I think that popular support is terribly important. I think that people who oppose sensible nuclear arms control ought to pay the political price, which is political oblivion, as far as I am concerned.

■ *CHAIRMAN DELLUMS:* I deeply appreciate that latter comment because I have been saying to the American people, whenever I have the opportunity to mount the podium, that the one factor that can be inserted into this equation that has the potential to bring constructive change is public opinion. If the American people do not speak loudly, clearly, and unequivocally on this matter, then those of us in the Congress who are advocating constructive alternatives to the madness of the arms race will be without a solid constituent base, which will undermine the effectiveness of our arguments on the floor of the House and the Senate. I appreciate the fact that you are willing to take such a strong public position on these critical issues of human survival.

Regarding the question of verification, will more sophisticated technology increase the problems of verification? Do we have the technical capability at present, and in the immediate future, to verify a limitation on strategic nuclear weapons?

■ *MR. WARNKE:* Let me speak first to the verification of the SALT II treaty. SALT II, of course, was negotiated with verification uppermost in our minds. The provisions were worked out so that we could be sure that we would know whether or not the Soviet Union was complying. It is interesting to note that the entire American position on verification eventually was accepted by the Soviets. As far as verification of SALT II is concerned, I have absolutely no doubt of its verifiability.

There are certain limitations as to what you can do in the field of arms control because of the verification problem. For example, being able to verify the total number of missiles would be better than being able to verify just the total number of launchers. I would hope that, as the arms control process continues, we can get more and more verification provisions and greater cooperation by both sides.

On-site inspection is frequently cited as being the ideal. On-site inspection really does not do you an awful lot of good on some arms control treaties. It would not add significantly, if at all, to the verifiability of SALT II. Instead, what we have are certain counting rules. For example, I mentioned the fact that the SS-18 has a maximum of ten warheads. Since we do not know of any other way to verify it, we count each SS-18 as having ten warheads even though we know that some of them have only one. Similarly, we count as launchers of MIRVed missiles every launcher that has ever housed or launched a MIRVed missile, even though we know some of those launchers contain a missile that has a single warhead. In sum, we over-count. It would be better if we could count with complete accuracy.

As we get further along, I hope that certain cooperative measures can be adopted. You have pointed out that the technology increases in all areas. It does, but our verification technology also improves at all levels. In addition, our photo-reconnaisance capability is almost unbelievable in its ability to detect what is going on in the Soviet Union.

Verification by on-site inspection is important and very valuable on something like a comprehensive test ban because there the essential problem has to do with a seismic event. The seismic detectors pick up a type of seismic event, so the question becomes, Was that an earthquake or was that an underground nuclear explosion? They are able to locate where that event took place, so you can send an inspection team with the necessary equipment to determine whether or not it was an underground nuclear explosion. That is an important type of on-site inspection that we were able to negotiate with the Soviets in the comprehensive test ban talks.

■ *CHAIRMAN DELLUMS:* In this country, some of the most potent lobbyists against the test ban are the scientists who are doing research projects in this area. I have talked with many who have raised important questions with regard to the test ban issue. You mentioned in your remarks that the SALT negotiators worked out the problems of a test ban. Would you elaborate upon that?

■ *MR. WARNKE:* Back when we started the comprehensive test ban negotiations, we thought we had three major negotiating problems. One of them was the question of on-site inspection. The second was Soviet insistence that there be an exception for what is referred to as peaceful nuclear explosions. The third was that we felt it was important to station national seismic stations on the territory of the other side. In other words, we would station on Soviet territory American seismic stations able to detect seismic events, and they would station theirs on ours. All three of those problems were effectively worked out by the end of 1977, so there is no reason why we could not speedily complete a comprehensive test ban. All that holds us back is that apparently we do not want to do it.

What are the reasons that are given why we should not do it? One is that we would not be able to detect very, very small explosions. Our detection capability would be able to reduce the magnitude of those explosions down to a level at which they would not give any significant military advantage to the other side. Another reason that is given is that we have to continue to test our stockpile; otherwise, confidence in the reliability of the stockpile would deteriorate. Well, I say three cheers for that. The less confidence that both sides have in the reliability of their nuclear weapons, the less chance there is that either side will ever use them.

■ *MR. BINGHAM (D-N.Y.):* Does it make any sense to have these so-called intermediate nuclear force (INF) talks going on limited only to the European area?

■ *MR. WARNKE:* It makes no sense, except in the context of the existing SALT restrictions. I noted with some relief that Secretary of State Alexander Haig said last July in a speech to the Foreign Policy Association that the administration recognized that the intermediate theater nuclear talks had to take place within the framework of SALT. I took that to mean that the administration recognized that the existing negotiated, though unratified, restrictions had to remain in force because it otherwise would be an exercise in futility. Even if you eliminated the entire question of these intermediate-range weapons—let us say that they liquidated all of their intermediate range missiles, such as their SS-20s, their SS-4s, their SS-5s, and we did not deploy the Pershing IIs or the ground-launched Cruise missiles—it would make no difference if each side is free to go ahead and add to the numbers of strategic warheads.

Every Soviet ICBM can strike every target in Western Europe that can be hit with an SS-20. An ICBM can cross the ocean, but it does not have to. It can stop off in Western Europe and destroy it. Similarly, our 10,000 strategic warheads can destroy every target that could be hit by the 572 warheads on our planned European-based missiles.

■ *MR. BINGHAM:* I am not quite clear how it makes sense, even within the context of SALT.

■ *MR. WARNKE:* If, in fact, we can reach an agreement with regard to these intermediate range theater nuclear forces and if, at the same time, we do something to formalize adherence to the restrictions of SALT II, then it gives us a basis for further progress. The administration, unfortunately, is on record as saying that the SALT II treaty is fatally flawed. I find it curious that they insist on abiding by the provisions of a fatally flawed treaty, but, nonetheless, that is the political situation. I take it that the administration feels that it could not at the present time send SALT II to the Senate. Suppose that we were to go ahead and negotiate an agreement that substantially eliminates the intermediate-range theater nuclear forces? Add that to the provisions of SALT II. Negotiate with the Russians for a further addition to the treaty that says that for the next five years, we are going to cut between 5 and 10 percent of the forces each year. Then you would have something that appears to conform to what the administration says it wants. I am certain that such a treaty could be speedily ratified by the Senate. Then you could go ahead with further quantitative and qualitative restrictions.

■ *MR. BINGHAM:* Does it make any sense for us to maintain that the French and British nuclear forces are to be left out of the calculation in discussing what is a reasonable balance in the European theater?

■ *MR. WARNKE:* I think it is quite clear that the Soviets will not leave those forces out in their own consideration of what sort of an agreement they would be prepared to accept. We cannot negotiate for the British and the French. I think there is very little chance that they will both come into these negotiations because their forces are so small that any substantial cutback would eliminate them entirely, but that is a decision that is theirs to make. What we ought to do is tell the Europeans that we are prepared to accept any agreement that is good enough for them. Obviously, that agreement on the part of the Soviets would have to reflect, on their part, some consideration of the French and British forces.

■ *MR. BINGHAM:* What is your reaction to the latest Soviet statement regarding the deployment of theater nuclear weapons?

■ *MR. WARNKE:* As I said earlier, I did not think much of it. Obviously it is a negotiating ploy. I do not think we can take seriously any negotiating proposal that is made in a public speech. That is not how negotiations take place.

My problem with it is that Mr. Brezhnev did not say that he was prepared to stop production of the SS-20s, but only that he was prepared to stop deploying it in the European part of Russia. If he deploys them east of the Urals, he can still strike Western European targets. Then, since it is a mobile launcher, he can move it back west at any time he so decides. In any event, in any place east of the Urals, SS-20s can strike all Japanese and Chinese targets, so we would be doing no favor to the Chinese or the Japanese by accepting a proposal that says that there can be an infinite number of SS-20s but that they will all be located in areas where they can strike you.

■ *MR. BINGHAM:* That suggests to me again the unreality of this business of trying to have an agreement separate from the strategic agreement.

■ *MR. WARNKE:* I agree. We always contemplated that negotiations on these types of missiles would be part of SALT III. As you recall, there was a protocol to SALT II, but it expired at the end of last year. That protocol said that each would not deploy systems like mobile launchers. Each would not deploy ground-launched or sea-launched Cruise missiles until the end of 1981. Then there was the statement of principles and guidelines for SALT III that said that these protocol items would be a priority item for negotiation in SALT III. These are inseparable from the overall central strategic system. It does not make an awful lot of difference to the Soviets whether the Kremlin is blown up by a warhead that came from the Federal Republic of Germany or whether it came from the Great Plains of the United States. It is still an American missile, and there is an American finger on the button.

■ *MR. BINGHAM:* The Soviet argument is that the existing forces in the European theater are approximately in balance because they take into account our warheads that are to be carried by short-range missiles or relatively short-range aircraft. Is that a reasonable position for them to take?

■ *MR. WARNKE:* I think that public positions tend to be unreasonable, and I regard that as an unreasonable position. You can add up these figures in a whole variety of ways. The way in which they end up with rough equality, something in the neighborhood of 950 to 975 on each side, is by including many of our airplanes and excluding virtually all of theirs. This does not include a number of Soviet planes that are capable of carrying out nuclear missions but does include all the American planes. Those figures are not accurate, but I must say that our figures do not amount to much either.

■ *MR. BINGHAM:* You quote former Secretary of Defense Harold Brown on the subject of a "limited" nuclear war to say that there can be no such thing, but then you couple that with a reference to Presidential Directive 59. How was Presidential Directive 59 consistent with the view that there can be no such thing as a "limited" war?

■ *MR. WARNKE:* I think essentially it is inconsistent with the view that there could be a "limited" nuclear war. I think that Harold Brown did a brilliant job of trying to explain an unreasonable and unworkable policy. Presidential Directive 59 was explained by some of its proponents as being directed to the proposition that we could fight a "limited" and "protracted" nuclear war. Those are adjectives that have no reality when you are dealing with nuclear weapons.

■ *CHAIRMAN DELLUMS:* Represented as the bottom line of this administration's rationale for proceeding with the arms race is the fact that we have not gone to war with the Soviet Union because we have stayed strong; that, in order to maintain a nuclear deterrence, we must continue to advance the level of our strength. Can you respond to that comment?

■ *MR. WARNKE:* I do not think that anybody who has studied the subject would be in favor of eliminating our nuclear weapons. I would not want to depend on Soviet charity or philanthropy to prevent them from exploiting that advantage.

The question is, What do we need in order to have an effective deterrent against the use or threatened use of Soviet nuclear weapons? What I would answer is, We have plenty, and we don't need any more. What we ought to do is explore every possibility for effective nuclear arms control, such as a nuclear freeze, arms reductions, and qualitative control. What our current policy looks like, I am afraid, is not an effort just to maintain a deterrent, but an effort to build up a nuclear war-fighting and war-winning capability. That is the risk, and if we follow that course, I can guarantee the other side is going to follow it too. As a consequence, the nuclear abyss comes closer and closer.

■ *MR. BEILENSON (D-Calif.):* Should we be concerned about going ahead with ground-launched and sea-launched Cruise missiles? I guess those were covered in the protocol, which has now expired.

■ *MR. WARNKE:* I think it is a mistake on our part to go ahead with the deployment of ground-launched and sea-launched Cruise missiles. They are small. They are very hard to detect. They do not require complicated launching mechanisms. One of the parts of the October 2nd Reagan strategic program that troubled me most was the idea that we would equip our general-purpose submarines with sea-launched Cruise missiles. We do not need additional warheads to destroy the Soviet Union. If we go ahead with that kind of a deployment, many consequences will ensue, none of them good.

In the first place, you degrade or perhaps eliminate the mission of the general-purpose submarine. If it is going to be loaded up with sea-launched Cruise missiles, it is not going to be a very effective attack submarine. It will not help us maintain the sea lanes. That Cruise missile is not going to be useful in trying to attack Soviet shipping. It is preprogrammed, and its little brain tells it to go to some point in the Soviet Union and blow up.

The second problem is that then every ship—not only submarines, but every ship—becomes a potential strategic nuclear delivery vehicle. In a sense, it is the sort of development that took place when we deployed MIRV back in 1969. It is fine as long as you have them and the other side doesn't have them. But unless we plan to start a nuclear war within the next three or four years, we can guarantee that the Soviets will match us in sea-launched Cruise missiles. When that occurs, then every fishing boat off the coast of New England has to be regarded as a possible carrier of Cruise missiles rather than cod fish. I do not think that is going to improve our security.

4

WHAT IS STRENGTH IN THE NUCLEAR AGE?

Richard J. Barnet

■ ■ ■

Richard J. Barnet was educated at Harvard College and Harvard Law School. He worked in the Arms Control and Disarmament Agency but resigned to become co-founder of the Institute for Policy Studies in Washington, D.C., where he is currently a senior fellow and an occasional consultant to the Department of Defense. His books include *Roots of War: The Men and Institutions behind U.S. Foreign Policy; Global Reach: The Power of the Multinational Corporations;* and *Real Security: Restoring American Power in a Dangerous Decade.*

THE DANGER OF nuclear war in the 1980s is awesome. Not only are inherently more dangerous weapons being built—vulnerable missiles with built-in pressures to "use them or lose them"—but nuclear weapons are being inevitably drawn into life-and-death struggles around the world. The first Cold War, we can see in retrospect, was a relatively peaceful affair. Despite the cosmic ideological issues over which the United States and the Soviets occasionally threatened to blow up the world, the half dozen men or so in Russia and America with a finger on the button never had any compelling reason to push it. The perceived need to avoid nuclear war was greater than either side's concern over the outcome of any particular confrontation.

The list of flashpoints for nuclear war is a long one—a statesman on the order of Idi Amin or some other despot with a ravaged brain; terrorist groups, with or without a cause; sophisticated criminals engaged in private enterprise blackmail. All have plausible reasons to acquire, or to make the world believe they have acquired, nuclear weapons and the will to use them. The materials and technology for creating nuclear weapons are ever more widely available.

These developments greatly increase the likelihood of new U.S.-Soviet confrontations. In future confrontations we cannot always count on the Soviets' backing down; their record of restraint in a crisis (even those they provoke) is a reflection of their relative military weakness in the past. Having achieved rough parity with the United States in military power, their national security managers are now much more likely to think as their U.S. counterparts think: "We can't afford to back down and be exposed as a pitiful, helpless giant." Thus, the happy accident that the world has survived the first years of the nuclear era is unimpressive evidence that we can avoid nuclear war in the coming era, for world power relationships are changing faster than we can comprehend and the arms race has become an entirely new game. The impending new stage of the military competition is likely to make the world of the 1970s look in retrospect like a Quaker village.

It is evident that, in the present political climate, "zero nuclear weapons" is merely a rhetorical goal, whether the rhetorician is the president of the United States or a spokesperson of the peace movement. With the spread of nuclear weapons and nuclear technology the call for physical abolition of all nuclear weapons—without regard for the political, moral, and psychological changes that must accompany radical disarmament—merely heightens anxiety and breeds cynicism.

To avoid an utterly catastrophic holocaust more than 95 percent of present stockpiles would have to be destroyed. Since we have long passed the point at which putting the weapons physically out of reach would make us much safer, most people have lost sight of what disarmament is supposed to achieve. Because we cannot visualize an alternative road to security except through stockpiling arms, we focus on the risks of disarmament rather than the advantages. Even the most minimal arms agreements involve the issue of transferring trust—from weapons we do not understand and cannot see but believe in, to shadowy foreign leaders whom we have been taught to distrust. Since the purposes of disarmament are unclear and the implications uncertain, most people prefer to stay with the world we know or think we know than to enter a world in which we put our trust in the sanity and decency of people rather than in the power of machines.

There has been no disarmament because the assumptions of the arms race have been almost universally accepted. Most people, including most people who favor disarmament, accept the premise that more weapons mean more security, that alternative systems of security not based on making hostages of hundreds of millions of people are utopian, and that the survival of the United States as a sovereign actor in the world justifies mass murder, poisoning of the earth, and hideous mutation of the human species. We do not seem to be able to generate the moral passion to rid the world of arms because we ourselves are psychologically dependent upon them.

The standard nightmare for our national security strategy is a Soviet attack or Soviet blackmail. If we fall short of the magic number of nuclear weapons, it is argued, Kremlin leaders may think that they would suffer "only" 10 million or 20 million or 50 million casualties if they push the button; they may then conclude that running the world with the United States out of the way would be worth it.

There is nothing in Soviet behavior, history, or ideology to suggest that the model of the Soviet leader waiting by the button until the computer predicts an "acceptable" casualty level is anything but a convenient fantasy to support an unending arms race. It is said that it is a harmless fantasy, a kind of insurance policy against Armageddon. But, unlike an insurance policy, the arms race directly affects the risk. By preparing for an implausible war we make other scenarios for nuclear wars—by accident and miscalculation—far more probable.

We have erected an elaborate system of war prevention— people in submarines are submerged for months waiting for the word to destroy 300 cities or more with the touch of a button; banks of computers are expected to behave significantly better in communicating critical information than those that produce the billing foul-ups in department stores; cool rational leaders are expected to make the most agonizing decisions in a crisis, without information or sleep. Anyone who ponders this system can understand why growing numbers of scientists state flatly that if the arms race continues nuclear war is now inevitable.

What is a practical alternative for the 1980s to a national security strategy based on ecalating the arms race? Arms limitation agreements can create a positive political climate in which it becomes possible to move toward an alternative security system—but only if certain requirements are met. The first requirement is that the agreement makes both sides feel more secure. Since partial limitations on nuclear weapons may appear to favor one side or the other, as the opponents of Salt II have alleged, the more comprehensive the limitations the more stable the agreement. Second, the new arms relationship should have clear economic payoffs for both sides. Third, the principle of "rough equivalence" should be extended not only to numbers and characteristics of weapons systems but to other aspects of the military relationship, including the right to acquire bases and to threaten the homeland of either power from such bases. Fourth, the explicit purpose of the agreement should be to remove ambiguities about intentions.

The more that these agreements require significant internal changes in both societies, the better reassurance they provide. Clear political commitment in the direction of demilitarization is not easy to reverse and thus offers the most reliable indication of national intentions. A substantially emptier parking lot at the Pentagon or at the Ministry of Defense in Moscow and the conversion of defense plants provide better indices of national intentions than satellite photos of missile silos, as important as they are. If Soviet consumer production began getting the priority attention now available only to the Soviet military-industrial complex and their tanks began to look as dowdy as their hotel elevators, one could reasonably conclude that something important had happened. A serious program of conversion would require the leaders of both sides to confront powerful interests with a bureaucratic and ideological commitment to the arms race. That itself would be impressive evidence of a turn toward peace.

The single most important measure toward fulfilling the four criteria I have proposed would be a mutually agreed-upon moratorium on the testing and deployment of all bombers, missiles, and warheads. Such a moratorium would be verifiable by existing intelligence capabilities on both sides. During that period, the signatories would undertake to negotiate a formula for making deep cuts in their strategic nuclear arsenals along the lines recently proposed by George F. Kennan. The mutual moratorium, not unlike that which preceded the negotiation of the atmospheric test ban, would enable the negotiators to keep ahead of technological developments and would create a much more favorable climate for the ratification of long-term agreements.

The greatest perceived threats are not the weapons already built, although they are more than adequate to destroy both societies, but the weapons about to be built. New weapons systems convey threatening intentions. However, a freeze on all new nuclear weapons systems would clearly indicate that both sides indeed intend to stop the arms race.

If the United States is to reverse the decline in its power and security, we must recognize that the uncontrollability of the arms race is the greatest threat we face. War is not a national security option in the nuclear age. If our strategy for war prevention fails, everything fails. Whether the survivors number in the millions, or tens of millions, the American experiment will be over. In thirty minutes we will have cashed in two hundred years of history and perhaps put an end to all history. There is no longer a way to base U.S. security on the threat of nuclear war without running enormous risks of having to fight a nuclear war. No national security objective can be served by such a war, for it would destroy our country and quite possibly civilization as well. America and Russia continue to stumble toward war. The greatest security threat of all is the fatalistic belief that the war no one wants cannot be avoided.

The Soviet Union is most likely to commit aggression under two circumstances. The first is when it senses that its own security is slipping away and makes a military move, as in Afghanistan, to stabilize its shaky domain. The more the Soviet Union feels its relationship with the United States is unstable, the more likely it is to make such a military move. The second circumstance in which the U.S.S.R. might well use military power is when the temptation to do so is overwhelming because of the political vulnerability of the United States. The United States should therefore build situations of strength, but the source of such strength is not more military hardware but strong political relationships. Ironically, the rush to rearm is weakening our most important relationships—the ties with the nations of West Europe and Japan. We need a much clearer definition of the national interest in the Third World and a much closer collaboration with the rest of the industrial world on new rules for developing a just international economic order. Our failure to project power stems from excessive spending on behalf of military strategies that cannot work and insufficient spending on political and economic strategies that can work.

We fear the triumph of socialism in other countries so much that we continually tie the national destiny to doomed regimes and undermine our own legitimacy as a force for freedom and democracy in the world. It is ironic that, at the very moment that the Soviet Union has lost much of its ideological force, the United States is reviving ideological diplomacy. Our decline in power is not a consequence of our failure to build more missiles but of our failure to manage our own society.

PART TWO

FOREIGN POLICY, NATIONAL SECURITY AND THE MILITARY BUDGET . . .
Arms for what ends?

■ ■ ■

We should have such an empire for liberty as she has never surveyed since the creation; and I am persuaded no constitution was ever before so well calculated as ours for extensive empire and self-government.

Thomas Jefferson to James Madison
April 27, 1809

■ ■ ■

THE BUDGET PROCESS is a fiscal reflection of the priorities of the government in power. In a very real sense, the budget is also a public expression of our concern—or lack of concern—for human dignity, personal freedom, and the public commitment to care for the less fortunate among us in this society and around the world.

For too many years the Congress has deferred to the president its responsibility to investigate, analyze, and formulate the policy choices upon which budget decisions ought to be predicated. The result has been a blind acceptance of misinformation, exaggeration, and hyperbolic pronouncements about the nature of U.S. security needs and a generally enthusiastic endorsement of a jingoistic, interventionist approach to developments in the Third World.

The military and national security budget proposals presented by this administration for fiscal year 1983 were, in my judgment, a moral affront to what this nation proposed to be when it embraced the Declaration of Independence, the Constitution, and the Bill of Rights. As members of Congress, we have an obligation and a constitutional duty to challenge the policy and budgetary assumptions upon which these proposals are based and to pose constructive alternatives that speak, as Abraham Lincoln once said "to the better angels of our nature."

If American democracy is properly to function as the expression of the people's will, then the people must have full access to all the facts and viewpoints so that they can make the proper assessment as to what is truly in their best interests. Once informed by the "unarmed truth," the American people will be better able to judge regarding the vital issues of peace and freedom, economic and social justice for all—at home and abroad.

The witnesses presented in Part II examine the foreign policy and national security assumptions that underpin the military budget. In Chapter 5, Marcus G. Raskin provides an overview of U.S. policy since World War II based, in his view, on five goals: to maintain a dominant economic, political, and military position;

to control national, regional, and international disputes; to create a sound international currency based on the U.S. dollar; to use military power as a primary means of asserting U.S. will; and to define multinational corporate and military deals as central to the national interest. He argues that arms control negotiations have, in fact, provided the rationale for weapons expansion, both nuclear and conventional. Stressing the need to take these policy discussions to the people of the nation, he calls for a thorough reevaluation of U.S. foreign policy assumptions.

In Chapter 6, former Senator J. William Fulbright decries the increasing "Pentagonization" of our foreign policy, the shift to a nuclear war-fighting strategy, and the rank inexperience of our current national leaders. He emphasizes the danger in the current misunderstanding and lack of perspective on Soviet intentions and actions.

In Chapter 7, Professor Walter LaFeber analyzes what he terms the new U.S. "isolationism"—a determination to undertake international actions alone and without consultation in regional, international, or even allied contexts. He calls for the reassessment of U.S. policy assumptions, especially in Latin America, and a switch from a military- to an economic-based foreign policy, asserting that the reliance on military power is a misuse of real U.S. strength.

In Chapter 8, Michael T. Klare outlines one of the more pernicious components of this "isolationist" foreign policy. He details how our escalating global arms sales are politically and economically destabilizing to Third World countries and are driving the Soviet Union to sell arms in order to maintain their influence throughout the world.

In Chapter 9, Professor Franklyn Holzman graphically details the administration misrepresentations of Soviet strength, debunking the "spending gap" as being as false as the "missile gap" of 1960. He anticipates Part III with his argument that we have not been outspent and Part IV with his argument that we may spend our economy into oblivion. □

5

U.S. FOREIGN POLICY . . . Imperialism and Military Power

Marcus G. Raskin

■ ■ ■

Marcus G. Raskin graduated with honors from the University of Chicago and its Law School. He served on the Special Staff on the National Security Council and was a member of the U.S. delegation to the 1962 Geneva Disarmament Conference. He was a co-founder of the Institute for Policy Studies in Washington, D.C. His books include *The Vietnam Reader* (with the late Bernard Fall); *Washington Plans An Aggressive War* (with Richard J. Barnet and Ralph Stavins); *Being and Doing;* and *The Politics Of National Security.*

BECAUSE THERE IS undeniably greater interdependence in the world, American leaders—and various elites such as newspaper editors, university and religious leaders, and military and certain labor leaders—often seek and easily find justification for becoming involved in entangling activities. Nevertheless, the dangers of imperial adventure for American society are greater than ever before. Adventurism tends to obscure the economic, regional, and racial problems within the United States. There is a tendency on the part of leaders to defer dealing with internal problems by taking up imperial wars or grand global alliances. When this choice is made by leaders, foreign and national security policy becomes a prime cause of internal decay. The Reagan administration's public policies are systematically dismantling the equity base of American society. Furthermore, they are depriving the federal government of its responsibility to build and maintain the infrastructure for a prosperous economy, while they commit the American taxpayer to at least a $1.6 trillion defense budget for the next five years. This internal starvation is being carried out to support foreign policy objectives that are either outmoded, counterproductive or harmful to American national security.

Since World War II, American national security elites have formulated and carried out five imperial principles in their foreign policy:

1. *The United States (but not necessarily the American people) must maintain or obtain the dominant economic, political, and military position in the world.* Accordingly, the agencies of government are to be a facilitating mechanism for exploiting and controlling the resources and markets of the world, both in the short and long term. America's leadership is to be suspicious of any nation or group of nations that stands in the way of such dominance. Furthermore, the state apparatus is to secure the paramount place in the international arena of world economics for American-controlled multinational corporations, even as these corporations fly no flag but the one of profit, closing plants in the U.S. after depleting American communities.

Poor nations are required to play out their classic role. They are to produce goods and raw materials at low costs, while committing themselves to a mode of capital-intensive technology that is developed in the United States. Other nations, including more industrially developed ones, are encouraged to conform their social structure (even their eating habits) to lines that are acceptable to international banks, multinational corporations, agribusiness, and the U.S. national security bureaucracy.

Within the United States it has been the task of government officials to "iron out" differences among these players on the international field. In the past it was assumed by government officials that national security policy should primarily reflect military and diplomatic judgments. Economic considerations were hidden even from the actors, even though those factors were usually determinant in daily decisions.

Prior to the emergence of West European prosperity and the war in Southeast Asia, it was assumed that military and political affairs were identical with the economic wishes of the largest corporate and financial units of the society. In the Truman, Eisenhower, and Kennedy administrations, the hidden assumptions were that all decisions served the dominant economic interests, whether or not they were directly represented at government meetings. These assumptions did not turn out to be accurate. Free-floating interests, corporations like Occidental Oil, escaped the "guidance" of the largest corporations. Even more devastating was the fact that political and military considerations came to determine the judgments of the bureaucracy in the national security state.

This situation was viewed with alarm during the early period of the

Carter administration. Attempts were made under Secretary of State Vance to organize a foreign policy that was not totally dependent on military power. He also assumed that the interests of the largest American-based corporations could be more carefully rationalized and hence protected. They could be the cutting edge of U.S. foreign policy objectives. Reagan's policy aims at sustaining the present resource allocation between the white and nonwhite nations. This policy can be most clearly seen in the United Nations, where the United States consistently votes against those trade and economic development resolutions that might lead to a more equitable distribution between the poor and rich nations. Reagan's torpedoing of the Law of the Sea Treaty is the classic example of this national selfishness.

The Reagan foreign policy has not shown the flexibility in execution that was initiated by Henry Kissinger and Richard Nixon in 1970-71. They attempted to establish a new international club, with rules fashioned by only the most powerful. Kissinger operated this international ruling club, comprised of Communist leaders, capitalists in multinational corporations and banks, oil sheiks, and democratically elected leaders. He assumed that approximately *500 people* were able to control the destiny of the world. Thus, the task of American leadership was to perpetuate this form of "stability" by finding the means of intimidating or cajoling club members to hold back insurrectionary groups, liberation movements, or any serious jockeying and change in the pyramidal status among members of the club. Kissinger assumed that this was the way to protect American preeminence. While previously it was assumed by American leaders that the Soviets and the Chinese favor insurrection and liberation movements, his operative assumption was that the Russians and the Chinese could be managed to support the *status quo* and the present distribution of operational power in the world. This balancing act was thought to be a necessary condition precedent to "détente."

2.   *The American security system is aimed at controlling all manner of dispute—to mediate it or, where necessary, to "enflame" it.* Thus, for example, in the Middle East or in India and Pakistan the American defense policy was to sell arms to both sides and train officers of opposing sides in military and paramilitary assistance programs. It was thought that the United States could exercise influence through its arms technology. It was also thought that local wars could be fought to U.S. specifications by controlling the spare parts to both sides, as in the India-Pakistan dispute. Through such manipulation, the national security bureaucracy hoped to judge which nation, or which of several nations, could operate as its "deputy" in a particular region of the

world. For example, Iran, under the Shah, played the U.S. deputy in the Near East.

This foreign policy system prevails in the Reagan administration, with changes only in nuance. The issue of anti-Communism is obviously a central part of American foreign policy. But, as important as the backdrop of anti-Communism is, there is the question of perceived national security "threat" and "mischief." These terms are important in coloring the judgment and actions of American government officials. The question of "threat" is, of course, a highly subjective one, fraught with problems of judgment and class bias. In an imperial period, "threat" means anything that thwarts the will of the powerful. But not everyone in an imperial nation is powerful or perceives in the same way. The assessment of a foreign "threat" is different to David Rockefeller from a Mississippi tenant farmer or a pregnant mother in a suburb. An imperial national security policy finesses the issue of threat by assuming that the United States is under continuous threat because it has intervened all over the world. During the Kennedy period, for example, the Defense Department assumed that there were seventeen "threat" situations to the United States.

"Mischief" situations are also grist for national security action. It is assumed that the United States must counteract the "mischief makers." Secretary of State Dean Rusk was fond of pointing out that while we were asleep for eight hours, two-thirds of the world was awake, and some of "them" were making mischief. Concepts such as "threat" and "mischief" buttress the imperial responsibility. Besides ideological ramifications, the material ramifications of this point of view are central to the operations of the present foreign policy. They are a boon to arms sales. According to the Department of Defense, arms manufacturers, and the Department of the Treasury, an ancillary benefit to the United States is that a hard-sell arms assistance and sales program helps the United States in easing trade deficits. This aspect has grown more important as the United States finds itself in a continuing monetary crisis.

Throughout the postwar period, national security policymakers assumed that the American presence should be felt directly through permanent military engagement, or indirectly through the client-state system. The direct engagement system, in which American troops and weaponry are present, has given bureaucrats and the military a sense of international bureaucratic omnipotence. Imperial leadership assumes that the presence of troops is evidence of strength. The reverse is true. Military presence reflects weakness, vulnerability, and insecurity. Was American "influence" in Southeast Asia greatest when Khanh and Ky were the rulers of South Vietnam because the United States had 500,000 troops there?

The presence of so many forces, whether in West Germany or Southeast Asia, is an indication of weakness. As a general rule, the presence of American troops on foreign soil is a statement that the United States has no other immediately effective way to influence the course of events. The intervention, for example, of Soviet troops in East Germany is a statement of Soviet fears and vulnerability. The Soviet concern is that the East Germans might follow a foreign policy that could be at odds with the Soviet Union and perhaps more congenial to neutrality. Even when there is no war, when troops of one nation are stationed in another, a tinderbox situation will develop over a period of time. Either the military forces become the lightning rod for internal nationalist sentiment, or they are the basis of a *causus belli* with competing third nations who view the presence of troops beyond another's border as evidence of hostile and imperial intent. Where shifts in domestic opinion occur, American military engagement abroad places the United States in an embarrassing situation. For example, Congress was chastised by Secretary of State Kissinger because it refused aid to Turkey during the Ford administration.

The use of indirect or neocolonial modes of control is more popular among policymakers. Indirect programs are tied either to military assistance and covert activity, or to economic credits and resource markets. An assumption by those who favor neocolonial modes of control is that the United States finds it economically and politically less expensive to train others to fight than to send its own troops. Historically, the Republican congressional foreign policy has been based on a client-state system. The late Senate Minority Leader Everett Dirksen of Illinois once explained American foreign policy in Asia during the Eisenhower period by saying that it was predicated on Asian boys fighting Asian boys. It is also assumed that client troops of one nation can be used in another nation to put down an insurrection. The classic case was President Lyndon B. Johnson and Secretary of State Rusk getting Philippine and South Korean troops to fight in South Vietnam. Another form of indirect engagement is the use of military advisors and assistance programs to put down insurrections, as with the Huks in the Philippines or the FDR (Democratic Revolutionary Front) in El Salvador.

Economic and paramilitary coercion was the method of indirect engagement in Allende's Chile. A study of how international bank credits to the Allende government dried up during its three years in power, while Chile continued its high level of imports, shows a classic case of economic coercion. Credits and loans to Chile ended when Allende came to power. The "indirect" mode has far-reaching effects. One consequence is that, once this policy "succeeds," the United States is drawn into a web of dependency in which the winning group seeks military and economic assistance to defend itself against its own people.

This process weakens constitutionalism and strengthens bureaucratic fascism, unadorned by control from the people or parliament.

Within the United States such "victories" reinforce bureaucratic and corporate patterns that favor militarism, manipulative violence, bribery, and control "from the top." The elites who operate American national security institutions (as well as those climbing the bureaucratic ladder in them) are hardly averse to teaching—and learning—from their Brazilian, Pakistani, or South Korean counterparts. To what extent their patterns of violence are emulated by the American bureaucratic "teachers" is more than an academic question.

Some have argued that indirect engagement aids the United States in understanding the world. This argument is usually advanced by those who favor covert intelligence or covert operations run by the CIA. Paradoxically, where the United States is not interested in infiltrating another nation or building up a spy network or economically dependent system, it will be less likely to misperceive the complex cultural and political forces of that nation. The covert or overt presence of national security operatives in another nation who are involved in rigging elections, bribing, or murdering are hardly people who are able to report on the activities or independent actions of the "host" nation. If another nation's system is manipulated by the United States we cannot begin to know the true aspirations and feelings of the "host" nation because we are too busy trying to turn it into a puppet.

The national security and corporate institutions undertake to control what they do not begin to understand. Often one agency of the United States finds itself supporting an agency or an institution of another nation at cross-purposes with those of another American agency. This happened as a matter of course during the Indochina war. Strict adherence to a policy of state nonintervention is the surest guarantee of comprehending and judging a society and its leadership actions.

The U.S. alliance structure is predicated on a supine Congress that allows an executive great discretion while imposing virtually no limits. Once Congress reasserts its historic role, the present alliance structure must be transformed. Internationally, as contradictions within the alliance develop into open disagreement, as nations in the alliance turn to the Left or become xenophobic, it will be harder for the national security bureaucracy to maintain an alliance posture built on Cold War, anti-Communist, and nuclear war assumptions. It should be noted that the Soviets are faced with exactly the same set of crises within the Warsaw Pact nations.

3. *United States foreign policy has depended upon the need to ensure a sound international currency system in which the American*

dollar is the preeminent medium of exchange. Ever since the Bretton Woods Agreement of 1944, that effectively ended the gold standard and tied world currencies to the value of the U.S. dollar, it was assumed that the dollar was the paper that was "as good as gold." This assumption was seriously eroded through military spending, American subsidization of military alliances abroad, and the expansion of U.S. corporations, which paid substantially less taxes to the federal treasury, while laying greater expenditures for their worldwide protection onto the American middle and working classes.

Both liberals and conservatives have been reluctant to protect the dollar by cutting military spending, changing the alliance system, getting corporations to pay an equitable share of their taxes, developing a full employment economy, or controlling the staggering amount of debt that now stalks all American institutions and most of the American people.

4. *The most dangerous side of U.S. foreign policy continues to involve armaments, especially nuclear weapons.* Weapons are seen as the primary means of asserting the will of the state in the international arena. Military and foreign policy experts remain committed to the so-called flexible brushfire war concept—adding to it the military dictum to "get there firstest with the mostest." Indeed, military and foreign policy planners seem to have learned only this cliché from the Vietnam experience. Such policies, while basically brutal, are often sugar-coated with liberal rhetoric. They may be found in official documents about nuclear arms control, or in the argument that brushfire war capability is necessary so that nuclear weapons do not have to be used. While lip service is given to the dangers of the arms race, arms control negotiations act as a spur to arming. As we learned through rather bitter experience, there is a chicken-egg relationship between the defense system and the predilections of policymakers to commit war. The enlarged apparatus and "responsibilities" of the bureaucracy, the new weaponry, the military ideologies fostered by certain "think tanks," and the national security agencies have encouraged active military involvement abroad.

The problem of the Reagan leadership is the classic twentieth century question of brinkmanship—how to threaten with nuclear weapons, or armaments generally, sanction the build-up in them, and codify a system of war and negotiation that will guarantee that weaponry will be used in a controlled and "rational" way.

5. *American foreign and national security policy takes the international bureaucratic arrangements, special deals of military bureaucracies within the United States, and concessions made to global corpo-*

rations and banks, and asserts that these are commitments and "interests" that Congress and the American people must support.

Although the self-serving talk of personal, commercial, and bureaucratic interest was exposed by the Indochina War, the exposure has had little effect on American policy. But, because the nation as a whole has begun to question the assumptions of the defense budget, the role of the CIA, and so forth, there is far less automatic support for the pretensions that have controlled for so long the minds and behavior of our leaders.

Since 1945, the American trip abroad has cost more than $2 trillion in defense and alliance building. But the social and political world is changing in ways that suggest that the United States has failed to buy either security or hegemony. The Reagan administration is reminiscent of King Canute commanding the waves to turn back.

How should foreign policy be conducted? Obviously, I do not exclude transnational discussions and explorations that go beyond state relations. I would argue that the long-term possibility for any relatively stable world system must be predicated on transnational relationships of "people to people" groups. Thus, for example, cities in the United States and cities abroad could work out their own relationships, economically and socially; or workers in one country could relate their common interests to workers in another nation.

Second, as the alliance system is replaced or allowed to wither, the chance for coordination and consultation among nations could take place within the United Nations. Consequently, the United Nations could be the major forum for carrying out the business of foreign policy. The United States would then no longer consider it a place in which to isolate itself, as it has so often in the recent past. The United States would not threaten withdrawal. Instead, it would seek to abide by the rules of the United Nations, the General Assembly resolutions, and the U.N. Security Council deliberations. The United States would take some responsibility in developing a world common law.

It is also important to remember that a foreign policy grows out of the needs, aspirations, and forces within the United States. Thus, so long as a cultural and political hegemony existed that muted alternative voices and interests, only the most powerful economic, bureaucratic, and military interests were heard. But in the wake of the Indochina War defeat and a changed cultural and economic context in which Congress may repudiate sterile bipartisan national security policies and "executivism," it is not likely that the policies of the Cold War can be long sustained. The policy question that immediately arises is whether a new foreign policy can be developed that will protect American society, as it works out its fundamental economic and social differences. Is it possible to develop a foreign policy that does not protect the Rockefeller interests any more than it would protect the interests of the unorganized and the wretched, the urban worker and the farmer, but that will protect the United States against military attack? To do so requires a return to President Washington's principle of no permanent attachments.

One of the major problems of the last generation was caused by the assumption that the United States has permanent attachments or ties to particular nations and that it must conduct its foreign policies according to a system of pacts and alliances. Prior to World War II, American diplomats and politicians viewed this course as antithetical to the interests of the United States. World War II and then the Cold War changed this perception. The United States undertook at least forty-six alliance and pact commitments, and it came to identify those with whom it had such commitments as the "Free World."

In 1960, those people who favored arms control over disarmament argued that arms control was the only sensible way of operating in the world. They argued that arms limitation could be achieved, whereas disarmament was utopian. One commentator believed that a stable armaments world could be attained if the United States kept just 100 to 200 missiles. Another, Leo Szilard, argued that fewer than forty was sufficient. He called it "the sting of the bee." The horror of the present arms race is that those who would favor a cutback to 100 to 200 missiles would be accused of being radical unilateral disarmers.

Unfortunately, arms control proposals have not put a brake on the arms race. Instead, they have been used as part of the defense rationale to continue the arms build-up of new weapons in the nuclear and conventional war area that we intended to build. The bargaining chip argument commits us to weapons we do not necessarily want to build. They are thought of as unnecessary and therefore negotiable. What might have been possible in 1960 does not now seem to be possible because of the sheer number of weapons, the proliferation of them to other nations, the increase of a vested interest in them as a result of deformed economic structures, and a situation in which the animosity among nations increases the pressure to keep the arms race going. For example, the poor relationship between China and the Soviet Union continues the arms race between them and also adds fuel to those who believe that the United States must be an armed mediator in their dispute, just as the suspicious French seem to be moving *beyond* a passive deterrent.

In the United States, serious public opposition to the arms race was quiescent until the Reagan administration. The result was disastrous, with the United States increasing its arsenal to over 30,000 nuclear weapons and insisting on making the low-yield nuclear weapon an "ordinary" weapon that would be treated conventionally. By making nuclear weapons "everyday" weapons, the United States has shown that it is tied to their use in "limited" wars. It remains tied to first-strike options on the strategic level as well. What is important to ascertain is whether their preparation or use, as outlined in the Nuremberg obligation and various U.N. declarations, can be made part of the lives of bureaucrats, citizens and policymakers. This is hard to accomplish, except through grassroots activities.

While it may be late, there remains a strategy for obtaining disarmament that could be effective and that calls upon the most legitimate symbols and social groups of the society. The American society has to set limits on its national security state. One must be thankful that the antinuclear movement is changing the present elitist debate about arms control and disarmament. It is shocking that until 1982 there were no more than a few dozen people outside the national security bureaucracy who had any familiarity with the nature of the arms contemplated —and in being—and the arms race we are ever escalating. The number still remains woefully small.

Congress has a primary responsibility in changing this situation. Congress should undertake official hearings on the cost of the arms race, whether it is related to anyone's security and whether there are means to secure the United States without the kind of Frankenstein defense system that has developed over the years. In this context, I asked four questions in 1975 that I think are still pertinent:

1. If the United States were now to stop any further production of nuclear weapons and missiles, would it be any less secure?

2. Should not American government officials be held to a standard of personal accountability, outlined in various laws, so that aggressive war will not be a part of the national security bureaucrat's kit?

3. Should people in the armed forces be able to unionize for wages, hours, and morality, setting forth a code of ethics that would *exclude* the use of genocidal weapons and participation in aggressive wars?

4. Should military personnel have the power to limit the mode of weaponry and destruction by abiding to an oath of conduct that eschews such weaponry and that acts as a control over unconstitutional wars of aggression?

While such questions must now be opened and debated in society as a whole, it is still necessary to press for disarmament arrangements through the national security bureaucracies as they are presently organized.

It remains possible to establish the movement for general disarmament in three stages. As a first stage, the United States must undertake unilateral steps, such as banning future missile production and the production of uranium and plutonium. Outmoded alliance commitments used to justify elaborate military force structures must be transformed. A process of "agonizing reappraisal" and reconsideration must be instituted in the bureaucracy so that policy decisions for disarmament will not be sabotaged. This will make possible a second stage that will include regional disarmament arrangements to limit and then exclude foreign troops, nuclear weapons, and missiles from different regions of the world.

The context for discussion on disarmament must now begin in the U.N. Security Council, with the permanent members laying out the basis for determining the questions and concerns of disarmament. The United States should take the lead in convening a U.N. Security Council meeting with a series of studies about disarmament—how to achieve it, and how to preserve true peace in the world. These disarmament proposals would be debated in the council for at least a year, during which time an agreed-upon position would develop. That position would include these steps: What nations should do on their own without inspection; the reduction of missiles and nuclear weapons, unilaterally and through negotiating their abolition; the development of inspection techniques and collateral forms of inspection; budget examinations as suggested under the Helsinki Accords; and the reduction and abolition of armaments over a period of ten years. Past plans correctly called for the staged reduction of armaments in which the great powers would reduce their forces first, in the context of a worldwide disarmament and arms control plan. Less heavily armed nations would then be more likely to follow suit.

In a third stage, the success of so-called confidence building measures would cause national leaders to move to the abolition of weapons and armed forces, except for purposes of internal order. Such plans should now be exhumed and studied by Congress in the light of current needs and realities. It should be noted that certain new plans have been proposed that demand careful study because they include the actions of nongovernmental groups and citizens (e.g., the plan for general disarmament put forward by nongovernmental groups with transnational and United Nations organizations). Presently the world is spending $700 billion to $800 billion a year on "defense." There is no security or budgetary relief in sight. Our choices are stark and obvious.

A proper and effective congressional role in foreign policy can be restored only if Congress goes directly to the people and makes clear that Congress and the people are engaged in a process of developing modern directions in foreign policy. Thus, foreign and national security policy would leave the secret situation rooms of the CIA and the Pentagon, or the board rooms of great corporations and the State Department, to become an open, messy, but democratic process. And probably with far wiser results.

6

NATIONAL SECURITY AND THE REAGAN ARMS BUILDUP

J. William Fulbright

■ ■ ■

Former U.S. Senator J. William Fulbright was a Rhodes Scholar, a university president in his thirties, and a distinguished chair of the Senate Foreign Relations Committee from 1959 to 1975. His books include *Old Myths and New Realities*, *The Pentagon Propaganda Machine*, and *The Crippled Giant*.

THIS MILITARY BUDGET is the largest in our history, certainly in peacetime. It calls for more than a $250 billion authorization for fiscal year 1983, and the administration has indicated that we can anticipate an expenditure of $1,600 billion over the next five years. This figure is so far beyond our capacity to comprehend that it leaves us stunned and paralyzes our ability to protest.

The nuclear development program within this budget contemplates an expenditure of some $222 billion over the next six years, according to the Center for Defense Information. The implied purpose of this program is to gain nuclear superiority over the Soviet Union. This program, together with existing programs, will result in some 17,000 new and more powerful nuclear weapons during the next ten years.

This budget, together with the propaganda to sell it to the public and to the Congress, has the effect of shifting the focus of our policy from that of deterrence of nuclear war to the waging and the winning of a nuclear war. For more than thirty years, we and our NATO allies have thought—certainly I thought—that the possession of some thousands of nuclear weapons by each of the superpowers was an effective deterrence to war, as it has been.

This military budget is so large and the emphasis upon nuclear weapons so strong—and the rhetoric about the Soviet threat is so extreme—that one cannot resist the feeling that we are preparing to fight and to win a nuclear war. No one in the administation has ever said this directly. It may be that they conceive of their tactics only as a form of psychological warfare and that they are playing games with the Soviets in the hope that they will behave more to our liking.

If this is the case, it is a dangerous game and could easily get out of control and lead to a disaster. It is not only dangerous, it is costly and threatens the stability and the soundness of our domestic economy. Furthermore, if it is a psychological game, it is a complex and delicate operation requiring experience and subtlety in its execution, qualities that are hardly the hallmark of this administration.

The military budget, with its focus upon the paraphernalia of warfare, diverts our attention from what should be the primary concern of our policy—that is, the intention of the Soviet Union. There are two principal elements to be considered in our relations with the Soviets—their military capability and their intentions toward us.

In the Anti-Ballistic Missile Treaty of 1972, we and the Russians agreed, in effect, that there is no known effective defense against a nuclear attack by either party. We cannot prevent them, nor can they prevent us, from releasing inter-continental ballistic missiles, and we should accept that in formulating our foreign policy.

On the other hand, it may well be possible for each of the great powers to influence the other's intentions, even though they cannot prevent the release of ICBMs. This is the essence of the policy of détente as conceived by President Nixon in 1972 with the first SALT treaty and the several other agreements in other areas including trade, space, medicine, and educational exchange. All of these joint ventures had the possibility, or I believe the probability, of influencing the intentions of both parties. In fact, I think they did.

Unfortunately, these promising efforts were thwarted by the Jackson-Vanik Amendment to the 1974 Trade Bill, which linked developments in détente with Soviet human rights practices, and by a number of other events in recent years under the principle of linkage. When the United States refused to ratify the SALT II treaty agreed to in Vienna in 1979, the effort of détente could be considered suspended or finished. The only prospect for improvement in our relations with the Soviets, I believe, is in a return to the process of negotiation and agreement begun in 1972.

The implication of the military budget that most concerns me is that it indicates that this administration has no desire to revive the SALT process and believes that it can preserve the peace by a massive increase in our military establishment featuring nuclear weapons. I believe that is an illusion, that it cannot succeed, and that if it does not lead to a war, which it probably will if pursued, it will at least impoverish us. The idea of the Secretary of Defense that military expenditures are a good social welfare program, as he has stated, I think is simply nonsense.

In order to obtain the support of the Congress for this huge military budget, the spokesmen for the administration exaggerate the expenditures of the Soviets and they understate our own strength. Beyond that, for many years, the character and the motives of the leaders of the Soviet Union have been distorted by the propaganda of our government and the rhetoric of our leaders to such an extent that a dispassionate and open discussion of these questions has been avoided in the Congress.

If we are to avoid the kind of mistakes that led to World War I, it is essential that we give much greater attention to the study of the intentions of the Soviet leaders and try to influence those intentions in a manner favorable to the avoidance of a war. In the climate of détente it is possible at least to consider and to discuss the means to influence those intentions, but I am quite certain that building more arms, as this military budget provides, is not the way to influence those intentions in the way desired. I believe today, as I did ten years ago when the SALT I treaty was before the Senate, that a program of agreements about arms control, research in medicine, agriculture, and joint ventures in space and educational exchanges is designed to, and can have, a powerful infuence upon the intentions of the Soviets toward the United States, and *vice versa*.

I would like to bring to the attention of the committee General George Washington, our first president, and his Farewell Address. Many people overlook this part of that address, because there are other aspects of it that may have been more appealing. He wrote in his address: "The nation which indulges towards another an habitual hatred or an habitual fondness is in some degree a slave. It is a slave to its animosity or to its affection, either of which is sufficient to lead it astray from its duty and its interest." That is exactly what I think we have allowed our hatred to do in this case.

In a more recent context, one of the great psychiatrists, Erich Fromm, wrote:

> The lack of objectivity, as far as foreign nations is concerned, is notorious. From one day to another, another nation is made out to be utterly depraved and fiendish, while one's own nation stands for everything that is

good and noble. Every action of the enemy is judged by one standard—
every action of one's self by another. Even good deeds by the enemy are
considered a sign of particular devilishness, meant to deceive us and the
world, while our bad deeds are necessary and justified by our noble goals
which they serve.

That statement reminds me of the incident in November 1979, after
we had more or less laid aside the SALT II treaty. Mr. Brezhnev was
very anxious for the Europeans and the United States not to proceed
with the Cruise missiles in Western Europe. He made a speech in East
Berlin offering to withdraw troops and tanks from Central Europe as
an inducement for us to consider not going forward. I consider this was
a legitimate offer of negotiations at least. President Carter at that time
denounced it as a trick meant to deceive us, as a fraud, and so on. In
other words, he dismissed it brusquely. He didn't say, "Well, that's
interesting. We might talk about it or perhaps we could do more." It
fits exactly this feeling, this idea that Fromm had. Because it was a good
deed, an offer that people other than ourselves would have thought was
an opportunity to negotiate, it was considered particularly devilish and
particularly deceptive and was so denounced.

In 1969, General David Shoup, former commandant of the Marine
Corps and a hero of the war against Japan in the Pacific, wrote in *The
Atlantic Monthly*, "America has become a militaristic and aggressive
nation," and developed at considerable length a description of how the
military-industrial complex has acquired a dominant influence in our
government and how it operates today.

George F. Kennan, a former ambassador to the Soviet Union and
Yugoslavia, a distinguished historian, and the preeminent authority on
the Soviet Union in this country today, has examined at length our
relations with Russia and how we might influence their intentions for
the United States. At Dartmouth College on November 16, 1981 he
said:

> I find the view of the Soviet Union that prevails today in our governmen-
> tal and journalistic establishments so extreme, so subjective, so far
> removed from what any sober scrutiny of external reality would reveal,
> that it is not only ineffective but dangerous as a guide to political action.
> This endless series of distortions and oversimplifications; this systematic
> dehumanization of the leadership of another great country; this routine
> exaggeration of Moscow's military capabilities and of the supposed
> inequity of its intentions; this daily misrepresentation of the nature and
> the attitudes of another great people . . . ; this reckless application of the
> double standard to the judgment of Soviet conduct and our own; this
> failure to recognize the communality of many of their problems and ours,
> as we both move inexorably into the modern technological age; and this

corresponding decision to view all aspects of the relationship in terms of a supposed total and irreconcilable conflict of concerns and aims; these, believe me, are not the marks of the maturity and realism one expects of the diplomacy of a great power; they are the marks of an intellectual primitivism and naïveté unpardonable in a great government—yes, even naïveté, because there is a naïveté of cynicism and suspicion just as there is a naïveté of innocence.

... [I]f we insist on demonizing these Soviet leaders—on viewing them as total and incorrigible enemies, consumed only with their fear or hatred of us, and dedicated to nothing other than our destruction, that, in the end, is the way we shall assuredly have them—if for no other reason than that our view of them allows for nothing else—either for us or for them.

The essence of our problem with the Soviet Union is not their capability to do us harm with their nuclear weapons, about which we can do very little, but it is their intention, about which we can do a great deal. If we insist on viewing the Russians as total and incorrigible enemies, that is the way we shall have them, for that view allows for nothing else; and I believe down that road we will find catastrophe. We must recognize that our own policies have a direct and powerful influence upon the intentions of the Soviets and upon the ultimate outcome of our rivalry.

■   ■   ■

■ *CHAIRMAN DELLUMS:*   You stressed that the rhetoric of this administration is becoming so extreme that one cannot resist the feeling, to use your terms, that we are preparing to fight and win a nuclear war. What do you think can be done, and should be done, to reverse the direction of potential superpower nuclear conflict?

■ *MR. FULBRIGHT:*   One of the few things I can think of is that the Congress should assert its duty and its prerogative to raise questions about the validity of the position of the executive. But anyone in elected office today is perhaps reluctant to challenge the administration's assumptions on defense needs openly because of what happened in the McCarthy period when, if you raised your voice at all, you were smeared and denounced. The Russians were assumed to be absolute devils: Nothing about them was redeemable; they ought to be eradicated from the face of the earth. If you did not agree you were a "ComSymp" or you were disloyal; you were a traitor.

The Congress is the only body in our government that can effectively counteract or influence the executive, an executive in which the top men in our government have so little experience. There are many representatives with much more experience and knowledge than the top officials of the Reagan administration. The Secretary of Defense's appearance before Congress, presenting the posture statement of the Defense Department, virtually threatened war. He said it is no longer sufficient to plan for one-and-a-half wars; we have got to plan for several wars to be fought at several different places, places of our own choosing and not of the enemy's, and so on.

That kind of statement is extremely provocative. I can imagine how it makes us look around the world. We complain about the fact that our European allies and others are not sympathetic to our views. I do not know how they could be, when they read that sort of thing. We make those statements day after day. The Russians talk peace, however much they mean it; we seem to be talking war. The Europeans reacted very negatively to the president's idea about a "limited" war.

■ *CHAIRMAN DELLUMS:*   As you know, the interpretation of Soviet intentions is often used as a rationalization for escalating the arms race and for expanding the military budget. In your testimony, you alluded on several occasions to the American lack of perception and understanding concerning Soviet intentions. What is your assessment of Soviet intentions in the global arena—in Europe, in Asia, in Africa, and in Latin America?

■ *MR. FULBRIGHT:*   I think the Soviets intend to maintain their strength and to be capable of looking after their defense. They have been invaded three times in my lifetime; in World War I and World War II by the Germans, and during the Russian Revolution by the United States, France, England, and Japan. The Russians' intention is to do everything possible to defend their homeland, as they call it. They are extremely concerned about defending what they now have. I do not believe that their activity means that they are contemplating attacking Western Europe or us. I think they have more than they can handle with what they already have; they are having great difficulty even maintaining that.

They have become embroiled in Afghanistan, and, of course, they have already been in Poland, so I think they have their hands full. I do not think, in other words, that they are contemplating an attack upon us or Western Europe or upon anything that they would consider or, certainly, we would consider, of vital importance to us—for example, the Persian Gulf. I think the last thing they intend to do is to attack it.

That does not mean that if we alienate, as we have, the Iranians and others, they will not take advantage—they are already doing business with Khomeini and getting oil from Khomeini, and they will continue to do that. I do not think they are going to move militarily, which would be provocative to us and give us an excuse to respond militarily. I think they will go to great lengths to avoid provoking us into military action, doing all the while everything they can to take advantage, through diplomacy and otherwise, of their opportunities either there or anywhere else in the Third World.

■ *CHAIRMAN DELLUMS:* Do you think that George Kennan is on the right track when he calls for a 50 percent across-the-board reduction in all nuclear weapons?

■ *MR. FULBRIGHT:* He is saying that we have already overbuilt our nuclear stockpiles on both sides to such an extent that it has become an absurdity and they ought to be reduced. There would still remain effective deterrence on both sides because these ICBMs now number in the thousands. I think it is a good start.

It is somewhat the same general idea of the nuclear freeze, only it goes a little further as a starting point. Both of them, I think, contemplate that this is the beginning of a process of negotiations. The significance of détente and SALT is the process of continuing negotiations. This probably should go on forever or for as long as these two countries continue as independent countries and continue in the natural rivalry that results from size, history, and differences in their ideas about how to organize society.

■ *MS. SCHROEDER (D-Colo.):* Have you found it a little ironic in a democracy that, in the eyes of the so-called experts, we are not supposed to talk about the nuclear freeze or we are not supposed to do this through the democratic process?

■ *MR. FULBRIGHT:* I think that is a reflection upon their inexperience. Just think about who these people are at the top of our government. What experience do they have? Naturally, whether they recognize it or not, self-consciously, they know they have no experience. They know they do not know what they are doing. Therefore, they do not trust and do not want anybody to discuss it. On what grounds does a man who spent thirty years in the movies come and tell experienced members of Congress what to do about Russia?

■ *MR. BEILENSON (D-Calif.):* Do we need to look at the Soviets as a benign society? Should we be concerned about the extent of their military buildup, which to many of us—and even those who share your point of view—seems excessive, more than they need for purely defensive reasons?

■ *MR. FULBRIGHT:* That is a very interesting question. That is dealt with to some extent by Mr. Kennan and others. What we overlook is the situtation of the Russians. We are now linked as allies of their traditional enemies, nations with whom they have had wars in the past. They are surrounded by about fourteen or fifteen countries, any one of which has been or is inclined to be critical. Of course, they don't have the power, but at least they are not friendly and would invade if they could. They are unfriendly, in other words, in contrast to our situation with two relatively weak, certainly militarily weak neighbors, and the oceans to protect us. So, you have a very serious question. What is reasonable from their point of view as a defense? Obviously, anyone would consider, I think, that a much greater number of such things as tanks and so on if you are thinking about waging a war as opposed to deterrence, would be justified.

As for nuclear weapons, which is the deterrence part that concerns us particularly, I do not think they are out for that. I do not accept it. Admiral LaRocque has stated that the Pentagon and CIA figures are often presented in such a way as to give the impression that the Russians have spent much more than we have. What he does is to take the amount of our own and our allies—the Germans, the French, and the British. Admiral LaRocque makes the point that it is not true that the Russians have greatly overspent us. If you take the Warsaw Pact countries and the NATO countries, including us, there is at least equivalence and no serious imbalance in that.

The Russians are oriented primarily to their defense and are not eager to have a show-down with us militarily. In fact, they will go very far not to do so. But I always say they also are going to take advantage of opportunities where we alienate people. If we line up with the old *status quo* dictators in Latin America or South Africa or anywhere and there is a revolution, the Russians are going to be sympathetic to the revolution. They have done that nearly everywhere.

■ *MR. BEILENSON:* I think it is fair to say that the Russians are pretty much alone and isolated in the world, whereas we have a substantial number of dependable allies. We and our NATO allies spend at least $20 billion a year more on defense than do the Russians and their Warsaw Pact allies. We and our NATO allies have at least 600,000 more men under arms than do the Russians and their Warsaw Pact allies.

■ *MR. FULBRIGHT:* People don't know that. The way you hear the Secretary of Defense talk you wouldn't believe it, unless you look at it. You say we have lots of friends. I think we have had in the past, but if we keep going down this road, I do not think we are going to have many. I do not think this budget is making any friends in Europe; in fact, I think it is scaring them to death.

■ *MR. KASTENMEIER (D-Wis.):* Would you agree that this administration appears absolutely convinced and sanguine about its position? It is totally uncompromising, more than any other administration we have seen in the last generation, with respect to foreign policy. Do you see any redeeming value in this administration in its pursuit of foreign policy and defense policy?

■ *MR. FULBRIGHT:* It seems to me that getting an administration with as little experience as this one has is the fault of our system. No other system in the world would produce leadership at the highest level with no experience. What you are saying is a reflection of that lack of experience—this stubbornness, this conviction, and so on, that arise not from any knowledge or experience with the Russians but from some illusions that they have acquired in Hollywood. People don't like to talk about this because it is, in a sense, embarrassing. This is the fact.

7

FOREIGN POLICY ASSUMPTIONS OF THE REAGAN MILITARY BUDGET

Professor Walter LaFeber

■ ■ ■

Walter LaFeber is Noll Professor of American History at Cornell University, where he teaches U.S. diplomatic history. He is recognized as a preeminent scholar on the foreign policy of the Cold War era. His books include *America, Russia, and the Cold War, 1945-1980*; *The New Empire: An Interpretation of American Expansion, 1860-1898*; and *Inevitable Revolutions: The United States in Central America*.

IT SEEMS TO ME that too often we become enamored with the numbers and argue about them without realizing that certain assumptions in the budget lead to the numbers that we discuss. The most condemnatory judgment to be made of the Reagan administration's military policies, in my opinion, is that they are making it impossible to attain the foreign policy objectives that the president seeks to achieve. The most important of these objectives, according to the president, are world order—especially protecting developing areas from radical revolution—and the restoration of alliances and partnerships with like-minded nations to bring about and insure world order.

Instead of creating better world order, the military policies of the Reagan administration are driving revolutions in areas such as Central America increasingly to the left. Instead of restoring alliances and partnerships with like-minded friends, the military approach is not only frightening many friends, it is driving the United States toward a foreign policy that, as a historian, I can best describe as "isolationist." I emphasize this word isolationist because it is my understanding that Secretary of Defense Weinberger has used it to describe the opponents of the military budget; he called them isolationists. It seems to me that the term "isolationism" much better describes, in the context of American history, Secretary Weinberger and the Reagan administration itself.

Let me first talk about some of the assumptions of the Third World policy. The effect of the Reagan military policies on revolutionary areas has been self-evident, especially in Central America. If the past three years are a guide, the U.S. attempt to exert military pressure against the Nicaraguan government and the Salvadoran revolution will necessarily drive both toward more radical solutions and move them away from stated U.S. interests in the area.

The problem goes deeper than just present military policy. U.S. policy toward Latin America has not been reviewed fundamentally, and no important new initiatives put forward, since the early days of the 1960s when the Kennedy administration began the Alliance for Progress. The Alliance contained two premises that deserve attention now because the Reagan administration policy is beginning to follow similar policies. The first was and is the belief that a large program of U.S. investment and trade can create growing economies that will short-circuit revolutionary movements. In the Alliance, such U.S. aid was projected as part of a ten-year, $100 billion effort. In the Reagan administration, this approach has resulted now in the $350 million Caribbean Basin project.

I want to note the results of the Alliance's policies in Central America and how they led to the Organization of American States—that is, the attempt to impose a military solution in that area. The three Central American nations that enjoyed the largest economic gains in the 1960s, as far as per capita growth rate was measured, were Nicaragua with 5.3 percent, Guatemala with 3 percent, and El Salvador with 2.8 percent, despite an extraordinarily high birth rate. By the late 1960s, the Johnson administration was so pleased with Salvadoran economic development that North American officials called El Salvador the "model" for other Alliance nations to follow. These three nations, of course, have become the most revolutionary in the region. The Central American country that had the lowest growth rate annually, 0.8 percent, was Costa Rica. It was and remains, as well, the most democratic and stable.

The moral of the Alliance experience for the Caribbean Basin plan seems clear. United States economic aid can help nations such as Costa Rica, whose governments are committed to distributing the aid equitably. The assistance cannot work, no matter how many strings are attached or how many U.S. advisers oversee the program, if the aid benefits primarily the military-oligarchy elite and if the gap between the rich and poor widens until it can be bridged only by revolutionary actions. A turn toward revolutionary alternatives was precisely the response that appeared in Nicaragua, Guatemala, and El Salvador during the 1960s. U.S. officials at that time responded as the Reagan administration is now responding; they tried to use military means to destroy the symptom, the revolution, instead of dealing with the causes, the military-oligarchy elite that did little to help the poor.

The other part of the Alliance thus came into focus as large-scale U.S. military involvement in Central American began. Between 1950 and 1963, for example, Guatemala received only $5.3 million in military aid, but the amount doubled to $10.9 million for the period from 1964 to 1967. For Nicaragua, the figures were $4.5 million during the first thirteen years and $7.5 million in the next three. Increased numbers of U.S. military advisers moved into the area, particularly into Guatemala. But Washington's policy of militarizing the Alliance to deal with the revolutions had the opposite of the intended effect. Local troops, armed with U.S. weapons and trained in counterinsurgency techniques by North American personnel, began to alienate their own people with indiscriminate shootings and torture.

By 1970, after nearly ten years of the Alliance for Progress, the economic part of the program was virtually dead, but the military part thrived. Its growth, however, did not short-circuit the revolutions in Nicaragua, El Salvador, and Guatemala. Instead, by this time the roots of the present revolutions in those three countries had appeared. The Alliance's economic and military policies, and particularly the military policies of the late 1960s, thus helped create the revolutionary problems that the Reagan administration has inherited.

It is one of the sad ironies of recent U.S. foreign policy—and an indication of how little the present administration understands or is willing to come to terms with the lessons of the past—that President Reagan is following the same type of policies, especially in the military area, to control revolutions that had actually helped to create those revolutions in the first place. It is the diplomatic counterpart of trying to use gasoline to extinguish a gasoline fire.

U.S. policy toward Latin American has been increasingly militarized during the post-1945 years and especially since the 1960s. It is impossible to argue, however, that during these years the United States has been able to use its military power for the positive, constructive purposes in the area. To the contrary, the use of such power, whether covertly or overtly, has worsened, not improved, the environment for U.S. interests.

There is no persuasive evidence that large military expenditures will control the indigenous revolutions in that region. To the contrary, strong historical evidence suggests that larger U.S. military expenditures and a wider involvement in the Caribbean-Central American area will drive those revolutions to the left, increase the amount of their indigenous support, and make it less likely that our friends in the hemisphere will cooperate with our policy. Millions of dollars spent on devising military responses clearly have not and, if the past is any guide, will not resolve problems in the area that require, above all, diplomatic solutions. Such spending has allowed us to maintain the traditional North American illusion that raw power can supersede political imagination and economic commitment. In this, if not in other respects, U.S. policy in Central America and Vietnam is similar, although the Vietnam experience should have destroyed such an illusion utterly.

The traditional belief in the diplomatic efficacy of the military leads to the second and final point I wish to make: The administration's military spending plans fit a foreign policy that, in the context of our history, can be characterized as isolationist. This point is of importance because Secretary of Defense Weinberger recently said that opponents of his five-year, $1.6 trillion budget were trying to turn the country toward "isolationism." Secretary Weinberger badly misused that term. Historically, U.S. isolationism has not meant turning inward or away from the world. We did not, in a mere matter of seventy years after 1789, conquer a continental empire and then, in the next one hundred years, become the globe's greatest power by turning away from world affairs.

In our history, isolationism has meant freedom-of-action, and especially the freedom to use unilaterally controlled power whenever we saw fit to do so. This is a definition that can be incontrovertibly supported by evidence from the last two hundred years of our history. In this sense, U.S. foreign policy officials may have often talked like internationalists, even in the 1950s after we began making such commitments as that to the North Atlantic Treaty Organization, but we have acted traditionally isolationist.

We never acted more like isolationists than in 1954 when we helped remove our ally, the French, from Vietnam and moved into the region with unilaterally controlled U.S. power; or when we unilaterally overthrew the Guatemalan government that year; or in 1956 when we unilaterally moved against three of our closest allies—England, France, and Israel—to stop their invasion of the Suez Canal and Egypt. It reveals a great deal about how we have misunderstood our past, and have inaccurately used labels in the present, when we realize that officials who emphasize the use of unilateral power and downgrade negotiations (as we have downgraded negotiations in Vietnam and Central American affairs) have successfully called themselves "internationalists," while those (such as Senator Fulbright and George F. Kennan) who wish to control the unilateral use of American power to strengthen our alliances and to negotiate seriously with our adversaries have been termed "neoisolationists." Any objective reading of American history indicates that it is the Reagan administration—with its clear attempt to use an immense military budget to *recapture* the unilateral *freedom-of-action* approach that characterized the 1950s—that is following an isolationist policy. Americans never acted more isolationist than when they followed a unilateral policy in Vietnam—or we should add, when they spend trillions of dollars on military forces instead of strengthening regional alliances and negotiating seriously with the Soviet Union for a freeze on such forces.

The Reagan administration is attempting the impossible; it is attempting to recapture the past. In the 1950s, the United States was able to follow an isolationist policy because it had overwhelmingly superior force with which to threaten adversaries and discipline allies. This situation changed drastically after 1960. Inevitably, Allied and Soviet power became much stronger relative to U.S. power. I use the word inevitable because it is clear that the 1945 to early 1960s era was an aberration in our history and in world history. The United States enjoyed incomparable power during those years because it had been the only major power to survive World War II not only intact but with tremendously expanded economic and military capacities—including a virtual monopoly on nuclear weapons. By the 1960s those capacities were being matched by friends and foes. The ultimate tests came in Vietnam and then in Nicaragua. We discovered that, although our unilateral power certainly remained immense, it was insufficient to determine the winner of those two revolutions, and that when we turned to allies for help, we found that they were not following us.

A number of times the president and other key officials have, consciously or unconsciously, misstated or misinterpreted the basic facts of our experience in Vietnam in order, in my judgment, to change or remove our memories of that experience. They have used history ignorantly, but not benignly; their use of the past aims to recast the 1960s and 1970s as history that can be undone.

Their use of a five-year, $1.6 trillion military budget aims at the recapturing of unilateral U.S. power of the 1950s, as if the intervening two decades did not occur. A 640-ship Navy, particularly a Navy that depends on *Nimitz*-type carriers, a Rapid Deployment Force that can supposedly work independently of our closest allies, a first-strike force of Trident II submarines, and MX missiles in relatively unhardened silos, as well as a marked hesitance to negotiate arms ceilings or freezes with the Soviets—all, to me, are signs of an attempt to recapture the power to follow the isolationist policies of the past.

It would be a worthy attempt, perhaps, if history could be repealed, at least at an acceptable cost, but it cannot be repealed regardless of cost. The conditions of the 1950s can never reappear, and the idea often heard in recent months—that if we really want to act with unanswerable power at any point on the globe, we can find the resources to do so —is a mere wish from the past that ignores the realities of global power during the past twenty years. The Pentagon military planners recently recognized this misuse of the past when, according to press reports, they told civilian officials that in order to carry out the possible military missions assigned to them in the late 1980s they would need another $750 billion in addition to the planned $1.6 trillion to be spent over the next five years.

Even that additional amount will not allow the new isolationists to exercise unilateral U.S. power wherever and whenever they wish. Soviet leaders will, as they have in the past, further regiment their own people and their bloc satellites, such as Poland, to stay abreast of our military power. Allies and neutrals will, as they have in the past, devise economic and political responses that make U.S. military power less effective—as the neutrals did in the matter of oil and as our European allies have in the matter of East-West trade.

These problems were anticipated more than three decades ago by a distinguished conservative voice. Walter Lippmann warned that, even with its then overwhelmingly superior power, the United States could not base its diplomacy on a worldwide military containment. Such a military policy, Lippmann declared, was "not suited to the American system of government," and "even more unsuited to the American economy which is unregimented." Such a military emphasis, Lippmann prophesied, would necessarily weaken ties to our "natural allies" in the Atlantic community and force us to base our security on "satellites, puppets, clients, agents about whom we can know very little." Lippmann fully understood the necessity of countering Soviet power. That was not and is not the issue. Rather, he objected to the military emphasis in U.S. policy not because, in his words, "it seeks to confront the Soviet power with American power, but because the policy is misconceived and must result in a misuse of American power."

If that assessment was proven accurate during Lippmann's lifetime, as I believe it was, it is even more true now. Recent attempts to deal with indigenous revolutions on a military level have been unsuccessful and have, indeed, too often produced the radical revolution our power tried to prevent. Unilaterally controlled military power worked in the unnatural world of the 1950s but less well thereafter. It is important that we learn from this history so that we will neither ignore nor conveniently try to rewrite it, as President Reagan has tried to do, and that we understand our own revolutionary background, our economic resources, and our more humane values so that, once broken free of the isolationist, military view of the world, we can exercise more constructively our influence and power.

■ ■ ■

■ *CHAIRMAN DELLUMS:* Could you comment on U.S. and Soviet leadership statements concerning nuclear arms reductions? Do you think that these are really the policy positions of these leaders, or are they simply rhetorical smoke-screens for an ongoing Cold War?

■ *MR. LaFEBER:* I think with some perspective we can say that when the Soviets make this kind of a proposal, they are serious about the negotiation process. I believe that it would be a tragedy if the United States did not try to seize this initiative and to begin, at least, to talk.

There have been a number of times in the last twenty to thirty years where this type of situation has occurred. It occurred in the 1950s several times, most particularly in 1953 and 1954, when the post-Stalinist leadership offered to have wide-ranging talks with the Eisenhower administration, which turned it down. Winston Churchill later said that this was one of the great mistakes in the postwar era.

In the early 1960s, once again and quite clearly, the Kennedy administration undertook a large policy of armament instead of negotiating about those arms, at least until after the Cuban Missile Crisis. Then, in the early 1970s, we unfortunately did not negotiate on certain kinds of arms the Soviets were willing to negotiate on, such as MIRV missiles. In the late 1970s, of course, the Soviets were willing to accept SALT II, and the Carter administration was not able to get SALT II ratified by the Senate. I think when we look back at this with some perspective, historians are going to be very puzzled why, over and over again, the Soviet Union seemed to be willing to talk, at least, about these particular issues of armaments, arms freeze, disarmament, and the United States has always been reluctant to respond in a positive and helpful way.

■ *CHAIRMAN DELLUMS:* What are your thoughts on how this administration's policy on Europe, Asia, Africa and Latin America differs from that of previous administrations, and how does this analysis bring you to the conclusion that this administration, on an increasing basis, is establishing an isolationist foreign policy?

■ *MR. LaFEBER:* I think it is quite clear, for example, in the way that we have dealt with our European allies on such issues as East-West trade and the problems over Poland. There is a very deep disagreement over how to approach the Polish issue between ourselves and what Lippmann called our natural allies in Europe.

I think there is a great danger that, as the Europeans and the United States are unable to work out a common agreement on such issues as Poland, it is going to be easier for the Reagan administration to argue, "Let's go it alone—if the NATO partners do not like what we are doing about Eastern Europe, then we should develop a military strength that can work independently of them; if they do not like what we are doing in the Middle East, (which they certainly have not liked in recent years), then we should develop a Rapid Deployment Force so that we can move unilaterally in the Middle East; if they do not like what we are doing in Central America, (and it is quite clear that a number of West European governments are at cross-purposes with us on Central American policy), then we define them out of the situation" and, as Secretary Haig said, "We will deal with this problem bilaterally." Given the power ratio in this area, that really means we will deal with it unilaterally, it seems to me.

Given our experience in the last fifteen to twenty years, it seems to me that this would be a highly unfortunate policy. American strength, regardless of how much money we spend on the military budget, is not going to be what it was in relation to other powers in the 1950s when we were able to act unilaterally. We are going to depend more and more on our friends in Western Europe and more and more on our friends in Asia, such as the Japanese. We are going to need regional partners such as the Venezuelans and the Mexicans. To define them out of the diplomatic equation, and then to say that we will develop the power to act independently of them, is an extremely short-sighted and, as I use the term, isolationist policy.

■ *CHAIRMAN DELLUMS:* Your testimony seems to indicate that you think the current administration's spending projection is out of line with its stated purposes. At first blush, the average lay American would think that the expenditure of $1.6 trillion over the next five years is consistent with the increasing sabre-rattling messages that this administration is sending forth. Can you go into that?

■ *MR. LaFEBER:* I think Americans expect too much from their military spending, and I think that they tend to measure those expectations in terms of a past that we can never recapture. To me, this is one of the great propaganda victories of the Reagan officials—that they have essentially been able to appeal to this past and, as I indicated in my statement, to rewrite the past, so that Americans can think that somehow we can recapture that past. But we cannot act in Guatemala, for example, as we did in 1954; we cannot act in the Middle East as we did in Lebanon in 1958; we cannot face down the Soviets in a missile crisis as we did in 1962.

I would argue that this is a highly unreal expectation of the past, that those particular years will never be recaptured, and that regardless of how much money we spend on the military, the Soviets will do everything possible to stay up with us. We will end up bankrupting ourselves and, if not bankrupting ourselves, getting our social priorities badly out of balance. And we will alienate our best friends who do not want to follow this particular kind of military policy.

It seems to me that we must understand, and I think that Americans are increasingly better understanding, that this kind of military budget does not buy security if that security is, as most of us think it is, the good old days of the Eisenhower years and the early Kennedy years. Those days are gone forever, and $1.6 trillion or $2.3 trillion or however many dollars you put on this is simply not going to recapture that kind of a world.

■ *MR. CONYERS (D.-Mich.):* There are myths to be demolished in terms of foreign policy: First and foremost is the myth that "the Commies are coming," which undergirds every fuel-up for military increases since World War II. The other is a "friend or foe" attitude that we seem to take into our international relations. If you are not with us all the way, then you must be an enemy, and we will treat you accordingly. So I ask in this connection, is there time—are we operating in a span of years in which we have to act feverishly or desperately or urgently, or are we not?

■ *MR. LaFEBER:* The nature of the danger has grown not only because of the new generation of weapons systems—that is the one thing that we know and talk about, as indeed we should. It is possible that the Trident II submarines will appear in 1989, for example, or that the MX system will be built. I hope not; I hope you people will be able to stop them. It seems to me that their existence is going to be a highly destabilizing influence.

There is a second part to this problem that you allude to that I would like to talk about. On both sides of the East-West conflict, what we used to call in the 1940s and 1950s the "two camps," the Soviet camp and the American camp, can no longer be called two camps anymore. A pluralism has erupted in the world. We see this certainly in Central America; we are now confronted with it. The Soviets are also seeing it. They are seeing it particularly in Poland. It is not going to be long before they see it elsewhere—they have it already in Rumania and Hungary. The East Germans and the West Germans are talking very differently and acting very differently than they did ten years ago. One of the things that concerns me as we talk about the numbers of the arms budget and the new generation of weapons, is that we are missing how the world is becoming destabilized because we are not talking to the Soviet Union and to other nations about how to handle this pluralism and the eruption of nationalism that is occurring in Eastern Europe, in Latin America, and in Asia.

We must begin some kind of dialogue with the Soviets that reaches an understanding about how to handle these parts of the world—not in the sense of our inviting the Soviets to talk about Central America, anymore than they are going to invite us to talk about Poland. That is nonsense. But we must understand each other so that we will not react hastily and without thought and without understanding as more and more of these parts of the world come unglued, as they certainly did in the 1970s and as they certainly will in the 1980s. This is a political problem, it is a cultural problem, and it is an economic problem. We have to think about that as much as we think about the military.

8

OPENING THE FLOODGATES . . . "Arms Diplomacy" of the Reagan Administration

Michael T. Klare, Ph.D.

■ ■ ■

Michael T. Klare took his B.A. and M.A. degrees from Columbia University and his Ph.D. from the Union Graduate School. He is a fellow at the Institute for Policy Studies in Washington, D.C., and author of *War without End* and a forthcoming book on U.S. arms sales to the Third World.

UNDER THE PRODDING of President Reagan, U.S. arms export policy is undergoing a thorough transformation: Whereas President Carter perceived military sales as an unsavory and hazardous activity requiring tight governmental control, his successor views such transactions as a benign and advantageous adjunct to U.S. security policy. Under his Administration, he declared on July 9, 1981, "The United States views the transfer of conventional arms . . . as an essential element of its global defense posture and an indispensable component of its foreign policy."

On this basis, Reagan rescinded the "arms restraint policy" established by Mr. Carter in 1977 and announced a new policy favoring increased arms aid to America's friends and allies. To reassure those analysts who feared a massive increase in weapons deliveries to volatile Third World areas, Reagan affirmed that adoption of the new policy "should not be seen as heralding a period of unrestrained military transfers." Despite such assurances, however, U.S. arms sales reached record levels in fiscal year 1982—at $21.3 billion, more than double the $10.7 billion figure for 1981—and appear headed toward even greater heights in 1983.

The Reagan arms sales effort is noteworthy not only for its volume
—already greater than that of any administration since World War II
—but also for the sophistication of the munitions being shipped abroad.
Among the major transactions concluded by Mr. Reagan in his first two
years of office were:

— *Saudi Arabia:* Five AWACS radar patrol planes and seven KC-
135 aerial tankers, plus ground stations and auxiliary equipment
worth a total of $8.5 billion;

— *Pakistan:* Forty General Dynamics F-16 fighters worth $5 bil-
lion, plus ten Cobra helicopter gunships, improved TOW antitank
missiles, and a variety of other gear;

— *Egypt:* Forty more F-16s, bringing to eighty the number now
on order from Cairo, plus four E-2C Hawkeye electronic spy planes,
and a host of other modern weapons;

— *Venezuela:* Twenty-four F-16s plus other gear for $655 million,
representing the largest and most conspicuous U.S. sale of high technology military hardware to a Latin American country.

— *South Korea:* Thirty-six F-16s worth $1.1 billion, plus a wide
range of other military systems and the technology to "co-produce"
many other U.S. arms.

These sales are symptomatic of the new U.S. policy of providing our
latest and most advanced weapons to friends and allies in the Third
World. Similar deals are expected soon with other prominent U.S. clients, including Israel, Turkey, Jordan, Morocco, Oman, Sudan, Tunisia,
Thailand, and Malaysia. In light of this munificence, Senator Christo-
pher Dodd (D-Conn.) noted in 1982: "The Reagan administration seems
willing to sell more highly sophisticated weapons to a wider variety of
countries than any previous administration."

For Dodd and other critics of the Reagan program, this apparent
willingness to confer modern arms on any Third World power able to
produce the necessary cash reflects the absence of any rational guidelines for the selection of appropriate recipients. Reagan's policy of making sales "on a case-by-case basis," Dodd complained, "really amounts
to no policy at all." But administration officials insist that these sales *do*
reflect a coherent policy. "The United States cannot defend the free
world's interests alone," Mr. Reagan explained in 1981. Because of the
unremitting growth of Soviet military power, "The United States must
. . . not only strengthen its own military capabilities, but be prepared
to help its friends and allies to strengthen theirs through the transfer
of conventional arms and other forms of security assistance."

In numerous speeches and policy declarations, administration officials
have consistently hammered home the same basic argument: The Soviet

Union and its "surrogates" have expanded their presence in the Third World, thereby jeopardizing vital Western interests—particularly oil and other strategic raw materials—and requiring in response a concerted American counteroffensive. Arms transfers play an important role in this effort, then-Under Secretary of State James L. Buckley affirmed, by enhancing the self-defense capabilities of nations with which we share close security ties and by facilitating access by American forces to military facilities abroad. Seen from this perspective, arms transfers are not "morally reprehensible" as charged by some, but rather "a vital and constructive instrument of American foreign policy."

On this premise, the Reagan administration has flooded the Third World with large quantities of America's most advanced and capable weapons systems. From all available indicators, moreover, the administration plans to pursue U.S. "arms diplomacy" abroad. An estimated $10 billion worth of arms were awaiting final action on September 30, when fiscal year 1982 drew to a close, suggesting that fiscal year 1983 will set new records in the weapons trade. (If added to the other transactions concluded in 1982, this $10 billion would have raised the 1982 sales total to $31.2 billion, exactly double the amount of the previous one-year record, set in 1975.) Furthermore, this administration introduced a plan to speed up the processing of arms requests and to water down existing congressional constraints on military sales to the Third World. "Security assistance is not doing the job it should," National Security Adviser William Clark declared, and so "we are planning a priority effort to improve the effectiveness and the responsiveness of this vital component of our national security strategy."

Unless checked, this policy will result in a massive flow of highly capable arms to a host of Third World countries. Typically, these nations will claim to be acquiring arms in order to deter Soviet or Soviet-sponsored aggression; it is more likely, however, that they will be used for other purposes entirely—to further regional ambitions, to put pressure on rivals, to subdue hostile minorities and dissidents, to enhance the authority of the military. In all probability, moreover, these deliveries will be matched by comparable sales of French and Soviet equipment, leading to an intensified arms race in many Third World areas. If the tumultuous events of 1982 are any indication, these local arms rivalries will periodically erupt in armed conflicts of explosive violence—threatening, in some cases, a regional conflagration and possible superpower intervention.

It should be apparent from all this that the Reagan policy on arms sales is altering the world military equation in some significant and potentially hazardous ways. Unfortunately, Congress has been relatively quiescent on the arms sales issue after failing to block the AWACS sale to Saudi Arabia, and the arms control community has its hands full dealing with Reagan's nuclear programs. Failure to address the conventional arms issue, however, could have perilous consequences later, when all the transactions now in the discussion stage result in deliveries to potential belligerents. In order to discern the risks embodied in the administration's arms sales policy, it is important to identify the changes Reagan has made to existing policy and then to consider the impact of these changes on global arms trade patterns.

The best way to distinguish the changes in U.S. arms policy decreed by President Reagan is to look first at the "arms restraint" policy established by the Carter administration in 1977. As a candidate, Mr. Carter pledged to "reduce the commerce in weapons" if elected president. Then, following his inauguration, he ordered the State Department to review U.S. arms programs and to propose new measures for their control. After several months of internal debate, the department produced a series of recommendations that formed the basis for Presidential Directive Number 13 (PD 13), the Carter administration's basic statement on arms transfers, which was made public on May 19, 1977.

Carter enunciated a new principle in PD 13 under which U.S. arms export programs would be governed: Instead of viewing military sales as a normal instrument of U.S. policy, "the United States will henceforth view arms transfers as an exceptional *foreign implement,* to be *used* only in instances where it can be clearly demonstrated that the transfer contributes to our national security interests." (Emphasis added.) The United States would continue to satisfy legitimate requests for arms on the part of allies, he affirmed, but when evaluating such requests "the burden of persuasion will be on those who favor a particular arms sale, rather than on those who oppose it. To implement this "policy of arms restraint," as he called it, Carter imposed several specific sweeping controls (with many exceptions):

1. *Arms Sale Ceiling.* The total dollar value (in constant 1976 dollars) of U.S. arms transfers to the nonexempt countries from fiscal year 1978 onward would not exceed the $9.3 billion attained in fiscal year 1977.

2. *Arms Sophistication.* The United States would not be the first supplier to introduce into an area "newly-developed, advanced weapons systems which could create a new or significantly higher combat capability."

3. *Arms Modification.* The development or "significant modification" of advanced combat systems "solely for export" was prohibited.

4. *Arms Promotion.* U.S. government personnel assigned to embassies and military missions abroad could no longer help representatives of U.S. arms firms sell their product to foreign governments.

5. *Human Rights.* In deciding on proposed arms transfers, the United States would attempt "to promote and advance respect for human rights in recipient countries."

Much criticism has been leveled at these guidelines—both from those favoring tougher restraints and those favoring reduced government control—but the fact remains that Carter succeeded in halting the steady upward climb of U.S. arms exports. According to the Department of Defense, total sales under the Foreign Military Sales (FMS) program dropped from an average of $15.3 billion in fiscal years 1975-76 to $8.8 billion in 1979. (It should be remembered, however, that the demise of the Shah in January 1979 resulted in the cancellation of $8 billion worth of Iranian arms orders, thereby accounting for a large chunk of the 1977-79 reductions.) Carter also slowed the export of high technology weaponry to some Third World areas and cut back on deliveries to several nations accused of persistent human rights violations. On the other hand, Carter repeatedly used legal waivers to PD 13 to permit high technology sales to major clients like Saudi Arabia and Egypt, and human rights considerations did not appreciably affect deliveries to such key allies as South Korea and the Philippines.

Ultimately, the success of Carter's policies rested on his ability to persuade other producer nations to restrain their own sales. His policy directive of May 19, 1977 stressed the need for "multilateral action" to ensure real cuts in global arms trafficking, and top administration officials were sent to several foreign capitals in an effort to promote cooperation in this area. U.S. and Soviet negotiators subsequently met at what were called the Conventional Arms Transfer (CAT) talks, but they made little progress before Washington called off the talks to protest Soviet adventurism in Africa and the Middle East. Given the lack of reciprocity on the part of America's competitors and the worsening international climate, President Carter was well on the road to scrapping his arms restraint policy when Mr. Reagan was chosen to replace him.

Once taking office, Mr. Reagan moved swiftly to impose his own arms policy. Many of the major transactions described earlier were concluded during his first months in office, and Under Secretary James Buckley was delegated to draw up a new statement of principles. Mr. Buckley's draft proposal was first aired in a speech to the Aerospace Industries Association on May 21, 1981, and subsequently incorporated into Reagan's policy directive of July 9, 1981.

Like the Carter directive that it replaced, the Reagan statement of July 9th is based on a number of fundamental propositions, particularly that the greatest threat to world stability is the growing military assertiveness of the Soviet Union. Consistent with this outlook, Mr. Buckley enunciated a new governing principle: Instead of arms transfers being viewed as an "exceptional foreign policy implement," they are to be considered as "a vital and constructive instrument of American foreign policy." The adminstration will continue to weigh the merits and hazards of pending transactions on a case-by-case basis, but favorable consideration will normally be given to transfers which help enhance "the state of preparedness of our friends and allies." The Reagan policy substitutes its own criteria for Carter's controls on arms sales:

1. *Ceiling.* Abolished. Pending arms transactions will be judged on their own merits, irrespective of their effect on the total dollar value of U.S. exports.

2. *Sophistication.* No further restrictions. Sales of high technology arms will be governed by "their net contribution to enhanced deterrence and defense" rather than by fears of a local arms race.

3. *Modification.* No further restrictions. In fact, the Reagan administration will actively "encourage" U.S. firms to design equipment for the Third World market.

4. *Promotion.* No further restrictions. Reagan mandated U.S. officials overseas "to provide the same courtesies and assistance" to arms firms as to other U.S. companies seeking business abroad.

5. *Human Rights.* No longer relevant. Decisions on arms transfers will be made on the basis of a nation's strategic requirement, not its record on human rights.

Reagan went beyond these changes, introducing several new elements into the arms program that reinforce this shift toward a relatively permissive, export-oriented policy. To begin with, the United States will now offer loans for the purchase of American arms at "concessional" rates (i.e., at a lower percentage rate than the U.S. government must itself pay to borrow money). Noting that "in today's economic climate a number of nations cannot afford to acquire military equipment on commercial terms," Under Secretary Buckley announced that Washington would sell arms to some U.S. allies at interest rates as low as 3 percent. Such measures, which constitute a form of indirect subsidy by the U.S. taxpayer (since the Treasury will have to borrow the money at much higher rates of interest), will obviously make it easier for over-extended Third World nations to buy arms that they otherwise could not afford. (Among the nations deemed eligible for such concessional rates in fiscal year 1982 were Egypt, Turkey, Pakistan, Thailand, Kenya, Somalia, El Salvador, and Honduras.)

The adminstration is also making a special effort to boost U.S. military sales to certain Third World areas that have not recently been major markets for American arms. A major target of this drive is Latin America, which in recent years has obtained much of its front-line equipment from Europe (where credit terms are softer and political requirements less stringent). In order to win back this market, Reagan has gradually eliminated most human rights restrictions imposed in the 1970s and has authorized sales of new, high technology weapons—such as the F-16s sold to Venezuela—that could not be exported under the Carter guidelines.

Washington also seeks to increase U.S. sales to South Asia, Africa, and Southeast Asia. These efforts are certain to stimulate increased marketing activities in these areas by other major suppliers, especially France and the Soviet Union, thereby producing a significant long-term increase in high technology deliveries to the Third World.

Finally, and most significant, Mr. Reagan has made arms sales his principal weapon in a new contest for influence in the Third World. Military exports, Andrew Pierre of the Council on Foreign Relations noted recently, "are a major component of America's approach toward competition with the Soviet Union on a global basis, perhaps the major instrument for action overseas." In line with this approach, Reagan has approved high technology sales to many Third World countries that had not previously been allowed to purchase America's latest arms, including Pakistan, Morocco, Tunisia, Sudan, Somalia, Bahrain, Oman, and the United Arab Emirates. The administration has also authorized the sale of sophisticated military hardware to China and hinted at similar sales to Iraq and Algeria if these countries would leave the Soviet orbit. These moves are certain to provoke comparable moves by Moscow, leading to an intensified arms race in many Third World areas.

President Reagan has declared repeatedly that arms exports enhance U.S. national security by strengthening the defensive capabilities of America's friends and allies. But while it is no doubt true that selective sales to close U.S. allies can in some cases enhance the common defense, it is also apparent that such exports can *undermine* U.S. security by spurring local arms races in volatile areas and by encouraging ambitious regimes to embark on military adventures. By employing arms transfers as an instrument of Cold War competition, moreover, Reagan is certain to aggravate local disputes in many Third World areas, thereby increasing the risk of a regional conflagration and a possible superpower confrontation. Presumably Washington hopes to put Moscow on the defensive through these tactics, but it is just as likely that they will produce a reaction in kind and thus expose the whole world to an increased threat of war.

President Reagan's plan for opening the floodgates on U.S. arms exports to the Third World may diminish U.S. security far more than it will strengthen it. Yet there appears to be only modest opposition to this in Congress and relatively little concern in the arms control and disarmament communities. To some extent this reflects the growing concern over Reagan's plan for nuclear modernization, but it also reflects an inadequate appreciation of the potential risks embodied in the adminstration's arms transfer policy. If any real progress is to be made toward global peace and security, it is obvious that conventional arms transfers will have to be viewed with the same level of concern as is nuclear weapons proliferation.

9

ADMINISTRATION MISREPRESENTATIONS OF SOVIET MILITARY SPENDING

Professor Franklyn Holzman

■ ■ ■

Franklyn Holzman obtained his Ph.D. at Harvard University. He is a professor of Economics at Tufts University and a research fellow at the Harvard Russian Research Center. His books include *Foreign Trade under Central Planning* and *Financial Checks on Soviet Defense Expenditures.*

IN HIS STATE of the Nation message on February 18, 1981, President Reagan said: "I believe that my duty as President requires that I recommend increases in defense spending over the coming years. Since 1970, the Soviet Union has invested $300 billion more in its military forces than we have."

This so-called military spending gap is calculated by the CIA, which also tells us that Soviet military spending currently exceeds ours by 50 percent. These two gaps are represented in Figure 9-1 published by the Department of Defense. The $300 billion gap is represented by the area between the Soviet dotted line of expenditures and the U.S. solid line from 1970 through 1979. The 50 percent gap is the percentage by which the dotted Soviet line exceeded the solid U.S. line in the year 1979.

These gaps are based on calculations by the CIA of Soviet military spending valued in current dollar prices. Failure of the U.S.S.R. to publish information on its military expenditures has posed a difficult problem for the intelligence community. I have great respect for the effort and ingenuity with which the CIA has attempted to penetrate

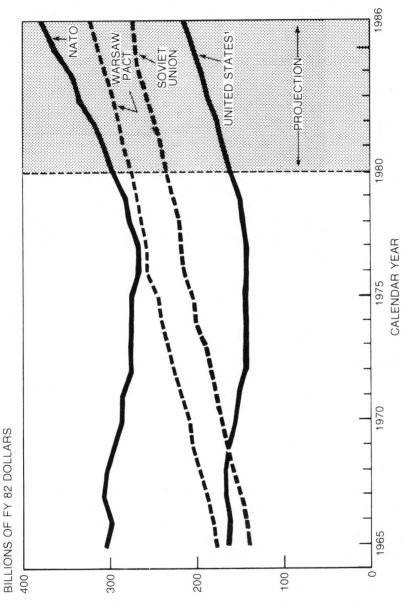

COMPARISON OF NATO AND WARSAW PACT TOTAL DEFENSE COSTS

BILLIONS OF FY 82 DOLLARS

400

300

200

100

0

1965   1970   1975   1980   1986

CALENDAR YEAR

NATO

WARSAW PACT

SOVIET UNION

UNITED STATES¹

←PROJECTION→

¹SOUTHEAST ASIA INCREMENT EXCLUDED (I.E., VIETNAM COSTS)
Xeroxed from: Department of Defense, *Annual Report*, Fiscal Year 1982

this veil of secrecy. The CIA faces many obstacles, many data gaps, and many difficult choices of methodology in the construction of its comparisons of Soviet and U.S. defense expenditures. It is, in fact, impossible for them or anyone else to come up with totally unambiguous and unbiased results. I do, however, disagree with some of the choices that the CIA has made and that lead their estimates of Soviet spending to be higher than I believe is warranted. Moreover, their estimates are often misrepresented by government spokesmen, the press, and others in ways that further exaggerate the military spending gaps. What I would like to do here is offer an alternative view and to draw some implications from this revised picture.

Before doing so, it is reasonable to ask, Why compare defense expenditures; why not just look at individual items of expenditure? The answer is that one cannot add tanks, planes, soldiers, research and development, operations and maintenance, and so forth. Total expenditures provide a generalized measure of a nation's effort, which has literally hundreds of separate dimensions. It must be stressed, however, that defense expenditures measure the cost of the inputs into defense rather than the outputs; hence, they do not tell us how effectively the funds have been spent. So, if two nations have equal military expenditures, but one spends wisely and the other unwisely, the former will be better prepared for hostilities than the latter.

The first problem with the estimates is that the CIA's process of estimating U.S.S.R. weapons' costs overstates their dollar value. The CIA relies on dollar valuations to compare the two defense establishments. As the CIA acknowledges, and I quote from a CIA pamphlet,

> Dollar cost calculations tend to overstate Soviet defense activities relative to those of the United States. Given different resource endowments and technologies, countries tend to use more of the resources that are relatively cheap and less of those that are relatively expensive for a given purpose. A comparison drawn in the terms of the prices of one country thus tends to overstate the relative value of the activities of the other.

In other words, the CIA admits that its dollar comparisons exaggerate Soviet defense spending relative to our own. This so-called index number effect is not difficult to understand. The Soviets pay their soldiers a very low wage and, partly for this reason, have more than twice as many as we do. When we value their almost 4.5 million person army at our average pay scale of close to $20,000, the result is a very high estimate of Soviet spending. The *reductio ad absurdum* of this methodology is the recently revealed CIA estimate of Chinese military spending in dollars, which purports to show that the Chinese government is currently mounting a defense effort equal to our own. This bizarre estimate results largely from valuing the enormous Chinese army at U.S. pay scales.

The proper procedure is to calculate expenditures in the prices of both nations, in this case in rubles as well as in dollars. The dollar estimate provides an upper limit of Soviet expenditures, the ruble estimate a lower limit. An average of the two, usually a geometric mean, may be calculated if one wants a single figure.

Experts on the Soviet economy, presented with the ruble and dollar comparisons just cited, are always surprised that there is so little spread between the two. For virtually all other sectors, the spread is much greater. For total gross national product, the spread is 49 percent, for example. There is a good reason why this is so. It is because the CIA has far fewer ruble prices of weapons than are available for civilian products.

In the area of weapons procurement, the CIA admits to having only approximately 150 prices for over 1,000 different weapons or, perhaps, one price for every ten products. This means that in making the ruble estimates, most weapons have to be valued first in dollar prices and then converted into rubles with just the few ruble prices that are available. This implies that the ruble comparison is, in large part, a dollar comparison and, therefore, is not as low for the U.S.S.R. as it should be. In light of a statistical study of this general phenomenon that I have recently come across and called to the attention of CIA economists, I would guess that if the agency had the thousands of ruble prices required to make an unbiased comparison, the Soviets would not be outspending us by much, or at all, measured in ruble prices, and that a geometric average of the dollar and ruble measures would show them currently outspending us by, say, only 15 to 20 percent rather than by 50 percent. It would also imply that the Soviet ten-year spending trend is considerably lower than estimated by the CIA and, for the first half of the 1970s, was probably below that of the United States.

This would significantly reduce or eliminate President Reagan's $300 billion decade spending gap. In suggesting these revisions of the two spending gaps I am assuming that in every other respect, the CIA estimates are perfect. In fact, I believe that other sources of bias exist.

There are two other important aspects of the military spending gap problem. Let me begin by quoting from one of former Secretary of Defense Harold Brown's Annual Reports: "We are fortunate in having prosperous and willing allies who can help counter-balance the Soviet effort. The Soviets are not so fortunate. Moreover, they have felt obliged to allocate up to twenty percent of their total defense effort to the Far East and the People's Republic of China."

The second part of this statement has to do with the Soviet defense effort directed at China. When CIA estimates of comparative defense spending are quoted, these are always taken to represent the "confrontation" between the United States and the U.S.S.R. But, in fact, Secretary of Defense Brown says that up to 20 percent of the U.S.S.R.'s military expenditures is not directed at the United States. At various times, the corresponding CIA estimates have been 20, 15, and 10 to 15 percent, respectively. Soviet expenditures allocated to the Far East have primarily supported a three-quarter million man army on the Chinese border. Soviet expenditures used to pay and support this large army have not been available over the past decade to produce tanks, planes, and missiles for use against the United States and its allies. In fact, were the Sino-Soviet dispute to be settled amicably tomorrow, it is a fair bet that given the seriousness of the current Soviet labor shortage, that the number of personnel in the Soviet armed forces would be rapidly reduced by 500,000 or more men. Removing the Soviet expenditures directed at China would not conflict with U.S. government practice at the end of the Vietnam War.

What does taking account of the People's Republic of China do to the CIA's gap estimates? If, say, 15 percent of Soviet military expenditures are directed at China, then the current gap is reduced from 50 to 27.5 percent and President Reagan's ten-year gap is reduced by $220 billion to only $80 billion. If these figures are subtracted, not from the CIA's official dollar gaps but from those implied by a ruble-dollar geometric average calculated from the CIA's own ruble estimate, the current gap falls from 50 to 13 percent, and President Reagan's ten-year gap disappears. If, finally, a further adjustment could be made for the deficiencies of the CIA's ruble measure, mentioned earlier, then I believe that the results would show the Soviet military expenditures directed at the West currently do not exceed U.S. military expenditures and that over the decade we have outspent them.

One further major adjustment remains to be made. So far as I know, the CIA makes no official estimates of the military expenditures of the other-NATO and other-Warsaw Pact nations. Hence, virtually all discussions based on CIA military spending estimates implicitly make the wholly unrealistic assumption that these two nations confront each other in a two-nation world.

In fact, we number among our allies more than fifteen nations that include, after the United States and the U.S.S.R., five or six of the strongest industrial states in the world. The Soviet Union's allies are six in number, of which only three are of any military or industrial significance. The largest of these, Poland, is in the kind of shape as to inspire the hackneyed remark, "With friends like these, who needs enemies?"

Generally accepted estimates by the International Institute of Strategic Studies put other-NATO military expenditures in 1980 at $94.9 billion, or almost six times higher than the other-Warsaw Pact's $16.7 billion. In fact, other-NATO has outspent other-Warsaw Pact by so much over the 1970 to 1979 decade that the CIA's $300 billion gap in the U.S.S.R.'s favor over the United States is turned into an almost $250 billion gap in NATO's favor. If we add to this $250 billion gap the adjustments made above for Soviet expenditures directed at China and for the dollar-ruble average, then the excess of NATO relative to Warsaw Pact expenditures over the decade must have been somewhere in the neighborhood of $550 billion.

The picture I have just painted is very much at odds with the conventional wisdom—which is that the U.S.S.R. and its allies have been engaged in a massive military buildup that has enabled them to reduce or eliminate our military superiority and, moreover, that this has been accomplished by virture of spending much more on defense than we have. If I am correct that there has been no military spending gap in the Soviets' favor, and I am quite sure that there has not, how is it possible to reconcile this finding with the alleged Soviet military buildup advantage?

There are two possible ways of making a reconciliation, and it is my guess that both are relevant. First, perhaps the military buildup, and the degree to which the Soviets have caught up with us, have been exaggerated. As I mentioned earlier, there are hundreds of dimensions to a military effort, and those who sound the direst warnings concentrate their attention on areas in which Soviet progress has been most rapid.

Further, the emphasis is usually on numbers—quantity rather than quality. As Harold Brown put it, the United States defense effort represents, in part, a "sacrifice of quantity for quality." This view was recently echoed by a CIA spokesman before the Senate Armed Services Committee in 1980, where he stated that U.S. military equipment tends to be produced with "more sophistication, more quality, better performance, more safety, more highly designed, more quality control, more across the board than Soviet equipment," and, he added, "it costs more." Listening to the pessimists, one would never know that the United States spends almost three times as much per soldier in training and maneuvers than the Soviets do or that our missiles are more accurate, that our submarines are superior to theirs, and so forth. To sum up this point, I do not doubt that the Soviets have been catching up, but I wonder if the degree to which this has been the case has not been overstated. Second, if the Soviets have been catching up, how has this been possible if they have not spent more than we have?

Earlier, I noted that the military expenditure comparisons measure the cost of the inputs and the cost of the effort but indicate nothing regarding the effectiveness with which these inputs have been utilized or the wisdom of the expenditure choices. If this nation has been spending money less wisely, in terms of our needs, than the Soviets have, in terms of their needs, then the Soviets could catch up without outspending us.

I am not a military expert, and I cannot speak on the basis of my personal evaluations, but there has been so much written in the past few years regarding the waste and the misdirected expenditures in our defense program that I do not think I need to prove the case. Some general categories of wasteful spending often mentioned are: the so-called gold-plating of weapons; introducing technology that is so complex and so expensive that it can neither be easily operated by our service personnel nor properly maintained; introducing too many competing models and changing models too often, both of which prevent reduction of costs; allowing weapons suppliers very high profits and cost-overruns not due to inflation; and, finally, the "pork-barrel"— maintaining facilities and programs that no longer serve a military function but are good for some representative's constituency. Evidence of inefficiency at the NATO level is the fact that the balance of forces in Europe does not appear to reflect NATO's much higher levels of military spending.

Let me come to the moral of my story. If my revisions of the military spending gaps are correct, they provide support for the critical view with which many in the Congress are now approaching the military race. First, since it seems unlikely that the U.S.S.R. could be as far ahead of the United States and NATO as the administration contends, it is important to weigh our pluses in the same balance as our minuses, in order to get a more judicial evaluation of where we are. A very skeptical approach to the administration's claims that the Russians are ten feet tall is warranted.

Second, if the reason that the U.S.S.R. is catching up is due to waste and inefficiency on our part, then it makes less sense to throw hundreds more billions of dollars at defense, at the expense of so many of this nation's major civilian priorities, without drastic revision of the military decision making processes. Preventing the waste of $50 billion in cost overruns, misguided programs, and the like is as good a way of financing our military buildup as $50 billion in new taxes or a $50 billion larger national debt. Finally, it is worth considering that, while many in this country view the Soviet Union and its allies as outspending us on defense per the CIA scenario, I think that it is highly probable that the Soviet Union views the spending competition in the terms in which I have presented it—that is to say, much more unfavorably to itself. If true and if, in fact, the U.S.S.R. views itself as having to take on almost singlehandedly the whole Western industrial world plus China and Japan, then the motivations behind its buildup must be less ominous than the administration has painted them. Our approach to the Soviets should be more alert to this fact.

■ ■ ■

■ *CHAIRMAN DELLUMS:*   Are we arming ourselves to go to war and to ruin our economy simply because of bad arithmetic?

■ *MR. HOLZMAN:*   I think that is partly true. When we analyze Soviet military spending in dollar amounts, the CIA's estimate method tends to overstate the case. On the other hand, when they look at us in rubles, they tend to overstate our defense effort. In dollar prices, their large army looks very expensive, although it is cheap for them. On the other hand, when they look at the cost of producing our very highly sophisticated equipment, it looks enormously expensive to them. It would probably cost them two or three times what it costs us to produce high technology equipment. So they think we are spending a lot more. The two nations could actually be equal in military power and each one think the other is ahead. That is one of the dangers of the economics of this whole exercise.

■ *CHAIRMAN DELLUMS:*   How would you react to the assertion that the expenditure of $4-plus trillion over the next ten years would weaken rather than strengthen the nation?

■ *MR. HOLZMAN:*   I would agree that if there were to be a long-run military strategy and that if we are not likely to go to war in the next five years or so, our greatest long-run strength would be the strength of our economy. Withdrawing resources from the rest of the economy and putting them into the military tends to weaken the rest of the economy, the civilian part of the economy, which is really what makes us grow. We do not grow from investing money in missiles and tanks and so forth. The civilian part of our economy has been starved. Our rate of investment is much lower than in most of the other industrial countries of the world. Our R&D is fairly extensive, but so much of it goes into the military sector and so little into the civilian sector that we find ourselves being out-competed in the things in which we already were ahead of other countries.

Furthermore, there is the question of the morale of the nation. The

United States is currently in a situation in which, in order to get the resources for the military, we are cutting back on all of our social programs. Morale is one of the things that is seldom discussed in analyses about relative Soviet-U.S. military strength. An exception is James Fallows's book, *National Defense*. One of the most crucial dimensions is the morale of soldiers. For example, the Israelis, in fighting the Arab nations, have shown how a few people with tremendous morale can outfight much larger armies than their own. I think that the morale in this country is really very low. If the economic situation worsens, and morale is lowered still further, we would be weakened militarily.

■ *CHAIRMAN DELLUMS:* We always talk about how much of a percentage of GNP the Soviets are spending on military hardware. Aren't the Soviet defense industries less efficient, from your vantage point; and second, isn't it a fact that the Soviet GNP is roughly half of ours?

■ *MR. HOLZMAN:* Yes. The CIA, the only U.S. agency that currently calculates Soviet GNP, estimates Soviet GNP in rubles to be almost 50 percent of ours for 1976, the last year in which they made the estimate, and roughly 75 percent in dollars. You see, the dollar valuation makes it bigger. The CIA takes a geometric mean of these, which puts the Soviets at about five-eighths of us, or 62 percent. The CIA's estimates are that the Soviets are spending 12 to 14 percent of their GNP for defense. For technical reasons that I feel would be inappropriate for discussion here, my own feeling is that the estimate is probably too high. It is probably not more than 10 or 11 percent of their GNP, but it is still much higher than ours.

Military expenditures of this magnitude are very hard on the Soviet economy. It is probably harder than it is on our economy, partly because it is a larger percentage and they are poorer to begin with, but also because when they establish their military economy, they really run it very much like we would in wartime. During World War II, we rationed and made sure that all of the best resources went to the military industry. In the Soviet Union the military get the best engineers, the best scientists. They don't ever have a bottleneck. If the military industry needs steel, it will be taken away from the civilian industry. If you want to get 1 percent more military spending in the Soviet Union, you probably are going to hurt the civilian economy by 1.5 or 2 percent in order to get it. I think the crucial thing is to realize that both countries hurt their civilian economies very badly by increased military spending. The Soviets probably hurt theirs much more than we hurt ours; it is very hard on them.

■ *CHAIRMAN DELLUMS:* How would you suggest that we go about challenging the budgetary assumptions that the CIA and the Pentagon are making with regard to Soviet and Warsaw Pact spending? What documentation will be required, and what documentation, from your vantage point, is available to us in order to make that case?

■ *MR. HOLZMAN:* Since I am the only one challenging these estimates, I don't know what else can be done beyond what I have done. One of my biggest handicaps is that I am not cleared to seek classified information. I know that when I have argued with them, their technicians have been fairly friendly to me. In fact, they invited me over to have a seminar with them and people from other agencies that deal with military spending. I argued all afternoon with them, but the crunch comes when they say to me, "Well, if we could show you some of these classified things, we could convince you." I am not convinced that they could convince me. My own view is that the points I have made are general methodological points and that they hold true.

There are, I believe, several other possibilities of exaggeration in the CIA figures. Whenever one has to make estimates that cannot be precise, judgment comes into play. And in situations in which national security is at stake, judgment would, I believe, tend to err on the "worst case assumption" side. When a technician is trying to figure out how many tanks are produced from a satellite photo of what is believed to be a Soviet tank factory, I would think that he would err on the high side. Similarly, when an American firm assesses the dollar cost of a Soviet plane or tank, I would guess that, to the extent that judgment is involved, again it would be on the high side. On the other hand, as I argued in a 1980 article, there is a tendency, in valuing U.S. equipment in rubles, to value our very high technology equipment at a lower price than it would have cost the Russians to produce it, if they even could. "Worst case assumption" strategy is a common human foible, and I do not put the CIA in a special category when I suggest that it may be susceptible to it also.

So I think there are probably many exaggerations of this sort in the CIA figures, but unless somebody can get in there and work with the CIA and evaluate everything that they do, a lot of possible exaggeration will remain hidden. But my points, the general methodological ones, I think, hold regardless. Those expenditures in China just do not hurt us. *The fact that the Department of Defense put out a chart showing that total NATO really outspent the total Warsaw even including China is a telling verification of the falsity of the claim that Warsaw Pact is outspending NATO.* I do not know how one can argue against this; it is just so obvious, it isn't even funny.

PART THREE

REAGAN'S MILITARY BUDGET . . .
Where are we going?

■ ■ ■

I am tired and sick of war. Its glory is all moonshine. It is only those who have neither fired a shot nor heard the shrieks and groans of the wounded who cry aloud for blood, more vengeance, more desolation. War is Hell.

General William Tecumseh Sherman
June 19, 1879

■ ■ ■

IN PART I we examined the Reagan administration's preoccupation with war fighting instead of peace making and the new strategic weaponry it is proposing. In Part II we analyzed the often faulty foreign policy assumptions that provide the justification for this strategy of nuclear brinkmanship, and we looked at the consequences of a blind determination to make the military our principal instrument of foreign policy in the Third World.

Conventional arms sales and first-strike nuclear weapons are not the sum total of this irrationality and of the waste, danger, and absurdity contained in the administration's arms budget. The military budget requests of the Reagan administration represent a commitment to a foolhardy attempt to reassert U.S. dominance throughout the world. They are a perfect reflection of the administration's view that social, economic, and political problems can be solved by bullying friends and adversaries in the Third World, and by cowing our European allies and adversaries with threats of a nuclear first strike.

Militarism and adventurism cannot resolve the issues that give rise to war. This is not a naïve, idealistic assertion, but a calculated view of fitting solution to problem. Sending a battleship to the shores of El Salvador will not still a people's yearning for freedom from oppression and terror. A Rapid Deployment Force cannot forestall future Iranian revolutions. New aircraft carriers are worthless in a strategic conflict with the Soviet Union and unnecessary if we implement a foreign policy that respects the right of independent nations to control their own internal affairs. More tactical airwings, airlift capacity, ships, tanks, trucks, troops, and munitions will not quiet voices crying out for economic justice, human dignity, and political freedom.

Yet the Reagan administration is committed to a military force build-up that is calculated to stifle these cries, projecting U.S. military power around the globe. The nature, parameters, and weaponry of this force projection are analyzed in Part III.

In Chapter 10, Rear Admiral Gene R. LaRocque, U.S.N. (Ret.)

details the preparations for nuclear war fighting and argues that the development of first-strike weapons destroys the entire concept and strategy of deterrence. Pointing out the increasing danger ahead as conventional weapons become intermingled with nuclear ones in all our land, air, and sea units, he urges the implementation of a no-first-use pledge by the United States. He calls for the development of a coherent, logical foreign policy and the military posture to accompany it.

In Chapter 11, Dr. Jeremy Stone critiques the administration's cornerstone policy of developing a nuclear first-strike capability. He enumerates the reasons why the policy is doomed to economic, political, and military failure.

In Chapter 12, Professor Earl C. Ravenal cuts to the heart of the military budget problem. Detailing how the military budget is spent, he makes the case for drastic cuts in conventional force deployments. Such a policy, based on a noninterventionist foreign policy, would immediately save $60 billion to $100 billion in the first year of implementation, and $2.25 trillion or more in the decade of the 1980s.

In Chapter 13, Dr. Paul F. Walker sensibly argues that the military budget should have the goal of creating an adequate defense for the United States. He notes the mischief and expense that could be avoided by abandoning sophisticated and dangerous weaponry, triple redundancy (having a deterrent in all legs of the nuclear "triad") of strategic forces, a 640-ship navy, and other elements of the Reagan military build-up. □

10

PREPARING TO FIGHT A NUCLEAR WAR . . .
The Reagan Arms Budget
Rear Admiral Gene R. LaRocque, U.S.N. (Ret.)

■ ■ ■

Admiral Gene R. LaRocque is director of the Center for Defense Information, which publishes *The Defense Monitor,* a periodical in the field of military policy.

THE REAGAN ADMINISTRATION'S new military budget is premised on the idea that we should be preparing to fight and win a nuclear war. President Reagan's *Budget of the United States Government Fiscal Year 1983* spells this out: "U.S. defense policies ensure our preparedness to respond to and, if necessary, successfully fight either conventional or nuclear war." Secretary of Defense Caspar Weinberger testified before congressional committees about the need to "prevail in nuclear war." The idea of nuclear war fighting is now central to U.S. war plans.

Winning a nuclear war and defeating the Soviets is a pipe dream. Neither we nor they can win a nuclear war. This is the fundamental truth of military affairs today. It is a bitter pill to swallow, particularly for military men. The traditional role of the military in all countries is to prepare to win. The military profession, to be blunt, has always sought superiority. Military men are understandably uncomfortable with notions of military balance or equilibrium.

Preparations to fight and win a nuclear war are a central part of the $222 billion package of strategic weapons the President announced last year. The fiscal year 1983 military budget is a nuclear war budget, and I think we should make no mistake about that. The funding for strategic nuclear forces would climb 43 percent between fiscal years 1982 and 1983, twice as fast as the spending for conventional forces.

The implications of the recognition that we cannot and should not be prepared to fight and win a nuclear war go far beyond just the nuclear weapons program in the new budget. Most of our conventional forces are planned for war with the Soviet Union. But I submit that *any* war with the Soviet Union is going to be a nuclear war. Once started, it is almost inevitable that a small nuclear war will rapidly become a big nuclear war. Neither we nor the Russians will permit the other side to get the upper hand in battle, and escalation is inevitable. General Bernard Rogers, the Supreme Allied Commander in Europe, recently said that he believes there can be no such thing as a "limited" nuclear war and that "the use of theater nuclear weapons would, in fact, escalate to the strategic level, and very quickly."

Reagan administration budget presentations are filled with bellicose rhetoric about imminent war and deadly peril. If you believe that we can fight and win a nuclear war with the Soviet Union and that such a war is looming on the horizon, then plausibly you may support the new military budget. In other words, if you think we are going to war tomorrow and are in favor of planning to fight a war with the Soviet Union, then there is some logic to this budget. If however, you do not believe we can win a nuclear war with the Soviets or anybody else and if you do not believe that war is around the corner, then you may exercise your own sensible judgment on this nuclear war budget. My own view is that the country does not face the kind of national emergency that this budget alleges. Tragically, however, the budget may contribute significantly to the creation of such an emergency.

Of course, some of the rhetoric is the typical oversell of the Pentagon officials, who, in order to get public and congressional support for large military budgets, believe their message must be delivered dramatically. While I do not doubt their sincerity, I do doubt their wisdom.

In the nuclear area, we quite safely could adopt a freeze on the production of nuclear weapons. A freeze could be negotiated mutually with the Soviet Union. The United States today has more than 30,000 nuclear weapons, about 12,000 of which can be exploded on the Soviet Union. This is far more than sufficient to destroy the Soviet Union, even if they strike us first. If all the nuclear weapons the president has requested are produced, we will be able to explode 20,000 nuclear weapons on the Soviet Union by 1990. We simply have no offensive or defensive need for all these very expensive weapons.

I would at the minimum eliminate the MX missile, the B-1 bomber, the Trident II missile, the sea-launched Cruise missiles, the Pershing II and the ground-launched Cruise missiles for Europe. I would also eliminate the expanded Continental Air Defense program, expanded ABM programs, expanded civil defense programs, and the new effort to acquire antisatellite capability. This would save about $13 billion in budget authority in fiscal year 1983. As I say, this is a minimal effort to control the escalation of unneeded nuclear weapons. A total freeze on new production of nuclear weapons and delivery vehicles would save about $20 billion in fiscal year 1983.

The first priority for military expenditures should be to insure that existing military forces and personnel and weapons are utilized in the most appropriate and efficient manner. I have supported and continue to support those expenditures on military manpower, operations, and maintenance that insure an appropriate peacetime level of readiness. But on this issue of readiness, there is a lot of disagreement. It is a far more complicated issue than most people seem to think. I know that "readiness" has become a catchall phrase that everyone has rallied around. But as with all good themes, I think this readiness theme is grossly overdone.

First, we must recognize that there are significant differences between wartime and peacetime. We simply cannot afford the human and financial costs necessary to maintain continuously a level of readiness for war that would be appropriate only if war were imminent. Some compromise level of less-than-perfect readiness for war must be maintained.

Second, measuring readiness is one of the toughest things for military men to do—to tell whether or not an organization or other entity is truly ready for combat. The posture statement of the Joint Chiefs of Staff recognized this difficulty when they stated: "There are no simple techniques for measuring readiness; some factors are readily measurable, but others are less tangible and require subjective judgment." I fear that a lot of activities that really have little to do with genuine readiness are being pushed these days because of the popularity of the slogan.

Third, I do not really know what readiness for nuclear war means. It certainly cannot mean that we are ready to conduct a victorious nuclear war because that is impossible. We may pretend that spending X billions of dollars will make us ready for nuclear war, but even if we spend our entire federal budget for nuclear weapons and nuclear warfare, it must be obvious that we can never be ready for nuclear war.

Fourth, former Defense Secretary Brown put a new light on this when he said, before he left the Pentagon:

I have seen many commanders of U.S. military forces in the field over the past three-and-a-half years, and I haven't found one who says, "I'd rather have the Soviet equipment and the Soviet state of readiness of equipment; I'd rather have the Soviet forces than the U.S. forces."

He also went on to say that "that's the measure of readiness, not some paper comparison." It is very difficult to measure readiness. But the furor about alleged unreadiness of U.S. armed forces has been a product, I think, partly of this partisan debate over military strength during the 1980 elections. The surprising fact of the matter is that the Soviets are at a lower level of readiness than we are.

Apart from their unsuccessful combat activities in Afghanistan, the Soviet military have had no combat experience for thirty-five years. On the other hand, the U.S. military were in Vietnam for ten years. We were in Korea. We stopped off in the Dominican Republic. Thus, we have had a lot of combat experience, being almost continuously involved in war since 1945. Of U.S. active military officers today, almost all have had some form of combat experience.

The Soviet Union has a large number of divisions, but its ground combat forces, as a whole, are in a poor state of readiness. Apart from those Soviet divisions occupying the restive East European states, barely 10 percent of the other Soviet ground divisions are combat-ready, and two-thirds are at greatly reduced strength, as Secretary of Defense Weinberger reported in the 1981 version of his booklet, *Soviet Military Power.* The Defense Intelligence Agency has also stated: "The Soviets rely on mobilization of reserves to supply much of their warfighting capability." My conclusion is that the picture of the Soviet war machine as poised to march tomorrow to victory on battlefields around the world is absurd.

My conclusion is that we should make sensible increases in spending to ready our forces for combat. We should not be stampeded into excesses. We should also question closely the argument that this military budget cannot be cut without reducing readiness for war.

One fundamental reason for what are termed readiness deficiencies is that, militarily, we are spread too thinly around the world. The United States is the only truly worldwide military power with hundreds of military bases thousands of miles from home. The Soviet Union has nothing remotely resembling our worldwide military establishment. When we try to be dominant militarily everywhere, simultaneously, it is inevitable that we will fall short of that goal. Even if the military budget were doubled, we could not be militarily superior everywhere in the world at the same time. On the matter of readiness, incidentally, there is no budget line item for readiness, but the Pentagon regularly comes to Congress and suggests that any cuts in the budget will impact adversely on readiness. That has to be a value judgment because there is no line item. There is nothing you could add or cut that is specifically for readiness.

Our inability to make tough choices on our huge overseas military commitments is the main reason the Reagan military budget presentation seems to lack coherence or logical structure. It was Frederick the Great who noted that "he who would preserve everything, preserves nothing." The nostalgic idea that we can win a nuclear war is coupled with the nostalgic idea that somehow we can control events around the world if we are strong enough militarily. There are far too many problems around the world that the United States cannot resolve or control by military force. Most of the problems of other countries are not military problems. Nevertheless, we must spend whatever is necessary to defend U.S. territory.

But is the U.S. defense budget really for the defense of the United States? Most of the so-called defense budget, nearly 70 percent, is to provide men and weapons to fight in foreign countries in support of our allies and friends and for offensive operations in Third World countries. The entire U.S. Army and most of the Air Force are equipped, armed, and manned to fight in foreign countries. And a major portion of the Navy is built, trained, and equipped to project our military power to foreign countries. The historic and continuing mission of nearly 200,000 Marines is to fight in foreign lands.

Another big chunk of the defense budget is the 20 percent allocated for our offensive nuclear force of bombers, missiles, and submarines whose job it is to carry nuclear weapons to the Soviet Union. These strategic forces are clearly not for defense; they exist to conduct offensive warfare. In the Secretary of Defense's listing of these strategic nuclear forces, he explicitly lists them as offensive strategic forces, not as defensive strategic forces. On the decision of President Reagan, these missiles, planes, and submarines can be launched to destroy the Soviet Union in a first-strike attack, or they can be launched in retaliation against a Soviet attack on the United States. Our strategic forces play no role in the defense of the United States, but we hope they will dissuade the Soviets from attacking us first.

Actual defense of the United States costs about 10 percent of the military budget and is the least expensive function performed by the Pentagon. It is accomplished by one of its relatively small components: the men, missiles, and aircraft of the Aerospace Defense Command, formerly the Continental Air Defense Command. Its job, of course, is to detect and destroy any aircraft *en route* to attack this country. It is also supposed to detect the incoming attack from missiles, either from submarines or land-based missiles from the Soviet Union. A sophisticated array of radars, computers, satellites, and communication nets are in constant operation by skilled crews to detect and report these missiles. Although the warning systems do nothing to defend the country after a missile attack has been launched, they do make it possible in theory for the president to launch our missiles at the Soviets while theirs are en route to the United States. Knowing this, the Soviets may be deterred from launching an attack. Perhaps this justifies the entire cost of the forces dedicated to defending the country; in other words, the 10 percent of the military budget is probably justified in helping to deter an attack.

Nearly everyone agrees that we ought to spend whatever is necessary to defend the United States, but it is clear that we are actually spending 90 percent of our money to fight in foreign countries—70 percent for those conventional forces to fight in foreign countries and 20 percent to send nukes to the Soviet Union. I do not argue that the military budget should be slashed by 90 percent. Some forces to deliver nuclear weapons to the Soviet Union and some forces to fight in distant countries and at sea undoubtedly contribute to the defense of the United States and to the deterrence of nuclear war. But I do argue that if the taxpayers and the Congress realize that the lion's share of the defense budget is not for defense, they may examine more carefully the administration's military spending program.

As a final suggestion, I would like to propose the creation of a Congressional Office of Defense Appraisal (CODA). Today there is no place in government where the total picture of military affairs is considered —where all relevant military and nonmilitary aspects are integrated. I received a visit the other day from one of the biggest television producers. He is trying to do a study on how U.S. strategy is actually arrived at, how it is derived, and who is involved in making U.S. military strategy. Is it driven by the acquisition of weapons, is it driven by ideas, or is it driven by what the Soviets or other countries do? He is finding it exceedingly difficult to come to grips with just how U.S. military strategy in this era is developed.

A new Congressional Office of Defense Appraisal could provide for the first time a centralized, coherent integration of U.S. military strategy, available resources, and military spending. Today's piecemeal approach allows the national security bureaucracy and the military budgets to grow rapidly, while no attempt is made to insure that the strategy, the forces, and the spending are mutually supportive. A new overview organization should also assess the impact on the economy and on American society of the military establishment and the massive increases in military spending.

A friend of mine in the Treasury Department told me that last year, for the first time in the history of this great nation, the Treasury Department had established an office within the Treasury Department to examine the impact of military spending on the U.S. economy. You would have thought we would have been doing that a long time ago.

■   ■   ■

■ *CHAIRMAN DELLUMS:*   General Rogers of the Supreme Allied Command in Europe has stated that there could be no such thing as a "limited" nuclear war and that the use of theater nuclear weapons would, in fact, escalate to the strategic level and very quickly. If the notion of theater nuclear war is absurd, then there can be no such thing as theater superiority, in terms of nuclear weapon capability, since any war would escalate to a strategic nuclear confrontation. Therefore, if we bilaterally freeze nuclear weapons at this particular moment, we are not freezing in Soviet superiority as the administration claims—or American superiority, for that matter. Is that correct?

■ *ADMIRAL LaROCQUE:*   Your observations are simple but profound in implication. Superiority has lost its meaning in terms of nuclear weapons in Europe. It is unmeasurable in quantity, quality, or anything else to talk about superiority.

We have today over 6,000 nuclear weapons in Europe, many of which can be hurled against the Soviet Union. Those are all nuclear weapons in NATO, in Europe. The Russians, it is true, have intermediate range missiles. They have 300 of those SS-20s and some SS-4s and SS-5s in Russia that can reach Europe. Both sides have enough to destroy each other, but regardless of which side fires first, there will be no winners—only a destroyed Europe will remain. So, to talk about superiority in the old-fashioned way of trying to fight and win a battle or even to fight and win a war is ridiculous.

We must first of all slow the increases in nuclear weapons and then begin to think about stopping all increases and then begin to reduce. I think it is specious for President Reagan to say that "we must only discuss reductions in nuclear weapons." He does not want to talk about slowing the increases or even leveling off on one side or the other or both sides simultaneously. Instead, he talks about this grand moment when we are going to begin to reduce nuclear weapons.

■ *CHAIRMAN DELLUMS:*   Do you believe that the United States and the Soviet Union could contain a conventional confrontation?

■ *ADMIRAL LaROCQUE:*   There is absolutely no way for a conventional war or for a nuclear war with the Soviet Union to be contained. Any war we have with the Soviet Union will inevitably be a nuclear war because we have nuclearized our Army divisions, our air wings, and our Navy warships, over 70 percent of which carry nuclear weapons. Nuclear weapons have become the conventional weapons of our armed forces today.

We do not differentiate significantly between conventional and nuclear weapons. Among the most effective weapons we have today against enemy submarines are nuclear weapons. Back in 1964, when I was the captain of a guided missile cruiser in the San Francisco bay area, our primary air defense weapon was nuclear. That was eighteen years ago, when we had only a fraction of the nuclear weapons we have today.

Any war we have today with the Soviet Union, even if it starts conventionally, will rapidly escalate to nuclear war. So, jumping from the beginning to the end, any combat we have with the Soviet Union in Europe will end in the destruction of the United States.

■ *CHAIRMAN DELLUMS:* President Reagan, the Secretary of Defense, and the Secretary of State have on a number of occasions communicated the idea to the American people that we can fight a clean, surgical, well-controlled, carefully defined, "limited" nuclear war. Is this a realistic concept in the decade of the 1980s?

■ *ADMIRAL LaROCQUE:* There is absolutely no way to control a war once you begin using nuclear weapons. We found, Mr. Chairman, in the South Pacific, when we were testing nuclear weapons in the atmosphere, that when we exploded a hydrogen weapon or any kind of nuclear weapon, a phenomenon known as EMP, electromagnetic pulse was produced. This electromagnetic pulse blanked out all communications for a period of time. It was not terribly significant in those days because we were using vacuum tubes in our communications with our ships and aircraft. When you fire nuclear weapons into the atmosphere today, however, that electromagnetic pulse will wipe out almost all of our communications because we are now using solid-state integrated circuits and silicon chips and this EMP is a disaster to any such form of communication equipment.

The former chief scientist of the Army recently pointed out to me that one nuclear weapon exploded 200 miles over the center of the United States—just one nuclear weapon 200 miles up—would blank out all communications in the United States. He also said that electromagnetic pulse wipes out computer tapes. It wipes them blank. Since much of our air defense and other weaponry is controlled by the use of computers, there is probably no way that we could communicate with our own forces in Europe once the first nuclear weapons begin to fall, much less with the British and the French, our allies, to get them to stop or start. Certainly, there would be no way to communicate with the Soviets. So, people who talk about controlling a nuclear war once it starts simply don't know what they're talking about.

■ *CHAIRMAN DELLUMS:* Admiral, are the concepts of mutually assured destruction or deterrence still valid concepts?

■ *ADMIRAL LaROCQUE:* The concept of a mutually assured deterrent, which somehow metamorphized to mutually assured destruction over the years, was a useful device when we had most all the nuclear weapons and when we could clearly destroy the Soviet Union before they could destroy us. Today, since both sides have the capability to destroy the other and both sides have the capability or are building the capability to try to destroy the other side's capability, it "puts a hair trigger on the reactions at both sides," in Paul Warnke's words. I think we ought to reexamine the whole strategy of mutually assured deterrence. We must move away, on both sides, from this confrontation that says, "If you shoot, I'll shoot," because that is the hair-trigger element. I think it is an outmoded idea. We are going to have to learn to live with the Russians, and they are going to have to learn to live with us—or we and the Russians are going to die at about the same time.

■ *CHAIRMAN DELLUMS:* What constitutes, in your estimation, an acceptable level of deterrence?

■ *ADMIRAL LaROCQUE:* If both sides had only the weapons that could be used in retaliation, that would be an acceptable deterrent. The problem before us today is the shift in this administration's philosophy away from deterrence to one of war fighting and war winning.

■ *CHAIRMAN DELLUMS:* We hear these terms "limited options" and "flexible responses" when a number of your colleagues from the Pentagon appear before the Armed Services Committee to talk about nuclear war-fighting strategy. Can you comment as to what you perceive to be the efficacy of ideas such as "flexible response" and "limited options." What do these terms really mean?

■ *ADMIRAL LaROCQUE:* What they mean to me is that for the last twenty-five years, military analysts, mostly outside the Pentagon but to some extent within the Pentagon, have under a facade of slogans built more and more nuclear weapons, far beyond any we possibly could use for deterrence. What they are saying is that with regard to flexible response we are going to fight in Europe as long as we can with conventional forces. Then we are going to respond flexibly with tactical nuclear weapons, and then flexibly respond with strategic nuclear weapons. They have built in a graduated escalation that they have then defined as their option to move on up. Once nuclear weapons begin to fall I don't know who is going to have the authority to exercise those options.

I see no way that you can implement "flexible response" or "limited options." It is sort of a war game idea. Really it is so much pap fed to the public in America and everywhere in the world to make them think that nuclear weapons can be used rationally. They cannot be used when one begins to examine the reality that they cannot be limited.

I participated in war games when I was stationed at the Pentagon. We would fight conventionally under flexible response for a little while and then drop a couple of nuclear weapons. As soon as we dropped a few, the game was over because there was no way to measure the response on the Soviet side, no way to say accurately how many they are going to fire at us nor what will happen on our side. So the game ends. Oh, you could say, "Well, we can measure the results if a thousand fell on Europe." You can measure the destruction, but you cannot measure a course of action after you have fired two or three nuclear weapons in Europe by either side, and it has never been done in a war game.

In history we have only exploded one nuclear weapon at a time. Nobody has any idea of what is going to happen when you fire thousands of nuclear weapons in one area in a short period of time. It is just beyond our comprehension. We have not been able to war game that in the Pentagon.

■ *CHAIRMAN DELLUMS:* Admiral, given the relative strength of the United States and the Soviet Union, do you perceive any risk to the United States as we build up our strength?

■ *ADMIRAL LaROCQUE:* The Soviet Union can destroy us, and we can destroy the Soviet Union, so we are constantly at risk. But we do not diminish that risk by adding more and more nuclear weapons and more accurate nuclear weapons and weapons that can respond more quickly. We increase the risk when we do that. We ought to be building a force that is simply a retaliatory force, one that says to the Soviet Union, "If you strike us with one nuclear weapon, we are going to blow you up, we're going to destroy you." That's the kind of force that we must have today. They could have the same kind of force and then both of us could relax on the assumption that the other side is not going to strike first.

■ *CHAIRMAN DELLUMS:* What are your thoughts as to how the Soviets might respond to our acquisition of the MX missile and the Trident II missile, given the Soviet's extraordinary reliance on ground-launched ICBMs?

■ *ADMIRAL LaROCQUE:* If we go ahead with that MX, that superaccurate, very large weapon on the MX, and the Trident II missiles, we are into a whole new era of nuclear weaponry with the Soviet Union. It puts us more firmly on a collision course for a nuclear war because the Soviet Union is going to have to respond in kind.

If there is one thing we have learned in the thirty-five years of the arms race with the Soviet Union, it is that whereas we have been ahead by three to five years in the development of every major strategic weapon system, they have followed along behind. What they want to achieve, apparently, is some form of parity with us. They are simply not going to let us be perceived as having more accurate, more powerful destructive weapons than they have. If they can get to that position and stay there, and if we do not keep trying to go ahead of them in that regard, we will have a chance to reduce the tensions that exist between our nations—and that, I think, is the key element.

In many ways, the nuclear arms race has gotten beyond the point of a military argument. It has become a political argument, and it ought to be taken out of the terms of who builds what weapons or how many. We need *now* a political solution. That is why I think your efforts, Mr. Chairman, in holding these hearings are so very important in helping to raise this beyond the idea of simply bean-counting who has what or who has the highest technology or who can do what with nuclear weapons. We must have a reduction of tensions between the United States and the Soviet Union in order to move away from nuclear war.

■ *MR. BEILENSON (D-Calif.):* What kind of a nuclear strategy should we have, pending the day when we start learning to get along with the Russians?

■ *ADMIRAL LaROCQUE:* It appears increasingly clear to military men that nuclear weapons themselves are really not weapons any more. You cannot use them in the way that we used to be able to use weapons. It is a boomerang weapon; it kills the enemy and it kills you, too. The only strategy that you can have is one that is based on not using nuclear weapons.

■ *MR. BEILENSON:* Has there been a shift in Soviet strategy with respect to reliance on mutually assured destruction, or has there been a shift in their nuclear strategy over the last five or ten years in response to what we are doing?

■ *ADMIRAL LaROCQUE:* I think the Soviet Union has tried to stay up with us. I have not seen in our close observation any change in Soviet strategy. It has been one primarily of deterrence, and that is reflected in the fact that they have a large number of very heavy, old-fashioned, land-based missiles. Most of theirs are still liquid-propelled. They have kept their submarines pretty well in their home ports. Nowadays that is not significant because they can now fire some of their missiles from their home ports to the United States.

But what we have seen from the Soviet Union that is different in the last several years are repeated statements from the leadership in the Soviet Union saying that nuclear war will destroy all of us. Nuclear war will destroy any country that is involved in a nuclear war. There will be no winners in a nuclear war. We have not heard that type of statement repeated in the United States.

There has been some talk about the Soviet Union shifting to a nuclear war-fighting capability. I do not think there is any evidence of that in the forces that they have built. There is certainly no evidence of that in the public statements from their leadership. I think that we in the United States, and particularly in military circles, are suggesting that the Soviets have moved to a war fighting strategy and, therefore, we should change ours. I think that we were first in developing the idea of a nuclear war fighting strategy and we are the *only* country where there is any evidence that such a strategy is being prepared—*the only country!*

■ *MR. BEILENSON:* The most disturbing thing you said was your suggestion that nuclear weapons had become the conventional weapons of today in the sense that they are fully integrated into our armed services in various parts of the world. You suggested that we could not get into a fight with the Soviet Union without moving to nuclear exchanges. Do we have some selectivity in terms of what weapons we use and don't use? Can we fight someone other than the Soviets without using nuclear weapons even though they are integrated into our armed forces?

■ *ADMIRAL LaROCQUE:* Yes, we can. I was limiting my remarks to the conflict with the Soviet Union. We have a dual capability in our ships, in our army divisions, and in our air wings that can be used for fighting against Ghana or El Salvador, although we have to exercise a certain amount of caution when we do that so that we do not integrate our nuclear forces into the act. For example, in 1958, when we sent a division or more into Lebanon, we in the Pentagon realized to our horror that going along with that division was its organic nuclear unit, so we rushed out messages to not land the nukes in Lebanon. I do not remember the details now whether they actually got ashore or not.

What I am suggesting is that nuclear weapons are now organic to each unit. If you are a battery commander or a wing commander, it is easier to accomplish your objective by using the nuclear instead of a conventional weapon. Presumably, the president is supposed to release all nuclear weapons. Theoretically, there is a whole chain-of-command. There is a permissive action link. It is all geared so that when the chain-of-command receives the word it passes on down to the local commander and he goes ahead and uses the nukes.

■ *MR. BEILENSON:* So, nuclear weapons can be used in Europe by U.S. forces without presidential approval?

■ *ADMIRAL LaROCQUE:* I believe it could happen. They should not be used. But all we are dealing with here is presidential approval.

There is no key that the president turns to unlock the devices in Europe. We have nuclear weapons spread all over the world. We are the *only* country in the world that has nuclear weapons in a foreign country. We still have them in Turkey and in various parts of Europe. We have nearly 5,000 weapons in Germany alone. They have to be sufficiently ready to be used, and it would be interesting to get a direct answer from the Pentagon on how a commander in the field is prevented from getting nuclear weapons out for use. It is a positive sort of thing. Once the request is generated from the field, it goes back to Washington; then the president says yes; and then the chain-of-command goes back and says, "The old man said yes—it is okay." And then they go ahead and do it.

■ *CHAIRMAN DELLUMS:* Your information indicates that the B-1B bomber program would cost roughly $40 billion—100 planes at $400 million a copy. The Reagan administration is attempting to sell this program to the Congress as a $20 billion program, roughly $200 million per plane. Would you comment on those two figures?

■ *ADMIRAL LaROCQUE:* Either figure is ridiculously high for an airplane whose sole mission is to carry more nuclear weapons to the Soviet Union. It is not going to get there very quickly. It will get there in six hours instead of eight or ten hours for the B-52. But in either case, it will be after several thousand nuclear weapons have already exploded on the Soviet Union.

The $20 billion figure that the Pentagon has come up with may have been what was thought to be a reasonable figure to start with because it was so big that it surely would cover all the costs. But the Center for Defense Information got alerted to some studies by the Congressional Budget Office, which had examined this very carefully. They came up with some good arithmetic to show that the total cost of this program would be nearly $40 billion. Then we went back over their figures, and we could find nothing wrong with the way they had arrived at them.

Anybody today who says you can build a weapon for what the Pentagon says it is going to build it for, and have it built in ten years at that cost, must be dreaming because they do not—they cannot—they never have —built them for the cost they say they are going to build them for.

■ *CHAIRMAN DELLUMS:* The argument in support of the MX missile on the part of the Pentagon was that our fixed-base ICBMs, on an increasing basis, are becoming vulnerable to Soviet attack. Therefore, we have to move from a stationary ICBM mode to a mobile mode, which is the MX missile concept. The president now throws out all of the basing modes but argues diligently to keep the missile warhead itself, the Mark 12-A. We understand there will be another warhead developed in Livermore, California, that will use less plutonium. Does not the retention of the ten-warhead MX missile itself, as opposed to this mobile mode, constitute a first-strike weapon?

■ *ADMIRAL LaROCQUE:* I think you are absolutely right. It is a first-strike weapon the way it is configured. It does not have to be, but it is and it has the accuracy and the explosive power to destroy Soviet missiles. The Soviets know it. It is touted as having that capability with the accuracy given by the Pentagon. It cannot be perceived by anybody as other than as a first-strike weapon. But all weapons systems, once they get started in the bureaucracy, begin to have a life of their own. I think this administration is caught up in a life of its own with the MX missile. In addition, it was a campaign promise by the president when he was running for election. He liked the missile, though I suspect he knew very little about it then, and I don't know how much more he knows about it now.

At a minimum, the Congress ought to say that we are simply not going to give you another nickel until you can show us why this basing mode is an adequate basing mode for the MX. Tell us what the costs are. They do not know what it is going to cost us to put that in the ground.

Dr. Scoville and I pleaded with President Carter to try to remove that element of the MX that would make it a first-strike weapon, but they insisted on leaving it in during the last administration, and this adminstration is simply carrying it on.

■ *MR. CONYERS (D-Mich.):* Is there growing support in our own military leadership for the views that you have articulated here so well?

■ *ADMIRAL LaROCQUE:* I do not think there is particularly growing support within the active duty military forces. I wish there were. If there is growing support, it is not evident. That is understandable. It is very difficult to speak out on these matters when you are on active duty. In many ways, I would prefer they did not because what we prize most highly in the military is loyalty in the chain-of-command. They ought to be doing what the commanders want.

On the other hand, on the outside—those of us who are retired—yes, sir! There is a growing number of retired military officers who share the views that I have expressed this morning. I have a deputy director, Rear Admiral Gene Carroll—thirty-five years in the Navy, active-duty carrier pilot. He shares those views. Major General William Fairbourn, of the Marine Corps, out in Salt Lake City, is associate director of the Center. I get letters from generals and admirals every day now who encourage us in the work that we are doing. It is absolutely a new element though, that these people have come to the fore and suggested that nuclear war is simply no way to go. I could come up with a list of fifteen or twenty flag officers. Admiral Noel Gayler, a four-star admiral, has been outspoken on this issue. He is going off in April to Cambridge to participate with the International Physicians for the Prevention of Nuclear War and to speak against nuclear war. He was commander of the Pacific theater for four years, and he was part of the strategic targeting group out in Omaha for several years when he was on active duty with the Navy.

■ *MR. CONYERS:* We are not talking about an ideological point of view, or whether you happen to like the Navy better than the Army. We are talking about life on the planet Earth. I was hoping that you might tell me that some of your former colleagues in the military leadership capacity could look at these issues from the perspective of American national security and say this is a danger and that this is going the wrong way; and that nuclear war fighting policies can actually weaken our security.

■ *ADMIRAL LaROCQUE:* I wish that it were possible to conceive of the military coming up with sort of an overall rational view of this. But, you know, we have really three navies, we have a half dozen armies, we have three air forces, and each of those components within the services is fighting for a bigger share of the budget, more airplanes, and so on. Each of the services—the Army, Navy, Air Force, and the Marine Corps—is competing against itself as well as each other.

I do not think we can look to the military to solve this problem. The military sees its role as preparing to fight a war, to win a war, and the more and better weapons they get, the more they think that improves their chances. But we are in a new era now where civilians have to get into it and tell the military, "We do not want you to fight a nuclear war." That is, I think, going to have to come from outside the Pentagon, sir.

■ *MR. CONYERS:*   The problem that I am confronted with is that those same military people that you suggest should not indulge in this are precisely the ones who come over here and load up the entire membership with the whole irrational logic of more is better and nuclear is best. I do not have any way of debating it, except to quote from these proceedings. I cannot say that I should leave it to them because they are the ones who come over with the briefcases and sit for hours and hours before all of these committees, persuading the majority of members that this is in the national interest. They are the ones who sell these things. They are the ones who sell these fantastic, affirmative nuclear policies and materiel. So I cannot say, "Gentlemen, let the civilians decide this," when it is the military itself that is participating in this debate at the highest level.

■ *ADMIRAL LaROCQUE:*   The military has been very effective in this. They are joined with the industry components who tend to benefit also from the procurement of these new weapons. I know the Pentagon is successful when they come over here. I recall some training periods we used to have, when I was in the Pentagon, before coming over to testify. We would get the admirals in a room, maybe fifteen or twenty, and there would be sort of a skull session, just like a football game—flip charts and everything. I can remember particularly in one case there was a Senator Allen Ellender of Louisiana, who is now deceased, and they would say: "When you're testifying before Senator Ellender, don't talk about any harshness with the Soviet Union. If you have to say anything, talk about competition. He loves the word 'competition.' "

Everybody on Capitol Hill is examined carefully—their profiles and so forth. We know just how to deal with them, what to provide. In many cases we provide the questions and answers for the members of the committee, particularly the chair. It is all pretty much set up ahead of time.

That is why I have suggested that the Congress needs an Office of Defense Appraisal. It has the Office of Technology Assessment. It has the Congressional Budget Office, which does very well in that small segment on the military. But it really needs a defense appraisal office of its own, so that the Congress can ask these basic questions and come up with its own appraisals. The issues are much too important to be left exclusively to the Pentagon.

11

REAGAN'S POLICY CAN'T WORK

Dr. Jeremy J. Stone

■ ■ ■

Jeremy Stone graduated from Swarthmore College and received his Ph.D. in mathematics from Stanford University. He has been a research mathematician at the Stanford Research Institute and a research associate at the Harvard Center for International Affairs. He is currently director of the Federation of American Scientists. His books include *Containing the Arms Race*: *Some Concrete Proposals* and *Strategic Persuasion*.

To understand where we should go in strategic force planning, it is necessary to understand where we have been and where we are. For a third of a century, the driving force behind American strategic planning has been the feeling that we could prevent Soviet aggression in Europe only by threatening to escalate to strategic nuclear attacks on the Soviet Union. For that same third of a century, with every passing year, the credibility of such attacks has steadily declined as the Soviet capacity to retaliate has grown. What are we to do in these circumstances?

Today we find that the average citizen understands quite well the infeasibility of our surviving such escalation to nuclear war. When our federation circulates the Hatfield Resolution (asserting that the United States should not base its policies or its weapons programs on the belief that the United States can limit, survive, or "win" a nuclear war) we get broad support and spontaneous help. The problem is that many officials in the Reagan administration believe that the only way to defend Western Europe is precisely to pretend or threaten that we can indeed limit, survive, or "win" a nuclear war.

Those officials who do not so believe that we could limit, survive, or "win" a nuclear war seem to be motivated by a fear that perhaps the Soviet Union thinks it could limit, survive, or "win" a nuclear war and that, accordingly, we would lose some kind of force, authority, or will if we did not adopt the same conception or misconception. Compounding the issue is the rate of spending on defense in the Soviet Union; it is a high rate of spending that, for whatever the reason, raises questions in Washington about Soviet long-run intentions.

Thus, those of us seeking to hold the line against war fighting policies are faced with three different problems: (1) the definition and redefinition of American policies; (2) the proper characterization of Soviet attitudes; and (3) the correct response to the Soviet defense build-up.

It is becoming increasingly difficult to explain American policy because it has to be discussed in euphemistic terms. The public debate will not permit candor about war fighting plans. To some extent this has been true for years. When Secretary of Defense James Schlesinger threatened nuclear first-use in Korea, more than 100 members of the House of Representatives co-signed a no first-use resolution of Congressman Richard Ottinger. Within a few days, when the administration explained to them that we had been threatening first-use for years in Europe and that it was indeed a mainstay of our policy, most of these members of Congress withdrew their names from the resolution. They did not know the policy because the United States had never been eager to emphasize in public what was well known to all students of the subject.

In order to get a somewhat more candid statement of both the fears and the aspirations of the Reagan administration than can be found in its posture statement, I have dug up a statement of Secretary of the Navy, John Lehman, who was formerly deputy director of the Arms Control and Disarmament Agency, which I believe reflects the real underlying desires and attitude of the administration. Basically, Mr. Lehman is arguing that in the present period much of the world "wherein lies the vital interests of the United States and its allies, is now for the first time outside the nuclear umbrella." He then says: "In the full world realization of Soviet nuclear superiority, can anyone seriously believe that we would take the escalatory step to nuclear weapons in the event of a European conflict?" In other words, he fears that we no longer have the capacity to credibly threaten to initiate the first use of nuclear weapons. As a result, he calls for accelerating development of the MX missile and a multiple-aim point basing mode; accelerated development of ballistic missile defense for our ICBMs in a mobile mode and advanced manned long-range combat aircraft; accelerated development and deployment of the Trident II long-range SLBM; and a host of other strategic expenditures.

The point I want to bring to the attention of the committee is what he feels are the goals of these expenditures because it is these goals that are the premises that the committee is striving to surface. I believe these are, in fact, the goals of the Reagan administration.

First of all, he would like a forthright declaration that it is U.S. policy to maintain the capability to prevail in a nuclear war if such takes place, regardless of who the adversary might be. He wants more than a stalemate; he wants to be sure that we would prevail.

Second, he wants no adversary to be permitted to maintain an advantage, particularly in nuclear capabilities, that provides them with military options and, hence, political leverage unavailable to the United States. This is to say, in effect, that we should have every capability that they have. Since the two sides are not symmetrical in their structure, it would mean that we would again have to acquire a measure of superiority in every area of weapons.

Third, he advocates that the United States maintain plans and capabilities to carry out nuclear strikes of selective targeting breadth and scale. Moreover, the United States will procure weapons suited to selective and flexible targeting, including more accurate guidance for all weapons systems, in order to gain the capability to limit collateral damage around precision targets and to increase the kill probability against hardened targets without yield. In short, he wants war fighting capability.

Fourth, he wants our triad of strategic weapons to be modified to provide a dimension of depth over time. He goes on to explain that any capability for fighting a nuclear war should include the capacity to execute controlled military strikes weeks and months after an initial exchange. He feels this four-step program, outlined above, would restore logic to our strategic policy and end destabilization.

This official, who is now the Secretary of the Navy, and was the deputy director of the Arms Control and Disarmament Agency, is calling for a reestablishment of the strategic superiority that we had in an earlier era. I would like to give nine reasons why this policy is not necessary and is bound to fail.

In the first place, in a contest between even roughly comparable opponents it is just not feasible for one of them to maintain the capacity to escalate to nuclear war while coercing the other one not to respond. The fact is that each of these superpowers can achieve and maintain the ability to match the escalation of the other. In this regard, Mr. Lehman and the Reagan administration are pursuing the resurrection of a strategic advantage that is long-gone and irretrievable.

Second, if even limited attacks were to take place with tens, much less hundreds or thousands, of nuclear weapons—and both sides now have thousands—command and control over nuclear weapons would deteriorate so fast that unlimited nuclear war would become a virtual certainty. There is no way to have this command and control stretching for weeks or months after nuclear war starts. Tens of nuclear weapons, much less hundreds, would blow all the light bulbs and all the electricity and everything else that would be necessary to maintain "limited" war. I believe that fifty nuclear weapons would be sufficient to destroy all the command posts and methods of controlling the nuclear weapons systems that we have built up.

Third, local conflicts are going to be decided by local factors. Each superpower will have advantages, geographical and otherwise, in some areas, but not others; just as the Cuban Missile Crisis on the one hand and Afghanistan on the other, were decided by local conventional advantage, so also will future crises.

Fourth, does this mean that Western Europe and the Persian Gulf are doomed because they are nearer the Soviet Union? That is Mr. Lehman's fear, but my feeling is, not at all. There are a lot of other factors that prevent Soviet expansion besides our threatening to escalate to general nuclear war. We have massive conventional capabilities in Europe and could put up a very good fight. In addition, even if the Russians were to prevail in successful aggression, it would so stir up the United States and the West as to produce an entirely different kind of world. Their inevitable fear that a successful aggression would stir us up, ally us with China, and lead us to take actions in a new, accelerated arms race is a tangible form of deterrence that should not be overlooked.

Fifth, notwithstanding what we build and what we say, there will always be the risk of nuclear escalation that neither side wants. We do not have to threaten to escalate to nuclear war to get some of the deterrence associated with the fear of nuclear war.

Sixth, are these kinds of deterrents enough? On the whole, it appears that they are because the Soviet Union is not that highly motivated to run open risks of conventional war with us, which I believe has been shown by the historical record of almost four decades.

Seventh, the risk of confronting Soviet threats of invasion or subversion with nuclear options is so great as to exceed the dangers of any other Soviet action itself. A policy of threatening to escalate to nuclear war every time something goes wrong is eventually going to act itself out in the very escalation threat, and when that happens, we can lose our entire nation. By contrast, no successful Soviet aggression in the conventional field has that character. We would continue. History would not end. We would step up our efforts to retaliate in other conventional ways.

Eighth, even those members of the Congress who do not share this reasoning are going to be forced to its conclusion. The constituency and consensus for threatening first use in nuclear weapons is vanishing rapidly. Expenditures based on those threats are not going to be supported by the Congress. The United States is going to have to reconstruct its strategy for dealing with the Russians around less than nuclear threats.

Ninth, it is becoming abundantly clear for both superpowers that economic strength is as important as these kinds of military threats. If the defense budget becomes an important element in the high interest rates that may cause economic collapse, then it seems the Defense Department will bear a heavy burden on weakening the alliance and the country.

In sum, the Reagan policy, fairly reflected by Mr. Lehman, is wrong, unnecessary, and counterproductive. It represents a redoubling of efforts as the administration loses sight of its goals, but it should not be a surprise. This administration has within it and around it that small group of strategists that always gave nuclear force too much emphasis, that knows how to play the "war game" because it does not know what else to do.

I would like to quote at this point a revealing recent statement by Herman Kahn, director of the Hudson Institute, who is repeating precisely his recommendation of twenty years ago and is, indeed, making some very candid statements about what is going on. He said, this past January:

> The U.S. needs to obtain a "not-incredible" first-strike capability. It is not necessary to build a fool-proof war-fighting system, systems that cannot be proved to be unworkable may be workable enough, that is, "not-incredible." . . . The Reagan Administration differs from its predecessors in that it is willing to spend money on non-cosmetic, war-fighting capabilities, but it is still unwilling to spend enough money on a high-confidence war-fighting system.

Then he went on to say:

> An understanding that the nuclear doctrine can be changed is overdue. A serious high-level public discussion of nuclear doctrine is impossible in this country, mainly for political reasons. Very few senior U.S. military officers are capable of expounding and defending U.S. nuclear doctrine.

This is a pretty pickle if very few military officers can expound and defend the doctrine and if it cannot be discussed in public. He continued:

> Perhaps the most practical solution is to do and say only things which are politically feasible and avoid initiating discussion of more complex and realistic nuclear issues. One must, of course, be prepared to answer if a discussion is initiated.

This confirms what I said earlier: The policy has become so esoteric and so politically unattractive that it cannot be discussed any more in public. Nevertheless, its goal is to strive to secure the crediblity of being able to threaten the Soviet Union with nuclear strikes as a method of deterrence.

Nowhere is the administration's zaniness more evident than in its approach to civil defense, an approach characterized by a statement of T.K. Jones. Mr. Jones is now the Deputy Undersecretary of Defense for Research and Engineering. He said recently in an interview about civil defense and nuclear war: "Everybody is going to make it, if there are enough shovels to go around. The shovels are needed to build primitive shelters in the countryside for the evacuated population." He went on to suggest that our nation would recover in two to four years from a nuclear war if it had a Soviet-style civil defense. This statement is so bizarre and outrageous that he is being threatened by the Foreign Relations Committee with a subpoena to come and say it before them in their committee.

Based on this approach by T.K. Jones, the administration wants to move 150 million people in a crisis into evacuation areas. This idea made little sense twenty years ago, when I developed one of the first plans for doing that at the Hudson Institute, when it was then put forward as a premise for nonincredible first-strike threats. I did not agree with it then, and I was happy to learn that the civil defense officials did not agree with it either when I briefed them on it.

This idea makes even less sense now because in the interim the Soviet Union has moved from a few bombers and no ICBMs to 6,000 one-megaton warheads—which is more warheads than we have cities, villages, and hamlets in this country. There are only 5,000 places in this country that have even 5,000 citizens in them. Those one-megaton warheads are more than fifty times the size of the Hiroshima bomb.

There are so many reasons that this strategic evacuation scheme does not make sense that it is a little hard to enumerate them, but perhaps I should sketch some of them quickly.

First, the scheme is based on the fear that the Soviets have an evacuation program that would somehow embolden them. I do not believe that they have put this civil defense program in motion with the view that they could then credibly threaten to survive a nuclear war and to use this as part of a nuclear war strategy. We could neutralize such an effort and such threats with the nuclear weapons that we have available. If evacuations take place within either of these superpowers, no matter what happens to the population, all the cities will be destroyed. If all the cities will be destroyed, it is not going to matter much what happened to the immediate survival of all the populations because there will not be the survival machinery that is necessary to maintain the population.

I once had a debate with T.K. Jones on television about this subject. I realized then that he had not studied as closely as he should have the literature of strategic evacuation twenty years before. The best experts at the Rand Corporation at that time were very sensitive to the problems of postattack economic viability. They understood quite well that if you save more people but fewer cities, you could be worse off than if you saved fewer people because the whole problem was the relationship between the survival industry and the people that the survival industry was supposed to support. Our job is not to persuade the American public that it could survive a war just because the Russians may have a misconceived idea that they can. Our job would be to persuade them that they cannot—not to persuade us that we can. Citizens are not going to be willing to leave their homes for host areas in a crisis. In any case, no president is going to order this evacuation because the evacuation will undermine the president's bargaining situation. Crises in Cuba, Afghanistan, El Salvador, and Iran are not going to be resolved by crisis evacuation. Evacuation is not going to insure survival of the nation.

I am appalled to discover that even the Carter administration, in a now declassified summary of its thinking about crisis evacuation, listed the three purposes of the evacuation plan and gave as the first two bargaining purposes and war-game purposes rather than prudential purposes. The Carter administration said, first, that the program that it was thinking of—a much smaller program than the Reagan administration has in mind—should assist in maintaining perceptions of the balance favorable to the United States. Second, the strategic evacuation program should reduce the possibility that the United States could be coerced in crises. The evacuation program's purpose for saving lives was third, and there the administration was rather modest in its hopes. Unlike the present administration, they just said that the program should "provide some increase in the number of surviving population."

This administration is claiming that you can save 80 percent of the population with this crisis evacuation plan. But it is also arguing in its pamphlets that civil defense is needed for bargaining purposes. I think administration officials are aware that this civil defense program has the potential to involve every citizen in this country in a personal, direct way with nuclear war. They sense, correctly, that the arms control movement and the peace movement are salivating over the prospect that this civil defense program should be put forward and should involve citizens in thinking about nuclear war. The arms control movement and the peace movement do not approve of this program, but they would be delighted to have a letter about it sent to every citizen in the country.

In my judgment, the attitudes toward nuclear war of this administration are really quite bizarre and frightening. Mr. Meese, who is second only to the president in influence in this area, was quoted as saying that nuclear war is something that might not be desirable. The former director of the Arms Control and Disarmament Agency, Eugene Rostow, in his response to the Foreign Relations Committee in his confirmation hearings, when asked about whether a country could survive nuclear war said, "Japan, after all, not only survived, but flourished after the nuclear attack." Needless to say, we had two nuclear weapons for Japan and the Russians have 6,000 one-megaton warheads for us.

The present chair of the Defense Science Board, Norman R. Augustine, said that risking nuclear war escalation would be better than being overrun—that is, having some of our allies overrun, in a conventional war. He said:

> Of course, that [escalation] is the $64 question. The thought is that if one controls the use of nukes very carefully and engages targets that are of a military nature, and that don't do major damage to civilian populations, then the enemy would be persuaded, perhaps, not to escalate unduly. There is risk in this and that is the real danger. On the other hand, if one is just being flat overrun in a conventional war, this option may not be that bad.

The Arms Control Agency has a general Advisory Committee. Its executive director, Charles Kupperman, said recently: "Nuclear war is a destructive thing but still in large part a physics problem . . . . It is possible to survive and prevail over the enemy." So it goes, on and on. It seems reasonable to suggest that the crazies are in charge of the nukes.

This hearing does not permit time to discuss Soviet attitudes or the insane psychology of risking nuclear war with them whenever anything untoward occurs. The fact is that most administration officials, like most members of Congress, have never been to the Soviet Union. They do not have the slightest idea of what the Soviet Union is like, the good or the bad, of which there is plenty of both, as in every country. Eighty percent of the House has never been to the Soviet Union, 60 percent of the Senate has never been to the Soviet Union. Eighty percent of the

Politburo has never been to the United States. The ruling political bodies of these two countries have spent a third of a century arguing about nuclear war and arming to the teeth, without taking the trouble to visit the site of their anxiety. They all know the importance of the slogan, "Know the enemy," and they all know that they should visit dams in their states, but nobody takes the trouble to get any first-hand sense of what the arms race looks like from the other part of the mirror.

In the most fundamental sense, I think this administration is irresponsible in its approach to nuclear weapons. Its spokesmen show every sign of not having the intellectual capacity or the desire to visualize what nuclear war would be like. When they do try, like T.K. Jones did, they come up with answers that defy common sense.

Make no mistake about it, our republic can be lost. Everything our Founding Fathers worked for 200 years ago can be destroyed by one administration in one day. While I leave it to members of Congress older than myself to confirm this, I would venture to say that no administration in the last twenty years could compile a list of statements so complacent—and so unnerving—about nuclear war as we could compile from this administration. On that basis, I would say that, if America had a recall procedure, this administration should be recalled.

■   ■   ■

■ *MR. DYMALLY (D-Calif.):* Is there a Soviet threat as perceived by the administration, or is this all psychological warfare?

■ *DR. STONE:* There is a Soviet threat. The whole question is what is the nature of it, how should it be confronted, and what is it a threat to do? In the last third of a century the nature of the quarrel and the nature of the threat have been so exaggerated that it seems that either side is about to attack the other on twenty-four hours' notice as soon as the light goes green. Each side has built up nuclear weapons now as if that were going to be the solution to what are really conventional threats and conventional quarrels.

I think the Soviet threat is much more political. It is interesting when you talk with German politicians who are right on the front line. They do not expect a nuclear attack; they expect the weight of this military build-up to make itself felt in political terms. If that is true, and to the extent that it is true, we are going about resolving this challenge in the wrong way because the nuclear build-up is upsetting our allies and because it is undermining the basis for our showing the same stability and force on our side of the line.

■ *MS. SCHROEDER (D-Colo.):* I read the booklet that was distributed in my area about how to dig a trench in your front yard, and it even described how to shelter your portable toilet from the street. Heaven forbid we should not be discreet during this time. It was insane. It was like we were going to camp.

■ *DR. STONE:* It seems to me that all these local civil defense officials in all these congressional districts should be holding hearings on whether they can cope with these directives. Citizens should be encouraged to participate in discussing this whole matter.

■ *CHAIRMAN DELLUMS:* Robert Aldridge stated that to pursue a ballistic missile defense strategy is to negate totally the whole notion of deterrence. Further, because the Soviet Union is forced to evaluate not our motives but our capability, if we develop a ballistic missile defense system along with all these other first-strike weapons, the Soviet Union has to perceive us as clearly developing not only a preemptive first strike but a first-strike capability that the Soviets would not even be able to respond to if we did put a ballistic missile defense system in place. Could you respond to that?

■ *DR. STONE:* I agree with the thrust of that. It took arms controllers ten years, from 1962 to 1972, to persuade these two superpowers of that same point that you just made. By 1972 the two sides had agreed that if either side built an antiballistic missile system, the other side would just build more warheads to overwhelm it. So they agreed to stop. That treaty has served us very well for ten years, and it would be a really unfortunate disaster to lose that treaty. I am very concerned that this administration may be moving toward terminating that treaty or trying to make changes in it.

■ *CHAIRMAN DELLUMS:* For the record, I believe it is terribly important that we expose the reality that this administration is aggressively moving toward developing a ballistic missile defense system that negates the ABM (antiballistic missile) treaty, negates the whole notion of deterrence, and moves us closer to a hair-trigger situation. So, at this point, is the concept of deterrence still viable? If so, what do you perceive to be an acceptable level of deterrence?

■ *DR. STONE:* The one thing I know for certain is that we have far more than we need and that both sides do. As you lower the amounts on both sides, the political situation would improve to the point where you could lower it still further. Then you are on the track to working out completely different kinds of relations, which is going to happen as new generations come to the fore. We have 10,000 warheads rather than 400 warheads at the ready now, so we can start moving down to 400, the number McNamara said was sufficient for deterrence. That is only 4 percent of 10,000, so just to get there, we would be able to get rid of 96 percent of what we have. There is plenty of room for arms reduction.

■ *CHAIRMAN DELLUMS:* This administration has suggested that because of the "errors of previous administrations" the United States is paying a very heavy price in terms of risk, as regards equivalent nuclear power. Do you believe that the United States is, in some way, at risk from the Soviet Union regarding our comparative nuclear strength?

■ *DR. STONE:* The two sides are equal in the most fundamental method of measurement—that is, each side can destroy the other after absorbing an attack from the other. So each side can retaliate devastatingly to the other side. In that sense they are both equal and will remain equal. This is the only measure of equality that I consider to have much importance. If you have to ask who is behind, both superpowers are behind. The reason they are behind is that, if a nuclear war occurred, these two superpowers would be blown to bits, but Bolivia would not be blown to bits and neither would Australia. The whole planet may suffer, but we know that we are in the line of fire and that the Soviet Union is in the line of fire, so these two superpowers have gotten themselves into a unique fix.

■ *CHAIRMAN DELLUMS:* As members of the Armed Services Committee and the Foreign Affairs Committee, we often hear the phrases, "flexible response," "limited options," and "surgical strikes." Are these concepts realistic, or are they figments of the Pentagon planners' imaginations?

■ *DR. STONE:* We have always had, and there is no harm in having, the ability to fire less than the full armory of nuclear weapons that we have. If that is what is meant by flexible response or surgical strikes, that would not be so harmful. However, by the time they have dressed this up in the terms you have talked about, they have in mind doing the selective strikes that Secretary Lehman was talking about in response to conventional attacks from the Russians. They have in mind saying to the Russians: "Well, we admit that if you invade Europe, we can no longer massively retaliate against you, as John Foster Dulles threatened, but we are going to retaliate selectively against you with these surgical strikes, and that is why you shouldn't invade conventionally."

My fear is that these conventional outbreaks of violence in Central

Europe can always occur. They can even occur through revolutions in East Germany without deliberate Soviet intent, but for whatever purpose they can start. It is not in our interest to escalate this to general nuclear war. We can lose our sons and our allies in a conventional war, but we lose our families and everything in a total nuclear war. Why should we always be threatening to escalate to general nuclear war? It is not practical. It is not sensible.

12

CUTTING
THE DEFENSE BUDGET

Professor Earl C. Ravenal

■ ■ ■

Earl C. Ravenal graduated *summa cum laude* from Harvard University and won the Henry fellowship for graduate study at Cambridge University (England). He obtained an M.A. and Ph.D. in international relations from the Johns Hopkins University. He was president of an industrial corporation, was director of the Asian division (systems analysis) in the office of the Secretary of Defense, and is currently professor of international relations at the Georgetown University School of Foreign Service. His books include *Atlantis Lost: U.S.-European Relations after the Cold War* (co-author), *NATO's Unremarked Demise,* and *Foreign Policy in an Uncontrollable World.*

No FEDERAL BUDGET—at least, perhaps, since Calvin Coolidge—has been good news. But President Reagan's budget for fiscal year 1983 is the most provocative in living memory and has inspired more than the usual criticism. The criticism has about it an air of desperation, as if the deficits and the depredations will have irreversible effects on the economy and, beyond that, on society and the future of governance in this country.

The administration now projects overall federal spending of $762 billion for fiscal year 1983 and $803 billion for fiscal year 1984 and at this writing admits deficits, respectively, of $96 billion and $83 billion. Others, including the Congressional Budget Office, say that the spending will be almost 10 percent higher and the deficits will be double that over the two years. The precise figures do not matter. In any case, they are elusive and subject to almost daily adjustments. The point is the magnitude of the nation's insolvency and the factors that are causing it.

Among the notable features of the Reagan fiscal year 1983 budget, the most egregious is the vast increase in defense spending. In terms of spending authorization (the figure I will use throughout), there is a 20 percent increase—from $214 billion in 1982 to $258 billion in 1983. At this point, considering the extent of the insolvency and surveying the alternatives (further steep cuts in entitlements and domestic government programs, higher taxes, recourse to the money markets or to the "printing press"), even partisans of the Reagan administration have begun to part company and insist that budget balancing moves include a "fair share" of defense cuts.

But the critics of defense spending, old and new, fail to understand the anatomy of the defense budget—"where the money is"—and to that extent disqualify themselves from offering constructive alternatives. If you don't diagnose accurately, you can't prescribe effectively.

Item: Senator David Durenberger, a Republican from Minnesota, makes headlines by unveiling, after the better part of a year's effort, a detailed 195-page counter-budget that would junk some plague-ridden weapons systems (such as the Army's AH-64 attack helicopter and Hellfire antitank missile and the Navy's F/A-18 fighter-bomber), substitute fossil-fueled aircraft carriers, cancel some continental air defense, and tighten the Army's force structure—among other individual items. But this gestation of an elephant has produced a mouse: a mere $3 billion of cuts for next year and $26 billion over five years.

Item: An editorial ("Asking for the Moon on Defense," *The New York Times,* February 12, 1982), echoes the sounds of the proponents of "military reform": Cut "big-ticket" items; "increase the a number of weapons systems by shifting part of the build-up to more austere, less expensive ships and planes"; improve the "readiness of general purpose forces"; scrap the volunteer army and move to conscription.

Item: Democrats for Defense, a group of former high-level Carter functionaries, find their savings in building oil-fired aircraft carriers (or fewer, or smaller, ships) instead of nuclear ones and eliminating the B-1B bomber and most continental air defense. Indeed, they have virtually given up on overall savings, since they approve the level of the Reagan defense budget (which Carter himself would have reached soon after Reagan if he had been given the opportunity) and offer a mere rearrangement of some "priorities." (For example, they would spend even more on readiness, lift, and forces for Europe.)

The critical syndrome is familiar and depressing. In some ways, the illusions of the critics are just as harmful as the disastrous course of the administration and its hawkish supporters. Why do liberal defense critics hold to these miniscule and illusory critiques? The cast of mind is so pervasive that it must be more than negligence. Rather, it is a systematic self-deception that proceeds from deeply held intellectual and political positions. These critics would like to think that they can avoid the stark choices: cutting their favored "conventional" forces and letting allies drift, fend, or cope. They want to believe that all can be put right but that we can still defend the world in the way to which we, and others, are accustomed. What they are telling us, ironically, is that we could have containment without tears, the fruits of rearmament without the penalites.

I want to present a comprehensive critique of the Reagan defense program—its rearmament, its renewed international militance, its impetus to intervention, its ruinous domestic costs—on the broadest possible basis. My argument is based on the capacity of our society, economy, and political system to bear the extraordinary efforts—whether conceived as "necessary" or not—that the Reagan defense program imposes upon them; the disproportion of those defensive efforts—whether well-intentioned or not—to the purposes of this nation and this society; and the tension that is caused between our Constitution, our tradition of limited government, and the great costs and impositions needed to support an ambitious foreign policy. This is a critique of defense spending that relates to our foreign policy. The argument is simple: The defense budget is the price of foreign policy, and we just cannot afford our foreign policy.

This is not the standard critique, and it is easy to misunderstand. If I seem to accept the "conditional necessity" of present defense programs—that is, their appropriate relation to the present foreign policy framework—it is only, in the end, to reject *both* the defense programs and the foreign policies.

There is an integral connection, after all, between foreign spending and domestic spending—between defense expenditures and the health of our society, economy, and political system. All activities of this society, in the end, must be financed with savings, or exactions, from private efforts and organizations. Resources have a price; they are scarce, by definition. Our economy now lacks the resources for the renewal of our industrial base and the maintenance of our standard of consumption; for the restoration of our competitive power and the employment of our people. The needs are so great, and the impositions of four years of Reagan deficits—some half-a-trillion dollars—are likely to be so enormous, that there is really only one place where a sufficient remedy can be found and that is in the reduction of defense spending.

The notorious bank robber Willie Sutton could have given the appropriate advice: You have to go where the money is. Critics of defense who would make cuts would be well advised to take Willie's advice. But to get such savings in the defense budget, you have to *know* where the money is.

First of all, strange as it seems, the real money in the defense budget is not in the conspicuous, exotic toys—the "big-ticket" items—particularly strategic nuclear systems such as the MX missile and the B-1B bomber. Those two systems, for example, will account for $4.5 billion and $4.8 billion respectively in fiscal year 1983; together, that represents 3.5 percent of the administration's 1983 defense request.

Equally strange, perhaps, it is not "waste" or "fat" that makes any noticeable difference. David Stockman's careless remark that the Pentagon was a "swamp" of waste and inefficiency might have been a reassuring swipe of rhetoric to the critics of the Pentagon. But waste and fat will come to only a few billion dollars a year in defense budgets that are going to three-quarters of a trillion dollars a year by the end of a decade. As Eugene McCarthy used to say about the Pentagon: "It isn't the fat that ought to worry us, it's the lean." The sad fact is that the waste is not so easily recoverable. Despite some commendable efforts in and out of the Pentagon, waste in the procurement and deployment of forces and weapons is, over time, virtually a constant.

Finally, all those expert and detailed invocations of "military reform" would not produce the decisive savings they promise. The real defect of these proposals is not what they promise, but what they cannot deliver. A few military horror stories—and there are many to choose from—do not add up to a conclusive critique, and a handful of therapeutic adjectives are not an effective remedy. Those cheap, sensible weapons must reach their targets, and possibly return, in an intensive battlefield environment. It is not dim-witted generals and grasping defense contractors—the stuff of current mythology—that are putting up the price of our forces and weapons. It is determined, capable enemies and the requisites of modern combat. Our choice, therefore, is reduced to either fighting in those environments and against those adversaries or not.

Where is the money, then—money on the same scale as the budget deficits we want to cure? It is not in the individual weapons sytems, which are the isolated line items. It is in the large aggregate forces and, in turn, in the broad missions of these forces in the world—the categories that all the microstudies cannot identify or "pinpoint." Here is a skeletal anatomy of the administration's fiscal year 1983 defense request of $258 billion. The *way* you analyze that budget is what makes the difference. First, the types of forces, then their regional orientation.

Strategic nuclear forces, including (as they should) their full share of support and overhead, will come to about $54 billion. This figure *includes* the early requests for the MX missile and the B-1B bomber. It is "only" 21 percent of the defense budget. This must surprise those who are brought up on the notion that the "bad" weapons must also be the expensive ones; that forces that kill large numbers of people must be the ones that are bankrupting us, too.

The fact that is so hard to get across to most critics of defense is that is it the popular "conventional" forces that cost most of the money. General purpose forces—land divisions, tactical airwings, surface naval units, and lift—account for $204 billion, 79 percent of the defense budget and those are the general purpose forces we already have, not even the additional ones the Reagan administration would like to create.

Defense dollars are best expressed in terms of some of the forces they buy—and, ironically, the rougher the estimates, the *better*. An Army division—whether equipped as now or somewhat differently—will cost over $3.75 billion a year to keep, and we have sixteen of them. A wing of tactical aircraft—whether filled out with those notional "rugged, simple" planes or those "fragile, gold-plated" ones—will cost $1.5 billion a year, and there are forty-five of these equivalents. The Marine Corps—whether reorganized or not—will cost over $16 billion a year. The full cost of deploying one aircraft carrier task force—whether nuclear-powered or oil-fired—in the western Pacific or the Indian Ocean or the North Atlantic or the Mediterranean—will be over $11 billion a year, and our present strategy requires us to keep four or five forward.

One might ask: Do these forces have to cost that much? The answer is: Virtually, yes. These aggregates will not change much with technical tinkering—unless we want to eliminate parts of them, and that is a choice most critics will not face.

The most important cross-section we can make is a geographical attribution of these general purpose forces—what their missions are, what allies they support, what regions they defend. Despite the protests of Pentagon budgeteers—and there are some conceptual problems in making regional attributions of general purpose forces—we must make them, or we cannot understand what our forces are for. As Secretary of Defense McNamara's systems analysts used to say in the 1960s: "It's better to be roughly right than precisely wrong." Europe will take $129 billion, Asia $39 billion, and other areas and the strategic reserve $36 billion. Given a reasonable projection of current cost growth, over the decade to 1992 Europe will cost us $2.25 trillion.

What this brief anatomy lesson ought to demonstrate is that defense budgets are not for nothing—they are *for something*. The dollars are to buy forces; the forces have missions; the missions are in regions where the United States has defensive commitments or putative strategic interests; the strategic involvements, in sum, are practically equivalent to the nation's foreign policy. The money, then, is ultimately in our alliance commitments, our forward defense, our global stance. Therefore, defense budgets cannot be cut significantly without consequences for their objects: our alliances, our foreign policies. A *serious* proposal to reduce the defense budget—commensurate with the magnitude of our solvency problem—entails reduction of our commitments, especially in Europe. If we would cut, we have to decide what we would do without.

It should not have taken Senator John Tower, a staunch defender of the Reagan defense budget, to make this point for defense critics—and from the deck of the newly commissioned aircraft carrier *Carl Vinson*, at that. He said (at Newport News, Virginia, March 13, 1982): "If Congress insists on these cuts, Congress must be able to identify which commitments we will no longer be able to honor." Then he went on to say, with perfect logic: "If reductions in defense spending are forced upon us, I will attempt to cut force structure—namely, Army divisions, aircraft wings, battle groups and the like."

But the critical syndrome is practically impervious to this logic, though logic, which is a two-edged sword, could be put to good use. Hardly any of the defense critics seem to understand the connections that run all the way from defense dollars, through forces and doctrines and military strategies, to national strategies and foreign policies—that is, to the defense of regions and the protection of allies. Editorialists, politicians, and experts out of office do not so much make arguments; they "position" themselves in the debate, in true Madison Avenue fashion. They ask, first and sometimes solely, how they can address important-sounding subjects and still maintain their credibility in the foreign policy establishment and the military analysis community. The way to do this is to acknowledge gravely the unalterable necessity of maintaining the familiar alliance commitments and the familiar global status and yet to display meticulous knowledge of how our complicated, expensive weapons systems work—or fail to work. The formula is: Keep the expansive global missions, nitpick the hardware and sharpshoot the "waste." But that exercise is wearing thin.

True, some critics talk about "cutting commitments." But they cannot be serious as long as they confine their intent to disowning a few Third World dictators or abandoning a few strategically worthless areas —objects that are not taking any American forces now, anyway. To be serious about cutting defense spending, you must talk about America's major alliances—particularly NATO, which is costing us $129 billion a year, or half of our entire defense budget.

Unfortunately, among the half-dozen critics who have begun to talk about Europe, the preponderance are hardliners who are not, as good conservatives, addressing our nation's solvency crisis but are simply disgusted with European neutralism, nuclear pacifism, anti-Americanism, and commercial greed. They threaten to dump Europe and to concentrate on the sea lanes, the Persian Gulf, or even the Western Hemisphere. This talk finds an echo in quasi-official administration utterances, such as those of Fred C. Iklé, Under Secretary of Defense for Policy, in a roundtable discussions in *The New York Times* (March 14, 1982):

> We want to get away from the Maginot Line mentality for the defense of Europe, which piles most of our military assets at one front . . . [and make an] effort to strengthen the southern flank, to develop a capability for deterring aggression in the Persian Gulf area . . . . [I]t is in our interest to improve Atlantic security in the Caribbean . . . .

Such proposals are intriguing straws in the wind, but two things are wrong: First, they proceed from the wrong motives; they are often expressions of pique and spite. Second, they are often conditional—that is, just bluff used to get the European allies to come to their senses and make a larger and more docile contribution to their defense.

True, the Europeans cannot seem to decide whether they are more afraid that the United States will not defend them or that it *will* defend them. But shaping the European debate should not be the American purpose. The underlying points are these: First, *if* America wishes to continue its role of global containment, it must defend Europe, and Europe, indeed, will remain the key theater. That is a fact that is decreed by our adversaries (adversaries we acquire through the adoption of a large part of the world as our own area of interest) and by their interests and objectives. Second, there is a real difference in geopolitical and political situations on the two sides of the Atlantic that leads inevitably to divergent strategic perspectives and divergent preferences for defense. Understanding this problem, and even sympathizing with the European perspective, will not change the policy orientations, let alone the underlying situations.

Even now, with all we are spending, neither our nuclear nor our conventional defense of Europe is whole; our allies are not confident of our protection. Our nuclear umbrella has been leaky since the attainment of parity by the Soviet Union. Those who concede this but reflexively opt for "improving our conventional defense" have the burden of not just prescribing that we must do more but predicting that this is likely to happen. That is another story. This is not to advocate the instant abrogation of the alliance but simply to recognize that after thirty-three years NATO is like some old, unused medicine on the shelf: The bottle is still there and the label remains the same, but the contents have long since evaporated or spoiled.

A few critics seem to apprehend the true dimensions of the situation and the real dilemma that arises from it. But even they are reluctant to draw the indicated conclusions. Stephen Rosenfeld of *The Washington Post* (February 12, 1982), surveying Secretary of Defense Caspar Weinberger's budget submission for 1983, asks, almost plaintively: "Is there not . . . a middle way that is not simply a response entailing the fashionable general bow to a strong defense followed by the crossing-out of the specific items that constitute a strong defense? That is not, in a word, a cop-out?"

I'm afraid the answer is: No. There is no *middle* way that is not just a stereophonic illusion—some noise hovering between the actual sources of the sound.

The choices are not conceptually obscure, just tough. An ultimate resolution of the dilemma that is wracking this country—that we cannot afford our global strategy—must involve a rather wholesale remedy. We need a determined assault on the federal budget, and that can only involve a large-scale, long-term cut in defense spending on the order of $60 billion to $100 billion a year from current levels. That is, we need a noninterventionist foreign policy and the strategies, forces, and defense budgets that would express it.

Our predicament will not end in one or two budget seasons. It is one of historic proportion—nothing less than the situation of a mature "imperial" power (I use the word descriptively, not pejoratively) beset by multiple challenges but unable to generate sufficient resources for the defense of its extensive perimeter. The question is whether the United States will have to go beyond minor and superficial adjustments and confront the entire "paradigm" of its national strategy—the way we have conducted our strategic business in the world since the beginning of the Cold War.

The elements of this paradigm can be stated as "deterrence" and "alliance." Both elements have been put to the service of containing Communist power and influence. Deterrence means the maintenance of a balance or, better, of strategic nuclear arms with our principal global adversary and the provision of a nuclear umbrella over our allies and various other countries. Alliance is a shorthand expression for forward defense; it implies commitments to protect countries that occupy strategic positions or have sympathetic social and political values. From these commitments derive deployments, bases, and military assistance and other support for proxy regimes and client states.

What kind of foreign policy will be appropriate to the world that is shaping up, to a large extent despite our efforts? And what foreign policy will conform to the limits that America's domestic situation places on the projection of its power?

When we ask those questions, we see that there is a real alternative.

In an appropriate foreign policy, both of the cardinal elements of the present American paradigm would have to change. Instead of deterrence and alliance, we would pursue war-avoidance and self-reliance. Our security would depend more on our abstention from involvement in regional conflicts and, in the strategic nuclear dimension, on what I would call "finite essential deterrence."

Our military program would be designed to defend the most restricted perimeter required to protect our core values. Those core values are our political integrity and the safety of our citizens and their domestic property. Obviously, that is a much smaller perimeter than the one we are now committed to defend. Precisely because America's stance in the world is essentially defensive, we would benefit from a compartmentalization of deadly quarrels between other nations. Of course, we will still have a variety of international interests but those interests themselves will often be confused. We might even find ourselves on both sides of disputes.

A counter-budget constructed on these noninterventionist assumptions about American foreign policy is not tricky, elusive, or arcane. It does not require detailed expertise in weapons characteristics or intimate knowledge of quirks of procurement. It is not particularly sensitive to minute inside information on costing. When we are talking about $4.5 trillion that the United States may spend over a decade, large aggregates will do very nicely to illustrate the differences that policy can make. Nor does the proposal of this alternative imply that we are about to adopt it soon. It is an illustration of a horizon, and that may be enough to instill some sense into our deliberations on the defense budget.

To implement a noninterventionist policy, I propose an alternative force structure. It would provide the following general purpose forces: 8 land divisions (6 Army and 2 Marine), 19 tactical air wing equivalents (11 Air Force, 2 Marine, which are equal to 4, and 4 Navy), with 6 carrier task forces. With the addition of a diad of strategic nuclear forces (submarines and stand-off bombers), it would require approximately 1,250,000 personnel (Army 390,000, Air Force 360,000, Navy 360,000, Marine Corps 130,000). The total defense budget, at the end of a period of adjustment, would be about $145 billion a year in 1983 dollars. In contrast, we have the Reagan administration's requested authorization for 1983: 19 land divisions and 45 tactical air wing equivalents, with 13 carrier task forces—about 2.1 million personnel; and $258 billion.

Here is the blunt comparison: At the projected rate of increase, at the end of a decade we will have a $715 billion a year defense budget, and cumulative defense spending during the decade will be $4.5 trillion. A noninterventionist policy and the appropriate force structure would cost a third of that in 1992, and its cumulative cost, over a decade, would be $2.25 trillion.

It has been fashionable among liberal critics to look at defense budgets in the terms of a Herblock cartoon—as the products of paranoid ideologues, bloated Pentagon brass, corrupt suppliers, rocket-rattling secretaries of defense and state. Would that it were true. Then the solutions would be relatively easy; and perhaps that is why people believe these caricatures.

But the Reagan administration did not invent its problems. Actually, this administration is trying to implement the defense objectives it inherited. As Secretary of Defense Weinberger put it in his maiden presentation to Congress, the Carter administration grossly underestimated the demands that Soviet challenges put on the tangible military responses of the United States. Above all, it systematically underfunded its own defense programs, leaving a cumulative shortfall of several hundred billion dollars for the incoming Reagan administration to make up.

Taken as a relative or conditional judgment, there is a certain wry justice in Weinberger's statement. If you ignore the rhetoric, overlook some of the nuances, and leave out of the calculation those policy objectives that have little consequence for military forces or defense costs, you could judge that what is wrong with Reagan's foreign and military policies is not that they are much different from Carter's, but that they are much the same. The Reagan administration is just the latest in a long line, Democratic and Republican, from the beginning of the Cold War, that has promoted the American "paradigm" of large-scale deterrence and extensive forward defense or alliance. All it is trying to do is spend what it takes.

In a perverse sort of way, the Reagan administration has rendered a service. What it has done, despite itself, is to prove that it is inevitably expensive to defend half the world against the other half, and that a determined, consistent attempt to do this will wreck our economy and warp our society.

13

A LEAN, MEAN MILITARY BUDGET

Dr. Paul F. Walker

■ ■ ■

Paul F. Walker holds a Ph.D. in political science from M.I.T. He was an intelligence specialist in Soviet affairs with the U.S. Army Security Agency, has worked for the Arms Control and Disarmament Agency, was research director for the Union of Concerned Scientists, and is former director of education and programs for the Physicians for Social Responsibility. He is a charter member of the Boston Study Group and one of the co-authors of the group's book, *The Price of Defense,* recently reissued in paperback under the title *Winding Down.*

OUR NATIONAL SECURITY planning has always presented us with a formidable challenge: How to provide the best national defense for ourselves, our allies, and our interests abroad, while at the same time not being destabilizing so as to provoke conflict and not spending so much as to undermine our economic well-being. This challenge is particularly important and pressing today in view of two primary facts: (1) the continuing development and deployment of highly sophisticated nuclear weapons capable of destabilizing deterrence and (2) defense costs escalating to near-prohibitive levels, where peacetime spending will likely soon surpass the height of World War II military costs in 1945 in real terms, accounting for inflation.

General allegations from the present administration that the defense budget is bare-bones and that it cannot be reduced without inhibiting national security are at best misleading and at worst threatening to the democratic spirit of this country. It is incumbent on all of us to seek to discern the foreign policy objectives of appropriations requests, relate those to specific force sizings, and, finally, to support production of the most effective weapons systems essential to meet those force demands.

It is our responsibility to put the horse before the cart, not to fall victim to technological fascination with new weapons systems without first posing the questions: To what purpose, and is it the safest and most effective appoach?

It is my thesis that much of current military planning fails to justify itself fully on solid rational grounds. Instead, we develop and purchase weapons systems and size forces to fit arbitrary political demands, false perceptions and obsolete military customs. A few examples, each with serious budgetary implications, will illustrate my point.

It is difficult to pinpoint explicit changes in policy, but certainly by the early 1970s, for example, in James Schlesinger's congressional testimony, nuclear doctrine had shifted in two significant ways: (1) No longer was assured destruction (300 megatons) in only one leg of the triad considered sufficient; rather it was argued to be necessary in all three legs; and (2) the theory of "limited" nuclear war rose to prominence in debates over nuclear deterrence objectives.

This first development, the demand for triple redundancy, is driving such programs as the MX missile in an attempt to overcome the perception of vulnerability or, as it is called a window of vulnerability of land-based missiles. The second development, limited nuclear war fighting strategies, is driving the stockpile of nuclear warheads ever higher and higher.

If one accepts Presidential Directive PD 59 and the nuclear war fighting doctrine it embodies, then there appears no foreseeable limit to the production of nuclear weapons systems. The goal of striking tens of thousands of targets in the Soviet Union and elsewhere over variable time-frames and infinite permutations is the key to propelling a dangerous and expensive nuclear arms race forward. That is where we find ourselves today.

In short, the fiscal year 1983 defense budget projects production of 100 MX missiles, 100 B-1B bombers, 12 Trident submarines outfitted with Trident missiles, the Trident II missile, 3,800 Cruise missiles, sea-based Cruise missiles, improved C^3I, and more civil defense. Some of this, I would argue, is positive investment. The more we can assure adequate, safe, redundant control and communications in nuclear forces the better. Some of this investment is well-based in policy but lacks ideal system design. I would argue that the Trident submarine falls into this category. Preserving the invulnerability of our sea-based deterrent is essential, but I predict that one or two years from now we will all be saying that we must cut back Trident production because it was the wrong boat and we should have realized that five years ago.

One might define my third category for current nuclear systems procurement as wasteful. In here falls the B-1B bomber and civil defense. We are procuring 3,800 Cruise missiles to be carried on board our workhorse performer, the B-52, well into the 1990s. The air-launched Cruise missile systems will give bombers stand-off capability, precluding the need for much penetration in heavily-defended Soviet air space. Yet, this year's report by the Secretary of Defense argues that the B-1B is needed "to penetrate enemy defenses." In light of this apparent incongruity in strategic thinking and of the advanced technology of Stealth bomber development, the B-1B procurement, some $40 billion overall—higher today at $400 million a copy than it was under the Carter administration when it was projected to be $100 million a copy —should be rejected. The report adds that the B-1B also will have a most important conventional role. This is very important. It may be that we are being asked to fund a strategic nuclear bomber that will more likely be used in nonnuclear roles as the B-52 was used in Vietnam.

Civil defense does not deserve much attention. It is like the story of the alcoholic—a little may be healthy, but a lot is wasteful and possibly life-threatening—thus giving only the impression rather than the capability of surviving nuclear war.

A fourth and last group of nuclear systems in my categorization includes weapons both wasteful and dangerous; the MX missile and the Trident II (D-5) missile. These two systems are not being developed and deployed to overcome vulnerability and to enhance stable deterrence, as some would like us to believe. Rather, they are designed as hard-target killers, effective primarily in a nuclear first strike; they are so described in the internal military-industrial debate.

The MX missile, in particular, is a camel sold as a horse. It is large. It carries a lot of weight, much more than a horse, but it is impractical, immobile, and does not suit the purpose. Intended to "reduce the vulnerability" of ICBMs, it was developed to emphasize size and MIRV-ing under SALT constraints. Smaller missiles such as the "common" and "mostly common" missiles, competing with the MX during its design phase, would have been much more suited for mobility and sea-based deployment modes if we had decided that we needed a new missile. I would recommend cancelling MX missile procurement, some $4.5 billion in fiscal year 1983, with full-system costs at well over $30 billion. Of course, full-system projections of MX costs at this point are very difficult to make until we see a basing mode. Trident II missile research also should be cancelled at $367 million.

Nonnuclear conventional forces comprise some 80 percent of annual defense spending and raise many issues that require serious discussion. In the fiscal year 1983 report, the Secretary of Defense lists 427 ships in the U.S. Navy active fleet. That does not count reserve ships. This is slightly more than half of what we floated at the height of the Vietnam

War in 1968. Administration plans are to build up to 640 ships by the early 1990s, necessitating the construction of about 150 new ships. The total cost is well over $100 billion. Included in this figure is $6.9 billion in fiscal year 1983 for two additional nuclear aircraft carriers in the 92,000-ton *Nimitz* class and for annual Navy and Marine aircraft production approaching 200, in order to expand from twelve to fourteen Navy air wings.

The Defense Department states boldly that this naval plan is based on the determination "to restore and maintain maritime superiority over the Soviets" in order to wage several wars worldwide against "the Soviet military empire." Such planning is based on several false assumptions: (1) that we have somehow lost naval supremacy; (2) that overwhelming maritime superiority enhances national security; and (3) that aircraft carriers around which the current fleet is designed continue to be the most effective way to build and deploy navies.

To the first point: The Soviets are ahead in numbers of naval ships by almost 50 percent, and they are evolving into an effective blue-water navy, a departure from their former coastal defensive strategy. But they are far from attaining any form of maritime supremacy. In terms of ship tonnage we still outweigh the Soviets almost two to one. The number of major U.S. surface ships, from frigates to aircraft carriers, is about equal. The size of our navy support ships, replenishment ships, amphibious ships, and fleet support is more than double theirs. The Soviets outnumber us in smaller coastal vessels, frigates, and antiship patrol submarines—mostly defensive systems.

To the second point: The United States, since World War II, has been an important naval power, necessitated partly by geography, partly by far-flung interests overseas. The goals of the Navy have been: (1) to provide floating airbases for light and medium bomber aircraft; (2) to transport troops and their support for amphibious assaults; and (3) to provide antiaircraft and antisubmarine defense of shipping lanes to Europe and Asia during a nonnuclear conflict. Never has the goal been to perform all of these functions simultaneously in many parts of the globe, except now.

We can continue to fulfill the above goals with a no-growth Navy, maintaining approximately a 400-ship fleet. By escalating to the proposed 640 ship fleet, I suggest we will undermine security in the following ways: (1) the heavy expense will be damaging economically, although keeping shipyards at peak capacity; (2) the fleet will all the more portray a *Pax Americana*-type military and political image abroad—something I think we can ill-afford today; and (3) a widespread interventionary force, I would argue, may very well encourage U.S. interventions in the Third World.

My third and final point regarding naval forces is that large ships, such as a 59,000-ton *Iowa* class battleship or the 92,000-ton *Nimitz* aircraft carrier, are obsolete except for two functions: political shows of force, at which they are very good, and war fighting against lightly armed opponents, such as Vietnam or, perhaps, El Salvador and others. With the not-so-recent advent of increasingly effective antiship Cruise missiles, such large ships become literally sitting ducks for formidable opponents such as the Soviet Union. In the event of a nuclear war, they will be more of a liability than an advantage, drawing early and heavy nuclear fire. It is partly for these reasons that the Soviets have never invested in large deck carriers themselves.

At a minimum, the two nuclear aircraft carriers proposed should be stricken from the budget. The *Iowa*, the *New Jersey*, the *Missouri*, and the *Wisconsin*—World War II battleships all currently in mothballs— should be left there for wartime, and not peacetime, activation as originally intended. This would save as much as $2 billion. The *Iowa*'s renovations, for example, are costing close to half a billion; for the *New Jersey* it is about a third of a billion, with the other two ships scheduled within the next two years. We recognized the cost-ineffectiveness of battleships immediately after World War II in 1945, when two new *Iowa*-class ships, the *Illinois* and the *Kentucky*, 22 and 69 percent completed respectively, were scrapped.

Regarding land warfare, one of this year's major budget items is the new M-1 Abrams tank. Much has been written about its technical deficiencies, such as a trouble-prone drive train and turbine engine, especially in sandy terrain, its inability to dig itself in, and its tendency to either throw its tracks or wear them out prematurely, among other things. The M-1 tank will cost some $3 million each. The fiscal year 1982 budget authorized 665 M-1s. Total projections for over 7,000 M-1s will cost around $20 billion. I believe the M-1 tank to be a very questionable buy at this time, partly due to its unresolved technical problems but largely due to the evolution of tactical warfare away from large, expensive, vulnerable systems and toward more mobile, less vulnerable, concealable, and relatively inexpensive systems.

I have argued elsewhere that many antitank missile systems lacking in several ways for a number of years are now sufficiently reliable, maintainable in the field, and effective under adverse conditions to make the tank obsolete on the intense battlefield—not every battlefield, but the intense ones. There will always be tanks for certain types of limited warfare, but procurement of them in the thousands is cost-ineffective. The M-1 tank monthly production rate should not be increased from sixty to ninety, as we are doing. We should minimally reduce the total production request to the fiscal year 1982 level, about

4,000. Eventual cancellation of any further purchases of the tank, combined possibly with extension of the M-60 production, should be seriously considered.

The last force reduction proposal concerns the Marine Corps. I realize the Marines are somewhat sacred, having been mandated a minimum of three divisions in the 1947 National Security Act. Their primary mission is over-the-beach amphibious landings. To this end, we deploy some sixty amphibious warfare ships in the fleet and are proposing construction of ten more. I question the cost-effectiveness of this investment, especially in light of the high vulnerability of such ships to new antiship missiles. I believe most Marine amphibious commanders, certainly everyone I have spoken to, would agree that amphibious operations are impractical until the beachhead is fully "neutralized." This may be the objective of battleship reactivation in the new budget (i.e., use against lightly armed opponents). If one wanted amphibious attacks in the Caribbean, the battleship would neutralize a beachhead—in fact, many miles of the interior of a country—very quickly.

Some amphibious capability should always be maintained as a force option, but major beach invasions—by major, I mean, with 50,000 troops—became obsolete with the Korean Inchon landing in 1950. A couple of LSD-41s with air-cushioned craft are sufficient for any limited contingency, such as saving embassy personnel, for the foreseeable future. Another related question is whether we need to continue to maintain three Marine divisions. Here we are treading, once again, on sacred ground. A cutback to one division, which I have recommended in the past, although requiring legislation amending the 1947 act, seems, to me, reasonable.

In conclusion, I would emphasize the general point that the 1982 military budget and its five-year projection is inconsistent in many ways. It is inconsistent, first, militarily. Stable deterrence is stated as predominant in nuclear doctrine, yet the proposed systems that we have talked about are hard-target, war-fighting, potentially first-strike destabilizing weapons. Technology development shows us that the future lies with mobility and stealth in all battle situations, yet custom continues to dictate procurement of obsolete equipment. I cite the aircraft carrier, the tank, retrofitted battleships, 40,000-ton amphibious ships, and gold-plated fighter and bomber aircraft.

The fiscal year 1983 military budget is inconsistent politically as well. It is portrayed as part of a long-range effort to catch, match, and largely surpass the Soviets, thereby protecting the "Free World." It fails, however, to prove any serious Soviet superiority in most categories, devotes much of its resources to forces such as a 640-ship Navy, only peripherally related to the Soviet threat, and presents the image to the "Free World" of a power bent on military and political domination rather than enlightened leadership and coexistence.

The fiscal year 1983 budget is also inconsistent economically. It seeks to provide for the national security of Americans around the world, but in so doing it may inadvertently undermine the economic well-being of the country and a large part of its national security. I am not alone in deep concern over this problem. I do not believe we can afford, nor do we need, some $2 trillion—$40,000 per taxpaying family—over the next five years for national defense. Controlling defense spending, particularly given much of its highly questionable procurement, is absolutely essential for bringing the federal deficit and, thereby, the economy under control.

The following budget deletions would, at a minimum, save us almost $20 billion in fiscal year 1983 defense authorizations and about $100 billion in longer-term system costs. I have not gone into many other systems such as Pershing II. I have not costed-out naval ships, Cruise missiles, ballistic missile defense, and the like, which I think could also be added to the list.

Secretary of Defense Caspar Weinberger states in his recent report to Congress the following:

> Defense policy and military strategy have to be renewed to adjust to the changed world environment, overcome obsolete concepts and thinking, and take full advantage of U.S. and allied capabilities. But the best strategic thinking will be of little use unless it can be translated into concrete policy decisions, budgetary choices and specific strategic plans.

I agree with the secretary and would recommend that we all, including the secretary, take this advice more seriously in debating military policies this coming year. That is why I am pleased to see these hearings taking place.

I would be remiss if I did not conclude by referring again to nuclear weapons and arms control. It is not through unlimited arms build-up but rather the through maintenance of a lean and mean defense establishment, along with active, serious arms control and disarmament initiatives, that true national security will be realized. As a beginning, I would recommend, very briefly, the following:

1. An immediate bilateral freeze on the production and deployment of all nuclear weapons, which would begin to halt the quantitative arms race now;

2. A Soviet-American comprehensive test ban (CTB), with the other nuclear and nonnuclear powers signing as well, which would elim-

inate all nuclear testing and inhibit qualitative weapons development;

3.   A Soviet-American flight test ban on missiles;

4.   A Soviet-American ban on the testing and deployment of antisatellite systems (this year's budget states specifically that both countries are actively pursuing antisatellite policies);

5.   A return to the SALT or START negotiating tables with serious effort, more serious than we have had in the past, to strive for substantial reductions in strategic and tactical systems; and

6.   A more coherent nonproliferation policy that recognizes that our own nuclear weapons production, currently averaging about three a day, provides a leadership model for non-nuclear countries to follow.

■   ■   ■

■ *MR. BEILENSON (D-Calif.):*   You referred to a 40,000-ton amphibious ship. I did not know we had such things.

■ *DR. WALKER:*   The United States is first in amphibious capability. I chuckled when I read the Defense Department booklet, *Soviet Military Power,* which says that the Soviets have the second largest marine force in the world. It failed to point out that we have the largest *and,* of course, that ours is many, many times the size of the Soviet force. One of the important points is that amphibious warfare is one of the primary goals of our ships. We have what is called the *Tarawa*-class ships, about which you have probably heard. These are actually marine amphibious landing ships that are larger than the Soviet aircraft carriers.

■ *MR. BEILENSON:*   We have them now?

■ *DR. WALKER:*   We have five of them now and we have two scheduled in the budget that I have said we should reject. They are not in this year's budget but, rather, in fiscal year 1984 and beyond, probably close to $1 billion each. They were over $250 million each eight to ten years ago.

■ *MR. BEILENSON:*   In your presentation of some recommended fiscal year 1983 deletions, you have the authorization for fiscal year 1983 and then future costs. Under future costs for nuclear aircraft carriers, you have $30 billion. What are we talking about there—additional nuclear aircraft carriers or the eventual cost of the two that are being started now?

■ *DR. WALKER:* The eventual cost of the two. An aircraft carrier is difficult to cost too precisely, but the carrier itself is in the range of $3 billion to $4 billion, just to purchase the ship. A naval wing of eighty-six aircraft on board requires several submarines and several destroyers and cruisers to surround and protect the aircraft carrier. It also requires a replenishment group with oilers, aviation fuel and supplies to supply that whole fleet. Over the long run, it costs somewhere in the neighborhood of $10 billion to $20 billion at a minimum for every aircraft carrier purchased. The aircraft carrier is the first buy into a long run of further purchases that must be made, once the aircraft carrier is bought because it cannot protect itself without the fleet.

I would argue that we would be much better off with the Navy having a good number of destroyers and cruisers heavily armed with missiles but not having to protect the aircraft carriers. I would rather have them available to protect the ship lanes to and from Korea, the Philippines, Europe, or the Middle East in the eventuality of a major conflict.

■ *MR. BEILENSON:* It costs us something like $11 billion per year to support each single carrier force that is out for a year some place in the world, in the Pacific, or wherever?

■ *DR. WALKER:* That might be a little high but it is possible. The Navy gets about a third of the defense budget. It is interesting that the armed services—Navy, Army, and Air Force—break down about a third each.

Since we have land bases all over the world, the question is: Do we need five aircraft carriers in the Atlantic, five in the Pacific, one in the Indian Ocean, one in the Mediterranean, and several in dry-dock? The only reason one would need that number of aircraft carriers is for a major Soviet-American conventional conflict.

■ *MR. BEILENSON:* But the military disagrees. They are saying that this is a show of force because even they claim that if we ever got into a serious conflict with the Soviet Union, these ships—with these four-and-a-half acre decks—along with our recommissioned battleships would be destroyed in the first ten minutes of such a war. They could not be missed.

■ *DR. WALKER:* All you need is one aircraft to miss the deck or land sideways on the deck, and the ship is out of commission.

■ *MR. BEILENSON:* Or one Soviet missile, of which they have many thousands.

■ *DR. WALKER:* Exactly. I really think it is a very bad investment.

■ *MR. BEILENSON:* We are proposing to spend $75 billion over the next ten years for this Rapid Deployment Force in order to protect our oil interests, such as they may be, in the Persian Gulf. A lot of that goes to these big cargo planes that carry tanks, troops, and other supplies. Should these also be reduced?

■ *DR. WALKER:* I would argue that we need some foreign interventionary capability. We always need something to protect American citizens abroad and to evacuate Embassies. Our Marines went ashore in Lebanon a few years ago under peaceful conditions and were greeted there with no opposition. We need forces to undertake such limited operations, but we have more than that in our current amphibious Marine capability. We have it in the 82nd Airborne Division. And we have it in the 101st Air Mobile Division. We do not need a quick interventionary force some three times that, which is what the Rapid Deployment Force is all about. I cannot foresee the commitment of 50,000 troops or more in a quick one-week or ten-day period anywhere in the world that easily. In that way, I think the Rapid Deployment Force and all of its air-lift and sea-lift capability, is largely a mistake.

One of the other items I would cite would be heavy land-warfare systems that accompany the M-1 tank—things like infantry fighting vehicles, which are almost the cost of the M-1. I think that if we are buying them in large numbers, which we are, it is potentially cost-ineffective. I would rather see fewer heavy land vehicles (60-, 50- and 40-ton vehicles) and more weapons at one one-hundredth or one five-hundredth the cost, which give a much more mobile missile capability to the Army.

I would recommend—although I have cited here some $20 billion in immediate reductions that could be made this year—that the $260 plus billion budget we are talking about could easily be reduced by $50 billion, $75 billion, or perhaps even $100 billion. I will be so radical as to say that we would thereby improve security, we would not lessen it. We would not be able to meet the "Soviet challenge" everywhere on the globe simultaneously because, frankly, we do not need to do that nor should we want to do so. But it would still give us very safe and affordable security.

I want a good, lean, mean defense. I do not think one has to trust the Soviets to be in favor of arms control. It is a difficult, dangerous world we live in, and we have to be strong to defend our citizens. But we do not need to design bottomless pits filled with steel ships, tanks, and dollars.

■ *MR. CONYERS (D-Mich.):* Unless this is articulated in the Armed Services Committee, on which the chair, Mr. Dellums, serves, it is never articulated on the Floor of the House of Representatives. We never even get to this. I have never heard a cogent, rational explanation of the nature of the policy considerations that fuel this huge armed military apparatus that we are asked to fund. I think we are entitled to know more, and so are all of the citizens of this country.

■ *DR. WALKER:*   I couldn't agree more. Some of us—the Boston Study Group, many of my colleagues testifying, and many of you, I am sure—have tried to hammer home that someone first has to set foreign policy goals. What do we want to do? The Boston Study Group said we have to defend NATO. We have to defend Japan, our interest in Asia. We have to defend Israel and our interests in the Middle East. And we have to maintain freedom of the seas.

We did not say we had to have the immediate capability to intervene, on very short notice, anywhere in the world to meet any challenge of any type from any power. We have had a "2½ war strategy" at times in the past. In other words, they have had the general goals of driving the forces to wage two and a half wars at one time, full wars in Asia/ Korea and in Europe and half a war somewhere else. For a long time it was Cuba. I think, in the 1970s, it switched to the Middle East.

That is quite an extraordinary demand. This year's policy statement says we no longer follow that. We changed from a "2½ war" policy to what was talked about as a "1½ war" policy, although the forces did not change, under President Richard Nixon. He said we could no longer afford to cover both the Korean and European context at the same time, plus a Cuban or Middle East context. So he specified "1½ wars," although we kept the same forces.

I am not sure what that says about policy and force relevance. But we kept the European context and switched from Cuba to a Middle East context in the 1970s for the "half-war" contingency. This year's policy statement rejects that approach as well. It says, in general, that we have to be willing to meet any challenge, anywhere on the globe with immediate and decisive military forces. Similarly, as I pointed out with nuclear weapons, if one decides that one wants the ability to hit every single target in the Soviet Union, from railroad-switching yards to ball-bearing factories, in various permutations from one hit to several thousand hits, then the potential for additional forces become almost infinite. I think that meeting any particular threat around the globe with conventional forces means that your force ojectives become potentially unlimited.

PART FOUR

MILITARY SPENDING AND THE DOMESTIC ECONOMY . . . What's left to defend?

■ ■ ■

We annually spend on military security more than the net income of all United States corporations. This conjunction of an immense military establishment and a large arms industry is new in the American experience. The total influence—economic, political, even spiritual—is felt in every city, every State house, every office of the Federal government. We recognize the imperative need for this development. Yet we must not fail to comprehend its grave implications. Our toil, resources, and livelihood are involved; so is the very structure of our society. In the councils of government, we must guard against the acquisition of unwarranted influence, whether sought or unsought, by the military-industrial complex. The potential for the disastrous rise of misplaced power exists and will persist. We must never let the weight of this combination endanger our liberties or democratic processes. We should take nothing for granted. Only an alert and knowledgeable citizenry can compel the proper meshing of the huge industrial and military machinery of defense with our peaceful methods and goals, so that security and liberty may prosper together.

Dwight D. Eisenhower
January 17, 1961

■ ■ ■

DURING MY FIRST term on the House Armed Services Committee in the early 1970s, lobbyists from North American Rockwell Corporation made a presentation to the committee on the supposed virtues of the then newly proposed B-1 bomber. They turned to me, the first and only Black member of the committee, pointedly and patronizingly commenting on the number of jobs the B-1 program would create.

For $20.5 billion dollars, I was informed, 125,000 people would be hired. Quick mathematical computation showed that this was an expenditure of more than $160,000 per worker. As a former manpower training specialist, I told the representative of North American Rockwell that, for $20.5 billion I could hire 1,000,000 workers at $20,000/year or 2,000,000 workers at $10,000/year (then reasonable salaries) in public service jobs. This would leave half a billion dollars to administer the program and could accomplish a great deal in the public interest.

Upon hearing my analysis the company representative admitted I was right and said that he would never again use the argument that a weapons program was a jobs program. He may never have, but every day, on the House Floor, in full committee and subcommittee meetings, the argument is made again and again that military spending creates jobs. This argument was nonsense in 1973, and it remains nonsense today.

Many people credit military spending in World War II with pulling the United States from the depths of the Great Depression. Whatever debatable truth there may be in this, the economic havoc that was wrought by the Vietnam War and the continued operation of our permanent war economy since should have destroyed all belief in this myth.

Additionally, we should not lose sight of the fact that when assuming office in 1981, President Reagan, with the help of a compliant Congress, transferred approximately $50 billion from the human needs sector of the fiscal year 1982 federal budget to the military budget. In each subsequent year, further cuts have been made in domestic spending in order to finance continued growth in military spending. Aside from the broad economic impact of such action, real pain has been inflicted on real people who relied upon these federal programs for food, housing, health care, and education.

In Part IV, several prominent economists demonstrate the devastating impact of increased military spending on our economy and social infrastructure. Their arguments shatter the myth that military spending creates jobs and prosperity. They paint a very bleak picture, indeed, if our present course is not changed.

The road to positive, progressive change is through economic conversion—changing our economy from one based on producing goods for warfare to one based on producing goods that improve the quality of life. Such a redirection of our government spending could improve our mass transit, health care, and education systems; it could help protect our environment; it could enhance civilian technological advancement; it could promote the great potential strength, foreign and domestic, of the United States: its capacity to feed, clothe and educate. Aside from all of this, the government owes a moral obligation to those who have worked in the defense industry to retrain them and provide them with new jobs in a peace-oriented economy.

In Chapter 14, Professor Seymour Melman explains the inverse relationship between our increasing investment in the military budget and the continuing decline in civilian capital investment and technological improvement. He illustrates how the accelerating drain on capital will increasingly place the United States at a competitive disadvantage in international markets, further exacerbating the recession in basic steel, auto, construction, and other industries.

In Chapter 15, Dr. Gordon Adams makes three critical points: High rates of defense spending exacerbate federal deficits; deficits crowd out private borrowing and raise interest rates, simultaneously inflationary and economically depressing; military spending is particularly demanding on high technology industries, draining manpower and talent from the civilian sector of these industries and driving up prices for competitive civilian uses. He argues that only an informed citizenry can break the "iron triangle" of Pentagon planners, defense corporations, and key congressional committees that have protected and perpetuated these programs and ushered them through the budget process at the expense of our economy and foreign policy.

In Chapter 16, Marion Anderson gets to the core of the jobs/defense dollar question. Her testimony, taken in part from her work "The Empty Pork Barrel," concisely makes the case that Pentagon spending increases actually destroy thousands of jobs each year, even in defense-related industries. Particularly hard-hit are the traditionally unemployed and underemployed, especially women and minorities.

In Chapter 17, William P. Winpisinger reinforces Ms. Anderson's earlier analysis of the relationship between job loss and defense spending increases. Despite his position as president of the International Association of Machinists and Aerospace Workers, heavily represented in the defense industry, he calls for conversion and reordering of our priorities, based in part on the Machinists' experience that sustained increases in defense spending have resulted in continuing job losses. He also argues that a failure to effect a rapid curtailment in defense spending, thereby ending the drain on the recapitalization of U.S. industry, will result in U.S. economic and technological uncompetitiveness, further resulting in additional and accelerated job-flight from the United States.

In Chapter 18, Dr. David Cortright develops the ground rules for successful economic conversion planning, "beating swords into subways." He reminds us that the government must protect defense workers by notification, retraining, and income guarantees during the conversion period. He argues that large-scale capital improvement projects, such as mass transit, railroads, or solarization/weatherization, would create hundreds of thousands of primary jobs, with hundreds of thousands more jobs in secondary and tertiary industries. Through conversion the government can play a positive rather than destructive role in the economy and the world. □

14

MILITARY SPENDING AND DOMESTIC BANKRUPTCY

Professor Seymour Melman

■ ■ ■

Seymour Melman of Columbia University is professor of industrial engineering and co-chair of SANE. His books include *Our Depleted Society*, *Pentagon Capitalism*, and *The Permanent War Economy*.

FOR THE FIRST time in the history of industrial capitalism in the United States, this society is beset by an economic problem that has little to do with fluctuation in market demand or fluctuation in conditions of finance. For the first time the technical and economic capability of U.S. industry has a problem in producing goods of acceptable quality at acceptable price. Even during the Great Depression, from 1929 to 1939, the technical and economic competence of U.S. industry was never at issue. Given market demand and the investment of capital, American industry could and did produce goods as desired and of acceptable quality.

The deterioration of the competence of U.S. industry—and, hence, its inability to serve the market or to organize people for productive work—derives largely from the operation of a permanent war economy. A permanent war economy is one in which military activity is major and continuing and, at the same time, is counted as an ordinary part of the national economic product.

I propose to summarize the magnitude of resources used for the military undertaking in the United States, with special emphasis on the understanding that a military budget in a modern economy is a capital fund. By a capital fund I mean a quantity of money that sets in motion the resources ordinarily called fixed and working capital, as utilized in any industrial operation.

Fixed capital ordinarily means land, machinery, and buildings. The working capital needed for production encompasses raw materials, purchased components, energy, and the labor of all classes of persons whose work is required for an ongoing productive enterprise.

From this vantage point, it is important to understand the magnitude of what has been expended in the United States in the capital fund called defense. From 1946 to 1980, the Department of Defense budgets totalled $2,001 billion. The planned military budgets of the Carter and Reagan administrations from 1981 to 1986 will total at least $1,600 billion, probably as high as $2,300 billion. It is difficult to appreciate the meaning of such enormous magnitudes. Therefore, we need a way of comparing these magnitudes to an appropriate category: the money value of the reproducible national wealth of the United States as published by the Commerce Department in the Statistical Abstract of the United States.

From the tables of national wealth that are given there, we learn that the value of everything made by people on the surface of the United States—structures, machines, inventories of personal and business goods, including government equipment and facilities but not including the land—amounted in 1975 to $4,302 billion. Accordingly, the cumulation of military budgets from 1946 to 1986 amounts to 83 percent of the money value of what is manmade on the surface of the United States. Hence, that extraordinary magnitude tells us that the military budgets represent a quantity of fixed and working capital resources that could replace the largest part of everything made by people on the surface of the United States.

There is a second way to examine the magnitudes of capital used by the military with capital. The national civilian capital outlay in a given year is typically called the gross fixed capital formation. As published by the United Nations, we know these data (last available year, 1977) for the United States, Germany, and Japan, three of the key industrial economies in the world. In the United States, for 1977, for each $100 of gross fixed capital formation, $46 was separately expended by the military. In Germany for every $100 of new civilian capital formation, $18.90 was expended by the military, and in Japan, that figure was $3.70. These data define the concentration of capital resources in Germany and Japan for civilian economic purposes. That has direct impact on the quality of civilian industry in those countries and on their ability to produce goods of acceptable quality at acceptable price.

A third way of viewing the magnitude of resources used by the military was given to us by President Eisenhower in his farewell address, where he stated: "We annually spend on military security more than the net income of all U.S. corporations." Net income means the net profit of all U.S. corporations. The net profit defines a maximum capital fund that is left to the managements of firms after they have paid all their costs and taxes. Actually, the annual budgets of the Department of Defense from 1951 through 1981 exceed—each year—the sum of the net profits of all corporations. Hence the largest capital fund in the economy of the United States controlled by a single management is the annual budget of the Department of Defense.

This concentration of capital resources in the hands of the Department of Defense necessarily limits their availability elsewhere. This limitation has two facets: One is conferred by nature; materials or energy used in one place cannot, at the same time, be available at another place. A second limitation derives from the character of products of a military economy. Whatever usefulness may be assigned to them as for political purposes, military goods and services do not comprise a part of ordinarily understood consumption goods and services. Neither can the military products be used for further production. Thus, a nuclear submarine, a technological masterpiece, cannot be used to produce anything else. Hence, the sustained concentration of capital resources on the military goes far to explain what is otherwise a mystery: The United States, emerging from World War II as the major intact industrial system in the world, with an average output per man hour at least three times greater than that of Western Europe and Japan, finds itself thirty-seven years later with an industrial system and an infrastructure that is progressively less productive.

In order to account for this, we have to compare the magnitudes of capital withdrawn for the military with amounts of capital required for some important civilian purposes. I call your attention to an article that appeared in *The New York Times*, July 26th, 1981, titled "Looting the Means of Production" in which I identified a series of trade-offs. In the first of these trade-offs, 7 percent of the military outlays from fiscal year 1981 to fiscal year 1986 amount to $100 billion. That quantity of finance capital is needed to rehabilitate the U.S. steel industry so that it is once again the most efficient in the world.

As of the period 1975-79, 69 percent of the metal-working machine tools in U.S. manufacturing industry were ten years old or older. In Japan, that proportion was 39 percent. Hence, the question: What would be the cost of bringing the average age of metal-working machinery in U.S. industry down to the age of that in Japan? The program cost of the Navy's F-18 fighter, $34 billion, equals the capital investment required for modernizing America's machine tool stock to bring it to the average level of Japan's.

But if the economy of the United States, through the federal government, invests its capital resources, which are finite, in military items, then the civilian means of production cannot be available. The society —the economy—cannot have both.

Investment in military hardware rather than in new industrial tools has serious consequences for productivity. The single most important factor governing average output per person in manufacturing is the quality and quantity of the means of production that are used in industry—hence, the degree of mechanization of work and the skill with which the work is organized.

Consider the case of two key industries: first, the industry producing machine tools. In the latter part of the nineteenth century, high productivity machine tools designed and first quantity-produced in the United States were sold at half the price of comparable products in Great Britain, the homeland of the machine tool industry, even while the wage in the U.S. machine tool firms was a third and more greater than the wage in British industry.

Second: Consider what happened in the early 1950s in the U.S. auto industry. Professor William Hadley of Columbia University's Department of Mechanical Engineering asked in *Mechanical Engineering* (September 1956), "What makes America strong?" He found that, as one computed the price per pound of motor vehicles produced around the world, hence the price per pound of fabricated material, the U.S. "big three" auto makers not only paid the highest wages in the world, they also produced the least costly, lowest-priced motor vehicles in the world, measured as price per pound. That was possible because there was a constant stream of renewed mechanization of work and capital investment in productive operations that yielded such improvement in the average output per person as to make it possible to offset, on a regular, continuing basis, the rise in wages of labor and increases in other costs as well.

But that process came to a halt following the mid-1960s. From 1965 to 1970, the average annual rate of productivity growth was 2.1 percent in U.S. manufacturing; from 1970 to 1975, it was 1.8 percent; from 1975 to 1980, it was 1.7 percent. More than that, during each of these periods, from data made available by the Bureau of Labor Statistics, we know that the average annual rate of increase in productivity in U.S. manufacturing was the lowest rate of increase for any industrialized country in the world for which comparable data exists. The low and declining rates of U.S. productivity in manufacturing industry are a direct reflection of the lessened use of capital for the mechanization and other modernization of industrial work.

In addition to diverting investment away from new industrial spending, there is another major collateral consequence of the operation of a permanent war economy—the destruction of the incentive system that had, for more than a century, induced U.S. employers to minimize costs by purchasing new manufacturing equipment. That incentive system rested on the fact that the machinery-producing industries of the United States operated to minimize their own internal force. That meant that, as the wages and other costs in machine production rose, the producers of machinery attempted to offset those cost increases by improved efficiency in their own operations. As they succeeded in doing that, the prices of their machinery products did not rise in the same degree as the wages of labor. That meant that, for the users of machinery products, new machinery was increasingly attractive as a replacement for direct manual work in manufacturing production. That process was the core incentive acted out by the managements in U.S. industry, which led to a constant flow of new mechanization of work and, automatically, the growth of productivity.

However, the operation of a military economy brought other incentive systems into operation. The military economy, with its network of 37,000 prime contractors, functions by a system of rules that leads to cost maximizing. During 1980-81 the rate of price increase was about 20 percent a year for military products, by contrast to the 13 percent rate that prevailed in civilian industrial products.

Why does this happen? It is because of the preferred modes of operation mandated by the Department of Defense, especially the practice of historical costing. Historical costing means noting the average price of a product during a period of years, calculating the average trend line of that development, typically of cost and price increase, then extrapolating the trend to the time when a new product would be purchased. The alternative to that, of course, would be engineering costing —namely, considering alternative ways to design and fabricate the product and then selecting the least costly among the possible alternatives.

By the method of historical costing, all of the factors that had yielded increases in cost and price in previous years are accepted as appropriate. Extrapolating the cost increase generated by those factors makes an "escalator", constantly enlarging cost and price. Then the projected cost and price become not estimates of future development but targets for future development. The firms that became involved in such practices were also those producing basic manufacturing machinery, including the vital machine tool industry whose products are at the core of all metal working.

The pattern by which the wages of labor tended to increase more rapidly than prices for machine tools came to a halt in the late 1950s and 1960s and was replaced during the decade of the 1970s by a cost-maximizing pattern. Thus, in the United States, as average hourly earnings of industrial workers rose 72 percent from 1971 to 1978, machine tool prices rose 85 percent. That greater increase in the prices of machine tools marked a negative incentive to the users of machine tools to purchase new ones.

Contrast what happened in the United States during that period with the developments in Germany and Japan. In Germany, average hourly earnings rose 72 percent. The price of machine tools rose only 59 percent. There were still clearly substantial incentives to German industrial management that favored the purchase of new machinery. In Japan the condition is more striking: From 1971 to 1978, average hourly earnings rose 177 percent, while the prices of machine tools rose a mere 61 percent.

The Japanese pattern during the 1970s was similar to the one that was once ordinary in the United States. The consequences for Japanese industry were the same ones that had been traditional in the United States. Japanese industrial employers were offered massive incentives to purchase and to utilize new machinery of greater productivity. They have done precisely that. Therefore, they have been able to offset the larger part of the wage increases in Japanese industry that have been running at the highest rate of wage increases in any industrialized country in the world.

There is a further characteristic of the military economy as it impacts civilian industry—the employment of engineers and scientists in large numbers on behalf of the military project. I calculated the number of engineers and scientists serving civilian industry per 10,000 in the labor force for 1977. In the United States, it was thirty-eight per 10,000; in Germany, forty; in Japan, fifty. This "brain-drain" of scientific talent away from civilian to war-related research and development is a further indicator of the problem.

This concentration of capital of every sort on the military economy has brought about the sustained withdrawal of capital resources of every kind from the civilian economy, with the results that I have indicated elsewhere. Increases in imports of goods that once were produced in the United States translate directly into a permanent loss of productive livelihood for the people in these industries and the industries supplying them. Further, for certain commodities and industries, the proportion of the product sold in the United States during 1973-79, that was produced outside the United States, represents an import.

This sample of industries suffering production foregone in the United

States demonstrates the historic decay in the technical-economic production competence of U.S. industry. In order to live, a community must produce. It is an elemental task of every economy to organize people to work. The growing failure of the manufacturing industries of the United States to be able to organize people for work is a fundamental failure in the functioning of the American economy as managed by private managements and by state managements, as in the military sector of the economy.

Finally, there are no grounds for supposing that these developments can be reversed without a reversal in the causal conditions that have brought them about. That means that there is no way of restoring production competence, technically or economically, without a shift in the use of vital capital resources from military to civilian purpose in the United States.

From this vantage point the great issues of peace and the economy are joined. We must address the idea of conversion from the military to a civilian economy—not as a far-fetched ideal but as a vital imperative for restoring economic competence to U.S. industry.

■   ■   ■

■ *CHAIRMAN DELLUMS:*   A number of people who are critical of the expanding military budget have suggested that if we continue to pursue this course, we will bring about one of two consequences: Either (1) we will achieve a level of nuclear technology beyond our social institutions' ability to control; or, (2) because of this bloated, wasteful, unnecessary, and dangerous military budget, the bottom will drop out of our economy. Would you comment on that?

■ *PROFESSOR MELMAN:*   These are the best-case and worst-case conditions. If there is no nuclear war, then we are in the best-case. In that case, the deterioration of the economy will proceed. The permanent structure of unemployment in the industries that I have identified and in many other industries will grow. The interest rates will continue to be high and may very possibly increase. For example, financial economists examining the prospect for federal government deficits until 1986 estimate that the funding requirements of the federal budget will be so large as to draw on 50 to 60 percent of total private savings.

As the federal government draws on an ever-larger proportion of the available finance capital of the United States, the federal government becomes the major factor in setting the interest rate. Furthermore, that drain on finance capital constitutes a major competitive factor, *vis-à-vis* private firms and others, for finance capital and escalates the interest rates almost automatically. The consequences of escalating interest rates are baleful, indeed—they deter the construction of homes, the purchase of durable goods like motor vehicles, and all manner of industrial capital investment.

The worst case implied in your question involves a total economic collapse, even beyond the gradual decay implied in these analyses or the far worst case—the occurrence of nuclear war. I have no plans for a far worst case. There is no way to plan for no life, no way to plan for no production. We can only plan for life or production.

■ *CHAIRMAN DELLUMS:* One of our problems in discussing the trade-offs between defense spending and other spending is that monies are readily available for investment in the Defense Department but very little investment is forthcoming in other sectors. Do you feel that the decline in military contracts will, in and of itself, result in a rechanneling of investment to the civilian sectors, or will this money simply be transferred to more profitable ventures outside the United States?

■ *PROFESSOR MELMAN:* That question needs translation. Since the largest capital fund in American society is controlled by the state management, the president, his cabinet and by the central administrative office that governs the industrial network of the Department of Defense, we have to ask how would they—how will they—dispose of these capital resources?

Well, we have precedent for that. In January of 1969, one of the last official acts of Lyndon Johnson was to make available a special report from his Council of Economic Advisors on the U.S. economy after Vietnam. That report indicated that it was possible to draw up a list of major productive capital investments involving public responsibility areas that would take up all, and then some, of the resources then being used to operate the Vietnam War.

In our time, it is entirely reasonable to expect that the federal government could draw up a similar agenda. It would be a longer agenda than the 1969 agenda. It would have larger money magnitudes, not only because of inflation but also because of the deterioration that has proceeded within the civilian sector. We would find ourselves thereby addressing the renewal and the modernization of the major infrastructure items of American society—that is, replacement of water systems that have become polluted, of public transportation systems that have become incompetent, and of all manner of services and facilities that have gone into decay during the last thirty years. Furthermore, it is altogether reasonable to expect that such a capital fund could also be deployed with priority (for example, with low interest rates or productive capital investments of a civilian sort), particularly in industrial areas where the United States requires new production competence or where the production competence has gone into disrepair.

For example, there is not a single factory in the United States competent to produce an electric trolley. Electric trolleys are fine vehicles for many modes of transportation not only within but even among cities, not to mention suburban areas. It is a very economical mode of transportation—it is quiet, runs free of fumes, operates at modest costs, and is capable of being laid down at modest capital outlay compared with superhighways.

A substantial capital investment is required there. It is a matter of precedent and well within the feasible understandings of our economists and others to develop a program of productive capital investment that would replace the nonproductive capital utilization of a military economy. There is nothing in the military economy *per se* that determines the alternative use of that capital. That is a matter of social decision.

■ *CHAIRMAN DELLUMS:* What do you think it would take to get U.S. industry to realize the damage that military spending inflicts on U.S. industry? Is it possible to convert their thinking?

■ *PROFESSOR MELMAN:* Let us consider two sides in industry: management and labor. In many industries, management has finally gotten to feel the whiplash because middle managers have had to be fired—as steel plants were closed, as auto plants were closed, as other plants on the list of enumerated industries have closed. Even some of the senior managers, however much they have become devoted to making money by any available means, may well regret the circumstance in which they can no longer perform the classic productive functions. Engineers not employed in the military economy increasingly know that opportunity for productive employment rests with new civilian capital investment.

From the standpoint of the trade unions, the matter is crystal-clear for all the parties engaged in industry. The percentages that I suggested are minimum percentages of employment lost in the relevant industries. For the working people of the United States, this collapse of production competence is a personal collapse. It is the end of the possibility of productive livelihood.

Therefore, I look forward to a growing awareness among the trade unions of the United States—the members and leaders—to the understanding that there is a future for working people in the United States only insofar as productive resources are utilized in the civilian economy.

15

THE "IRON TRIANGLE" AND THE AMERICAN ECONOMY

Dr. Gordon Adams

■ ■ ■

Gordon Adams did his undergraduate work at Stanford University, was a Fulbright fellow at the College of Europe in Belgium, and received his Ph.D. in political science from Columbia University. He was senior research associate at the Council on Economic Priorities and has taught at Columbia, Rutgers University, and the City University of New York, among others. He is currently the director of the Defense Budget Project of the Center on Budget and Policy Priorities. He has published *The Iron Triangle: The Politics of Defense Contracting.*

MY ASSOCIATES AT the Council on Economic Priorities and I have calculated that the plan to spend $1.6 trillion on military arms over the next five years comes out to $20,000 per American household, a considerable financial burden which sends 50 percent of every individual's tax dollar to the Department of Defense. This is before we add in the costs of such programs as nuclear weapons work in the Department of Energy; the National Aeronautics and Space Administration budget, since a substantial portion of space shuttle missions are for military purposes; and the Veterans Administration. That pushes the proportion of tax dollars even higher.

The administration's program is disastrous for our national security for four reasons. First, the real world is rather dramatically different from the world the administration sees. Second, fortunately, most Americans' expectations from their government have changed dramatically from ten or fifteen years ago, and those changes are important in examining this problem. Third, and perhaps most seriously for the purposes of these hearings, the administration's military program is going to be a disaster for the American economy. That economy is no longer the same as it was twenty years ago, and we will all suffer as a result. Finally, there is growing frustration with the way in which the Department of Defense is buying its weapons. Let me just go through those four points in slightly greater detail.

First, America lives in a very rapidly changing world. Threatening developments around the world—in the Soviet Union and Third World countries—simply refuse to conform to the rhetoric coming from the administration. The mismatch between what is happening in the world and the rhetoric of this military program carries serious risks for national security.

With respect to the Soviet Union, a powerful, militarily capable Soviet Union has become a reality, despite massive U.S. strategic and conventional arms spending since the 1950s. A strategically equal Soviet Union is also a reality. It is important for us to keep in mind, however, in contrast to what the administration argues, that the United States remains significantly ahead in the strategic warhead count and in the accuracy of its strategic weapons.

Regardless of how one feels about this change in the world picture in the last twenty years, it is a reality. In the past, sound arms control policy has been a central aspect of American strategic thinking. It has been matched by Soviet policies, though each power has remained wary of the other.

The superiority that the administration now seeks, its often-claimed "margin of safety," is, in fact, chimerical in the nuclear age. Both sides, as a result, will move ahead with new strategic systems, including more counterforce weapons and more ballistic missile defenses, thus leaving both countries and their peoples with less actual security and a less stable nuclear relationship.

The administration's rhetoric about the southern tier of the globe is equally unrealistic and dangerous for world peace. The addition of seventy-five new nations to the United Nations since 1960 is one of the most profound changes in the world politics of this century, and changes are going to continue to take place in this area. In fact, revolutions and upheavals in the southern tier have complicated causes, many of them linked to precarious internal and external economies. The outcomes of these conflicts are unpredictable and, most important, not controllable by either superpower. It is self-defeating and dangerous for our relations with our allies, with the Soviet Union, and with the southern tier itself for us to assume that an arms build-up and an effort to impose U.S. military superiority is going to prevent these changes and avoid violence in the southern tier of the globe. In fact, even massive American intervention forces will simply not permit us to impose outcomes we desire on these events.

Second, public expectations of our government have changed. In the last ten to fifteen years, Americans have begun to realize that the government is neither omnipotent nor omniscient. The Vietnam War and the Watergate crisis have had a profound impact, not only on the national security community, but also on the way the American public perceives its government.

Third, the most serious crisis we face as a result of the military budget, and the one that I know is the principal focus of today's session of hearings, is the damage being done to the American economy. A study on the impact of military spending on the economy done by the Council on Economic Priorities and commissioned by the Machinists Union and the Coalition for a New Foreign and Military Policy concluded that the rapid and accelerating rate of growth of military spending is going to exacerbate our economic crisis.

The study makes three very basic points: First, higher rates of defense spending, inadequately financed through taxation, are exacerbating the federal deficits that the administration promised to eliminate. The deficits crowd out commercial borrowing, keep interest rates high, and add to inflationary pressures in the economy. Moreover, defense spending pushes additional demand into what is still a very heated sector of the American economy—high technology and aerospace industries—where the demand for raw materials, titanium, chromium, cobalt, machine tools, skilled engineers, and skilled machinists is very high and the supplies are short. As a result, increasing military demand for those goods is going to add to cost pressures for all commercial users of those same goods. As the commercial users seek to obtain the same raw materials, machines, and labor, they, too, are going to be forced to pass along their cost increases to the consumer.

As citizens, we face a double-barreled problem. On one side, defense spending will go up as the shortages are incurred. The taxpayer will fund the increase. On the other side, as consumers, we will be forced to pay higher prices for goods that commercial manufacturers have to make at higher prices because the same inputs of production are costing them more.

As the president's own Council of Economic Advisors put it in February 1982: "The substantial demand for resources in the durable sector for defense production may increase relative prices in at least some of the affected industries. Both the Department of Defense and private purchasers may have to pay more for goods in these industries." That is the administration's analysis.

Second, on the economic issue, the administration's commitment, if supply-side economics has any meaning at all, is to enhance the productivity and employment-creating potential of the economy. Capital shortages due to federal deficits, however, mean there is no money for private capital borrowing for industries of the future. In fact, private capital markets, housing construction, transit, energy industries, and the like have begun to complain about the shortage and high cost of capital. In addition, we invest 65 percent of our federal commitment to research and development in technologies that have absolutely no commercial economic payoff. Through NASA, the Department of Energy, and the Department of Defense, we are spending well over $25 billion on military-related technologies that no longer have spinoff for the commercial economy. I think the last time that we saw significant spinoff from the military sector to the commercial sector was probably the invention of Tang for the space program; Tang is now a popular drink on supermarket shelves. The problem with spinoff is that it goes no further than Tang.

Third, defense spending also creates problems for employment, one of the most serious issues we face in the American economy today. Within the defense sector itself, the unions that organize in that sector recognize that they are not adding new members. Over the past ten years they have been losing members, not because they are losing union elections but because their membership base is eroding as the capital intensity of the high technology defense sector increases. Over time, more and more technology, research, raw materials, and machinery go into each defense product, but there are fewer and fewer jobs.

Ten years ago, the McDonnell Douglas Corporation in St. Louis employed twice as many aerospace workers as it does today. It has cut its labor force in half in ten years. Today they do twice as much defense contracting business as they did ten years ago. That is a measure of this problem of capital intensity. Even within the defense sector new employment is a problem, as any defense contractor acknowledges. Outside the defense sector, of course, the American employment crisis is dramatic. There we see rates of 15 percent unemployment for women and 45 percent for Black teenagers, and those are the official government figures. Any resident of an urban area, as I am, knows that the crisis is more dramatic than those figures suggest. The average aerospace worker is simply not a twenty-four-year-old Black high school graduate mother of two living in the ghetto.

The federal government's Bureau of Labor Statistics has pointed out for several years that almost any other way of spending the federal dollar creates more employment where that employment is required. We have, in fact, what the economists call an opportunity cost problem. We are losing the opportunity to create more employment through other forms of federal spending.

My fourth general point concerns the issue of waste. While the administration argues that its military budget is going to improve readiness, the fastest growing part of the defense budget is for procurement, research, and development. These categories now comprise over 44 percent of the administration's defense budget. Procurement and research and development spending does not directly improve readiness. In fact, personnel, operations, and maintenance spending are all declining as a proportion of the total. Those are the areas where readiness is provided.

The administration also tells us that this is a reformed military budget. The so-called Carlucci Initiatives to control costs and stop waste, announced in 1981, are the basis of this claim, and yet these so-called reforms have turned out to increase procurement of weapons in almost every category of the Department of Defense budget.

Why did they do this? Because the reforms do not zero in on the sources of cost growth. They simply say we will budget realistically for cost increases in the future. We will use "realistic" inflation estimates, and we will assume the contractors are telling us true cost figures. The reforms make no effort to go into the problem of waste itself. In fact, as David Stockman has made very clear, one can find a swamp of $10 billion to $20 billion to $30 billion worth of waste in the Department of Defense budget.

How do we move to a rational defense strategy? We must begin to define the alternatives. Alternatives to current policy must go beyond the suggestions of the reform of military thinking and seek routes toward arms reductions in a more peaceful world in which, at the same time, all Americans feel their national security is adequately protected.

I want to suggest three areas where I think we can begin to look for alternatives. The first of these has to do with the U.S.-Soviet relationship. In contrast to administration rhetoric, I think it is very important to underline that the U.S.-Soviet military relationship is in a state of military parity, or military balance. Each side's armed forces have strengths and weaknesses that are asymmetrical. The United States, for example, has more warheads and greater accuracy. NATO leads in antitank precision guided munitions, while the Warsaw Pact, with a history of mechanized warfare, has a lead in tanks, and so on. We can go down an inventory of the balance, but what we end up with is with a situation of virtual military parity.

Current strategic efforts on both sides contain grave risks of escalating the nuclear confrontation between the superpowers and of destabilizing the deterrent relationship. The technology points in that direction. Both superpowers need to be urged to move toward arms control, arms reduction, and a nuclear freeze, which will increase the stability of the nuclear relationship between the two.

But the nuclear freeze is not enough. Initial steps toward stable deterrent forces have to be followed by negotiations toward reductions, which would lead to substantial cuts, down to perhaps even 200 or 300 delivery vehicles on each side, insuring adequate deterrence. The budget savings of the freeze itself would probably be on the order of $15 billion to $20 billion, while the savings of cuts would be more dramatic.

With respect to Western Europe, the combined military and economic power of NATO is vastly superior to that of the Warsaw Pact. A European arms build-up should not be accelerated, nor should we be putting pressure on our European allies to commit more spending to their own defense. They now spend adequately for their national security, and, as I say, the opposing forces are in virtual balance. Moreover, both sides seem to acknowledge and have acknowledged for years that Europe is not a likely arena for armed conflict. The risks are simply too great.

The United States and NATO, in other words, have a valid interest in arms reductions, both in terms of theater nuclear forces, which means halting the Pershing II and ground-launched Cruise missile programs, and in terms of eliminating planning for the use of chemical weapons in Western Europe, which would be disastrous in a windy, crowded urban environment and therefore, would have no purpose. The saving would be $2 billion to $3 billion over the next three years. Indeed, it is time for Europe, the United States, and the Soviet Union to begin the pursuit of serious, balanced, conventional force reductions in Western Europe. This, in turn, will have a direct impact on the American arms budget by reducing personnel associated with army deployment in Western Europe.

With respect to the southern tier, as I have pointed out, change is inevitable. But not every change or every conflict is a direct reflection of U.S. and Soviet tensions. Instead, it is important to urge this administration to begin to use diplomacy as a constructive alternative to further arms build-ups and military confrontations in the Third World.

One of the singular successes of the Carter administration in the southern tier was in Zimbabwe. Under pressure from the United States, the British and the participants in a bloody, gruesome civil war managed to get to the bargaining table, negotiate an agreement, hold elections, and, although those elections brought to office what was seen here initially as the most extreme candidate, the American government discovered that Robert Mugabe was a gentleman with whom one could do business. Zimbabwe is an ideal scenario for handling necessary and inevitable changes in the Third World countries, such as El Salvador.

Mixing in a good degree of diplomacy enables us to take a harder look at demand for such items as a 640-ship Navy based on building large carriers and bringing battleships out from mothballs, projects that are entirely wasteful and unnecessary. Current forces and smaller, less vulnerable naval vessels will provide adequate security. The Navy should be designed to protect legitimate U.S. interests, where necessary, and to be efficient for that purpose, but it should not constitute a global intervention force for total sea lane domination with the capability to fight naval conflicts in all oceans simultaneously.

The same holds true for the Rapid Deployment Force, where we could save somewhere between $6 billion and $10 billion in current budget authority. We have had a Rapid Deployment Force for some time, 180,000 Marines. Those U.S. Airborne and Marine units that now exist, current air-lift capability, and adequate attention to its readiness are more than enough to protect real U.S. interests. A larger force is simply not needed for almost any other contingency. In the Middle East, diplomatic initiatives, existing U.S. capabilities, and a reduction in U.S. dependency on imported oil would be a realistic response to a troubled situation we simply cannot unilaterally control.

As I have suggested in going through a number of these items, there are direct and immediate financial implications for the administration's fiscal year 1983 budget request. I might add that, for instance, cutting the B-1B bomber program, an almost willful violation of the Carlucci Procurement Initiatives' prohibition of "buying in" on weapons systems, would save $4.8 billion in fiscal year 1983 budget authority. Cutting the M-1 Abrams tank, and buying the A-10 plane, instead of the AH-64 helicopter gun ship, are examples of how, by correcting improper decisions, eliminating buying in, reducing the instability of the deterrent, reducing conflict focusing on Western Europe, and altering our strategy with respect to the Third World, we could save substantial amounts of money in the fiscal year 1983 and subsequent defense requests.

The alternative defense options I have suggested are not a reflection on all U.S. military forces, nor are they based on the assumption that the United States alone has created a risky and conflict-laden world. Instead, they aim at insuring basic national security and opening up the possibility for modern flexible defense options. They seek a more peaceful world and the liberation of enormous pools of resources in the budget to address the serious national economic and social problems that we face here at home—concerns that are, after all, the bedrock of our national security.

■　　■　　■

■ *CHAIRMAN DELLUMS:* You raise some very interesting questions. For example, if we eliminated all of the so-called dangerous weapons systems, we would reduce the military budget in fiscal year 1983 only by approximately $5 billion in outlays, and I think you said the figure was $20 billion in budget authority.

Therefore, in order to reduce significantly the military budget, one has to begin to deal with policy assumptions. With regard to Europe, I tend to agree with you that, on a scale of 1 to 10, the probability of a war breaking out in Europe is somewhere between 0 and 1. The fact that we could not contain a war in Europe is very important. Even if it began as a conventional war, it would escalate to theater nuclear war. That fact in itself is enough of a deterrent so that we would not go to war in Europe. What kind of savings do you perceive us being able to realize as a result of taking a much more realistic view of the "threat" in Europe?

■ *DR. ADAMS:* I could not give you an absolute dollar figure on those savings, but we could talk some numbers. If we decided not to accelerate the production and deployment of 700 or 800 F-16 Aircraft for Western Europe; if the Western Europeans on their side did not proceed with the Tornado aircraft program; if we did not proceed with M-1 tank construction and deployment; if we drew down and ultimately withdrew something on the order of 300,000 or more soldiers based in Western Europe and demobilized them—then I suspect that the overall budgetary savings would be substantial.

The administration suggests that at least $70 billion to $80 billion of its fiscal year 1983 budget is designed for programs that concern Western Europe and the NATO alliance. This $70 billion to $80 billion is substantial; if it were reduced even by half it would be a considerable savings.

■ *CHAIRMAN DELLUMS:* You made an interesting assertion earlier when you suggested that it is not a proper goal to suggest that our European allies increase the level of their defense expenditure. A number of our colleagues suggest that the trade-off for any significant reduction in military expenditures on our part has to be met by a corresponding increase on the part of our European allies. You argue just the reverse; would you amplify this point?

■ *DR. ADAMS:* I *am* arguing the opposite analysis. There are really two issues here: One is the argument that the United States pays a substantial burden for defending Western Europe, that our allies do not match that burden, and that they ought to do so. There is an implied moral imperative in that position that has nothing to do with the structure of the force balance. The other has to do with the "real numbers" game: What is the military relationship between the Warsaw Pact and the NATO alliance, and what does that force balance tell us about what would happen in the case of a conflict?

If we assume that this is not a likely arena of war, then we have to look at the numbers as they now stand and see if there is a serious imbalance at even that low level of probability. If you put current American forces together with NATO forces, there are some asymmetries, such as tanks and air defense. Antitank weapons, mine capabilities, and naval capabilities on the other side are an asymmetry favoring NATO. In my judgment the United States and the NATO allies, vis-à-vis the Warsaw Pact and the Soviet Union, are in a situation of military parity at a very high level of deployment and production.

The next step, I would argue, is serious negotiations between the NATO allies and the Warsaw Pact for the reduction of the force balance. Reducing forces obviates the need for anything beyond regular modernization of the reduced forces that will be already in place. A massive conventional build-up is unnecessary.

■ *CHAIRMAN DELLUMS:* With respect to Third World policy, some of us argue that this administration perceives the problems of the world as mainly military ones that must be resolved on a military basis —that is, if only the United States were to have enough troops, enough firepower, and enough nuclear capability, it could bring peace and stability to the world.

Some of us, especially those of us in the Congressional Black Caucus, challenged that assumption in the debates on the budget last year. We said that we perceived the problems of the world as economic, political and social, and that they have to be resolved in that context. If the American people desire to be competitive with the Soviet Union, then let our competition express itself in terms of who best can address the human misery of people in the Third World, as opposed to who can best develop the technology of death and destruction. Could you comment on that?

■ *DR. ADAMS:* The Third World arena is the subject of heightened tension and dispute, especially in Central America. What we see there is a simplistic attempt to choose the military option to deal with complex problems. The countries around the world spend, as a recent study by Ruth Sivard points out, $550 billion annually on their armed forces—salaries, maintenance, and the weapons that are purchased. It is a massive burden for their economies, which is the heart of the problem for Third World countries.

When the administration chooses the military option to deal with

Third World issues, it exacerbates that problem in three ways. One has to do with foreign arms sales. This administration has totally reversed a policy that was already weakened toward the end of the previous administration—that of prohibiting certain arms sales overseas. This administration has an active arms sales policy and these sales have two effects: First, they are used for internal repression, so the possibilities of growth, social change, development, education, and health in these countries are threatened. Second, the economic burden on those countries is tremendous. The cost in foreign exchange, in investments foregone simply to buy weaponry, is an enormous burden for every country in the Third World. The third problem relates to intervention forces. This administration has gone beyond the previous administration with respect to the Rapid Deployment Force. Instead of a force of 110,000, with airlift capability and prepositioned ships, current plans for the Rapid Deployment Force in this administration include 229,000 soldiers and a much larger number of airlift aircraft, both C-5As and KC-10 aircraft, to move that force, its supplies, its fuel, and its equipment overseas.

■ *CHAIRMAN DELLUMS:*   Could you comment on: (1) the arithmetic of the B-1B bombers and your cost estimates; and, (2) the efficiency and efficacy of the B-1B bomber?

■ *DR. ADAMS:*   I personally consider the B-1B bomber one of the classic cases of waste in the administration's military budget request. Strictly on its own terms, even before we raise the issue of spending funds on such things as Aid to Families with Dependent Children or educational subsidies or loans, the B-1B bomber is a classic waste of money and a classic case of "buying in."

The cost figure is a good place to start because the administration suggested that it will cost $27.5 billion (inflated dollars) for a fleet of 100 planes, or $20.5 billion in fiscal year 1982 dollars, which was the figure certified by the administration in January. That program has a troubled history of cost growth. When the initial B-1 was proposed in 1970, Rockwell promised a plane that would cost $40 million per copy. When the program was cancelled by the administration in 1977, it cost $107 million per plane. When Rockwell proposed a new long-range bomber force a year ago, they said it would cost $119 million per plane. As they negotiated through the spring on a contract price, they ended up with $195 million per plane (in fiscal year 1981 dollars). Adding the systems they will require for the bomber to function, both as an adequate penetrator and as a Cruise missile carrier, and adding more realistic inflation estimates, the Congressional Budget Office has estimated that it will cost $398 million per plane.

The first issue that has to be raised is the need for the B-1B. If we need it, obviously we should spend the money for it. But do we need it? The answer is a resounding no. It is a totally wasteful requirement. Right now, the American taxpayers, at a cost of $16 billion, are revitalizing 150 B-52s and building 3,400 Cruise missiles to position on those B-52s to do the same mission—that is, penetrate Soviet air space. Cruise missiles, as virtually any military testimony will tell you, are a much more adequate penetrator than any manned bomber so far tested. We are spending $16 billion for precisely the mission that the B-1B bomber is designed to do. The B-1B can perform that mission only until, at best, 1990, if not before. The Cruise missile program on the B-52, according to Air Force testimony by General Kelly Burke, head of research and development in the Air Force chief of staff's office, can do that mission until the twenty-first century.

If the mission is important, the system we are creating for $16 billion is adequate for that mission. Deprived of that mission, the proponents of the B-1B have designed what I have called the "bomber for all seasons"—an airplane that can do everything. It can penetrate Soviet air space, it can carry Cruise missiles, it can do conventional bombing, it can lay mines, it can provide air support for the fleet. It is a plane that has now been sold to every part of America's military services to justify the expenditure. For every one of those additional missions, we have other current aircraft in the inventory that can do the same thing. The B-1B is redundant for all of those missions.

The question then arises as to why we are buying the B-1B. Here we are dealing with something I have called the "iron triangle"—that is, that rather unique American policy network, the closed-off arena of information, access, and influence that links defense contractors to the Department of Defense and to certain key committees in Congress involved with defense procurement and the defense budget.

Inside the iron triangle, bomber programs have been lobbied for ever since the B-52 production line was closed twenty years ago, and they will probably continue to be pushed for as long as the Strategic Air Command feels it needs an airplane and Rockwell International or another company feels it needs a contract. The source of the B-1B lies more in the peculiar politics of our military procurement apparatus than any military mission. The cost to the taxpayer and the foregone $40 billion that could have been used to better purposes is going to be the price we all pay.

■ *MR. CONYERS (D-Mich.):* Does the Boston Study Group analysis agree with your views on alternative military systems?

■ *DR. ADAMS:* I think the general thrust of the proposals I have seen is in accord with what I have been saying. The Boston Study Group study makes two important assumptions, which I share. One of those has to do with the importance of stability and reductions in the strategic arena—that is, removing the perilous threat of nuclear war that hangs over both the United States and the Soviet Union, not to mention the rest of the globe. I think there are common sense, real world policies that can roll that deterrent relationship back to a level where it is stable and reducible, policies that I have suggested in my testimony. The Boston Study Group also suggests some in its study.

There is now growing agreement in the strategic community that there is ample room for stability and cutbacks, and grave risks in the development of technology such as ballistic missile defense, accurate warheads, survivable missiles, that moves in the direction of counterforce or war fighting scenarios. This technology is ultimately destabilizing because both sides will match each other step for step in the nuclear arms race.

The other assumption the Boston Study Group has made, which I also share, is that it is not the purpose of the United States to maintain forces that permit massive intervention in numerous overseas theaters simultaneously. That has to do with the southern tier problem I spoke of earlier. It suggests that things like a Rapid Deployment Force, additional divisions and air wings, and the like are simply not required for a decent American foreign policy. Again, there are common sense, real world alternatives to such a military force that guarantee an adequate American national security without the build-up being proposed by the administration.

■ *MR. CONYERS:* Are there any assumptions that you do not share with them?

■ *DR. ADAMS:* With respect to the Boston Study Group, I did not find many I did not share. In some areas they were weaker than they might have been—the European theater and communications, command, and control being two. There were areas where the book simply did not fully flesh out what they were talking about. But I do share its two principal assumptions.

■ *MR. CONYERS:* Have you noticed a "brain drain" in the American economic system, in that many of our talented engineers and even scholars are being drawn into the military sector at an increasing disadvantage to the private and public sectors?

■ *DR. ADAMS:* Yes, as I tried to suggest in my testimony, albeit briefly, we pay a dramatic opportunity price in the America. For our military budget it is very hard to count the number of research scientists, technicians, and engineers actually engaged in defense-related work because, ultimately, you have to look at time cards. You have to be able to say that person X in shop Y spent 40 percent of his or her time on NASA and 20 percent of his or her time on a toaster lever. In fact, current estimates with respect to our technical personnel suggest research scientists and engineers are about 30 to 40 percent employed in defense-related areas in the United States. We spend about two-thirds of our research and development dollars at the federal level on military-related research and development. In both of those cases, the proportions involved in military work in such countries as Germany and Japan are much lower. The Germans and the Japanese, instead, concentrate their public investment in research and development on civilian and commercial technologies and social problems—mass transit, housing construction, energy alternatives, and the like. Their personnel are also employed in that way and are simply not caught up in the military sector.

The consequences, in terms of economic growth rates, as we found in a study that we did for the Machinists Union, is dramatic. The German and Japanese growth rate varied in almost directly inverse proportion to the commitment of personnel and research monies to defense. To the extent we invested in defense, our growth rate proved slower than either the Germans or the Japanese. So the answer to your question is: Yes, there is a trend in that direction. The defense budget increase will increase the trend in that direction. The best and the brightest go into aerospace. It just seems to be more exciting to master the technique of missile avionics than it is to manufacture a car that will get eighty miles to the gallon.

16

THE EMPTY PORK BARREL

Marion Anderson

■ ■ ■

Marion Anderson was educated at Oberlin College and a consortium of universities in Washington. She is a former director of the Seminar on Congress and American Foreign Policy in Washington. Ms. Anderson is currently director of Employment Research Associates. Her most important studies on the interrelationship between the Pentagon budget and employment issues include "The Empty Pork Barrel" (parts of which are included in this testimony) and "Military Spending: All of Us Pay, Most of Us Lose."

I HAVE SPENT some years talking with representatives and senators about the arms budget and what it does to the economy. I noticed that one thing that happened time after time was that representatives or senators would say to me, "Look, Marion, I know we don't need the weapons system, I know it's gold-plated, but think of the jobs."

The "but the jobs" would terminate the discussion because, in their minds, what they were saying was: "I know the money isn't needed for additional weapons systems, and I know it's probably wasted from the point of view of even its military utility, but it's creating jobs. And since it's creating jobs, we are going to go ahead with it and please don't talk about it."

In 1975, we did the first edition of "The Empty Pork Barrel: Unemployment and the Pentagon Budget." What we have found over a period of years, and our research has now spanned the period from 1968 through 1980, was that every time military spending goes up, jobs disappear in this country. It is, in fact, the exact opposite of what the military contractors say here on Capitol Hill, which is, "Congressmen, vote for this wonderful weapons system because you'll get all these jobs in your District." What they do not discuss regarding all those lovely jobs being generated is from whom the jobs are being taken. I would like to offer a few basic statistical realities to counter these arguments.

During the 1977-78 period, the military budget averaged only $101.4 billion, well under half what Mr. Reagan proposes for this forthcoming year, and it cost an annual net loss of 1,015,000 jobs in the American economy. The states that contained 70 percent of the U.S. population lost jobs that year every time the military budget went up. Our current updating of this data indicates that with every increase of just $1 billion in the military budget, 9,000 jobs disappear in our own country. That is a *net loss* of jobs. It takes into consideration all of the jobs generated through military contracts and through military salaries.

The reason for this is straightforward. If people all over the country are paying high taxes, a substantial percentage of which goes to the Pentagon, they do not have control over that money. This means that they build fewer houses, buy fewer cars, take fewer vacations, and vote lower taxes for their state and local governments. These "expenditures never made" have a profoundly negative impact upon jobs in these areas of the economy.

A few specific examples should suffice. If you spend a billion dollars on retail trade, you generate 65,000 jobs. If you spend it on education, you generate 62,000 jobs; on hospitals, 48,000 jobs; on guided missiles and ordnance, 14,000 jobs. When you move money from the Department of Education to the Pentagon, for instance, or from a state like Michigan, which would spend it on education if we had the money to spend, *you are destroying jobs at about a three to one ratio.*

In order to analyze the job creating differential between military and civilian spending, we compared the jobs lost in these sectors of the economy with the jobs created by the armed forces and their contractors. The jobs foregone—never created—because of military spending were estimated in each state, for durable and nondurable goods production, residential and nonresidential construction, services, and state and local government. Then the number of jobs created by military contracts and military personnel was determined. The difference between the total number of civilian jobs foregone and the military jobs created equals the net job gain or loss for each state. *The results of the study show that increased military spending seriously depresses employment in the United States.*

The discovery of this negative impact undermines one of the most persuasive arguments that the Pentagon uses when it comes to Congress for its annual appropriation. Even if there were doubts as to whether the weapons would work, doubts whether the costs would worsen an already bad inflation, increase the national debt, and cause massive cuts in civilian programs—even given these problems, the military establishment still argues that expanding its budget would create more jobs.

However, the calculations have not been pursued to their logical conclusion. Since a dollar spent on military priorities is a dollar that cannot be spent on civilian priorities, it is not sufficient to discuss only the number of jobs that are created by military spending. One must also ask how that dollar would have been spent if the Pentagon had not received it—if instead it had been used by consumers to buy the goods and services that they needed or had been turned over to state and local governments to meet public needs. The answers are contrary to what most people would expect.

Military production has become technically very complex; it involves large amounts of expensive raw materials and even more expensive equipment. Therefore, less of the money spent goes toward hiring people and more goes toward buying high-priced equipment than when the money is spent on civilian purchases.

For example, the estimates on the MX missile indicate that for every billion tax dollars spent, 17,000 people would be hired, whereas the same billion dollars could have hired 48,000 hospital personnel. Table 16-1 shows the difference between the employment created by military and civilian spending in several categories. Table 16-2 shows the total difference in the economy between military and civilian spending.

If $1 billion is spent on civilian industry, 27,000 jobs are created; if spent on military industry 18,000 jobs. When $1 billion is spent hiring state and local government personnel—police officers, teachers, and fire fighters—72,000 jobs are created. When military personnel are hired, only 37,000 jobs are generated per billion dollars spent.

TABLE 16–1.   JOBS GENERATED BY ONE BILLION
DOLLARS OF EXPENDITURE.

Employer	Number of Jobs
Retail trade	65,000
Education	62,000
Hospitals	48,000
Newspapers	30,000
Apparel manufacture	28,000
Fabricated metals	16,000
Guided missiles and ordnance	14,000

TABLE 16–2. JOBS CREATED PER BILLION DOLLARS OF EXPENDITURE.

Sector Spending $1 Billion	Number of Jobs Created in Industry	Number of Jobs Created in Government
Civilian sector	27,000	72,000
Military sector	−18,000	−37,000
Jobs foregone by spending on the military	9,000	35,000

The Myth about Military Spending and the Economy

It has been a long-held myth that huge military spending creates jobs—one reason military budgets have passed Congress for decades with virtually no comment upon their economic impact. Like many myths, it had its genesis in historical circumstance. Everyone over fifty remembers the Depression and everyone under fifty has heard about it. The memories of long lines of destitute men waiting at soup kitchens and of Ph.D.s selling apples on street corners made an indelible impression on the American consciousness.

Then came World War II. Eleven million young men were drafted into the armed forces, and war factories were opened all over the country hiring unemployed men and women. Everyone had a job. So the concept that was stamped upon the collective memory of Americans was that the war ended the Depression, and therefore military spending created jobs.

No one said that the government spending $80 billion a year in 1941 on anything would have ended the Depression. The federal government could have replaced worn-out housing, run-down railroads, and decrepit hospitals. Any vast influx of investment and consumption into the system would have terminated the Depression. But most Americans just observed that when the war began the Depression ended and therefore assumed military spending must be good for the economy.

Myths die hard. It has taken years of the current economic malaise, the combination of high unemployment, high inflation, and high military spending, to cause people to reexamine their assumptions about the economy, to ask what makes it healthy, or unhealthy, and why.

The Jobs Costs of High Military Spending

How many jobs does the American economy lose when the military budget is high? In which sectors of the economy are people losing their jobs? Which states lose and which states gain when the military budget goes up?

In order to do the calculations, we applied a thirty-year analysis of the relationship of the military budget to key sectors of the economy. This analysis showed that when military spending went up, the following categories went down by definite percentages: durable goods, nondurable goods, residential construction, nonresidential construction, services, state and local government, exports, imports, producers' durable equipment, and federal civil purchases. In order to avoid any possibility of double counting, and to keep our data conservative, this study analyzed only durable goods, nondurable goods, residential construction, services, and state and local government.

Table 16-3 shows in dollar terms, for every billion dollars spent on the military, how much was not being spent in these key areas of the economy.

Having determined from this thirty-year study the percentages of each billion dollars that went to the Pentagon that would have gone to each sector of the economy, we were able to calculate the net number of jobs foregone—never created—in each of these sectors. To do this calculation, we determined first the number of civilian jobs foregone for each state and then the number of jobs created by military contract awards and military personnel.

TABLE 16–3.   EXPENDITURES FOREGONE BY SECTOR OF THE ECONOMY FOR EACH BILLION DOLLARS SPENT ON THE MILITARY.

Sector of Economy	Expenditures Foregone
Services	$187,000,000
Durable goods	$163,000,000
State and local government consumption	$128,000,000
Residential structures	$114,000,000
Producers' durable equipment	$110,000,000
Exports	$97,000,000
Nondurable goods	$71,000,000
Nonresidential structures	$68,000,000
Federal civil purchases	$48,000,000
Imports	$25,000,000

An analysis of all fifty states displayed in Table 16-4 shows that 70 percent of the U.S. public lives in states that suffer a net job loss every time the military budget goes up. *Every large industrial state in the country but Texas loses.* All of the Middle Atlantic states, the Great Lakes states, and the Midwest lose jobs. The South is split, with Florida, Louisiana, Arkansas, and Tennessee losing heavily while the rest of the South and the Southwest, excluding Arizona, gains.

TABLE 16–4.   STATES IN ORDER OF NEGATIVE EMPLOYMENT IMPACT OF MILITARY SPENDING, ANNUAL AVERAGE 1977–78.

State	Number of Jobs Foregone	State	Number of Jobs Gained
1. New York	−288,200	1. Kansas	+600
2. Illinois	−160,750	2. New Hampshire	+650
3. Michigan	−139,100	3. Maine	+2,350
4. Ohio	−131,900	4. Alabama	+3,550
5. Pennsylvania	−112,900	5. Connecticut	+3,950
6. New Jersey	−71,950	6. North Dakota	+4,450
7. Wisconsin	−71,700	7. New Mexico	+7,450
8. Indiana	−64,550	8. Utah	+9,350
9. Minnesota	−54,600	9. Kentucky	+11,100
10. Tennessee	−47,200	10. Colorado	+11,200
11. Florida	−40,150	11. Texas	+15,450
12. Massachusetts	−39,800	12. Alaska	+15,750
13. Iowa	−38,500	13. Oklahoma	+16,000
14. Oregon	−37,850	14. Maryland	+17,050
15. Nevada	−24,100	15. Washington	+20,200
16. Louisiana	−23,350	16. Georgia	+20,950
17. West Virginia	−18,950	17. Mississippi	+23,450
18. California	−13,800	18. North Carolina	+23,800
19. Arkansas	−12,300	19. South Carolina	+29,200
20. Nebraska	−6,200	20. Hawaii	+45,200
21. Missouri	−4,500	21. Virginia	+125,950
22. Vermont	−4,250		
23. Rhode Island	−3,650	NET JOBS LOST	−1,015,500
24. Wyoming	−3,050		
25. Idaho	−2,850		
26. Arizona	−2,850		
27. Montana	−2,300		
28. Delaware	−1,200		
29. South Dakota	−600		

The Net Loss States

Of the 70 percent of the U.S. citizens who live in states that suffer a net loss of jobs, the overwhelming majority of them live in highly industrialized states that do not contain large military bases.

Table 16-5 shows the job impact of military spending by region. The Great Lakes region suffers the most. In the states of Ohio, Indiana, Illinois, Michigan, Wisconsin, and Minnesota, 623,000 jobs were foregone. This region, the industrial heartland of the nation, showed a net loss of almost 170,000 jobs just in the industrial sectors of its economy —durable and nondurable goods production. With relatively few military bases to compensate and a very substantial number of jobs foregone in services and state and local government, this region was hit hard.

The Middle Atlantic region suffers heavily. New York loses more jobs than any other state in the country—a staggering 288,000. New Jersey and Pennsylvania have heavy net job losses, even though they both received substantial military contracts and contain military bases. The losses that they sustained in civilian industrial production, coupled with the very large number of jobs that they had to forego in services and state and local government, resulted in 72,000 jobs foregone in New Jersey and 113,000 in Pennsylvania.

During the period studied, the New England states were split. The region as a whole lost about 41,000 jobs annually, although Maine, Connecticut, and New Hampshire had slight net gains.

The Midwestern Plains states showed a varied picture. Although the region as a whole showed a net loss of 45,000 jobs, some states gained. The net loss states included Iowa, Missouri, Nebraska, and South Dakota. The net gain states were North Dakota and Kansas, as a substantial number of troops were stationed in those states.

The South Central states comprising West Virginia, Kentucky, Tennessee, and Arkansas suffered a loss of 67,000 jobs. Only Kentucky showed a net gain in this region.

The majority of the Mountain states lost jobs. Montana, Idaho, Wyoming, and Nevada all lost. Only Colorado and Utah showed net gains.

The Net Gain States

The states that showed net gains in jobs from military bases and industry, shown in Table 16-6, form a geographic band that begins in Maryland and extends south to Georgia (Florida is excluded), west to New Mexico (excluding Louisiana), and north to Utah.

The Southern region which includes Maryland, Virginia, North Caro-

TABLE 16–5.   NET JOBS LOST BY GEOGRAPHICAL REGION, ANNUAL AVERAGE 1977–78.

Region	Net Job Gain or Loss	Region	Net Job Gain or Loss
GREAT LAKES		MIDWEST	
Ohio	−131,900	Iowa	−38,500
Indiana	−64,550	Missouri	−4,500
Illinois	−160,750	North Dakota	+4,450
Michigan	−139,100	South Dakota	−600
Wisconsin	−71,700	Nebraska	−6,200
Minnesota	−54,600	Kansas	+600
Total	−622,600	Total	−44,750
MIDDLE ATLANTIC		NEW ENGLAND	
New York	−288,200	Maine	+2,350
New Jersey	−71,950	Vermont	−4,250
Pennsylvania	−112,900	New Hampshire	+650
Delaware	−1,200	Massachusetts	−39,800
		Connecticut	+3,950
Total	−474,250	Rhode Island	−3,650
SOUTH CENTRAL		Total	−47,750
Kentucky	+11,100		
Tennessee	−47,200	MOUNTAIN	
West Virginia	−18,950	Montana	−2,300
Arkansas	−12,300	Idaho	−2,850
		Wyoming	−3,050
Total	−67,350	Colorado	+11,200
		Utah	+9,350
		Nevada	−24,100
		Total	−11,750

lina, South Carolina, Georgia, and Florida gained 180,000 jobs. Maryland, Virginia, North and South Carolina, and Georgia had about 521,000 military personnel stationed within their borders. Almost 100,000 military personnel were living in Florida, but their presence was not sufficient to overcome the large job losses in construction and services.

Oklahoma led the Southwest section with a net gain of 16,000 jobs. Texas has fallen dramatically in number of jobs gained, from 133,000 in the 1968-72 period to 15,500 in 1977-78. New Mexico gained 7,450 jobs. Arizona, by 1977-78, had entered the ranks of the net loss states. Its heavy losses in construction, services, and state and local government were not counterbalanced by the troops stationed at its bases.

Of the Pacific states in the continental United States, only Washington is a net gain. California, the state with the largest population in the

TABLE 16–6. NET JOBS GAINED BY GEOGRAPHICAL REGION, ANNUAL AVERAGE 1977–78.

Region	Net Job Gain or Loss	Region	Net Job Gain Or Loss
SOUTHERN		SOUTHWEST	
Maryland	+17,050	Oklahoma	+16,000
Virginia	+125,950	Texas	+15,450
North Carolina	+23,800	Arizona	−2,850
South Carolina	+29,200	New Mexico	+7,450
Georgia	+20,950		
Florida	−40,150	Total	+36,050
Mississippi	+23,450	PACIFIC	
Alabama	+3,550	California	−13,800
Louisiana	−23,350	Oregon	−37,850
		Washington	+20,200
Total	+180,450	Alaska	+15,750
		Hawaii	+45,200
		Total	+29,500

country, has become a net loss state. Oregon has always suffered a net loss of jobs when military spending is high. Alaska and Hawaii both have a small industrial base and a large concentration of troops, so they have a substantial net job gain.

The Case of California

Between the 1968-72 period reported in the first edition of "The Empty Pork Barrel" and the 1977-78 period of the 1982 edition, dramatic changes took place in the job impact of military spending upon the state of California. *California moved from being a state with a net gain of 97,000 jobs, to a state with a net loss of over 13,000 jobs.* This shift has occured despite the fact that California's military contracts have grown substantially. However, the growth in the size of the military contracts did not generate enough jobs to counterbalance the enormous number of jobs foregone in services and in state and local government.

California is an excellent example of what happens to a big industrial state during a period of high military budgets. Even when military spending for contracts is high and a large number of troops are based there, it does not make up for the enormous job losses in the civilian side of the economy.

Loss by Sector of the Economy

Another way of analyzing the data is by seeing how many jobs are lost or gained within the different sectors of the economy. Every sector but durable goods loses when the military budget is high. The four areas where people have discretion over their expenditures suffer dramatically: civilian durable and nondurable goods, residential construction, services, and state and local government.

One of the first major expenditures people cut back on is building or buying a new home. This expenditure, the largest that most people ever make, is at the top of everyone's discretionary spending list. This means that hundreds of thousands of carpenters, bricklayers, plasterers, electricians, plumbers, and painters cannot find work, or cannot find it for enough weeks each year to support their families.

There is a vast ripple effect throughout the economy of millions of decisions not to put a new room on the house, not to take a long-awaited vacation, not to buy a new car, not to approve a local bond issue. The figures in Table 16-7 show only the beginning of the story. They do not show the jobs lost, or never created, in wholesale and retail trade as those carpenters, teachers, and automobile production workers look in vain for jobs, take lower paid jobs than their training entitles them to, and then as they both save and spend less money, cost other workers their jobs.

When a multiplier is used, the job effects of losing over one million jobs because of high Pentagon spending is at least another one millon jobs lost. The true job loss is over two million jobs. So the figures on jobs foregone reported in this study are very conservative.

The Economic Impact of Military Spending

Since the Vietnam War, the U.S. economy has shown signs of sustained deterioration. Productivity has been falling. Inflation has been rising. And unemployment rarely goes below 7 percent. The other menace to our economy—inflation—is also caused by high military spending. There are three reasons why high levels of Pentagon spending are inflationary.

First, when people are hired to produce military hardware or to work in the armed forces, they spend their incomes on consumer goods. However, military production does not increase the supply of consumer goods; consumers do not enter the marketplace to purchase missiles, submarines, or tanks. When there is an increase in the *demand* for goods (represented by the purchasing power of people employed on military contracts and as members of the armed forces) without a

TABLE 16–7.   JOBS FOREGONE BY SECTOR OF THE
ECONOMY, ANNUAL AVERAGE 1977–78.

Sector	Civilian Jobs Foregone	Military Jobs Created	Total
Durable goods	−537,050	+612,800	+75,750
Nondurable goods	−229,650	+45,400	−184,250
Residential construction	−380,650	+125,100	−255,550
Nonresidential construction	−226,450	+7,500	−218,950
Services	−1,563,400	—	−1,563,400
State and local government	−1,063,550	—	−1,063,550
Uniformed and non-uniformed military personnel employed in the United States		+2,194,500	
NET JOBS LOST			−1,015,550

corresponding increase in the *supply,* there is more money chasing a constant supply of goods. The result is higher prices and more inflation.

Second, the prices for basic raw materials are forced up by military contractors. As they work on a cost-plus basis, they can pay *anything* for limited resources such as steel, chrome, aluminum, and petroleum. However, civilian businesses rarely work on cost-plus and cannot pay such inflated prices. Some are forced out of business; others pass along the price rises to consumers, thus worsening the inflation.

Third, military spending has been an important reason for the deficit spending of the federal government. As the government has been unwilling to either cut spending or to raise taxes enough to balance the budget, the federal government has been borrowing almost $1 billion a week for years.

As supply of investment capital is finite, this borrowing by the federal government crowds other—largely civilian—investors out of the market and pushes up the interest rates for those remaining. The collapse in the automobile and building markets has been a direct result of heavy federal borrowing.

In 1981, we did a second study entitled "Neither Jobs nor Security: Women's Unemployment and the Pentagon Budget." In this study we found that women lose jobs in forty-nine out of the fifty states when the military budget goes up. Virginia is the only state in the country that increases jobs for women when military spending goes up. All the other states lose. In fact, in 1980, when the military budget was $135 billion, for every $1 billion that the military budget went up, 9,500 jobs for women disappeared. It cost women at that time 1,280,000 jobs.

Why does military spending especially hurt women? The reason is straightforward. On the one side of the equation, women are losing many jobs in services and in state and local governments where they have about half of all the positions. They also lose jobs in durable and nondurable goods production. On the other side of the equation, they do not pick up very many jobs in the military, because they are a very small percentage of the military. In fact, only 1 percent of all women working in the United States work either on military contracts or directly for the Armed Forces. So, cuts in federal programs especially hurt women, as do raises in the military budget, depriving women who are working on the jobs that they have, and depriving women who wish to work at jobs that they could have.

Blacks are also especially hurt through high military spending. In fact, there is not a single group in this country—women, men, Blacks, or whites—that gains overall when military spending goes up.

The deep problems of the American economy cannot be ameliorated until the military budget is cut and the money either left in the hands of citizens through tax cuts or spent on economically productive activities by the government—federal, state, or local.

We make the following recommendations. At this point in our country's history, we can say that the one sure way that any president and any Congress has of simultaneously increasing unemployment and inflation is to raise the military budget. I would like to suggest to the Congress and to the people that its members represent, that the way is now known to cure the two worst ills affecting our economy: unemployment and inflation. The way is simple and straightforward. The Pentagon budget must be reduced, substantively and substantially along the following lines:

1.   Cut $30 billion from the Pentagon's budget, thus allowing 300,000 Americans to have jobs again;

2.   Conduct a congressional investigation into the employment impact of high military spending, with special attention paid both to the sectors of the economy and to the states that suffer employment losses when Pentagon spending is high; and

3.   Pass legislation for the conversion of military industry to civilian industry to meet the urgent national needs of renewable energy, efficient mass transit, and a revitalized industrial base.

■   ■   ■

■ *CHAIRMAN DELLUMS:*   As you have moved around the country in an effort to reeducate American people, what has been the response when you have hit them with these startling statistics?

■ *MS. ANDERSON:*   People are very interested. What the audiences often do is to relax visibly in front of my eyes, once this myth is exploded. They seem to act as if to say: "Oh, now I understand!"

I think there is another rather important figure to be brought out, which also might make sense to emphasize to your colleagues. Even a $1.6 trillion five-year military program means that every working American, every family will work one out of the next five years at the Pentagon. That does not include the other taxes at all. That is not state taxes, that is not local taxes, that is not Social Security taxes, that is not taxes for EPA—nothing. That is just for the Pentagon. Audiences find that a rather startling thought too.

17

THE MILITARY BUDGET AND AMERICAN LABOR

William Winpisinger

■ ■ ■

William P. Winpisinger is a veteran of World War II and a committed union activist who rose steadily through the ranks of organized labor to become the current international president of the I.A.M., the International Association of Machinists and Aerospace Workers.

I WOULD LIKE to summarize a report that I think goes to the very heart of the questions that concern us. The study is "The Cost and Consequences of Reagan's Military Buildup." It was commissioned jointly by the Machinists Union and the Coalition for a New Foreign and Military Policy. The Council on Economic Priorities, in New York City, conducted the study and wrote this report, which I am offering for the record.

I would synopsize it by saying that, ever since Adam Smith, economists have warned that if resources such as capital and labor are used for the production of guns, fewer resources will be available to produce butter. Opportunities to create and strengthen civilian industries are sacrificed when resources are diverted to the military. That traditional economic logic has statistical support, without question. The Council on Economic Priorities found that, when comparing the economic performance of thirteen major industrial nations over the past two decades, those countries that spent a smaller share of economic output on the military generally experienced faster growth, a higher rate of investment, and higher productivity increases. Those, like the United

States, that carried a heavier military burden had poorer overall economic performance.

For years after the end of World War II the American economy appeared capable of sustaining these high arms budgets. In the last decade, however, the accumulated effect of heavy military spending, and particularly the hangover from the Vietnam War, helped to slow economic growth, pushed inflation ever higher, and left a great many Americans today unemployed and pounding the streets, looking for jobs.

Considering our continuing economic problems, it seems to us that President Reagan's proposal to undertake the largest peacetime military buildup in our history deserves more than just careful scrutiny. Would spending $1.6 trillion over the next five years make us safer from military threats? The administration's build-up primarily increases the number of hightechnology weapons we buy but fails completely to redefine the military policy of our country. This sophisticated weaponry being purchased by the Pentagon is often unreliable and typically costs at least twice the initial estimates—and testimony about this abounds everywhere. This makes accurate budget planning difficult and markedly reduces the funds necessary for carrying on normal training and maintenance in our country.

Decision making at the Pentagon is largely controlled by a self-reinforcing network of Defense Department procurement officers, military contractors, and some members of the Congress, particularly those from defense-dependent districts (or at least from what they perceive as being defense-dependent). Mismanagement alone accounts for somewhere between $10 billion and $30 billion a year in Pentagon waste, and that comes from no less an authority than Budget Director David Stockman, who has been known to be seized with moments of telling the truth.

The administration's case for expanded arms spending rests largely on the assertion that the Soviet Union has spent considerably more than the United States on the military over the past ten years. Yet, when we compare total NATO spending with total Warsaw Pact spending, as this study does, we come to exactly the reverse conclusion, even using the controversial CIA estimates. Additional funds for the Pentagon will not create a coherent defense policy, reform procurement practices, or eliminate Pentagon waste. Throwing money at defense is no more justifiable, as our president always tells us, than throwing money at social problems.

The economic consequences of buying more weapons will be substantial. Job, investment, and economic growth absolutely will be sacrificed. Technological progress will be distorted, and social programs aimed at decreasing human suffering will be cut. The high technology sector, an industry important to future American economic growth, will be hardest hit by these arms increases. Even before this build-up, electronics and aerospace firms supplying the weapons industry were functioning very close to their outer limits. We know because we represent a great many people who work in those industries.

The administration has called on industry to increase weapons output faster even than was done during the Vietnam War. To produce the substantially greater number of sophisticated jet fighters and missiles and other armaments that the Pentagon seeks, and is attempting to contract for, these companies must compete against some civilian firms to obtain scarce resources, not the least of which is technically skilled labor, key subcomponents, and, quite often, rare metals. Pitting military demands against civilian production will drive up prices without question, even as the economy recovers from the present recession, and could stifle the ability of U.S. technology firms to compete internationally.

Expanded military spending will not help solve our unemployment problem. Jobs created by arms production will go primarily to technically skilled personnel and few will be created for the semiskilled workers of the country who are most in need of jobs today. The regional imbalance of military spending will continue to shift employment from the older industrial regions of the Northeast and Midwest right down to the Sun Belt and the Southwest.

Social costs are also going to be quite high. The Reagan administration budget represents the most dramatic shift of national priorities since World War II. By severely reducing the civilian budget, the government will drastically limit investment in job-creating areas, like safe energy production, railroads, housing, and mass transit. Reductions in human service programs will add to the hardship of the nation's already poor citizens. Over 60 percent of those below the poverty line today receive almost no assistance from the so-called social safety net programs. The American people should not be asked to bear the burden of this outrageous build-up. Instead, they should insist on a thorough review of U.S. defense policy.

Our union has monitored over this period of time the ever-larger military outlays of the nation as a whole and the congressional reactions that always seem to argue that high defense spending has meant more jobs—and thus is good for the economy and good for the workers. This is, in my judgment, a thoroughly outmoded view.

Some years ago, we sat down and graphed out on a sheet of paper what we had witnessed. We found that military expenditures had escalated on a rapidly rising curve of billions of dollars at the same time that the number of jobs available to our members in industries that were the recipients of the billions of dollars turned in exactly the opposite direction. On completion, the graph looked like the mouth of a trumpet.

As America has continued this nuclear build-up, I, and many members of my union, have become concerned about the future of mankind. It is said that I am irresponsible: Because members of my union earn their living in the industries that build this junk, I am betraying their interests by being such an outspoken opponent of this nuclear madness.

I am an opponent because of all of the reasons stated by Professor Melman. Moreover, I have talked to workers represented by our union in most of the major defense establishments, and I have toured most of the facilities and talked to the people at their machines. I have found very few workers who did not understand the premise that no job, at whatever wage rate, is worth having if you stand in daily danger of being incinerated while you are doing it. That collective concern accounts for the rather dramatic growth of participation in this entire discussion by working people across the country. That awareness accounts for some of the renewed interest by the AFL-CIO and its ongoing search, through a committee on which I serve, for a rational position that can be taken by organized labor on this whole question.

I believe that our members understand that one of the bottom-line conditions that must be present for us to have an acceptable society is that workers must have the right to peace and the fruits of peace. That understanding is increasing, geometrically, in terms of the number of people getting the message. We see increased participation right across the board, certainly by our union, in the growing effort to avert a nuclear holocaust and to challenge any connection between the thought processes that say that because we have jobs in the industry we therefore must perpetuate it. Economic conversion is the answer to that, and Professor Melman presented that case very factually and very completely. Economic conversion is the path down which we will be traveling to deescalate the danger of eliminating human life from this planet.

■   ■   ■

■ *CHAIRMAN DELLUMS:*   Many people in this country perceive the major unions at one level or another being in support of defense spending: (1) Is that correct? (2) Is this because they see no alternatives? (3) What can we do to eliminate this problem?

■ *MR. WINPISINGER:*   There are some common misperceptions about the total position of the institution of labor in the country. Labor —the AFL-CIO as the labor center—is often characterized as being pro-defense spending. I find that to be untrue, beyond the point that is always made. Labor believes, categorically, that we need an adequate national defense. It does not believe we ought to expose our country to the risk of being taken over by some foreign power—not by the identified current enemies or by any potential ones in the future. That position gets stretched hither and yon by some of the observers who sometimes put words in the mouths of the institutions that are not always accurate.

There is a thorough inquiry now in progress by a committee of the AFL-CIO executive council on which I serve. We are looking at the total defense budget in a meticulous fashion never before done by the federation because we no longer think that we are getting reliable stories from the responsible officials in the country. We no longer can depend on what we are getting from the executive branch of government and continue just blindly saying that we want to defend the country and promote national defense.

I can predict that the posture of the federation at the top will moderate substantially over the course of the next year and beyond, in terms of withdrawing support from the kind of outlandish weapons build-up that threatens the very foundations of the world. I think we are going to see progressive—not spectacular, but progressive—changes in the attitudes about the proposals of this administration. Labor will be more solidly on record in the future about their precise posture on defense than at any time in the past.

This is a rather remarkable turnabout. Five years ago, when I assumed the presidency of the I.A.M., we were ensnarled in the same loose characterization that branded all labor as pro-defense. That was accentuated by the fact that we have so many members who work in the defense industries. However, visits to union halls around the country and extensive personal meetings with union members have resulted in quite remarkable revelations.

Transformation in attitudes comes by working at it, by disseminating information, by developing needed pieces of information that are cogent and understandable. We will continue to do that. To the extent that this committee reports to the total Congress in the same meaningful fashion, we will get better and better dissemination of information that the American people can understand. Union members, after all, are just like the entire public. I am satisfied that, if union members, by getting the facts, will react to this issue, then the broad base of the American public will react in much the same manner.

■ *CHAIRMAN DELLUMS:* Would you comment on the argument that our machine tool industry is being devastated by vast military spending?

■ *MR. WINPISINGER:* Throughout our study we used the term "gross domestic product," which we think is a more valid measurement on international comparisons than GNP. Gross domestic product, of course, is gross national product, taking out imports and exports, so that you have the bald picture of performance in each, as regards your domestic position. Military spending is a share of the gross domestic product, versus gross fixed capital formation as a share of gross domestic products. In the comparison of the so-called western industrialized democracies of the "free world" and all of our trade competitors in the world's marketplaces, it indicates conclusively that capital formation lags farthest behind in those countries that spend the most on so-called defense budgets.

The United States, not coincidentally, leads the parade. Japan trails at the end. Japan's fixed capital formation is miles ahead of what is indicated for the United States. It is true not only in machine tools but in a whole range of other very basic and fundamental industries in this country. If all of this is carried to its logical extreme, then it can be fairly said that while we talk about getting off of Third World dependencies for military equipment and so on, that we are actually ordaining ultimately an absolute Third World dependence because we will have so eroded and emasculated the industrial base of America that we will lack the plant and equipment to even build the stuff at some future time. That, in and of itself, is a catastrophe.

A lot of the starry-eyed intellectuals talk optimistically about the post-industrial society and the great service economy of tomorrow. In my judgment they have never satisfactorily answered the question: How can American workers maintain their living standards and life-styles by taking in each other's laundries for a living?

Again, the story is there. It is universal, and this is a comparison of all of our economic competitors. Civilian government spending has a percentage of gross domestic product versus real growth in the same study, and it shows again that those countries that spend the most in the civilian pursuits of their governments, to the exclusion of armaments, are experiencing the best growth, by and large, on gross domestic product expansion. In total compensation per-worker-hour on that basis, compared with real growth, the story is the same. Those countries that spend the least, those countries that compensate their workers the most, are experiencing better growth in their gross domestic product, something that seems to fly squarely in the face of a lot of the conventional wisdom of the economic community, particularly the likes of Milton Friedman and other architects of disaster.

■ *CHAIRMAN DELLUMS:* You mentioned that you agreed that we needed to engage in the process of conversion away from a war economy, in order to save U.S. industry. Do all of your industrial union colleagues agree? If not, what can we do to bring them around to thinking that conversion is a terribly important factor in saving American industry?

■ *MR. WINPISINGER:* Quite candidly, I doubt that there are too many in the labor movement—I am talking now about other labor organizations and others in the labor centers of our country—who are similarly persuaded at this point. I think much of the educational effort that is now in progress is going to bring them to that point of view ultimately, but I really feel that it is down the road a way yet. What we need to do is to continue to investigate the potential of this type of activity to dramatize the case.

I would predict that, down the road, there is going to be a—I don't want to say massive—but a much wider understanding of it than there is right now, and much broader support, in terms of supporting those legislators who think we ought to take the country in that direction. I would tell you right up front that anyone in the Congress who wants to go that way will have the undying support of our organization because we think that is the only future there is for workers.

Obviously, as long as members of my organization are hooked on building F-15s, F-16s, F-18s, and so on, and do not know where they are going to go from there, they have created a rather dead-end specter in their minds. When I meet with them, it is not unusual for the first remark to be: "You're against what we build. Therefore, you are against our jobs." I reply: "It is not that simple, so let us devote the meeting to developing some common understanding. As long as our government elects to pursue the purchase of this kind of hardware and you make it, your job is secure, but it is only limited security, and you are not doing anything in terms of fortifying yourselves for the future." I said to take the most way-out case: "What would you feel if, tomorrow morning, the heads of state in the world convened at some central point and engaged in a discussion about the balance of terror that exists and the potential for obliterating the planet, and, as a result, a declaration of peace was signed by the nations of the world? Where would your job be then?"

I then tell them that I think it is the job of the union, if it really has their long-range welfare as a source of concern, to be developing those plans and getting them in place for that potential eventuality or anything reasonably approaching it. In that context we can then try to put as much collective pressure on our national leaders as possible from our organization to terminate this nuclear madness and have a mechanism in place by which workers are assured a productive future in the interest of promoting the society, rather than blowing it up. We talk about conversion. We plan for it. Legislative proposals have been supported by our union to deal with that, and we will continue to do so because we think that is where the long-range welfare of the worker lies.

■ *MR. DYMALLY (D.-Calif.):* As you observe a rise in military spending, do you see a decrease in blue-collar jobs?

■ *MR. WINPINSINGER:* Absolutely. Ms. Marion Anderson from Employment Research Associates, under a commission from our union about three years ago, studied defense spending and its impact on Machinists Union jobs. We knew the general answer from work she had previously done.

We took the Machinists Union as a single entity and surveyed the situation from that vantage point. The graph that resulted was the mouth of the trumpet—increasing billions being spent and a dramatically decreasing number of available jobs. The conclusion was quite clear—any billion dollars appropriated to the defense establishment, allocated in any other way in the civilian sector of our economy, would have generated anywhere between three and fourteen times as many jobs. Defense is the poorest job generator of every dollar that is spent on anything we do as a society. That is powerful evidence. You would have to be a fool, or tantamount to one, to walk willy-nilly by that bald fact and maintain any support for squandering the resources of our country in that direction.

18

ECONOMIC CONVERSION . . . Retooling for Peace

Dr. David Cortright

■ ■ ■

David Cortright received his B.A. degree from Notre Dame University, an M.A. in Russian history from New York University, and a Ph.D. in public policy from the Union Graduate School of Antioch College. He was a research associate at the Center for National Security Studies and has been the executive director of SANE since 1977. His books include *Soldiers in Revolt*.

THE MILITARY BUILD-UP and its various inimical consequences for the economy have created difficulties that, in my judgment can be solved by paying more attention to the process of economic conversion. We must begin to search for and implement a method that can move us out of our dependency on armaments and toward a healthy and vital civilian economy.

Bills for economic conversion have been introduced in the various sessions of Congress by Congressman Ted Weiss, Senator Charles Mathias, and others. These bills generally contain some of the following provisions. The first is pre-notification of any impending closing. We need to have substantial lead-time in order to plan for the transition of a facility from military to civilian purposes. Similarly, we need to have as part of any economic conversion plan a process by which alternative-use plans can be devised at every major military plant and military base. A good exmple of this is the formulation at Lockheed Missiles & Space, in Sunnyvale, California, of a detailed plan prepared by the work force, the management, and the community development people in that region that says how these facilities at Lockheed Missiles & Space can be utilized for civilian purposes in the most efficient and rational manner by using the existing work force and capital structure. A second requirement of any bill for economic conversion is that kind of a contingency planning process. The various economic conversion bills that have been introduced over the years give defense contractors and communities the opportunity and mandate to prepare such contingency plans for the eventual transition of plants from military to civilian production. An essential part of that process of contingency planning is the involvement of trade union people, some elements of management, and community economic development representatives.

Finally, the third major ingredient of economic conversion legislation is a process of income and job guarantees for the workers themselves. As Bill Winpisinger and others have so frequently stated, the military and the civilians who work in these military plants, and who are in a sense conscripted to work for the national defense should not be made to pay the penalty of a transition to civilian priorities. The people at Lockheed Missiles & Space and at the military bases all around the country should have some guarantee that a transition to peace will not be at their economic expense.

Economic conversion legislation must have job protection and income guarantee provisions, such as we presently have in our automobile contracts and other industrial contracts. That kind of a provision is included in the Weiss legislation and should be seen as an essential part of the process of planning for a more civilian-oriented economy.

A comprehensive program of economic conversion would be immensely beneficial for our society. A number of studies already have been done. They sketch possible scenarios for conversion—for a true reindustrialization program—that would help to build up our civilian economy by reallocating portions of present military expenditures.

One of the best proposals along these lines was a study done in 1979 by the National Center for Economic Alternatives entitled "Jobs to People: Planning for Conversion to New Industries." This study points to a number of areas in our civilian economy that need substantial investment and then discusses the job dividends that might result from that investment. In the area of railroad development, for example, the study talks about a program to upgrade and expand rail corridors between our major population centers and to revitalize our passenger rail network. If we were to invest up to $7 billion a year in revitalizing our railroad system, which it certainly would require, we would generate as many as 164,000 jobs directly each year. In addition, 310,000 jobs would be generated indirectly in ancillary services and industries.

Another study also proposes developing a substantial annual investment in mass transit through the construction of metro-type systems, not just for one or two cities but throughout the country. If we were to invest just $3 billion a year in a substantial program of mass transit, we would generate 78,000 jobs directly and an additional 114,000 indirectly.

Other examples abound. The point is that the monies we now spend on the military in activities that create relatively few jobs and that exacerbate our inflation and taxation and budget priority problems should be redirected to civilian programs that would enhance our security much more assuredly than the proposed arms build-up.

A final example: A major part of our arms build-up is directed at equipping a Rapid Deployment Force that will allow us to intervene in the Persian Gulf to secure petroleum imports. But if we were to take even a part of the money that is going to be devoted to this Rapid Deployment Force—in the illusory and false notion that we can somehow secure our petroleum supplies by force—and devote that money instead to a program of moving toward alternative energy sources at home—toward weatherizing and insulating our buildings and developing mass transit programs and the like—we would be able to eliminate the need for Persian Gulf oil, generate many more jobs here at home, and more substantially guarantee our economic and national security.

The economic aspects of the military budget are vitally important and must be an essential part of any effort to try to reverse the arms race. Indeed, peace and prosperity have to be seen as complementary; we can have one only if we also have the other.

■　■　■

■ *MR. CONYERS (D-Mich.):* You have reminded me that in Detroit, the center of the automobile industry in the United States, we have experienced a serious planning problem with reference to developing alternatives to our dependency on this one particular part of industry, which is so large and pervasive in the Detroit area. Could you comment about the difficulty that we have found in coming up with alternatives?

■ *MR. CORTRIGHT:* It is not an easy problem by any means. I am somewhat familiar with the problems that some of the locals of the Auto Workers have encountered in trying to encourage this process in Detroit. The difficulties they face in trying to develop this process in one isolated community point up the need for a comprehensive national program. It is not possible for one industry or one plant in one city to develop a functional conversion plan without having some connection to an overall program.

The steps I sketched earlier with regard to existing conversion legislation fail to address the problem of a market. Even with a comprehensive planning mechanism in place and subsidies to the local communities to participate in this planning process, we also need to have a program initiated by the federal government that will guarantee that potential markets exist.

Thus a local plant will know that the federal government will be buying $7 billion worth of rail equipment or $3 billion worth of mass transit equipment on a yearly basis for X number of years. Planning at the local level can thus be geared into and connected to an overall national plan. It is really economic planning of a sort—one that can be democratically based and linked to communities with a bottom-up rather than top-down focus.

We already have economic planning today. It is a militarized version of it. It is time to shift this planning towards a civilian focus.

■ *MR. CONYERS:* Your discussion of conversion schemes is very important. The nature, the difficulty, the complexity, and the coordination that will be required are very much misunderstood. We have experienced this. There is probably not an elected official, not only in the metropolitan Detroit area but perhaps in the entire state of Michigan, who has not talked about the need for us to do something other than make automobiles.

But coming up with something effective and workable is enormously difficult. The first problem, on the most elementary level, that you experience is that the automobile industry depends upon steel. The steel industry happens to be having enormous difficulties of its own, presenting another complex international set of circumstances. As a member of the Steel Caucus in the Congress, I know that we sometimes say things diametrically opposed to those working to stimultate the auto industry. We are talking about more than the difference in distance between Detroit and Pittsburgh. Can you comment further on these problems?

■ *MR. CORTRIGHT:* The military budget is currently the only major comprehensive public works program, so people logically gravitate toward it. But there are bottlenecks and production problems even within the military sector. If we have problems in the military industry, then reduce Pentagon demands on industry and begin to shift toward civilian prorities.

I would not want to diminish for a second the enormous complications and difficulties involved in this economic conversion process.

Many people who advocate peace or arms reduction tend to avoid it completely and thereby create a political problem. Our brothers and sisters in the labor movement, who normally would support the goal of a peaceful foreign policy, are forced to stand on the other side because their jobs are directly at stake.

■ *MR. CONYERS:* Do you see any connections between economic conversion and the Humphrey-Hawkins Full Employment and Balanced Growth Act, legislation that was never implemented by the previous administration and that the present administration does not even acknowledge to be a part of federal law?

■ *MR. CORTRIGHT:* We had a number of discussions on this subject a couple of years ago with some of the trade unions, and there was reference then to the Humphrey-Hawkins bill. I do not know that there is an easy answer. Ultimately, in order to get to a level of reduced unemployment and move toward jobs creation in this society, we need to have a coherently and cohesively planned program of economic stimulus around the country. Setting targets and mandating training and the like is not sufficient unless we also address the question of demand. This has been absent from all federal programs, and it will probably continue to be absent for some years.

As we look toward what really is required to restore a peacetime, full-employment economy, we must have some level of economic planning and targeted federal involvement in creating a market and stimultating the development of production. It does not mean that the feds necessarily have to buy and build every railroad line or mass transit system, but they must make the dollars available to small businesses in cities and communities all around the country.

■ *MR. CONYERS:* I appreciate your response. The most important part of Humphrey-Hawkins was the balanced growth aspects. In my judgment, the Humphrey-Hawkins bill countenanced a conversion plan. If it did not, it would seem that one would certainly be appropriate to complement the implementation of such legislation.

■ *MR. CORTRIGHT:* You are correct. The creation of a program for developing jobs in the civilian sector is the central part of conversion.

PART FIVE

MORAL IMPLICATIONS OF THE MILITARY BUDGET . . . A citizen responsibility?

■ ■ ■

We as kids are constantly told to prepare for the future, by going to school, by getting good grades, and saving our money, etc. However, there is no one to guarantee us that there will be a future . . . . We finally would like to assert the hope that the adults of this world don't destroy the earth before we have a chance to change it.

Statement of young people, 6-18 years old, arrested at Lawrence Livermore Laboratory at International Disarmament Day blockade
June 20, 1983

■ ■ ■

THE ISSUE OF, and the need for, constructive nuclear arms limitation is the transcendent moral issue of our time. As Einstein foresaw, we have now reached a stage in the devlopment of weapons technology that threatens to destroy humanity and the planet along with it. This nuclear peril poses a most urgent threat and demands our immediate attention and our constructive response.

The Reagan administration's plan to put in place weaponry that blurs the distinction between tactical and strategic nuclear weapons, and between conventional and nuclear weapons, heightens this peril. This plan and its implementation make a nuclear confrontation between the superpowers all but inevitable.

Throughout the world, citizens of conscience are speaking out, demonstrating, and taking direct action in a collective citizen effort to force their governments to halt and reverse what Ms. Randy Forsberg, founder of the Nuclear Freeze Movement, characterized in our hearings as "the hubris, the arrogance, the almost criminal carelessness of the men who pursue this policy in their confidence that they can play 'nuclear chicken' forever without losing control of the situation once." From Japan to New York, from Moscow to Rome, from Greenham Common in Great Britain to the Trident submarine bases in Connecticut and Washington, dedicated individuals of high moral principle are defining a new foreign and military policy for the future. They are saying that more missiles mean less security; and that new missiles mean an end to foreseeable arms control; that the international politics of military confrontation is too dangerous and archaic for the world of the 1980s and beyond.

Military confrontation must become an anachronism in our lifetime and not just with respect to nuclear weapons. Within our own society and throughout the world, the concentration of resources on the development of both conventional and nuclear arms diverts vital resources from the world economy. Citizens throughout the world, and especially the young, view Washington's increasing bellicosity with alarm and fear. They look to the *people* of the United States to bring a sense of sanity and morality to U.S. foreign policy.

In Part V, the witnesses probe the moral implications of this state of affairs. They call not only for a reexamination of these policies but also for the active involvement of citizens of conscience in leading that reexamination. As one who has fought an often lonely battle in the Congress to expose and restrain U.S. militarism, I welcome their call to citizen activism.

In Chapter 19, Episcopal Bishop John T. Walker sets out very succinctly the twin aspects of this moral crisis. Beginning with the premise that the continued construction of nuclear weapons fulfills no legitimate need to "provide for the common defense," he notes that the burden of the shift of resources to build these weapons falls squarely on the backs of those least able to bear it.

In Chapter 20, Roman Catholic Archbishop John R. Quinn argues forcefully that a nuclear war cannot be reconciled with the theological concept of a "just war"—one that accomplishes more good than evil and that discriminates between combatant and noncombatant. He articulates the view that the continuing reliance on arms sales and military action actually breeds the causes of war—economic dislocation and the suppression of legitimate political movements to redress social grievances.

In Chapter 21, Roman Catholic Bishop Walter F. Sullivan criticizes the expanding military budget on three grounds: First, it spreads death and destruction throughout the Third World; second, it is a theft against the poor, both nationally and internationally; third, it is "killing our children" by breeding fear, cynicism, and bitterness among the future that is living within our midst.

In Chapter 22, Terry Herndon insists that our policies must have a moral consistency and that U.S. policy, and policymaking, should reflect a confidence in democracy. He calls for a national effort to teach the values of peace and nonviolent conflict resolution, chronicling the persecution suffered by those educators who have done so.

In Chapter 23, H. Jack Geiger, M.D., performs a verbal autopsy on the devastating medical consequences of nuclear war, pointing out the cruel hoax of the Reagan administration's plans for civil defense and its assertion that a nuclear war is "survivable." As a medical doctor committed to the preservation of life, he asks the fundamental question: "Do we have the right to end the species?"

In Chapter 24, Dr. Earl A. Molander evokes the potential promise of the democratic process as the key to reversing the perilous U.S. arms policy. He calls upon the citizens of the country to become aware and active, to educate their neighbors and political leaders, and to participate in the effort to return sanity to our foreign and military policy.

In Chapter 25, Philip Berrigan reminds us that we are all responsible for the actions of our government. He argues convincingly that this responsibility requires us to protest, dissent, and resist government policies that immorally push us toward the extermination of the planet. □

19

THE IMMORALITY OF THE ARMS RACE

Bishop John T. Walker

■ ■ ■

John T. Walker, the Episcopal bishop of Washington, graduated from Virginia Theological Seminary. Before coming to Washington, D.C., in 1966, his spiritual service spanned the pastoral and geographical spectrum from Detroit to Uganda.

THE NATURE OF the moral crisis of America's military buildup has two aspects. In the first instance, we are guilty, I believe, of building our fortress of safety on the backs of those who are the weakest among us and who are most vulnerable before the economic crisis that confronts all of us daily. The second aspect of the moral crisis is inherent in the very build-up of a mass of nuclear weapons. It is clear that the use of such weapons and the consequent indiscriminate devastation that would be unleashed on a civilian and defenseless population is unconscionable. The specter of multiple Hiroshimas in the latter fifth of this century is too painful to be contemplated by civilized human beings.

At the outset let me answer two inevitable questions that might be raised by some. We in the clergy are always asked why we are addressing matters that more properly belong to government and military officials—that is, political matters. After all, it is said, it is their job to protect us, and who knows better than they what our needs are.

I will grant that the government is charged to provide for the common defense and, further, that it is the job of the president and the

Congress to know what those needs are and to raise the necessary funds to meet those needs. However, in a democratic society, it is the responsibility of the people to make known their attitudes on those issues that affect their lives most directly. Certainly, the threat of depression and nuclear war have a devastating effect upon all of us.

I am not here as an economic, scientific, or military expert. I am here because I am called by the Church and the Lord it serves to address questions of injustice and matters of peace. The model is given to us by the prophet Isaiah, who calls his people back to the ways of economic and political justice. Isaiah writes, and he is bold enough to quote God:

> Is not this the sort of fast that pleases me; to break the bonds of injustice, to untie the knots of the yoke, to set free the oppressed and to break every yoke? Is it not to share your food with the hungry, and to shelter the homeless poor, to cover those you see without clothing, and not to turn away from your kin?

I believe that Isaiah's words are as appropriate today as they were nearly 3,000 years ago. They are applicable to the United States, the Soviet Union, Japan, West Germany, and every nation on earth. The greatest nations of the world, in the constant escalation of destructive weaponry, are taking away vital resources from the poor and the suffering, and shifting those to military budgets. That may be acceptable in the Soviet Union, but it is unacceptable in a democratic society that is not only charged with "providing for the common defense," but also charged to "promote the general welfare, to insure domestic tranquility and to secure the blessings of liberty to ourselves and our posterity."

The course we are presently on will do none of these. A nuclear war will not provide for the common defense. It will reduce us to rubble. Taking food, clothing, and shelter away from the needy will cause dislocation and unrest; it will not insure domestic tranquility. Nuclear war will not secure the blessings of liberty to ourselves or our posterity. It will produce a frightened, incoherent mass of self-centered and survival-oriented people clinging to one another, as indeed our earliest ancestors must have done in the caves. Because many of us take seriously the God of history, and believe that our God calls us to peace and will not tolerate injustice, we are committed to the same intolerance of war and oppression.

Let me give you some figures to document my assertions. The largest tax cut in American history took place in 1981, along with enormous federal budget cuts, most heavily in the areas of human needs and services. Recent studies indicate some of the shocking results of the tax cuts and the budget cuts. This year, in the 32 percent of households with incomes below $11,500, there is an income loss of $8 billion. For the 6.5

percent of all households making over $47,000, there is a gain of $9.2 billion. This would appear to be the Robin Hood story in reverse.

Along with such economic injustice, we hear the claim that the needs of poor people are to be met by the churches. The $8 billion loss by low-income households speaks for itself. No conceivable swell of charity on the part of the churches and all the rest of the private and voluntary sectors of American society can make up that magnitude of income shift from the poor.

We are not viewing an adequate increase of charity; rather, we are beholding unacceptable increases of injustice. My inner-city parishes are beginning to be overwhelmed by hungry, desperate people. In one city parish, the number of hungry people coming for emergency groceries has tripled since January of 1981. The number of hungry people coming for the parish's meals programs has more than doubled. But still more and more come. In that same parish, the incidents of person-to-person violence are increasing alarmingly. The number of such incidents happening inside the church buildings has more than doubled this year from what it was in all of 1981. I join with the Black clergy of the city who recently invited the president to walk those streets, and I ask that you walk those same streets to see for yourselves the suffering already in evidence.

I am concerned not only with unjust tax and budget cuts, I am concerned also with the stunning increases in our nation's reliance on military force for national security. Many of us have read Jonathan Schell's fine series of articles in *The New Yorker* magazine published in book form as *The Fate of the Earth.* He makes alarmingly clear that a nuclear war will have no winners, that the ecosystem of this fragile planet, our island home in space, will be forever destroyed should humankind be so stupid as to unleash the nuclear demons. At such a time, our nation should be leading the world in efforts to find alternatives to military solutions. But what are we doing?

We are increasing our military spending to $1.6 trillion over this five-year period. The House Budget Committee chair recently observed that, if you spent $1 million every day since the birth of Jesus Christ 2,000 years ago, you would have spent only half what is being proposed for military spending in the next five years in the United States alone. Much of that stupendous amount is slated for a new generation of nuclear weaponry and the capacity to fight a continuing nuclear war. But why? We already have more than enough nuclear weapons to make the radioactive rubble bounce several times. Furthermore, there is no such thing as a morally acceptable continuing nuclear war.

Isaiah quotes God as calling on men and women of religion to "shout for all you are worth, to lift up your voices like trumpets to call My people to account for their faults." It is in an effort to respond to that call that I say to you that the future of this nation and this planet simply does not lie in the immoral shift of the necessities of life from the most vulnerable among us to a military budget, or to those among us who already possess an abundance of all things.

I am trying to respond to that call of God when I say to you that the future security of this nation and this planet does not lie in more weapons. Our only future, our only security lies emphatically in fewer nuclear weapons. The first step in that essential direction is a nuclear arms freeze and a cut in the military budget, to make possible an increase in the national spending for human needs.

Please understand that I do not minimize the difficulties in all of this. The quest for peace is not a simple matter. There is a genuine disagreement on matters of defense. The American who rejects pacifism is no more an ogre than those who call for a freeze of nuclear weapons and ultimately for a reduction. We need, I think, to have an end to name-calling and proceed to discuss nuclear arms reductions and at least try a freeze. I am not sanguine about the Soviet government. There are ample demonstrations of their intent. I cannot believe, however, that the only course open to us is the madness of a continued arms race, at the expense of the humanizing programs that we have supported over the years.

Many of the world's helpless poor look to the United States to break the back of every roadblock to peace. I do not know the precise way to accomplish this. But I ask, in the name of God, that the Congress explore the avenue of a freeze and reduction of nuclear arms, and that you refuse further cuts in the area of human services and restore what can be restored, particularly those things that are essential to life on earth.

■　　■　　■

■ *MR. CONYERS (D-Mich.):* Bishop Walker, what are the moral implications of the arms race?

■ *BISHOP WALKER:* The moral implications of the arms race have to do with the fact that we have embarked on a global strategy that will, in the end, bring about the murder of many millions of innocent people on earth. I do not know how else to put that. I cannot put it more strongly than that.

■ *MR. CONYERS:* What is the responsibility of religiously inclined people and the religious leadership under those circumstances?

■ *BISHOP WALKER:* The responsibility of religiously inclined people, and particularly the religious leadership, is to take a firm stand, which I think many in the churches of America are now doing: Episcopalian, Roman Catholic, Baptist, and what have you. They are taking positions firmly against the continuation of the madness that is involved in the nuclear arms race, which is moving us more and more toward the possibility of a nuclear holocaust.

■ *MR. CONYERS:* What kinds of action do these firm stands take?

■ *BISHOP WALKER:* At the moment they take at least two forms. I think they take the form of more and more sermons addressing the issue. They take the form of more and more forums within churches and synagogues around the country addressing the issue. And they are going to take the form, I suspect, of more and more marches to Washington, D.C., to demonstrate solidarity with those who are opposed to war.

■ *MR. CONYERS:* If that does not work, will they have to take even further steps?

■ *BISHOP WALKER:* I suspect they may. Some already have taken steps. At least one Catholic bishop has taken the position that we ought not to pay taxes. That has not been a position that most of us have yet taken, but I think we may well have to move in that direction, if it comes to that.

The efforts at negotiations with the Soviet Union were an important matter to all of us. As far as I know, those efforts have been supported strongly by every major religious denomination in the United States in the last ten years at least, encouraging presidents and the Congress to proceed with such discussions as SALT I and SALT II. However, we must recognize that this is the first confrontation we have had with an administration that seems quite determined to escalate beyond the levels where we could claim that it was a matter of defensiveness. These weapons have become a real threat to the continued existence of peace in the world.

For at least a year the movement has been spreading within the churches of this country. It began in California and the Northwest, in New York, in Washington, D.C., and began to move across the country. However, I confess that all too often church people, myself included, are too silent on these major issues of concern. I have spoken out on many things; many Episcopalians have and many of the local church leaders have, on matters that related to Vietnam and the present crisis. I can name many who have done that. But that is only a drop in the bucket. When you talk about the vast majority of American religious leadership in American religious communities, we have been silent as a body.

■ *MR. CONYERS:* This new capacity to annihilate the earth must have among some theologians a religious nexus, and all I am asking you is this: Are there some to whom there is no nexus, no religious question, in that? If there are some to whom there is a nexus, what is that? Would you put a religious framework around this subject for me?

■ *BISHOP WALKER:* In 1949 and 1950, Dr. Miller of the Yale Divinity School began writing a series of books, as a theologian, on the whole subject of the moral implications of atomic war. That is not a new subject within the life of the Church.

But you cannot ignore the reality that this is a country with a pluralistic religious background. There are those on one end of the spectrum who are totally pacifistic, who believe that this is in keeping with their particular Christian or whatever religious heritage they may hold to. There are those on the other end who believe in what they call defensive weaponry. They put that within the context of religion; that is to say, they do not believe that God wills that people should sit by and let another people destroy them. They would argue very forcefully and very cogently on this subject. Although I do not always accept their arguments, they would argue that, from a Christian or religious perspective, before a person can sit by and let someone else destroy his or her family, that he or she must develop those elements that would protect them.

In between those two extremes, you have everything across the spectrum. You have those who have relegated the task to government and who are quite willing to challenge the government at times but not to say too much. You have others who want to march in the streets. You have others who want to withhold taxes, and I think that number is going to grow. But in this country, one cannot define religion in such a way that everyone interprets every aspect of religion in precisely the same manner. Nor are they prepared to accept even what I have said here before you today.

I think that what I have said is very mild, but I also think there are those within the religious spectrum of American life who would be quite willing to reject that and say that it is not in keeping with their religious understanding of God's demand upon humankind in the world —namely, they don't believe that they should sit by and let someone else overrun them. They are convinced the Soviets will do this. Therefore, we should build up our weaponry in order to prevent that. I disagree with that position, and I have so stated it.

All you have to do—and I know you have done this—is to look at the attitude of American people, religious American people, toward the feeding of the hungry. The work ethic comes into it and that is a Protestant position, so they will say: "Well, why don't they get jobs?" You can raise all the implications that you want about their not being trained or being able to get jobs, but they will still hold to that. We forget that human beings are very self-centered. I alluded to that in my opening statement—that people are very self-centered. They want to protect what they have. They are sometimes blinded by their self-centeredness into believing that all they need is a gun or a bomb to protect themselves from some external enemy.

20

"THE CROSS OF IRON"

Archbishop John R. Quinn

■ ■ ■

John R. Quinn did his seminary studies at the Gregorian University in Rome, where he earned three degrees in philosophy and theology. Ordained a priest in 1953, he became auxiliary bishop of San Diego in 1967, then served as bishop and archbishop in Oklahoma City before being named archbishop of San Francisco in 1977. He also served as president of the National Conference of Catholic Bishops from 1977 to 1980.

ALBERT EINSTEIN LAID bare the foundations of the problem when he said: "The splitting of the atom has changed everything except our modes of thinking, and thus we drift toward unparalleled catastrophe." Similarly, the famed German theologian, Romano Guardini, at the end of World War II, said that the preeminent human question for the last half of the twentieth century would be whether we could develop the moral capacity to control the power we had created. In the case of nuclear weapons we have created a vast military technology without thinking through its moral implications.

I am convinced that the Church, from a centuries-long tradition of moral analysis of war, has an irreplaceable contribution to make to the debate about that technology. I am equally convinced that the Church cannot be passive or silent in the face of the most dangerous public policy issue of our time.

The Church has a long-standing moral teaching on war, referred to as the "just war" theory. Some elements of this teaching go back as far as Augustine in the fifth century. Two key elements in the "just war" theory are the principle of proportionality and the principle of discrimination. Simply stated, the principle of proportionality requires that, for any war to be justified, the good to be derived from it must be greater than the evil involved. The principle of discrimination states that the indiscriminate killing of populations cannot be justified. Underlying the whole just war theory, of course, is the assumption that war is a very great evil and that it must be avoided until and unless there is no other course for the defense of the nation.

Far from being obsolete, the just war theory is eminently applicable to today's problems and serves to make unequivocally clear the utterly immoral character of nuclear war. When it is a question of war waged with nuclear weapons, warfare takes on a qualitatively new dimension. It is not a matter of merely conventional weapons on a larger scale. Nuclear weapons are qualitatively of a whole different order of destructiveness. Strategic nuclear weapons are uncontrollable once they are detonated. A second quality is their enormous and terrible side effects —their effects on genetic structures for untold generations, their irrevocable effects on our ecological systems, and their effects on the fundamental fabric of our social system.

Thus, on the basis of the two principles of proportionality and discrimination, it should be clear that it could never be morally justified to use strategic nuclear weapons. The good to be derived from their use is far outweighed by the incalculable evil involved, and they also mean the indiscriminate killing of whole populations.

A special question arises today in the case of what is called "limited" nuclear war. This implies the use of tactical weapons against military forces only. In addition, some have pointed out that some nuclear weapons have a lower yield than some large conventional weapons. These considerations would appear, at first sight, to give some moral justification to the so-called limited nuclear war or the use of tactical or battlefield weapons.

In considering the case of the so-called limited nuclear war and tactical weapons, the moral judgment cannot rest only on the two principles of proportionality and discrimination of the just war theory. One must also take into account the psychological factors involved. In other words, there has existed until recently a barrier in people's thinking against the use of nuclear weapons. That barrier may be called "firebreak"—a firebreak standing between conventional and nuclear weapons. The psychological firebreak lies precisely in the perception of the colossal qualitative difference between conventional and nuclear weapons. This firebreak, in turn, created a political barrier contained in the policy of nonuse; this policy dictated that nuclear weapons would never be used. All of this is now being challenged by current discussion of limited nuclear war and the explosion of nuclear weapons as a warning to aggressive forces. The political and psychological firebreak is in danger of being eroded, thus further increasing the possibility of actual nuclear conflict.

Taking into consideration the importance of the firebreak, I believe that:

> *even if* tactical nuclear weapons are controlled within limits of discrimination and proportionality, the very fact of their use today would come under moral criticism because it moves the legitimate order of combat into a new arena. Psychologically, it makes it an easier step for men to resort to nuclear arms. Once this new [nuclear] order of combat is legitimated, it contains potential levels which far exceed both discrimination and proportionality. Nuclear weapons are to be proscribed, not solely because of their size, but because they establish an order and style of combat for which we have no precedents or experience to control its conduct.
> (J. Bryan Hehir, *The New Nuclear Debate*, Council on Religion and International Affairs).

From the standpoint of moral judgment, then, the use of any and all nuclear weapons of whatever size must be clearly rejected. This means that even the so-called limited nuclear war cannot be morally justified.

At this point an obvious question arises. It is the question of legitimate defense. Given the present state of affairs, a closely related question is: If it is not morally permitted to use nuclear weapons, is it morally permissible to have them?

Regarding defense, for Catholic moral thinking there is no question about the right of a nation to its *legitimate* defense. This position was clearly stated by Pope Paul VI in his address to the United Nations when he said:

> As long as men and women remain those weak, changeable and wicked beings that they often show themselves to be, defensive arms will, unfortunately, be necessary.

Two months later, the Catholic bishops of the whole world, gathered at the Second Vatican Council, also stated:

> Certainly, war has not been rooted out of human affairs. As long as the danger of war remains and there is no competent and sufficiently powerful authority at the international level, governments cannot be denied the right to legitimate defense, once every means of peaceful settlement has been exhausted.

I note the use of the qualifier "legitimate" when speaking about defense. Because Catholic moral teaching holds and the Council also stated: "The possession of war potential [does not] make every military or political use of it lawful."

Now to the second question. If it is contrary to all moral principles to use nuclear weapons, is it morally permissible to have them? What this question does in reality is to raise the question of deterrence. Deterrence, at least until recently, has been understood as the ability to prevent or hinder action by threatening dire consequences or undesirable levels of risk.

While, in principle, the possession of nuclear weapons targeted at cities cannot be justified morally, there is some reliable body of moral opinion that would tolerate the possession of nuclear weapons, but only as an interim instrument of policy. This grudging toleration, and on an interim basis, is simply a recognition of the fact that, in the present international system, deterrence has until recently seemed to fulfill, even though in a limited degree, some positive goal. But we must emphasize that the high risks involved in this condition of preserving peace by the threat of terror and of total destruction make it a morally unacceptable long-term strategy.

The Vatican Council itself took a similar position. It noted that:

> Scientific weapons, to be sure, are not amassed solely for use in war. The defensive strength of any nation is considered to be dependent on its capacity for immediate retaliation against an adversary. Hence this accumulation of arms which increases each year also serves, in a way heretofore unknown, as a deterrent to possible enemy attack.

But the Council went on to note that:

> Whatever be the case with this method of deterrence, men should be convinced that the arms race in which so many countries are engaged is not a safe way to preserve a steady peace. Nor is the so-called balance resulting from this race a sure and authentic peace. Far from being eliminated [through the arms race], the causes of war threaten to grow gradually stronger.

Those words, written in 1965, can now be seen to be clearly prophetic. This escalation of forces to a first-strike posture underscores the compelling logic of the Council's prophetic observation that nuclear weapons, even as a deterrent, are not a safe way to preserve a steady peace.

This leads us to the grave moral obligation to move beyond the present situation. Among the reasons for this obligation are the fact that the arms race strengthens the underlying causes that lead to actual war. But a second reason for the moral imperative on all nations to stop the arms race and to reduce their nuclear arsenals is the scandalous, appalling fact that the excessive amounts of money being spent on this madness called the arms race is draining money from the alleviation of the unspeakable human suffering of the growing numbers of the poor and destitute around the world. The poor and the destitute who are citizens of these nations have a right in justice to the help of their governments in raising their standards of life to a truly human level.

The arms race is often promoted as a contribution to the security of nations and peoples. The fact is that the arms race does not ultimately contribute to security since, by straining the world economy and diverting resources from urgent human needs, it only intensifies international instability, it only intensifies the anger of the poor, and becomes, in fact, one of the major threats to security and stability.

No less a military hero than President Dwight D. Eisenhower commented as far back as 1953: "Every gun that is made, every warship launched, every rocket fired signifies, in the final sense, a theft from those who hunger and are not fed, those who are cold and not clothed. This is not a way of life. Under the cloud of war, it is humanity hanging on a cross of iron."

It should not be difficult to understand then why the Second Vatican Council declared: "The arms race is an utterly treacherous trap for humanity, and one which injures the poor to an intolerable degree. It is much to be feared that, if this race persists, it will eventually spawn all the lethal ruin whose path it is now making ready."

We cannot emphasize too strongly that nuclear weapons are not simply conventional weapons on a larger scale. They are qualitatively of a whole different order of destructiveness. Therefore a whole new attitude is called for regarding war—not only by the peoples of the world, by you and by me, but, most importantly, by the governments of the world. Governments cannot with moral justification discuss, plan for, and treat of nuclear war as if there were no qualitative difference. It is an entirely new reality and must be dealt with as such. Leaders and citizens of all nations, and especially of the major nuclear powers, must quickly come to the only possible conclusion there is: The future of the world is in peril unless nuclear weapons and all thought and threat of nuclear war are removed totally and entirely from our world.

Interdependence is perhaps one of the most striking features of our modern world. If no man is an island, no nation is an island, in terms of international relations. Given this fact of interdependence, it is not reasonable to place the burden of retrenchment and disarmament on only one nation. This is the grave moral responsibility of all the nuclear powers together. The Second Vatican Council put it this way:

> Peace must be born of mutual trust between nations, rather than imposed on them through fear of one another's weapons. Everyone must work to

put an end to the arms race, not indeed unilateral disarmament, but one proceeding at an equal pace according to agreement, and backed up by authentic and workable safeguards.

War, it has been said, is neither inevitable nor invincible, but its control is a continuous process requiring intellectual effort, political skill, and moral courage. Is it beyond the scope of dreams that the leaders of the great nuclear powers could take the risk of setting aside all the accumulated prejudices of decades, and perhaps centuries, to come together in complete mutual truthfulness and honesty, to once and for all rid the world of the nuclear menace, from which no one gains and everyone increasingly suffers? Are the risks involved in taking some such initiative any greater than the risks involved in continuing the grim path of nuclear escalation and proliferation? The world awaits the intellectual effort, the political skill, and the moral courage needed for a decisive termination of the arms race and of the nuclear proliferation that threatens to make it a monument of ashes.

21

DUPLICITY AND DELUSION IN AMERICAN FOREIGN POLICY

Bishop Walter F. Sullivan

■ ■ ■

Walter F. Sullivan is the bishop of the Catholic Diocese of Richmond, Virginia. Ordained a priest in 1953, he was an early member of *Pax Christi* and has been a leader in the Catholic bishops' effort to challenge the immorality of the nuclear arms race.

DURING THE FIRST months of 1982 I gave a number of talks to clergy, college students, parish, and ecumenical groups on the whole question of peacemaking. People are beginning to understand, for the first time, what nuclear war would mean for them and for the world. They are anxious, and they are frightened by what they see and what they hear. They, like myself, speak out of love for our country and concern for the human family. They search for what can be done to turn things around.

I want to stress three points. First, the present American policy on arms shipments continues to spread death around the world. Second, the proposed military budget is a theft against the poor of our country and the poor of the world. Third, the overemphasis on national security has had a negative effect on the attitudes and hopes of the young people of our country.

Our world has truly become an armed camp. Armaments are big business. Admiral Gene R. LaRocque has said: "We've made big business out of war in the United States. It is part and parcel of our society." In the last ten years, arms purchases have risen about 825 percent in the Middle East, 422 percent in Latin America and 3,500 percent in Africa. The United States leads the world in the sale of arms. In 1979, we sold over $10 billion worth of arms. As someone said in a discussion I had last week after a peace talk in Lynchburg, Virginia, we sell arms in order to lower the balance of payments. Our economy is geared toward preserving the *status quo* through the sale of armaments around the globe.

We should not be surprised that tensions have risen among nations. Our military weapons keep oppressive governments of the Third World in power. United States aid to military dictatorships that torture and imprison their own people and deny basic human rights make a mockery of American ideals of freedom and democracy. People are dying from the guns and bullets made in the United States. El Salvador is a prime example. Thirty thousand civilians have died in that small country since 1979. Archbishop Arturo Rivera y Damas recently said it so well: "Arms come from the outside, but the dead are all our people."

To be questioned, if not condemned outright, is a foreign policy that seeks a military, rather than a political, solution to human problems. Also to be challenged is a policy that promotes militarism rather than economic development around the world. Our country always appears to be on the wrong side of history. By supporting oppressive governments, we align ourselves on the side of power and wealth and alienate ourselves from the masses of people. We make suspect our own announced ideals of freedom, self-determination, human dignity, and justice for all.

With regard to the second point, the arms race is also to be condemned as a crime against the poor. Our Church has called it an act of aggression. For even when the weapons are not used, the very cost alone kills the poor by causing them to starve. Two-thirds of the world's population lives in poverty. The world's powers spend more than $500 billion annually on armaments. The arms race consumes vital resources. It deprives the poor of the basic necessities of life.

Last summer I saw at first-hand the terrible deprivation of people in Latin America. Peace will never be achieved in our world unless we first work for a just world order where human dignity and human rights are insured. True peace cannot be based on the power of arms, but on the power of justice. Human development must be the highest priority of our government, rather than the preservation of war machines and economic self-interests that keep people enslaved and dependent.

Fear tactics are used to justify every expenditure emanating from the military-industrial complex. I believe we have a duty to unmask the idolatry that places national security above all else. Are we really secure as a nation if, because of defense spending, the most defenseless of our own are made to suffer? How can we be secure as a nation knowing that our own needy and marginalized are being deprived of basic human services? How can there be any national will when so many are unemployed, when children are deprived of food, when the handicapped are again neglected, when the elderly must do without, when young people cannot receive an education, when the poor have health benefits taken away?

The list is endless of those citizens who no longer seem important. Yet, we wonder why crime has increased in our communities, why violence has become the favorite American pastime. When resources are transferred from welfare to warfare, our country casts aside millions of people who have a right to share in this nation's blessings. What message do we give to the world when we opt for the *status quo,* the privileged, at the expense of the powerless? We are beginning to appreciate the negative side of arms sales abroad when we experience first-hand here at home a defense budget that ignores the cries of our own people.

My third point is this: Living in a national security state, which I consider our country to be, under the growing threat of nuclear war, has had a disastrous effect on the attitudes and ideals of the young people of our country. During the past month I have talked with many high school and college youths in southern Virginia. A vast majority of them truly believes that a nuclear holocaust is inevitable. Unfortunately, some even see it now as part of God's plan for the world, an analysis to which I do not subscribe. A survey of attitudes of college students from a book entitled *When Dreams and Heroes Die* shows that most youth believe that they are "living on the *Titanic.*" They feel that the world situation is bad and will only deteriorate further. Pessimism then leads to a sense of helplessness. There are no dreams among our youth for a better tomorrow or for a meaningful future. Today's prevailing attitude is that you live for the day, get what you can, spend what you have, and have as little concern as possible for others. Dr. John Mack, a psychologist and psychiatrist, has found that adolescents are deeply disturbed by the threat of nuclear war; they have grave doubts about their future and their survival. They experience fear, cynicism, and bitterness. They feel unable to think ahead in any long-term sense. In summary, the arms race, the threat of no tomorrow, has caused the young people of our nation to grow up without the ability to form stable ideals or to have a sense of continuity with the past.

Many parents ask why the Church is not doing more for the youth. They feel a sense of failure in not being able to hand down religious and intuitive values to the young. What we all must realize is that, by living in a world with apparently no future, the values and the ideals of our families, of our society, and even our country, become totally irrelevant. I do believe that, for the youth, dreams and heroes have truly died, with nothing stable or meaningful to replace them. Certainly more guns, and more weapons and more killings, have signalled to our youth that our country is headed in one direction and only one direction, and that is eventual conflagration.

I stand with many others to protest the present arms policy of our country. For me, it is suicidal. It will only lead to our own capital punishment. Our weapons keep people in poverty and oppression. Our weapons tell the youth of our nation that they really have nothing to live for. Our militaristic policies fly in the face of our stated ideals of freedom and justice and democracy. Instead, they foster repression, injustice, and poverty.

The arms race does not form a more perfect union. The arms race does not insure domestic tranquility. The arms race does not provide for the common defense. The arms race does not promote the general welfare. And finally, the arms race does not secure the blessings of liberty to ourselves and to our posterity.

■　　■　　■

■ *CHAIRMAN DELLUMS:*　What is your position with respect to multilateral versus unilateral action on the issue of nuclear and conventional weapons disarmament?

■ *BISHOP SULLIVAN:*　I personally believe that nuclear weapons are immoral, but in all of my public talks I have said that I do not favor unilateral disarmament, I favor unilateral initiatives. I would like to see our country take some symbolic action to tell the world that we really are serious about peace.

The message coming from our government has the overtones, over and over again, that we are getting ready for war, and I am afraid this policy is going to become a self-fulfilling prophecy. I oppose unilateral disarmament because I think it is unworkable. I just believe that it will not happen. Therefore, I very much support what we call a bilateral nuclear freeze and other bilateral discussions for disarmament.

■ *CHAIRMAN DELLUMS:*　In its attempts to justify this massive increase in America's military budget, a number of us are suggesting that the tragedy of this administration is that it perceives the problems of the world as primarily military—that they should be solved in military terms. Many of us have taken objection to that. We are suggesting that, on an increasing basis, the world's problems do not lend themselves to military solutions. They are economic, political, social, and cultural and must be solved in those contexts. Your sophisticated analysis of our problems leads you to the same position. Given this similarity of views, how can we, from our respective positions, mobilize the American people and educate them to begin to understand the nature of the problems as you and I perceive them at this moment?

■ *BISHOP SULLIVAN:* I believe that the task of the Church is to raise the level of consciousness of our people about what is happening in the world today. When we talk about the oppression of the Third World and try to indicate why there is so much poverty, why it is that so many people are living under oppression, I try to relate how militarism and military solutions are ways of keeping people in poverty.

I do believe that the task of the Church is to raise the consciousness level of our people. We have to talk in terms of human rights and human dignity. We have to see that the world is a single entity, that we are one family, that the oppressions in the world are not going to create peace. If we do not have peace in the world, it is because we do not have a just world. So we need a just world order, a world that is more humane, in order to bring about peace.

In my judgment, the task is to make our people more aware of the relationships between peace and justice, economic development and disarmament. But these must go hand in hand. We will never have peace in the world unless we promote justice. But peace will never be achieved, I am convinced, through just duplicating and multiplying military hardware around the world.

■ *CHAIRMAN DELLUMS:* Bishop Sullivan, the Pope is an internationally known figure. How can the Pope assist in globalizing religious concern around the struggle to end the nuclear arms race? If I could ask you to be that presumptuous, as an American bishop, how would you advise the Pope to maximize his role in globalizing concern about the nuclear arms race?

■ *BISHOP SULLIVAN:* What the Holy Father has done is visit many countries of the world; he has personally seen the terrible poverty, and he is beginning to raise these critical issues. Of course, in his own country, he sees the whole question of Communist dictatorship, of what a dictatorship can do to individual freedom and human rights.

What I think has happened in the Church is that we find increasing opposition against nuclear armaments and the frightening consequences of what is happening in the world today. We find the voice of the Church becoming stronger and stronger, and the same is happening here in the United States. You are certainly aware of a number of bishops speaking out, from their own faith perspective. I feel it is very important that, when we talk about the whole question of militarism and nuclear weapons, we have to speak from a faith basis. In other words, I am not against nuclear arms just because the Pope tells me to be against them. I do that out of personal conviction. I think that is where we have to lead our people, to form their consciences. I see the whole issue as a right-to-life issue, a respect-for-life issue and, until we identify it that way, we will not make real strides.

■ *CHAIRMAN DELLUMS:* The nuclear bomb can abort all life. It would seem to me that those concerned about the right-to-life would certainly want to challenge the insanity of the nuclear arms race. We know that there are segments of the American religious community that have raised the issue of the right-to-life in rather narrow terms. You have raised it in much broader human terms. Do you anticipate that the Church will become much more active on Capitol Hill with regard to this particular threat to life, as have a number of people who have come to the Hill in more narrow terms to discuss the issue of the right-to-life?

■ *BISHOP SULLIVAN:* I would hope, first of all, that we would begin to convert our own people. I feel that is our primary obligation and responsibility. I see the value, of course, of political action. This is where the decisions are made. I am not so sure that we should parade up here as Church members, but as citizens who are concerned and who have a right to speak out.

But I do see that people are becoming concerned, people that you would never dream of doing so. These people are beginning to speak out from their own worries, fears and anxieties. I feel that what the Church needs to do is then to interpret and bring out the moral principles of what we stand for. I do see a form of coalescing on what I would call the whole right-to-life movement, that we have to be consistent. I do not think we can be only one-issue people. We have to be consistent all across the board on the sacredness of all life. As you said, a nuclear holocaust would abort all the people of the world.

■ *MR. CONYERS (D-Mich.):* Have I perceived correctly that the Catholic Church has become more active on the question of not only antinuclear activity but also on the question of oppressive dictatorships and governments, particularly in Central and South America? If so, why is that the case?

■ *BISHOP SULLIVAN:* In the area of the oppressive governments in Latin America, many of our American priests and sisters are missionaries in these countries, so they see what is actually happening.

They are working among the people, especially among the poor. They see a real dichotomy between their experience and what is being told to them, either by the press or by the American government as official policy. They see a direct contradiction. What is happening is that there is a real conflict between the position of the Catholic Church in communication with the Church in Latin America, which is very Catholic, and what seems to be the official position of our government.

Also, you mentioned the whole question of the arms race and armaments. The Church is beginning to speak out. What is really good is that individual bishops are speaking out from personal conviction.

■ *MR. CONYERS:* Is there a religious dogma, to which certain religionists subscribe, that precludes them from supporting their government's military escalation?

■ *BISHOP SULLIVAN:* For me, the religious issue is the dignity of the human person. That is revealed to us in the Scriptures—the equality and the dignity of every person under God. From that flow basic human rights. Among those rights is the right-to-life. You see that the Church is very much on the side of life. The Church is also identifying with the poor of the world, especially those in Latin America, where the Church has made a decision to be the public advocate for the poor.

What we find is that our government, through massive military expenditures, through the use of arms, is going directly contrary to our religious convictions, that innocent people are dying. Second, people continue to be oppressed in poverty because of these large military expenditures. It is very clear that someone has to speak out for those who cannot speak for themselves. That is why the Church is taking an advocacy role on their behalf.

There are many documents attesting to this from the teachings of the Second Vatican Council. Many statements of the Pope very clearly condemn the arms race and condemn the threat of nuclear holocaust. One thing we have to realize is that, just because the Church says something, it does not mean that automatically our Catholic people are going to believe it or accept it. In some way that has to be translated into their consciousness. The peace movement in the Church is coming from two directions: One is from official teachings, and another is from the experiences from the grass roots. These two forces are beginning to converge, and something is finally happening, thankfully.

■ *MR. CONYERS:* I agree with your assessment that it flows in both directions. One of the projects that has interested me and makes these questions so important is that I have begun to ask myself what is the religious connection? Wherein does it say to anybody that you are not fulfilling your Christian obligation if you support this incredible build-up?

■ *BISHOP SULLIVAN:* The problem in the Church, in justice issues and peace issues, is that we have compartmentalized our lives. We have emphasized religiosity and we have often claimed that one is religious just because he or she attends church on Sunday. But that is not enough, especially in the age of nuclear peril and rampant human injustice.

What has happened is that we do a lot of things in the name of religion. I think we oppress people in the name of religion. You can find your favorite passage in the Bible to justify almost anything you want to do, but we have to examine and analyze the entire picture. What has happened though, in defense of everybody, is that only recently has the nuclear question hit us over the head like a sledgehammer to attract our attention and cause us to say: "Hey, what is happening in our world? What type of world do we want? Why do we have to live this way? Why do we have to exist under fear?"

That is a starting point. The starting point is always the experience; it is not some religious truth on the wall over there. The starting point is your needs and my needs, the needs of your family, the people we live with, to try to find meaning in life. Suddenly our experience is telling us something very different. The important thing is to go back into our religious roots, to find answers and meanings in our basic beliefs.

To me, this is a human question. We keep emphasizing that this is a religious issue. It is basically an issue of all humanity. Whether a person is religious or does not practice any religion is not the point. We are all in this together. What we are beginning to say is that a lot of our differences are very unimportant if we are all "on the *Titanic.*" I would hope that we examine the human issues in light of our religious experience, which gives us, we hope, answers and meaning.

I believe that if the Church cannot come to terms with the peace issue and the justice issue, the Church is going to be completely irrelevant to people because it is not touching people where they are—in their experience, in their lives. At the same time, and this is the challenge, the Church has an opportunity to give leadership in presenting and perpetuating those true Christian traditions that are an integral part of Christ's teachings.

My personal belief is that I do not think my role is to preach to you. My responsibility is to preach to our Catholic people, to share my faith with them in an effort to turn this whole attitude around. We have to raise the conscious awareness of our people to what their religious values should be telling them.

■ *MR. CONYERS:* Do you have a view on how all this is going to work out?

■ *BISHOP SULLIVAN:* I am filled with hope. I look to the Holy Spirit. We have no option because it truly is a matter of life or death. It is as simple as that. Thankfully, people are becoming concerned.

I spoke one night in Pittsburgh at a parish. There were about 450 people. Many of them were elderly people, people who said: "I never thought about this before. Nobody ever told me. Nobody is speaking." That is what we need to do. It is my responsibility to try to proclaim the word with the clergy and our people, not to come here to try to convert you.

■ *MR. GRAY (D-Pa.):* I am a Baptist minister, by profession, as well as being a member of the House of Representatives. About three weeks ago, I had the opportunity to visit the Pope, His Holiness, to discuss a series of issues—ranging from the discriminatory and insensitive treatment that our government is pursuing with regard to Haitian refugees, and which the Catholic Church has been extremely active on, to the question of oppression in South Africa of Blacks, and also questions with regard to Latin America.

The trip was prompted by the fact that the Pope has spoken out very clearly with regard to specific issues of justice and that the whole question of justice is not simply an ontological one that is up in the heavenly realm somewhere. The Pope's speaking out on specific issues, such as Poland, has brought justice from the theological clouds down to everyday existence, where human needs are paramount.

In Philadelphia, this past weekend, there was a rally for disarmament that had over 15,000 people present. That was the first such rally that we have been able to have in Philadelphia in probably twenty years with that size crowd. It seems to me that a large reason for that has been the new social activism that I see emerging from the church community.

In this context, what has happened in the religious community to cause this new social activism? It is something that we have not seen in this country since the Civil Rights era, and maybe since some of the protests against our immoral adventurism in Vietnam. What has happened that has caused this new social activism by the clergy?

■ *BISHOP SULLIVAN:* There is no one single thing. What is happening throughout the world has made us more aware that we live in one world. Then the application begins to come home to what is happening to our own people. I do believe that the present policies of our government have certainly increased the fears and concerns of people. The religious community is beginning to identify, articulate, express concern, and really try to proclaim the basic values and needs of the poor, the powerless, and the victimized people of our society.

What I have found in the ecumenical community is a growing closeness of spirit and commitment. This is not just a Catholic question. The Catholics might be giving a certain amount of leadership and courage to others, but other denominations are also actively involved, in word and deed. Just a week ago at an ecumenical gathering in Richmond, where I was the keynote speaker, eight religious groups were represented there, planning for a statewide ecumenical conference on the whole question of peacemaking.

To me, it is a movement of the spirit. That is the only way that I can describe it. I always like to say what Saint Thomas Aquinas said: "You never have courage unless you first get angry or indignant. Something has to move people from apathy." So, I think there is a spirit that is beginning to well up in people's hearts and minds.

■ *MR. GRAY:* What do you think has made people angry, thus allowing this new spirit to billow the sails of faith?

■ *BISHOP SULLIVAN:* Most significantly, there is the insensitivity of our government. It seems to be unresponsive to the concerns that are being raised. So, the voices become more strident in saying: "What is happening?" I get very, very upset, personally, when I see and hear leaders of our government lying to our people. I cannot describe it any other way. I do not think that is the way to do things. I feel, as a citizen, I have a right to the truth. Our leaders should not equivocate. You do not justify a policy by not telling the truth.

Another thing that has motivated me a great deal is that in preaching about peace I begin to realize where the attitudes of our people are. We have a lot of conversion work to do. The prevailing popular attitude is more defense, more defense. That is the whole mind set. When you try to present an alternative position, or try to develop a whole new attitude, right away you are charged with being soft on Communism and told you ought to go back to Russia, as some people write and say to me. Others say that I am unpatriotic or "too political." So, in speaking out, it begins to heighten my own convictions.

■ *MR. GRAY:* As you well know, Bishop, there are some religious groups in America, often called fundamentalists, sometimes referred to as the Moral Majority and other names, who do not agree particularly with your viewpoint and the viewpoint of many people with regard to the arms race. They almost give to the arms race a sort of divine inspiration, that it is part of godliness to increase the maddening build-up of nuclear weapons. How do you deal with that viewpoint? How do you respond when they claim America as the citadel of godliness facing an ungodly world?

■ *BISHOP SULLIVAN:* I find that I do not take direct issue. I would make a mistake by running around going after the Moral Majority, or being critical of them. I am not sure what the Moral Majority is. I guess the opposite is the "immoral minority," to which, maybe, I belong. I think it is very much overemphasized. I feel that my primary task is to proclaim my convictions and not to attack other people. There are a lot of our people who believe in the defense budget and I accept that—as a transient reality. They are not bad people. But I do think persuasion and inspiration are the only ways we are going to turn them around, not by getting into arguments with them.

■ *MR. GRAY:* Finally, there is the inherent conflict between the ideal and the reality. T.S. Eliot once had something to say about the shadow falling between the two. How do you respond to the question, when it comes to the arms race and nuclear proliferation, that your position is a position of faith, which is the ideal, while the world is not an ideal place?

■ *BISHOP SULLIVAN:* Most of us are trying to achieve peace in our world. I do not disillusion myself by saying that the world will someday be absolutely peaceful. But that does not absolve me from becoming involved in the effort to make the world a more peaceful place in which to live.

The same would hold for poverty. It is a misuse of the Scripture quote: "The poor you will always have with you," to mean that God wants poor people to be poor and lets us go on our merry way. Obviously there will be continued injustice. There will still be violence in society, but to say, "I cannot do anything," is helplessness and hopelessness, and I cannot do that. If I felt it were hopeless, I would not get involved.

But I feel that my faith calls me to be a person of hope. If there are enough people who are willing to stand up, then I do think it will turn the whole situation around. I do not think it is an ideal; I think it is a way we have to live to survive. I think it is very real, and maybe because it is real, people are beginning to address the question.

■ *CHAIRMAN DELLUMS:* Of all of the very powerful things that you said, one factor that struck me profoundly was your delineation of the impact on the children of this society and the thought that they have deeply internalized that they are "living on the *Titanic*." I had to fight back my emotions when you made the comment that we have crushed the hopes and the dreams of our children because I draw the conclusion that people who have no hope and who have no dreams are dead people.

I think one could argue that, in pursuing this madness, we are, in very real terms, killing our children because we are killing their hopes, killing their dreams, and killing their future. It is a great moral failure in any society that contemplates action that destroys its own children and destroys its own future. That, to me, is an incredible indictment of our society and the policy we are presently pursuing.

22

EDUCATION, VALUES AND THE ARMS RACE

Terry Herndon

■ ■ ■

Terry Herndon received his B.A. and M.S. degrees from Wayne State University in Detroit. He taught in the secondary school system in Warren, Michigan, before going to Washington to work for the National Education Association where, on May 1, 1973, he assumed the duties of executive director, a position he held until his retirement in 1983.

WHAT ARE WE defending and securing for our posterity when we deny higher education to millions of young people, close schools for children, and add their teachers to the unemployed, so as to divert the money to a five-year enhancement of the world's most sophisticated conventional and nuclear arsenal—an arsenal that is already sufficient to destroy not only our enemies, but ourselves and the rest of the world?

To build redundant weapons with dollars stripped from the millions of children served by Head Start or from the millions served by Title I, to install the MX missile system with money wrenched from the education of handicapped children and aspiring college students, or to build computerized tanks that don't work with dollars from poor retirees is to forego the enrichment of life in favor of the termination of life. It is to abandon our proud legacy to our fear of a foreign power. It is to subordinate our confidence in the efficacy of democracy to a certain faith in military intimidation. It is to sacrifice our self-determination to reaction. These are sacrifices we need not make and ought not make. It is the wrong path. I do not have a single personal objective that is enhanced by a nuclear holocaust. I do not have a single personal objective that is advanced by annihilation of the Soviet people, and, yet, I am taxed and taxed to make that increasingly probable.

The United Nations study *Nuclear Weapons: Report of the Secretary-General* (Autumn Press 1980) opens with the observation that:

> It is obvious that the nuclear weapons arsenals existing today are many times larger than what the superpowers need for credible deterrence. Furthermore, their technological development makes it increasingly difficult to maintain the so-called balance of terror, and the risk that it will get out of hand is growing.

The "get out of hand" part is a source of great anxiety to me and many whom I represent. It may be more of a contemporary reality than a prophecy. The United States of America is a great beacon of prosperity, tranquility, and liberty, but we are showing the world an increasingly futile face. Our dependence on the implements of war seemingly threatens our will and our capacity to establish justice, to insure domestic tranquility, to promote the general welfare, and to secure the blessings of liberty. Moreover, it may provide more common jeopardy than common defense.

Clearly, the common defense is to be found only in the aggressive pursuit of peace. The imposition of a self-serving *Pax Americana* on the people of the world through military intimidation is impossible, and the persistent effort to do so does not promote our national security or our common defense.

Neither we nor the Soviets can rely on the seas to shield us from one another any longer. As the missile flies, we are only thirty minutes apart, and the span diminishes with each new technical development or strategic placement for launching devices. The wonders of science have brought us to the imperative that we grudgingly respect our reciprocal destructive power. Our windows of vulnerability are opened, but they will never be closed. We have only but to stop throwing stones if we are to survive.

I, and most of my colleagues in the NEA, see this reality and know that the security and well-being of our nation is enhanced by the instruments of peace and not war. We must persist with our commitment to the fundamental promises of our nation and extend this legacy to all of our people. Then, standing morally erect, we can offer to the peoples of the world a friendly, helping hand.

It is for the Congress to decide whether we will be the envy of the world or the anxiety of the world. The better course is the tougher course. It requires a solid and a fair economy; a healthy, well-educated and hopeful population; and, a stable, peaceful world order. The other is easy. It requires only arms, arms, and more arms.

■   ■   ■

■ *MR. CONYERS (D-Mich.):*   Is it accurate or fair for us to put this burden on the Congress? It seems to me that what we are really saying is that we have to change the Congress. Merely taking all of this accumulated testimony, which has never been put together in one spot before, and putting it on all of the members' desks—assuming that they read it—may change nothing, if I may be so bold to suggest that.

My experience is that it would not. So, these hearings have several functions: One, they call attention, intellectually and rationally, to an incredible peril that threatens the nation and the world. That alone would justify these hearings. Second, they serve to remind everybody who is wondering if we have taken leave of our senses that there are some people in the federal government who perhaps more accurately recognize what the situation is. Third, they pose the very difficult question, Where do we go from here? As the leader of the most progressive educational organization in the United States, it seems to me that your views on this would be very important to this committee.

■ *MR. HERNDON:*   The message that I am delivering to every group that I talk to is that every American citizen has the responsibilty to express himself or herself on this question. One of the extraordinary elements of life in a democracy is that each citizen shares in the responsibility for the direction of the government.

At the present time most Americans are either indifferent or perceive themselves to have little or no influence to exercise in regard to armaments and the military budget. I would exhort them to express themselves. I would exhort the members of the NEA to make the peace-war antithesis one of their most fundamental considerations in all of the political judgments that they make in the coming months and years. I have exhorted them to recognize that the NEA, like every other institution in the United States, cannot continue to set this issue aside as though it belongs to somebody else while we pursue our narrower interests. I believe that this is, in part, my responsibility.

On the other hand, there are those who do have the opportunity to cast votes in Congress. While I anticipate that there are many people in the Congress who will not be moved by the testimony, I do think that it is imperative that those who sit in the Congress use whatever influence is available to them in that quarter to bring some sanity to our national policy.

■ *MR. CONYERS:* Well, what about you people going out and defeating people that Mr. Dellums cannot persuade?

■ *MR. HERNDON:* I have indicated that I am going to take a shot at that. I believe I have to do what I have to and what I can do. With all due respect, I believe that you need to do likewise. I doubt that either of us will make a convert of the chair of the House Armed Services Committee. I have indicated that, failing that, we will endeavor to do our political part, but I do not intend to ignore him in the interim. I believe that I must speak.

I hold my own position on at least quasi-political terms. I have already had many letters of the type that you suggest would be addressed to you from people who suggest to me that we ought to let that lay and not alienate members of Congress who believe strongly in nuclear armaments because we want their vote on an education bill.

I think there will have to be large numbers of Americans, particularly leaders like myself and members of Congress, who are willing to risk being called a fool and the indictment of "peacenik" and perhaps even to wear it with pride. There must be a collective voice that wells forth from the people. Those of us who have leadership roles must use the platforms that are available to inspire that voice and to cause it to come forth.

■ *MR. CONYERS:* Is there something that can be done to deal with the issue of teaching war and peace in our educational system?

■ *MR. HERNDON:* I think there is something that can be done. But I am not terribly sanguine that it will be as universal as I would like. Education for war and peace does take place throughout the United States to varying degrees. One of the more interesting programs, and perhaps it is one that should be brought to your attenton, is carried out by the Stanley Foundation in Muscatine, Iowa. They have thoroughly internationalized the entire school curriculum, including physics, biology, social studies, literature, in all of its aspects. They spend a great deal of time and energy looking at cultural differences, cultural harmony, and international understanding as a basis of world order.

However, it is not likely that we will find many school boards throughout the United States putting their blessings on teachers who carry anti-defense budget positions into the classrooms of the United States. That would be perceived as propagandistic and would probably significantly enhance the measure of unemployment among teachers. But I am going to persist in my dialogue with school administrator organizations and with school board associations in an effort to find ways that we can work together to make that possible in more places.

■ *MR. CONYERS:* I deduce from that, then, that teachers who have a pro-defense bias are more secure in their employment in many public school systems than those who want to teach the question of war and peace without any bias?

■ *MR. HERNDON:* I describe the prevailing condition. I think that security and tenure go to those who create the fewest waves, and so the answer is yes. I think the more secure position for a teacher today would be to shy away from the issue altogether.

■ *MR. CONYERS:* Does the NEA defend those teachers who lose their jobs or whose promotions are jeopardized because they would dare teach the truth on this subject or even introduce it into the curriculum?

■ *MR. HERNDON:* The answer is an emphatic yes, to the tune of about $9 million or $10 million a year. All of that money is not spent on that question, but a chunk of it is spent on freedom of political expression, freedom of speech, and the other associated questions. We will defend those teachers; and, therefore, we will be indicted.

■ *MR. CONYERS:* Mr. Chairman, I must express some concern about a dimension that has been uncovered here of which perhaps the Chair was aware. It had not occurred to me until our distinguished witness's presentation that the teachers in the American school system can be jeopardized in the security of their professonal activities by merely introducing, or attempting to introduce, into the curriculums of the school system the subject matter of war and peace.

That is a dimension that those in the Congress who are on the Education and Labor Committee—and perhaps other kinds of committees, certainly the Congressional Black Caucus, whose constituents overwhelmingly populate many public school systems, and many of whose teachers are members of the NEA—ought to inquire into. I had no inkling before now that a teacher could lose his or her job by trying to promote a more intelligent curriculum.

■ *MR. HERNDON:* Might I embellish that point? One of the great difficulties in talking about education in the United States is that the schools are operated by some 12,000 to 13,000 different local authorities. You describe for me any hypothetical condition, and I will find for you a school district where it exists.

The question you posed inquires as to prevailing conditions: Is the prevailing pattern throughout the United States one in which a teacher would be more secure supporting the defense establishment or more secure in stirring up dissatisfaction with the defense establishment? Clearly, among those choices, the former is the more secure in the largest number of places. There are growing numbers of states that now have approved textbook selection lists. A teacher can be in jeopardy in some quarters for using materials that do not appear on those lists.

There are growing numbers of right-wing, anti-academic freedom committees, groups, and individuals who are spending a great deal of time and energy scrutinizing teaching materials and textbooks and endeavoring to persuade legislators and state education authorities to revise those lists.

One of the patterns that emerges among those groups and committees is that anything that questions the defense establishment is anti-patriotic and therefore ought to be purged from the list. There are a variety of traps to which the dedicated teacher is exposed. I stand on my summary response earlier—that the more secure course is to keep your mouth shut and let what happens happen.

■ *MR. CONYERS:* I just want to make sure you understand the difference between stirring up dissent about the war budget and trying to develop a more fully intelligent curriculum that deals with the matters of war and peace. It seems to me that that is a valid subject and, in this environment that you quite accurately describe, we need to be forming some committees to review book lists ourselves. We need to have educators who possess the skill and experience in teaching to argue that we can introduce the question of nuclear peril into the discussions.

■ *MR. HERNDON:* I certainly agree with you that it ought to be, if possible, a mandatory subject of study. Second, I have to observe that the difference between teaching the truth and exposing people to the truth, and stirring up trouble, may be more theoretical than real.

I have a passionate conviction that anybody exposed to the truth in regard to this issue will not maintain support for the present course of our government—that anybody exposed to the truth on this issue will be stirred up. In the defense of that teacher, we then get into the debate of whether the individual simply was exposing one to the truth or stirring up trouble. The NEA's position will, of course, be that they were exposing students to the truth and that they ought to be protected by the state in carrying out that responsibility. But there are numbers of places where the indictment will be that this was, in fact, stirring up trouble.

■ *CHAIRMAN DELLUMS:*   As you described our system of education, it seemed to me that it would be an interesting idea to draft
legislation that placed the federal government in a role of providing
incentives for the local school systems to embark upon a course of
education in the area of peace and nuclear disarmament. This may very
well be an appropriate role for the federal government. The government could make some resources available to the local school systems
and say: "If you pursue this course, we will provide *X* resources in order
to do it." Perhaps our responsibility at this point is to produce that kind
of incentive if we are committed to the idea ourselves, and to continue
to operate within the framework of the levels of jurisdiction of our
educational system.

■ *MR. HERNDON:*   I think that is an excellent idea. I think I could
add to it a specific variation. In the 1960s, when our society was extremely interested in enhancing its capacity in the sciences, we invested many millions of dollars to provide summer training opportunities for teachers so that they might be better equipped to return to the
schools and carry on more sophisticated instructions in the sciences.

I think it would be a very exciting time in the history of the republic
if the federal government decided to invest in equipping teachers to
teach about peace and to make available a summer program equivalent
to the old National Science Foundation programs for teachers to pro-
mulgate instruction in peace.

■ *CHAIRMAN DELLUMS:*   I would appreciate your assessment
of the Reagan budget priorities as they relate to military spending,
vis-à-vis the various aspects of the education budget at the federal
level.

■ *MR. HERNDON:*   The Reagan budget, in this setting, is appro-
priately called a moral outrage. I do not see any way to describe it other
than that. The circumstances in which human beings make choices
about their alternative futures is essentially a moral dilemma. In this
case we have the opportunity to choose between helping people and
building what I believe to be a redundant and awesomely destructive
military machine. We have opted for the latter.

I have long been intrigued by the equation that some of our more
militaristic citizens draw between the Cuban experience and contemporary El Salvador. They talk about the "bleeding hearts" who called
for understanding and compassion and friendly hands to Cuba fifteen
or twenty years ago and say: "Now, see here, we have a Marxist government in Cuba."

I think what they overlook is that we "bleeding hearts" lost that argument. Indeed, we contended for compassion and understanding, but the government pursued hard-line military confrontation, military intimidation, and as it is their hypothesis that was tested, I think we can now see twenty years later that it was a failure. What we have is precisely what we did not want, a Marxist government in Cuba. Now we are replicating that policy approach in Nicaragua and in El Salvador. We never seem to learn from history.

Clearly, if we wish to build here a bastion of freedom with the capacity to resist Communism, Marxism, or totalitarianism of any kind, we must have moral consistency and confidence in democracy and freedom. We need to develop a society that is capable of sustaining a democratic order and demonstrating its efficacy. We need to offer the kinder elements of our society to the Third World and to developing nations.

That means, obviously, that we ought to be doing a lot more in education. We really ought to reduce the military budget by enough dollars, at the very least, to sustain education at its present level. We ought to reduce the military budget by more than that because that is a decision worthy of consideration on its own merit. We ought to spend more on educational opportunity for our people because that is a decision worthy of consideration on its own merit.

■ *CHAIRMAN DELLUMS:* You have painted a very devastating picture. You mentioned that literally tens of thousands of students will be driven from college. I believe that we are about to give rise to a generation of young people—Black, other minority, poor white, working class white youth—whose percentage of those respective populations attending colleges and universities will probably be the lowest since the Great Depression.

We are talking about a whole generation of young children who, when they come out of high school, will have the doors of the colleges and universities closed to them because they do not have the economic wherewithal to matriculate, even though it has been an articulated basic value that education has been one of the ways up and out, in terms of making a better life for the future. Would you comment as to whether that is correct or incorrect, a distortion, or what?

■ *MR. HERNDON:* No, I think it is very accurate that the declining federal assistance for college education will have a disproportionate impact on the minority community. But I suspect that, in terms of absolute numbers, the largest number of people adversely affected will be white. Nevertheless, there will be a disproportionate impact on minority communities.

There is a related concern that I think deserves just as much attention and that is the child who is presently fourteen, fifteen, or sixteen years old, preparing now for the possibility of college some day. The impact will not be only on those presently seventeen and eighteen years of age. We are talking about an impact on minority populations and on large numbers of white children. That impact will be experienced over the next ten years if the present direction of government is not immediately reversed.

■ *CHAIRMAN DELLUMS:* Do you think NEA would be prepared to consider the possibility of challenging the military budget of the Reagan administration in fiscal year 1983? Would it be prepared to support any positive constructive alternative to that budget?

■ *MR. HERNDON:* The NEA in the past has worked with a number of people in the Congress and people in the Congressional Black Caucus on the various transfer amendments. We will do that in the future.

23

THE MEDICAL CONSEQUENCES OF NUCLEAR WAR

H. Jack Geiger, M.D.

■ ■ ■

H. Jack Geiger is Logan Professor of Community Medicine at the School of Biomedical Education, City College, City University of New York. He was previously chairman of the Departments of Community Medicine at the Medical School of the State University at Stony Brook, New York, and at Tufts University School of Medicine in Boston. He was a founding member of the Physicians for Social Responsibility.

ONE IMPORTANT WAY for the American people to approach the questions of the morality of the military budget, the arms race, and our nuclear build-up plans for the next ten years is to confront what would be the full meaning, in human and medical terms, of a single thermonuclear weapon. The United States has not had the direct experience of war in more than 100 years. Not since the Civil War have American cities in any area of the country been devastated, or shelled, or set afire, or suffered huge numbers of civilian deaths and injuries. We face a situation in which the only nation that has ever used nuclear weapons on a civilian population is the nation that is least prepared, by past experience of war or disaster, to understand what the effects of nuclear weapons are.

There is a terrible paradox in talking about the medical effects of nuclear war. Although I do it often, I have difficulty every time in using a word like "medical" to apply to levels of death, destruction, and devastation that are truly beyond our capacity to imagine. Again, it is common to talk about "victims" and "survivors." That distinction simply loses all meaning when we look at the consequences of even a small number of nuclear weapons.

In trying to understand what will happen, we face problems of both quantitative and qualitative differences from conventional weapons. To explode even a modest size thermonuclear weapon is to create a small sun on the surface of the earth, at whatever place the target is. This is an event that has no precedent, except for Hiroshima and Nagasaki— and they are inadequate examples of the current threat.

The Hiroshima bomb was twelve-and-a-half kilotons. A one-megaton bomb—not a very big weapon in today's arsenals—is equal to eighty Hiroshima weapons exploding simultaneously at the same site on the surface of the earth. A twenty-megaton bomb, the kind of weapon that is much more likely to be used in a population-targeted attack, releases the power of 1,600 Hiroshima weapons exploding simultaneously. Either one of these bombs is simply one of the 50,000 thermonuclear weapons currently in the combined arsenals of the two nuclear superpowers. There is another respect in which attempting to describe a thermonuclear war defies our imagination and our past experience. Any previous single awful event, no matter how horrible, has had effects that started to decay rapidly with time and could be mitigated by help from outside. What "saved" Hiroshima and Nagasaki and many lives there was the fact that the rest of society was intact and help could come in from outside. But in any likely nuclear scenario today, there will be no outside help because every other place and every other potential source of help will be similarly afflicted.

But even that scenario is wrong because we tend to think of a single event, when the likelihood is much greater that there will be one thermonuclear strike at ten o'clock in the morning and another one that will arrive in the midst of the resulting devastation at four o'clock the next afternoon or at ten o'clock the next morning or days or weeks later, since both the superpowers have submarines capable of staying under the surface for weeks or months. They all are presumably under instructions to make the assumption that a nuclear war has occurred and fire their missiles on their own authority if, when they do surface, they are unable after a considerable period of time to make contact with their own headquarters. Thus, we face the probability that two weeks, or three weeks, or four weeks after a nuclear war has begun and ended it will be begun again, or continued, by missiles fired from submarines.

Predicting the consequences of a nuclear blast over a city is not difficult. The physics and the biology are well-known and the same all over the world. Russian flesh burns at exactly the same temperature as American flesh. English children get leukemia at exactly the same radiation dose to the bone marrow as Japanese children. Yet, in doing this exercise, I always have the same difficulty—I worry that, for all of the details of this description, we are going to miss the essential nature of the event, the essential immorality of the event. It is as if, as an epidemiologist, I had gone to Germany to all of the concentration camps that were involved in the holocaust and somehow gotten all of the records, and plotted out month by month and year by year all of the deaths in the holocaust at Auschwitz and all of the other camps; then categorized the deaths—by cause—by execution, by hunger, by starvation, by beating, by disease and type of disease—by month and by year, and then plotted it all on graphs. It might, indeed, be possible to do that. To do so would statistically demonstrate the scale of the action, and yet doing that in itself would not communicate the *fundamental immorality* of what occurred there.

We face that same problem when we look at what a single thermonuclear weapon would do to any city. I can tell you how many people will be killed and how many people will suffer third-degree burns and how many people will die subsequently and what life will be like during and after the attack. But that only begins to approach the moral issue—that this is something no rational and moral human being could contemplate, much less do. But we must understand it to prevent it.

Fifty percent of the energy released in a thermonuclear weapon is blast, like that of a conventional weapon, but on a hugely larger scale. Another 33 percent or so of the energy released in a thermonuclear explosion occurs as heat, and only about 17 percent of the total energy in such a bomb is released as radiation.

The first thing that anyone, a real or imaginary spectator, would see is an enormous blinding flash of light that is many times brighter than the sun. It could cause temporary flash blindness in millions of people and, in some, permanent blindness due to retinal burns.

Next would come the blast. The blast effects are of two kinds. The first is *static overpressure,* the collapsing and crushing effect of an enormous wall of compressed air created by the release of the bomb's tremendous energy in a very tiny space. In effect, the sky is transformed into a gigantic shock wave, a huge hammer that collapses and crushes almost everything in the environment. The results are most intense, of course, at ground zero but are still measurable as far as twelve or thirteen miles away in the case of a one-megaton burst. The second kind of blast effect is *dynamic overpressure,* a term to describe winds moving at 600 to 700 miles an hour, seven times hurricane force, near ground zero, and still reaching velocities over 100 miles an hour at distances of five to six miles.

Blast—either static or dynamic—has three effects: First, it collapses and crushes even the strongest steel and concrete-reinforced skyscrapers within a radius of several miles. Second, it creates hundreds of thousands of flying missiles. Chunks of steel and concrete and wood and glass, all of the instantly created debris within six miles of the ground zero of a one-megaton air burst, will be set in motion at high velocities and cause enormous numbers of injuries as far as thirteen miles away. Third, it sends people flying because—while human beings will withstand those crushing overpressures fairly well—if they are out in the open, the winds will pick them up and hurl them through the air at high speeds. Those that are not turned into missiles will be in buildings that are crushed or under buildings that are collapsed.

The winds, even at four-and-a-half miles from ground zero, can pick up a 180-pound adult and throw him or her at the nearest hard object with a force two or three times that of gravity. At thirteen miles from ground zero, a relatively small chunk of debris will be travelling at a speed sufficient to create a 50 percent probability of skull fracture in anyone hit in the head.

Among the injured survivors there will be people whose bodies will be partially or totally crushed. There will be crushing wounds of the chest and the abdomen; skull fractures; people being impaled on debris or missiles being driven into people so that they have penetrating wounds of the chest and the abdomen; fractured spines and severed spinal cords and paralysis; ruptured lungs and rupture of the liver, spleen, and other internal organs; multiple lacerations with profound hemorrhage and shock. These will occur not only in the closer-in areas. An air burst eleven or thirteen miles away would turn a window into several thousand shards of glass traveling at speeds of several hundred miles an hour. For many persons those flying pieces of glass would be akin to a flying Cuisinart that would lacerate them and chew them up, even at that distance from ground zero. Second- and third-degree burns would occur by the tens or hundreds of thousands. People would be blinded, at least temporarily, as far as thirty-five miles away in all directions. People would be deafened by ruptured eardrums. There will be combinations of all of these injuries, and very often two injuries, neither of which is lethal, will be deadly in combination.

What is probably even more devastating to humans is the heat—a factor that precedes blast in the real sequence of events. First the flash, then the heat, then the blast. An enormous thermal pulse, starting at a temperature of twenty-seven million degrees Fahrenheit in the fireball, travels at just under the speed of light. Again, it is hard to find an image adequate to describe it. It is as if a giant sunlamp were created over the whole sky a mile or two from the surface of the earth, or as if there were a huge blowtorch applied to the whole environment. The effect of that heat, modified only slightly by the weather and by the extent to which people are protected by the shadows of buildings in the few seconds before the blast wave arrives, would be to create third-degree burns on a scale that we have simply never known in human history.

People within the first few miles of ground zero, if they are un-shielded, would simply burst into flame. They would be charred and turned into charcoal. Closer in, people would simply be vaporized—turned into gas molecules. All that might be left would be a shadow, such as that created by a soldier in Nagasaki in Figure 23-1 (see p. 253).

Even in a single city, the numbers of third-degree burns would be beyond our capacity to imagine. The heat flash will also, further out, set clothing afire, causing flame burns. On a clear day, people in a room five or six miles from a one-megaton air burst would see the windows melt and the drapes, wood paneling, wood desks, carpeting—almost every-thing in the room—burst immediately into flame. At this distance third-degree burns become a very serious problem. Closer to ground zero, the heat burns people and objects but creates no lasting fires because no buildings would be left standing for fires to consume and spread among and grow. But at five, six, seven, eight, and up to eleven miles out, considerable numbers of buildings and rubble are left in sufficient concentrations to fuel fires and cause enormous numbers of additional third-degree and second-degree burns.

Adequate medical treatment of any of these kinds of injuries from blast, or third degree burns such as those shown in Figure 23-2 (see p. 254), or radiation injury would require, for effective treatment, the most sophisticated technological resources that medicine now com-mands. They would require operating rooms, surgical wards, sterile areas, CAT scanners, and complex X-ray equipment, life support sys-tems, respiratory systems, and oxygen. For effective treatment, a single third-degree burn may involve all of these resources, require the partic-ipation of one hundred or more medical personnel for several months, and require as many as thirty surgical procecures during the months following that burn. It may consume for each such case, 300 or 400 units of blood, plasma, and glucose and enormous quantities of drugs and other medical supplies. Nothing like this is available in America today for the number of injuries a nuclear blast would create.

There are other consequences of heat and fire that should be men-tioned here. One is that there might be a mass conflagration, a moving fire, like a huge brush fire, driven by the winds. It would simply move this way and that in the blast-destroyed areas, in the areas where build-ings are still standing. Nuclear planners assume that a mass conflagra-tion of this kind would occur in cities, and that everything out to ap-proximately 4½ miles from ground zero will fairly rapidly, certainly ultimately, be burned. The consequence of moving fires of this kind is that people who are wounded but not lethally injured and those who

Figure 23-1.   The shadow of a vaporized soldier burnt into a plank wall approximately 2 miles from ground zero, Nagasaki.

Source: *Hiroshima-Nagasaki: A Pictorial Record of the Atomic Destruction* (Tokyo: Hiroshima-Nagasaki Publishing Committee, 1978), p. 268.

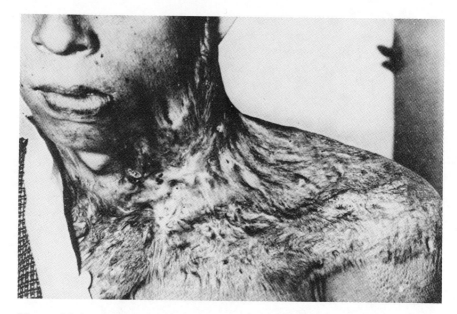

Figure 23–2.   Disfiguring scar tissue resulting from third-degree burns to a survivor of the Nagasaki blast. Photograph courtesy of Physicians for Social Responsibility.

are trapped in wreckage or who are unable to walk or run or crawl fast enough will die simply by being burned alive in a mass conflagration after the blast.

The other possibility is a fire storm. A fire storm is a tremendous stationary fire like a gigantic fireplace with a huge chimney draft extending up into the atmosphere. While it does not move, it burns with enormous heat and intensity in a single coalesced cone of flame. It sucks in cool air from the outside, consuming all of the oxygen in the immediate vicinity and creating large amounts of carbon monoxide and other toxic gases. The air sucked in may create convection force winds of 200 miles an hour or more.

A fire storm may create ambient temperatures of approximately 1,500 degrees Fahrenheit hours after the bomb has exploded. We know from the experience at Hiroshima, as well as at Hamburg and Dresden during World War II, where fire storms were started by conventional bombing attacks, that the only people who would be likely to survive are those who flee their shelters and the area rather than those who enter and stay in shelters. This is because in a fire storm people who have entered shelters would be simultaneously dry roasted and asphyxiated. The only effective shelters would be deep blast shelters of the kind that we build for missiles—if, in addition, they were thermally insulated, had independent oxygen supplies, and had some system of venting toxic gases. The construction of enough such deep blast shelters for even 10 or 15 percent of the population would consume the gross national product for several years and still probably would have the result (as we shall see) of simply postponing death rather than of accomplishing survival.

Finally, there is the problem of radiation. If we are talking about a one-megaton air burst, radiation is not very important for the target area although in the first mile-and-a-half around ground zero it would be lethal—but in that mile-and-a-half, almost everybody would already have been killed by blast and heat. The danger of radiation from an air burst lies in radioactive fallout after the blast. This is a slower and more delayed problem in which the chief difficulties are nonetheless real; they are the depositing of the fallout in the ecosphere and its concentration in the food chain.

If, however, we consider the effects of a ground burst or of a mixture of air and ground bursts—the most likely pattern in a nuclear war— then radioactivity becomes an enormous problem. In a one-megaton ground burst, the overpressures in the first several miles around ground zero would be even greater than with an air burst. The overall circles of destruction would be smaller. The effects of blast and heat would not extend as far. But near ground zero, a crater about three-quarters of a mile wide and three hundred feet deep, would be dug into the earth. All of those thousands of tons of soil, and all of the skyscrapers, buildings, and other structures in that area, which would be crushed into small particles, would ascend into the fireball, and would be made intensely radioactive. Starting in ten or twenty minutes, or an hour at the outside, they would descend as radioactive fallout, creating intense radioactivity not only locally but as far away as 300 or 400 miles, depending on which way the wind is blowing. There are standard calculations by our own government showing the effect of a one-megaton air burst on Detroit, distributing lethal radioactivity to Cleveland, and significant and dangerous radioactivity as far away as Pittsburgh.

There would be no way readily to distinguish between people who have had a lethal dose of radiation, and who will die no matter what anybody does medically, and people who have had only a moderate dose and might be saved by medical care. No one will know the magnitude of his or her own radiation dose. It will not be possible accurately to calculate it afterwards. The initial symptoms of small and large doses are the same and the kinds of sorting out that might be done in some other situation would be impossible.

The effect of radiation on people with burns is such that a modest

Effects of a 1-megaton blast

WIND SPEED	BLAST ARRIVAL	EFFECTS ON PEOPLE	EFFECTS ON PROPERTY
2,000 m.p.h.	Almost instantly	100 percent die instantly.	Total vaporization.
1,500 m.p.h.	0.6 seconds	100 percent die quickly from heat, blast, initial radiation.	Complete devastation; all buildings crushed.
330 m.p.h.	3.5 seconds	98 percent die quickly from heat, blast and initial radiation; 2 percent are severely injured.	Destruction of all except specially designed shelters, though skeletons of a few buildings stand. Extensive fire damage.
150 m.p.h.	9 seconds	50 percent die from burns and collapsing buildings; 40 percent are moderately to severely injured; 10 percent are safe inside shelters. Many will die later from radiation.	Most wood-frame houses and small apartment buildings collapse; reinforced-concrete structures are severely damaged. Extensive fire damage.
90 m.p.h.	19 seconds	5 percent die from burns, blast and flying objects; 45 percent are mildly to severely injured. 50 percent are safe inside shelters, but many will die later from radiation.	Small residences damaged severely, reinforced-concrete structures moderately. Extensive fire damage.
60 m.p.h.	28 seconds	25 percent are mildly to moderately injured from second-degree burns and flying objects; 75 percent are uninjured. Many will sicken or die later from radiation.	Small residences damaged moderately, reinforced-concrete structures lightly. Fire is a threat.

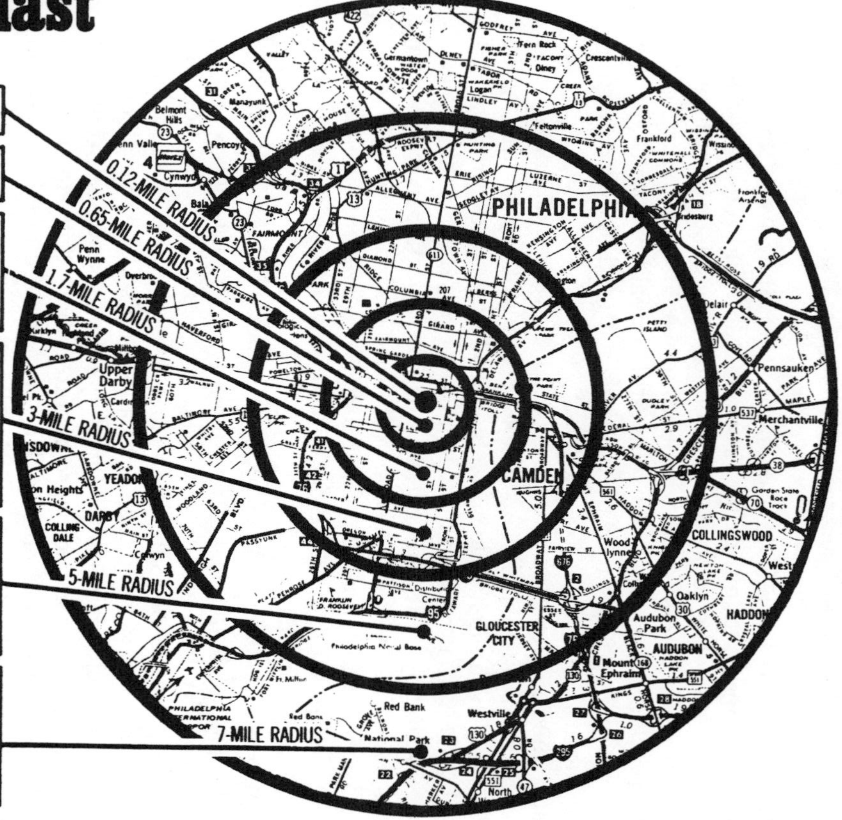

Figure 23–3.   One-megaton airburst over Philadelphia.

dose of radiation would double the mortality risk of a standard burn. A bigger dose of radiation would increase the mortality risk of a standard burn eight-fold. To put that in lay terms, a person who has only one-eighth the amount of burn that would ordinarily kill him or her but who is also exposed to radiation would probably die as a consequence of the combined effect. Similar increases in mortality result from all of the other combinations of blast and burn, radiation and burn, blast and heat, and the like.

The effect of an attack on Philadelphia is shown in Figure 23-3 (see p. 256). Most of the hospitals, the square dots distributed on the map, are in the zones of the greatest destruction. If ground zero is City Hall in Philadelphia in a one-megaton airburst, these would be a zone of total destruction with a radius of about a mile-and-a-half in all directions from ground zero and a total area of seven square miles.

Near the center of the this zone, the overpressures are incredible, 200 pounds per square inch. Out at the rim, they are down to twenty pounds per square inch, which will crush and collapse almost every structure, twist and shake and explode all of those buildings. The winds in that zone are 500 to 700 miles an hour. Almost nothing will be left standing. Subways will be crushed, tunnels will be crushed, bridges will collapse, ships in the river will sink. Winds at that speed are sufficient to pick up a locomotive and hurl it some distance.

In the first third or so of that zone, everything will be vaporized by heat or crushed by blast. In the rest of that zone the heat is such that steel and glass will melt and concrete will explode.

Radiation is lethal throughout this first zone. It would take about twenty-three seconds to get a lethal dose of radiation, even in an air burst, unless one were shielded by four feet of concrete and, of course, the concrete would likely be lying on top of you rather than be doing an effective job of shielding you.

People will be vaporized, broiled or crushed, have their internal organs ruptured, or be lethally radiated. In that zone 100 percent of the people will be killed, 98 percent almost immediately.

Next, out to 4.3 miles, conservatively, 50 percent of the people will be killed promptly and another 40 percent will be seriously injured. In the zone that has a radius of about three miles in all directions and covers an additional twenty square miles of Philadelphia, the overpressures run from twenty down to ten pounds per square inch. Ten pounds per square inch were sufficient to devastate the reinforced factories of Hiroshima and Nagasaki.

Concrete buildings, everything but the steel skyscrapers, will collapse. Brick and frame residences will be totally destroyed. The heat in this zone is such that aluminum siding will literally evaporate and windows will melt. Radiation is negligible.

A human being in this three-mile zone would be picked up and thrown or blown 300 feet or more at high speeds. There will be all kinds of crushing injuries and injuries due to hurled and blown debris. Fifty percent of the population in this area will die of blast alone. Almost all those who survive will have third-degree burns, and there will be spontaneous ignition of clothing.

The outer border of the zone, stretching to 4.3 miles from ground zero, encompassing an additional thirty-two square miles, demarcates the lethal zone, an area of total burnout. Within it, winds of 160 miles per hour will exist, and blast effects will still be sufficient to destroy heavy factories and blow the roofs off of lighter construction. Four-and-a-half miles away from ground zero, the heat in this zone will be sufficient to make asphalt roads melt, to ignite all of the cloth, wood, fabrics, bedding, and carpeting in buildings.

Effects on people again are due to the crushing and collapsing of buildings, and to hurled debris and hurled people, causing all kinds of trauma. In addition, there will be third-degree burns, flash blindness, and retinal burns. In this zone there will be 50 percent dead overall, 45 percent seriously injured. A subsequent mass conflagration or fire storm would expand the lethal zone five-fold—too large even to fit on this map of Philadelphia.

In a zone out to five miles there is an addditional eighteen square miles of destruction to Philadelphia. The overpressures are still huge and the winds are 125 miles per hour. Even at this distances, fires will start and the crushing and collapsing of residential structures will occur. One hundred percent of the people outdoors will get third-degree burns, and their clothes will catch on fire. Indeed, burn injuries at this point start to predominate over blast injuries because of all those spreading fires.

A zone with a radius of a little over six miles adds another fifty square miles of destruction. The winds in this area are still 100 miles per hour, hurricane force, enough to blow people out of buildings. There will be moderate damage to commercial and residential structures. The walls of skyscrapers in this area would still be swept away, and heavy industrial plants damaged. There still will be sufficient heat to cause third-degree burns. At this distance, somebody wearing a neoprene-treated nylon raincoat would discover that it was melting. Four of five people exposed will get third-degree burns, and, of course, there will still be people with trauma, blindness, and the like.

Approximately 10 percent of the people in a zone out to seven miles will die promptly. Forty-five percent will be seriously injured. Glass still will be flying at high speeds; 30 percent of the trees and utility poles will be down, blocking roads; people still will be blown out of buildings.

The heat will be enough to give one in every five persons a third-degree burn, and 70 to 80 percent of those people outdoors will get a second-degree burn.

If this were a twenty-megaton weapon, the level of destruction in all these zones would correspond to that of the first zone in a one-megaton blast, 100 percent destruction of the population and everything within. There is another way to spread first-zone destruction as widely as the seven-mile zone, or even more widely in Philadelphia or any city attacked. This would be through the use of multiple warhead weapons, the so-called MIRV weapons—such as our Minutemen III and MX missiles and their Soviet equivalents. One can disperse the damage and destruction with smaller warheads. They do not waste so much energy making the rubble bounce near ground zero and simultaneously burning and vaporizing it. They spread it out. Three 100-kiloton warheads, properly dispersed, may provide the destructive equivalent of a single one-megaton warhead.

In Philadelphia, at just one megaton, about 770,000 people would die; 1.3 million people would be seriously injured. For those 1.3 million injured people, what would be available in the way of hospital beds? There are 12,417 hospital beds in the Philadelphia metropolitan area, of which 1,046 generously could be assumed to be left intact, mostly on the further rims of the damage. In addition to those thousand beds, there would another 7,500 beds in the five rural counties outside of Philadelphia in all directions, a total of about 8,500 beds for 1.3 million seriously injured people.

In the United States, where we fill 80 percent of our hospital beds most of the time, 80 percent of those beds would already be occupied. So there would really be left only 1,730 beds for 1,330,000 wounded. Statistically, there would be 771 seriously injured people trying to get into each hospital bed that was available. This is an absurdity because most of the beds are twenty to thirty miles away. There would be no transport, no communication, no emergency vehicles, and no electrical power. The roads would be blocked and most of the environment would be on fire. That is simply one illustration of the problems that would confront those attempting to seek or to provide medical care.

The cataloguing of these injuries and the numbers of people who would be in trouble with third-degree burns, skull fractures, and similar trauma does not begin to indicate the total burden of illness that would be facing any surviving physician. Many of those injured would be dying slowly, over weeks. Many of the people in shelters would become ill and die. Literally tens of thousands of people in all of the bombed metropolitan areas would start to sicken and die if they ran out of their insulin, their cortisone, their digitalis, and the other drugs on which their lives now depend—and drugs would become rapidly and totally unavailable in the chaos that would ensue. Moreover, among all the uninjured survivors the normal incidence of coronary heart attacks, appendicitis, gastric ulcers, and other life-threatening illnesses will be continuing.

Whether people have lethal doses, moderate doses, or sublethal doses of radiation, they will all have the same initial symptoms, and there will be no way to sort them out or to distinguish them from those with similar symptoms of psychological origin.

Hospitals tend to be concentrated in downtown areas. Physicians are also concentrated closest to ground zero and, if anything, would be killed at rates greater than the rates for the general population. There have been numerous studies, my own and others, that show the range of physician survivability in a nuclear attack is from one surviving physician for every 350 seriously injured people to one surviving physician for every 1,700 seriously injured people.

If there were one surviving physician for every 1,000 injured and each physician decided to risk radiation exposure—feeling that his or her moral responsibility was to get out there and do what could be done immediately, even if that meant he or she might be dead within a week and therefore unable to take care of people later on—what would happen? If each physician magically located all of those thousand survivors with no loss of time, and if each physician spent only fifteen minutes on each patient for all purposes of diagnosis and treatment, and worked eighteen hours a day, it would still be three months before every patient was seen for the first time by a physician.

The vast majority would long since have died. Indeed, the vast majority of these seriously injured in every city will die without ever seeing a physician or health worker, and without even the administration of narcotics for the relief of pain. But even that calculation is an absurdity because we are talking about third-degree burns, skull fractures, ruptured lungs and other very serious injuries. A physician facing such injuries equipped only with his or her black bag—with no X-ray machines, intraveneous solutions, blood, caches of drugs, operating rooms, or the like—would be able to do very little.

When civil defense officials talk of survival and promise that large numbers of people will survive, they treat us as if we were simply ciphers in some kind of a biological body count. In fact, for human beings, the only real meaning of survival is social—in families, in communities, and in groups. Even the simplest social enterprises—keeping a family together, finding water, finding food, finding shelter, and staying alive—will be virtually impossible in a post-attack world, which piles misery on misery. There would be no social fabric in which the survivors could live.

We have data from studies in Boston and other cities by my medical colleagues that indicate that a significant percentage of adolescents and teenagers now believe they have no future, that they will never live to have children of their own, that there is no real point in planning, career planning, and the like. This may very well have something to do with the prevalence of substance abuse, of alcoholism, and of other kinds of problems in that age group.

To plan for destruction on this nuclear level is to deny to ourselves that what we are talking about is human beings and to make distinctions that deny our own humanity. There are neither capitalist babies nor communist babies. When we burn them up, they are all just babies. There will be neither rubles nor dollars left in the rubble.

We are talking about events on a scale that pose a new moral problem that mankind has not faced before, certainly in recorded human history: Do we have the right to end the species? The survival of mankind as a species may indeed now be at risk; nuclear weapons have made us the new endangered species.

Physicians are, by profession, supposed to be healers. It is a profound and painful experience even to report these data and to make these calculations. But it seems to me that the morally indicated course for physicians is to refuse to bow down to this pestilence and to strive our utmost to be healers. If humanity itself is threatened, then it must become everyone's task to end the threat—not merely politicians, not merely professionals, not merely physicians or other groups—and that, I hope, is the moral point of this statement.

■   ■   ■

■ *CHAIRMAN DELLUMS:*   Would you comment on the general assertion of this administration that fighting, surviving, and "winning" a nuclear war is a real possibility, and that we can actually defend ourselves as civilians against the devastation that you just so graphically illustrated?

■ *DR. GEIGER:*   I have studied the civil defense plans in detail, from this perspective, nationally as well as a series of local plans. The first conclusion, of course, is that nuclear war is not winnable, that nuclear war cannot be limited, and that nuclear war is not survivable in any social, understandable, commonsense meaning of that term.

Our major civil defense plan at the moment is the so-called crisis relocation plan, calling for massive evacuation of people from the cities. It is more than absurd; it is dangerous. The Federal Emergency Management Agency concedes that an effective crisis relocation plan will require "only" five days warning time—but people are aware that it takes only twenty-five minutes for a missile to travel in either direction between the Soviet Union and the United States, and only five to ten minutes for submarine-launched missiles.

The plan assumes that there will be some definable moment in the middle of a crisis when a government can rationally decide that things are serious enough to order a mass evacuation. It assumes that people will respond as they have in other disasters—hurricanes, floods and the like—that are more familiar, and will behave in an orderly and rational fashion. It assumes (in Washington, for example) that people with odd-numbered license plates will leave on a given day and everybody with even-numbered license plates will calmly wait until the following day. It assumes that people will not rush out to fill their automobiles with gasoline and create a huge, enormous traffic jam by that effort alone. It assumes that civil defense planners will know in advance where the bombs will fall, it assumes that the bombs will be accurate, and it assumes that one can specify in advance that there are "safe" areas.

It assumes that there will be adequate shelters for protection against radioactivity, and that shelters will have food, water, and sanitation for people by the millions in the so-called host areas to which citizens are to be transported. We know that this is not the case. The plan assumes also that people in the host areas will be happy to have all of these visitors coming, and we know that this is certainly not the case.

I believe the greatest danger, however, lies in the possibility that implementing a so-called civil defense plan for nuclear war will increase the risk of the very event the plan is designed to protect against. If we are involved in a major crisis with the Soviet Union, and in the middle of it we start to evacuate our people, or they start to evacuate theirs, that would be instantly detectible by each other's satellites and the most likely response would be for each side to decide that this is being done because: "They are going to fire their missiles and so we had better fire ours now," or vice versa.

The plan also overlooks the fact that it takes contemporary technology only twenty-five or thirty minutes to *retarget* a missile. If one really wanted to kill the maximum number of people, one would wait for the middle of the crisis relocation, when everybody is out on the highway and the smallest number were in shelters, and then retarget and attack.

There is yet another possibility. Suppose the crisis fades and is resolved and everybody goes back home. The civil defense agency's own literature acknowledges that they would never be able to get people in any significant number to evacuate a second time because people would say: "I went through that false alarm before, I'm not going through all of that again. Nothing happened. I'll take my chances."

Enemy planners can also read the U.S. civil defense literature. They could conceivably provoke a crisis, get the United States into crisis relocation, and then back off and have it resolved. Everybody would go back home. Then, three weeks later an adversary could launch the real attack. I have asked civil defense officials how they would plan for that eventuality, and they had nothing at all to say to me because they could not think of an answer.

The civil defense plans, finally, overlook the longer-term ecological problem. Even a moderate exchange of the present nuclear arsenals of the United States and the Soviet Union might, in the opinion of the National Academy of Sciences, destroy a significant amount of the ozone layer in the Northern Hemisphere. It is that layer of the atmosphere that protects us from penetrating ultraviolet radiation. The consequences of that ultraviolet radiation coming down for a period of eight or ten years are such that we can only speculate about it. It seems highly likely that crop growth would be seriously impaired. We know that people outside would have to be totally clothed or suffer serious burns after only forty-five to ninety minutes exposure to the sun. People would suffer flash blindness and, later, lasting eye damage as a consequence of the penetrating ultraviolet radiation unless they wore sunglasses, as well.

What the civil defense planners have overlooked, even for the short term, is that most of the other mammals would die. They would be blinded, and that makes it very hard for them to eat, let alone reproduce. In a recent discussion with civil defense planners, I took the planning mode that they are so fond of and offered them two suggestions, since they seem to believe that all problems can be solved by planning in advance. The first was that we manufacture in advance and stockpile sunglasses for all the cows, horses, pigs, sheep, and so on that we will need; the second, that we will have a plan for the post-attack period to designate human survivors with sunglasses as seeing-eye people, each of whom will lead around a cow, a pig, a horse, or whatever. One turns to this kind of nasty irony as a despairing response to the misleading, inhumane lying that civil defense plans represent.

The medical literature also describes the post-attack environment that civil defense planners have ignored: There would be epidemics, trillions of flies, millions of corpses. The flies, the mosquitos, the cockroaches are all enormously more radiation-resistant than mammals. The San Francisco area, for instance, would have 300,000 or 400,000 human corpses left, breeding maggots. The birds would be dead, so they could not eat the insects. It is difficult to write a better scenario for epidemic disease.

Most of the survivors, nationwide, would be concentrated in the places where there would be little food. Most of the remaining uncontaminated food would be in grain silos in North Dakota, Minnesota, and Iowa. The petroleum industry would have been destroyed, so there would be very little fuel. People will have the choice of using that fuel to haul grain from North Dakota to St. Louis, so that people in St. Louis will not starve, or saving it to try to grow next year's crops on which the future of survivors will depend—assuming that those crops will grow in the presence of ultraviolet radiation.

How does one then respond to a T.K. Jones saying: "All we need is enough shovels and everything will be all right," for example? This is a gross, unethical distortion. Well, we will need shovels to bury the survivors in a year or so, but I cannot think of any other rational purpose for them.

I think it is profoundly unethical for any physician even to participate in any kind of civil defense planning specifically related to nuclear war. The civil defense planners, it seems to me, are immoral in the same way.

■ *CHAIRMAN DELLUMS:* Would you give us some sense of what life would be like, in the shelter itself?

■ *DR. GEIGER:* Let us assume that we have a relatively good case in which people are some distance away from the attack point—perhaps upwind from one of the missile bases, not in a place that has necessarily been directly attacked. Let us say we are upwind from the SAC base at Omaha, or we are upwind from the ground burst on San Francisco, and that enough of us either lived there or have been evacuated in advance to get into the shelter that the civil defense people have prepared for us.

The civil defense calculations are that we will each have five feet by four feet of space. They do not allow for the almost inevitable overcrowding and maldistribution that will occur. Second, they do not tell us very clearly that we are going to have to stay in that shelter anywhere from two weeks to a month or longer, if we are in one of the high radiation contours.

Some people inside will already have had radiation exposure, and will have symptoms of radiation sickness, vomiting and bloody diarrhea. A very conservative estimate is that 30 percent of the population in a shelter will start to vomit. There will be no sanitation. It is difficult to write a better scenario for the epidemic outbreak in each shelter of respiratory disease, bronchitis, of gastrointestinal disease, and the like.

The most disgusting sample of the civil defense shelter literature that I have seen deals with the very high probability of profound emotional disturbance. One of the civil defense manuals says, in effect: "Some people in each shelter may become emotionally disturbed, hysterical or the like. What is needed is one calm person, first of all, to deal with those people. Secondly, what one should do is get them together in a group and have them talk out their problem."

Again, one can only turn to a kind of sick humor in talking about this. These are the plans, in reality, that are being made for use when people talk about sheltering. From those shelters, people will emerge into an environment with epidemic infectious disease and malnutrition—a society unlike any society that we know now.

There will be survivors. The most valuable people to those survivors, I think, will be medieval historians who know in some detail what life was like in the ninth, tenth, and eleventh centuries—how people grew food and how they sheltered themselves—because those are the skills that will be required.

Survival does not mean what the civil defense people tell us it means when they say some people will survive or more people will survive. It does not mean a resumption of anything remotely resembling the life we have today. It may mean simply the prolongation of death from disease or hunger over the following year or two.

■ *CHAIRMAN DELLUMS:*   Have there been any studies or have you been in communication with other physicians and scientists who indicate the same picture that you draw for America is essentially the same picture for the Soviets?

■ *DR. GEIGER:*   Admiral Stansfield Turner, when he was the head of the CIA, testified to Congress that there was no civil defense plan that he knew of in the U.S.S.R. that could conceivably protect the Russian population effectively against nuclear attack or, even more important, give the leaders of the Soviet Union the delusion that effective protection for their population and industry against nuclear attack was made possible by that civil defense plan.

One has to remember, when one hears about what is essentially being presented as a civil defense gap, that we have been suckered several times in the past in this nation by missile gaps and mineshaft gaps. The International Physicians for the Prevention of Nuclear War raised this issue with Russian physicians, including Dr. Ye. I. Chazov. He and his colleagues had two-and-a-half hours on prime time on the Soviet national television network and presented to the Soviet people precisely these kinds of material, as to what the consequences would be, and as to the futility of any defensive measures. This information has also appeared in Soviet newspapers and magazines.

24

DEMOCRACY IN MILITARY POLICY . . .
Leading the "Leaders"
Dr. Earl Molander

■ ■ ■

Earl A. Molander holds a Ph.D. from the University of California at Berkeley and is currently on leave from Portland State University, where he is associate professor in the School of Business Administration. He is the deputy director of Ground Zero. His books include *Responsive Capitalism* and *Nuclear War: What's in It for You?*

GROUND ZERO IS a nonpartisan, nonadvocacy nuclear war education project that sponsored Ground Zero Week—a nationwide week of community-based discussion and events designed to educate the American people about nuclear war. It involved over 1,000 communities and 30 cities, 300 college campuses, and almost 1,000 high schools. Ground Zero is headed by my twin brother, Dr. Roger Molander, who for seven years served as a member of the National Security Council staff, spanning the administrations of Presidents Nixon, Ford, and Carter. He had principal responsibilty for the area of strategic nuclear policy issues, and he and I have the responsibility for Ground Zero. Our primer, *Nuclear War: What's in It for You?*, has, just two days after hitting the bookstores, gone into its second printing.

I would like to recall for you a set of historical circumstances similar to those we find in the country today. About four centuries ago, Western Europeans found themselves in a dilemma. The Roman Church, the institution that provided the most necessary element of security at that time, the security of one's soul, had lost touch with the people. The experts in salvation, the clergy, were secretive. The people were being forced to pay heavy taxes to build large religious edifices in distant cities that they never saw. They were also badgered to buy indulgences against holy bones in the Church inventory in order to clear the way so their souls could be guaranteed a place in heaven. The latter practice reached such absurd proportions that in one German church, the arsenal of holy bones numbered something like 1,182,437. These common people were being told by the clergy: "Trust us, we'll give your soul security; just buy more bones."

Ultimately the people resisted the Church, the clergy, and prevailing religious beliefs. They took matters into their own hands and began a reform movement, not a revolution. That very same thing is happening in this country today. Rather than Martin Luther's ninety-five theses nailed to the Church door to call our attention to the problem, however, we now have ninety-five different freeze resolutions nailed to ballot measures, town hall agendas, and now the walls of Congress.

It is particularly noteworthy that this sudden groundswell of support for Ground Zero and nuclear freeze resolutions is not centered in major metropolitan areas. Rather, the major support for these initiatives is in small and medium-size communities that heretofore have not been at the cutting edge of any social movement—places like Spokane, Washington; Cedar Rapids, Iowa; and Rapid City, South Dakota.

I believe that these people feel the same sense of frustration that their ancestors felt 400 years ago. First, I think the numbers finally overwhelmed people. Megatonnage is just as incomprehensible after a while as megabones. Second, the concept of deterrence—"Trust us, we'll make you more secure if we can show the Russians this new weapons system or that new weapons program"—wears thin. When you have 10,000 nuclear warheads that can be delivered on the enemy in a matter of minutes, and you still do not feel secure, something is wrong. Third, today's sabre-rattling takes place in an already precarious international environment. While not greatly different than invocations of the devil himself in the old days, it does make people uneasy, as does talk of "limited" nuclear war and civil defense.

But I do not believe that these factors, or any of the variety of other national security-oriented explanations, are sufficient to explain the heavy rumblings out there in America on this issue. I think the explanation lies in the fact that a succession of elected officials and national security experts have promised more than they have been able to deliver, especially on the issues relating to the economy.

The American people have been subjected in recent years to a repetition of unfulfilled promises that are all part of the constellation of the American dream—of a secure and prosperous future for ourselves and our children. I cannot emphasize too strongly why I think the failures in the economy are key. What these failures have done is cripple the trust that the American people have in the ability of experts in the federal government to solve society's problems.

So much has been promised in this country over the years—in terms of a secure economic future when people can own a house, their children can go to college, and they can retire on a secure, inflation-proof income. Government efforts to reestablish this dream are not succeeding. This unhappy experience with the economy has raised in the public mind the fear that the ultimate threat to their personal security, nuclear war, may also be in the hands of experts who will do no more for their personal security than did the economic experts.

With the contemplation of this ultimate threat to their personal security, the volume of public outcry is not surprising. These are people who, in their silent way, entered the voting booths in 1980 and answered with a resounding "No!" to Ronald Reagan's question: "Are you better off now than you were four years ago?"

What is to happen to this concern? Let me suggest that the freeze proposals and the participation in Ground Zero Week are the first stage in a process in which the American people, like their ancestors 400 years ago, are about to take matters into their own hands and participate not just in the budgetary process but at all levels of policymaking.

If the rising tide of public concern about nuclear war, dramatized by public involvement here, can find the proper channels of expression and reach the appropriate audiences in an effective way, these positive consequences will result. There will be a broad-based public support for aggressive mutual efforts on the part of the United States and the Soviet Union to undertake whatever policy initiatives are necessary to reduce the risk of nuclear war. There will be restored confidence in the government's capacity to provide enduring security and peace for all Americans. There will evolve a public with "staying power" on the nuclear war issue—in other words, a public that will stay committed to finding a resolution of the current dilemma through such diversions as Soviet bad behavior, false starts in efforts to improve U.S.-Soviet relations, and efforts to co-opt or divert public concerns by opportunistic politicians and public officials.

If this concern is diverted, co-opted, blunted, or otherwise prevented from having real substantive effects, these negative consequences could result: alienation of the American people from national security policymakers; a repetition of the "tuning out" of the threat of nuclear war, just as the threat looms large, as we saw in the early 1960s; or easy derailment of important public, governmental policy initiatives and programs that would contribute substantially to peace and security.

If the public concern about nuclear war is to find a positive response, it must be nonpartisan and not politicized. It must be informed and not superficial. It must be committed and not capricious. And it must be sensible and not hysterical.

For this to occur, Ground Zero, as an educational effort, was created. However, the congressional and administration response to this public concern must be immediate and vigorous, or the interest and momentum that has developed in the last few months will be lost. We also risk losing the objective we all share, the involvement of an educated and aware American citizenry in a debate about government policy, as to how to stop nuclear war.

Ground Zero is a nonpartisan, nonadvocacy effort. My brother, our executive director, served in several administrations, most recently with a Democratic administration. I am a Republican who has run for public office in my home state. Professionally, I am a business school professor and a businessman. I believe it will take the kind of broad-based nonpartisan effort we have at Ground Zero—Republican and Democrat, Washington, D.C., national security expert and Portland, Oregon, businessman—to move to a positive resolution of this problem, both here in Congress and in the country as a whole. After all, the lethal dosage of radiation is the same for Democrats as it is for Republicans, the same in Washington, D.C., as it is in Portland, Oregon.

■ ■ ■

■ *CHAIRMAN DELLUMS:*   You mentioned in your opening remarks that this is a movement that is not emanating from the major cities but, in fact, from the small and medium-size cities. Why do you think that is the case, given that literally millions of human beings in the major cities would die in a nuclear holocaust?

■ *DR. MOLANDER:*   Perhaps in the major cities people have a lot of other issues competing for their attention. Perhaps they are a little more cynical about the possibilities of doing anything. I think that you have to look at the smaller and medium-size towns themselves for an explanation.

These are people who are the true believers in their government, in the American dream—the people who spend a lot of time thinking about their personal security and their families, and have always felt that the government had their best interests in mind as they pursued a common set of goals. I think you are seeing a sudden realization that what they have wanted, and what they had hoped for could be totally lost to a national security system that is not providing them the ultimate security that they had hoped for. It is because they come as sort of innocent people, hopeful, thinking that something can still be done about this issue, that they show the kind of optimism that has always prevailed out there in smaller cities.

■ *CHAIRMAN DELLUMS:* What do you perceive to be superiority, given the incredible level of nuclear capability that both the United States and the U.S.S.R. have? Would you also comment on this notion that we have to go up, in terms of the development and production of several additional thousand warheads, in order to come down?

■ *DR. MOLANDER:* That is, in essence, the question that is going to be posed to the American people as a whole. What we are attempting to do is not answer that question. We are a nonadvocacy group. I don't have a prescription. I don't have an answer to the comparability issue. What we have attempted to do in the book, and what we will be attempting to do in the week of activities in April, is to present, as best we can, the reasonable arguments on both sides.

How do you compare? What is superiority? Is superiority essential to insure security? I can't answer your question in terms of being an expert in the national security business. Remember, I am the lay person who has come here, in a sense—as many other people come here—with an expression of concern. Our hope is that the Congress and the president and the supposed experts on this issue will reach that resolution. I think our statement is one of tremendous concern, a desire to know more, and we will be ready to participate in answering that question, probably by the time of the 1984 elections. But I don't think that I, or the public at large, know enough right now to say conclusively what the answer is. I think that is why my organization exists in the first place.

■ *CHAIRMAN DELLUMS:* Suddenly, in the last few months, we have seen this massive grassroots movement. I think that there are three reasons why it exists. First, the European peace movement has been terribly important in focusing the American people's attention on the danger of nuclear weapons. Perhaps it is because people in Europe have lived through the devastation of war, whereas for us war has always been something that takes place in some other nation's territory. Our European allies, with literally millions of people demonstrating, brought this matter to the attention of the American people.

Second, and this is certainly no partisan, parochial statement, I think that both the arrogance and the bizarre nature of some of the comments emanating from this administration have also triggered this—for example, their notion that a nuclear war can be limited to Europe. The idea that we could have any kind of surgical nuclear strike in Europe is, in my estimation, at best, the height of arrogance and ignorance. The notion that we can detonate a nuclear device in the middle of a diplomatic crisis is, at best, bizarre.

Look at the annual report to the Congress by the Secretary of Defense, the posture statement of this administration that acts as a justification for fiscal year 1983 military budget. It says almost verbatim that one of the policy objectives in the budget is the creation of the capacity to fight, survive, and win a nuclear war. How frightening even to think these thoughts, much less to try to make them public policy.

Finally, look at the incredible military budget figures the administration proposes. At this rate of growth, by 1987 it will be over $422 billion per annum. By the end of the decade, we are talking about a half-a-trillion dollar military budget per annum. These figures are astronomical. Together with the European peace movement, statements about "limited" nuclear war and "winning" a nuclear war, this military budget has provided the catalysts for this kind of grassroots movement. Do you think this has anything to do with it?

■ *DR. MOLANDER:*   I essentially agree with your use of the term "catalyst." I don't think any of those three are the root cause. People in the United States sense a threat to their personal security. Until now, in a small town, if you were worried about your personal security, you bought life insurance. You locked your door. You made sure the roof didn't leak. You saved your money and so on, and that was going to insure a secure future. Then suddenly the possibility was introduced that all of that could be preempted by a nuclear war, when people had been promising you that you were secure. This—combined with the failure of the administration's economic promises—has brought matters to a head. You have to look at the root sense of what constitutes security for an individual in this society to find where it has all gone wrong.

■ *CHAIRMAN DELLUMS:*   Catholic Bishop Walter Sullivan has testified that, on an increasing basis, the young people in this country are without hope and without dreams, that they believe that they will be destroyed by a nuclear weapon prior to achieving adulthood. I wonder whether or not this feeling is pervasive among our young people and is expressing itself in the Ground Zero movement to challenge the arms race?

■ *DR. MOLANDER:*   To some extent, but that is not the whole of it. There certainly are a large number of young people involved in Ground Zero who are resisting the loss of optimism in the future that they see among their peers and have felt themselves, who want to do something but realize that perhaps there isn't going to be a future. I think it goes even lower down to children of the age of my own children, aged nine and eleven.

I am more concerned with young people within the larger population of young people who are not even thinking about this issue. It is their future, long after you and I are gone, that we may be mortgaging or taking away. For twenty years we have talked to them about this issue, and those who have learned about it have lost the sense of optimism, but I think the majority of young people in this country right now are not even thinking about the issue, are not really aware of why we have the weapons or why we want more or less in this program or that program.

I think that some kind of educational effort has to be initiated before you are going to see a broad base of support for a movement of this kind from young people. I think the real hard-core support, as I stated before, is among those people who are parents, those people who are looking to the future, who are in adulthood. It is not a grassroots youth movement of the kind that you saw in the late 1960s and the early 1970s against the Vietnam War.

25

"WE ARE ALL RESPONSIBLE."

Philip Berrigan

■ ■ ■

Philip Berrigan, a combat veteran of World War II, graduated from the College of the Holy Cross. He then entered religious life and was ordained a Josephite priest. He has devoted his life to working for the poor, for peace and for the attainment of human rights. His books include, *A Punishment for Peace* and *Widen the Prison Gates*: *Writings from Jails, April 1970 - December 1972*.

I WANT TO SAY something about the biblical, moral, and ethical implications of the nuclear arms race. It is a subject that most American Christians find very, very illusive.

Christ took literally the imperative to defend the helpless as in the parable of the Good Shepherd: "As God knows Me and I know God, in the same way I know My sheep and they know Me, and I am willing to die for them." John 10:14, 15. On Holy Thursday night, He anticipated precisely what would happen on Calvary the next day. "This is My body given up for you and this is My blood, the blood of the new covenant shed for you." The Eucharist and Calvary have this unassailable meaning: He gave his life that we might never take life, might never shed blood, might never experience the second death because we dared to do something that God would never do, kill another person.

In brief, those true to that tradition and teaching are, by definition, persons who strive to match the compassion and justice of God toward the poor, the ostracized, the helpless, the victims of human greed and cruelty. Today, as the whole human family lives on borrowed time in a kind of literal nuclear countdown, the victims are everyone, including the architects of nuclear insanity, the superpower rulers, the armsmakers, the technicians, and scenario writers and ideologues. These people are perhaps victimized most of all. They are ignorant, deluded, and mad—indeed, not knowing what they do.

First of all, the arms race is a cursing, of God and creation. It substitutes nation-state idolatries for the sovereignty of God; it accepts the bomb as peacemaker, instead of the Prince of Peace; it worships death instead of the life of the Resurrection; it treats the earth as an enemy to be subdued, raped, and robbed.

Next, the arms race is a perverse exhibition of unfaith and of moral weakness. It reduces to hypocrisy our claim as a Judeo-Christian nation, and it attacks fundamentally the moral universe that preserves humanity as humanity. Furthermore, it undermines the force that allows the human experiment to continue, and that is simply moral conduct. As a people, we have never faced the consequences of having incinerated hundreds of thousands of Japanese people or of preparing the thermonuclear end of the world.

Next, the arms race is an attack upon life and the right to life. Right now there is perhaps no living person who has not ingested some radioactive material where it incubates in genes and organs. As for our inalienable right to life, who can honestly in this room expect today a death apart from nuclear terror, flame and poison. In the opinion of many, we have already expended our human chances for survival—dependent as we are upon malfunctioning computer chips and a restrained interpretation of the next "broken arrow", to use the Pentagon term. (A "broken arrow" is an accident involving a nuclear weapons system.)

Next, the arms race is unfathomable waste. What has been the American outlay for war since 1946? It is well over two trillion dollars. Then add the projection of Reagan's five-year plan beginning this year, an additional $2.3 trillion. One can think only of the megamillions to buy the megatons to cause the megadeaths. It is an investment that rapes the earth of critical resources and bankrupts economies to secure but one mad objective—the prospect of nuclear suicide. It is a bottomless rathole into which we sweep wealth and lives in a frightful obsession with death and its byproducts.

Next, the arms race is poison. One American scientist, Dr. Ernest Sternglass, has estimated from official statistics that twenty million Americans have died from nuclear testing, mostly from our own but also from the Russian, Chinese, British, and French tests. Let me read the pertinent paragraph from his book, *The People of Three Mile Island*:

> In 1969, I pointed out that the statistics throughout the United States showed that there were probably some one-half million children who

died as a result of nuclear bomb testing since the atomic age began. With the latest statistics on total mortality published by the U.S. Public Health Service, and looking at the decline of death rates before the bomb testing began, we see the decline halted during the time of nuclear testing, and it is now resumed for all ages. It is now possible to say that the total number of Americans who died as a result of bomb testing is close to 100 times the number of people who died at Hiroshima, very close to 20 million people who died earlier than they would have if we had never dropped a bomb on Hiroshima and Nagasaki, nor done the bomb testing in Nevada, and in the Pacific and Russia in Siberia, and England in Australia. That has poisoned the atmosphere of the whole world.

Next, the arms race is not a paradox; it is a contradiction. We cannot both threaten with nuclear weapons and hope to avoid nuclear extinction by making the threat. Both intend to do something and intend not to do it. We cannot build nuclear weapons and then disavow their use. The inner logic of deterrence destroys deterrence. In fact, that logic drives one superpower to seek technical superiority and to embark upon the course of a disarming first strike—like the brother, who thinking that I was about to kill him in self-defense, was about to kill me in self-defense, and so I had to kill him in self-defense.

And then the other power follows suit until we possess insanity as reality—both superpowers on hair-trigger, ourselves by policy, and the U.S.S.R. by paranoia. Pershing II and Cruise missiles, for example, the Eurostrategic system that is a launch-on-warning system, illustrate this descent into pathology. They bring a disarming first strike to the very doors of the Soviet Union.

Next, the arms race is apolitical, subverting and holding in contempt the very objectives of politics, which would be, according to the Greek tradition, providing for the survival of the human family, providing the means for ennobling life, and providing for the next generation, the children.

Politics in its true sense is something like art. It remembers the dead and provides for the unborn. The current "deterrence" of the superpowers—unanalyzed and unscrutinized—comes down to this: It provides no reason at all for either side not to launch a first strike. To preserve such madness from debate and scrutiny, the superpowers will suppress public inquiry, cultivate public amnesia, loot their economies to build a doomsday force, and offer no one, least of all, the young, a decent option for survival. These are not the politics of capitalist or communist tyrants but of respective political systems gone mad.

Next, the arms race is legal. It is buttressed and sanctioned by the law at every turn. The international treaties—they are more rearmament than disarmament treaties—are legal. The vast profligate appropriations are legal. The criminal bluster of the politicians, so much like the spite of schoolyard bullies, is legal. The bombs itching to vent flame and poison on the world are legal. The applecheeked servicemen trained to ask questions later—when neither they nor anyone else is alive—are legal.

The whole lock-step toward a nuclear doomsday is unassailably and impeccably legal. The death of Hiroshima and Nagasaki were legal. The millions of fatalities, even American ones, from nuclear testing are legal. The prospect of global suicide is legal.

Yesterday, my brother Jerome—a doctor of literature, a college professor, and the father of four children—was sentenced to penitentiary for nonviolent resistance at the Pentagon. Clearly, my brother is illegal. He's a political felon. So are my brother Dan and myself, both under three-to-ten year sentences. We are illegal, but the Pentagon is legal; first-strike weapons like Trident, Cruise, and Pershing II are legal. And a nuclear holocaust is legal.

Finally, the arms race is either/or. Either we have peace, or we have annihilation. And if peace means disarmament, it also means disarming the system. Our economics and politics are fantastically unjust, irrational, and murderous.

From the standpoint of structure, it is they who spawn the bomb and threaten the world. Consequently, nonviolent resistance to the lunacy of nuclear brinkmanship must be at the same time a move for equitable economics and sane politics internationally, and a reversal of national sovereignty by which the superpowers place a higher value on national interests than they do on human survival.

And now, one last moral aspect that removes what I have said from the academic level. What I am trying to avoid is the curse of the intellectual—bartering in ideas but never risking for them. For after nearly twenty years of resistance to the "Big Brother state" in civil rights, the Vietnam War, and the arms race and after nearly five years in prison for civil disobedience, I am clearly of the conviction that if ideas are worth having, they are worth living for, and even if a need arises, they are worth dying for.

In brief, Americans must protest. They must dissent. They must resist. We are not all equally guilty of the colossal crime of nuclear gamesmanship, but we are all responsible. The Manhattan project was American—American atomic weapons bombed Hiroshima and Nagasaki. Over half of all nuclear testing—atmospheric and underground—has been American.

The leadership of this indescribable madness from nuclear monopoly to first strike has been American. Today, quite contrary to the Reagan version of reality, we kill still from Hiroshima and Nagasaki. We kill from nuclear testing, and we threaten humanity with nuclear doomsday, more than the U.S.S.R. We Americans are responsible. Responsibility means protest, dissent, and resistance. We must lead the retreat from the nuclear brink—not Western or Eastern Europeans, not the Japanese, not the insurgents who, by violent means, have rebelled against the superpower stranglehold upon their economies, their politics, and their lives—but Americans—by any non-violent means. Otherwise, we must question our very worthiness to live.

Gandhi wrote prophetically in the late 1940s in reaction to the atomic bombing of Japan that the only thing the bomb could not destroy was nonviolence. Martin Luther King, Jr., paraphrased him by saying that the choice was simply this: nonviolence or extinction. Those are profound and priceless insights, and they meant a nonviolence centered on the law of God, what Tolstoy called the law of life—compassion toward the helpless and justice for them. Paul says in the letter to the Romans there is only one law, and that law is love your neighbor as you love yourself. In this essential vision, justice would require obedience to God's law but to international law and national law as well, all of which brand the arms race as illegal and a crime against humanity.

Let me remind the Congress that the laws of war have been, for the most part, ratified by our Constitution or by specific acts of Congress, and that they are the law of the land. Furthermore, the United States initiated Nuremberg and executed German and Japanese war criminals because they did not commit civil disobedience.

In brief, divine and international law assert that we have global responsibilities that transcend and supersede national ones. Along this line of reasoning, which I judge absolutely elemental, we are civilly disobedient not when we break the laws insulating the deadly paper-shuffling at the Pentagon of those protecting any nuclear war plant or nuclear war fighting base (the laws that insulate them from scrutiny, that legalize them, and that moralize them), but rather when we don't.

Germans were civilly disobedient when they did not resist Auschwitz, Belsen, Dachau and Treblinka. Then the stakes were the lives of thirteen million people, and now the stakes are total.

So it is sisters and brothers in prison now for a reasoned and loving resistance who are in reality obedient to God's law and to secular law —it is they, and those heading for prison (I know scores of them), who are obedient to law in its truest sense. They restore the law from its absurdity and degradation. They restore it to law from being antilaw.

This is mere common sense as well as the most lofty reverence for law. What a crushing bit of nihilism it would be if the human family passed from life to extinction legally. Americans must resist. Our souls depend on it, and the lives of everyone depend on our resistance.

If we do not, then we risk what the Scripture calls the "second death"

—the fact of having quit on life to become an active partner with death. Paradoxically, the second death happens before the first. We will have died within before dying with everyone else. We will have affirmed suicide before becoming extinct.

The stakes are total—spiritually, physically, globally—for us the human family, the unborn, for the earth. The time is both late and now. Americans must lead in the resistance to nuclear weapons, even as we led in their fashioning, their production, their deployment, and their use.

PART VI

WHERE DOES THIS LEAD US?

■ ■ ■

There are at the present time two great nations in the world, which started from different points, but seem to tend towards the same end. I allude to the Russians and the Americans. Both of them have grown up unnoticed; and while the attention of mankind was directed elsewhere, they have suddenly placed themselves in the front rank among the nations, and the world learned their existence and their greatness at almost the same time. All other nations seem to have nearly reached their natural limits, and they have only to maintain their power; but these are still in the act of growth. All the others have stopped, or continue to advance with extreme difficulty; these alone are proceeding with ease and celerity along a path to which no limit can be perceived . . . . Their starting point is different and their courses are not the same; yet each of them seems marked out by the will of Heaven to sway the destinies of half the globe.

Alexis de Tocqueville
Democracy In America
1835

26

TRUE PEACE IS MORE THAN THE ABSENCE OF WAR

IN HIS ANNUAL report to the Congress for fiscal year 1984, Secretary of Defense Caspar W. Weinberger presented the Reagan administration's formal statement of foreign policy and national security goals and objectives. With regard to foreign policy policy, he stated (p. 15):

> While the threats and circumstances facing the United States, and the strategies and capabilities needed to meet them have changed over time, the nation's fundamental vital interests and the foreign policy needed to protect them have remained constant. They are:
>
> > To preserve our freedom, our political identity, and the institutions that are their foundation—the Constitution and the rule of law.
> >
> > To protect the territory of the United States, its citizens, and its vital interests abroad from armed attack.
> >
> > To foster an international order supportive of the interests of the United States through alliances and cooperative relationships with friendly nations; and by encouraging democratic institutions, economic development, and self-determination throughout the world.

> To protect access to foreign markets and overseas resources in order to maintain the strength of the United States' industrial, agricultural, and technological base and the nation's well-being.

He then went on (p. 15) to argue that:

> Our foreign policy naturally encompasses far more than military concerns. Likewise, the ability to promote our foreign policy and protect our vital interests depends on more than military power. It requires as well economic strength and technological advancement; the operation of our diplomacy and the flow of information about the United States abroad; and the political will and patriotism of a free people. We seek to integrate all these aspects of our national power with our foreign policy. But we also recognize that our economic and political power are imperiled if we lack the military strength to defend our interests.

The document continues:

> The Reagan Administration, like previous Administrations believes that the Soviet Union poses, and for the forseeable future will continue to pose, the most formidable military threat to the United States and its interests.

Weinberger then summarized the "highest priority national security objectives of the Reagan Administration," which include the need:

> [t]o deter military attack by the U.S.S.R. and its allies against the United States, its allies, and other friendly countries; and to deter, or to counter, use of Soviet military power to coerce or intimidate our friends and allies.

Further (p. 16):

> Our aim is to secure the strength needed to deter, or if necessary defend against, nuclear and conventional attack, as well as to discourage coercive use of Soviet military power. A sustained commitment to redress any significant imbalance will not only strengthen our deterrent capabilities but also will improve prospects for agreements on arms control and reductions." (p.16)

Finally, he argued that the tremendous increases in the Reagan fiscal year 1984 military budget request, far beyond last year's increases, are warranted:

> to inhibit further expansion of Soviet control and military presence, and to induce the Soviet Union to withdraw from those countries, such as Afghanistan, where it has imposed and maintains its presence and control by force of arms.

This rapid, substantial and sustained increase in the Reagan military build-up is also required, he argues (p.16), in order to:

foster a reduction in the Soviet Union's overall capability to sustain a military buildup by preventing, in concert with our allies, the flow of militarily significant technologies and material to the Soviet Union, and by refraining from actions that serve to subsidize the Soviet economy.

The document clearly demonstrates that this administration is irrevocably committed to a maximum militarization of the foreign policy of global containment and the escalation of the U.S. nuclear weapons arsenal to a first-strike, war fighting capability. The essential tragedy of this Defense Department posture statement is that very few of my colleagues in the Congress will trouble themselves to read it, and even fewer will question the policy assumptions on which the Reagan administration's military spending priorities and budget requests are predicated.

It was because of this combination of the failures of past policies, the contradictions and dangers inherent in the present policies, and the skewing of vital national budget priorities, that I embarked upon an extended effort to persuade my colleagues in the Congress and concerned citizens everywhere about the need to rethink and reevaluate foreign and national security policies, past and present, in order to devise constructive policy and budget alternatives to those currently being implemented.

The Ad Hoc Hearings on the Full Implications of the Military Budget, which formed the basis of this book, were a necessary first step in the awareness and education process. They also provided the documentary foundation for the development of constructive alternatives. In many instances the information and viewpoints presented in these hearings strongly reinforced positions I had previously advocated. In others, they expanded my own knowledge and understanding, and compelled me to reexamine complex problems from more diverse perspectives.

The information presented in the hearings, combined with subsequent working sessions among staff, defense intellectuals, and budget analysts, evolved into the alternative military budget that I introduced as H.R. 6696 and that I took to the Floor of the House of Representatives for full debate on July 20, 1982. It was a comprehensive, constructive alternative military budget to that proposed by the administration and the leadership of the House Armed Services Committee. It was the first such effort ever made during the Cold War era and may well have been the first of its kind in American history.

The alternative military budget that I presented to the Congress at that time, and which was submitted in an updated and expanded fashion in mid-1983, shortly before this book went to press, was based on an entirely different set of foreign policy and national security princi-ples, critical analyses, and value judgments than those advocated by the Reagan administration and many of its Cold War predecessors. It differs significantly from the Reagan administration's demands for rapidly ac-celerated increases in military spending for fiscal year 1984 and well beyond.

It also differs in concept and substance from other recent proposals that have surfaced in the wake of the so-called Dellums Alternative Budget proposal. It differs dramatically from any military budget "re-forms" proposed by the mainstream thinking in the Congress. Most of them are intellectually and politically comfortable with current Cold War assumptions and are content with limited modifications of exist-ing nuclear weapons systems and force structures. At the same time, they are also supporters of "real growth" increases in the defense bud-get. At root, I believe we must ask in response—"real growth" for what purposes?

It is also at variance with the budget-cutting proposals of the Wall Street banking and investment community, as reflected in their full-page ads and articles in *The Wall Street Journal, The Washington Post* and other newspapers and periodicals that appeared in January and February of 1983. They argued that the staggering federal budget deficits caused by Reaganomics and the Reagan administration's mili-tary build-up necessitate major reductions in military spending, but they offered no policy justification or structural approach for cutting the Pentagon budget.

A month later, former Secretary of State Cyrus Vance, former Secre-tary of Defense Robert S. McNamara, and other "moderates" in the permanent national security establishment issued a twelve-page memo-randum on the need for significant cuts in the Pentagon budget. Their proposals were based in part on policy and force structure considera-tions, but they were only a minimal first step in the effort to contain a runaway military spending program.

The central theme of our alternative, which this book documents, is that the Reagan administration military budgets have been based on incorrect policy assumptions, faulty analysis of problems in the contem-porary world, and incorrect budget priorities. We have learned from the mistakes and actions of the past, in order to craft a national security policy and military budget that is rational and moral and that guaran-tees the total security of the American people.

In my judgment, the United States faces a far greater danger from the internal disruption of its national economy, caused by an unwar-ranted arms build-up, than from any foreign foe, real or imagined. In my judgment, a valid national security policy must be constructed on the firm foundation of a healthy national economy that ensures economic justice and equal opportunity for all. This can occur only in a truly "American" society, where the government guarantees personal freedom from discrimination for all and where the government ensures an adequate and enjoyable quality of life through environmental protection and pollution control, national health care, housing, education, job-training programs, and other real human needs services, especially those designed to help the less fortunate among us—while at the same time protecting the nation from any aggressor.

Our alternative military budget is predicated on three fundamental principles: a noninterventionist foreign policy that stresses international cooperation and a firm commitment to the cause of human rights and personal freedom; a national security policy that is defined as the proper, restrained, deterrent defense of the United States and not the attempted domination of the world through overt or covert intervention in the internal affairs of other countries; and a doctrine of nuclear arms "sufficiency" rather than "superiority."

Based on my years of service on the Research and Development Subcommittee of the Armed Services Committee, and fortified by the expert testimony offered at our Ad Hoc Hearings, I am convinced that, at the present time, the United States has tens of thousands more nuclear weapons in its strategic and tactical arsenals than are necessary for any adequate nuclear deterrence. The United States has enough nuclear firepower to destroy the Soviet Union almost forty times over. In the nuclear age, how much is enough? How much is too much? This budget proposal attempts to answer these questions.

This budget proposal is also a first step toward mutual, balanced-force reductions between the nuclear superpowers in an effort to improve the diplomatic climate for serious and substantive arms reductions that can only lessen international tensions on all sides of the Cold War. *It is not a move to unilateral disarmament.* It *is* a concerted effort to achieve a minimal, but sufficient, deterrent force capability in nuclear and conventional forces, on land, sea, and in the air, until such time as a bilateral, mutually verifiable (including on-site inspection) series of arms reduction treaties can be negotiated and ratified by the nuclear superpowers and then, by extension, the other members of the nuclear weapons club as well.

Nuclear Weapons and National Security

The most immediate, pressing foreign policy and national security crisis at this moment in history is the global danger posed by the escalation of the nuclear arms race and nuclear weapons technology in recent years. We have an obligation to ourselves and future generations to reduce significantly, if not eliminate entirely, the risk of nuclear war. This must include the elimination of all plans, such as PD 59 and its various mutants, for a nuclear war-fighting strategy based on the premise of a preemptive first-strike, or the equally ludicrous notion that a "limited" nuclear war could be kept "limited." As witness after witness testified in our hearings, any "limited" war would quickly escalate to an all-out strategic nuclear exchange between the superpowers, resulting, at minimum, in the virtual annihilation of the Northern Hemisphere of the planet Earth.

The first constructive step in this direction is *the immediate, total elimination of all crisis-destabilizing nuclear weapons systems, on land, sea, in the air, and in space.* These are the weapons that make the world situation infinitely more dangerous and that actually breed greater insecurity rather than enhance our national security. The continued development of these first-strike, hard-target, time-urgent, non-verifiable weapons systems will inexorably force both superpowers to gravitate to a launch-on-warning nuclear strategy based on the Pentagon premise of "use them or lose them," and on the Soviet fear that the United States is undermining their capacity to establish a credible nuclear deterrence.

The crisis-destabilizing nuclear weapons systems that I proposed to eliminate include the MX missile, the Pershing II missile, the Trident II (D-5) missile, and the ground-launched (GLCM) and sea-launched (SLCM) Cruise missiles. Although they are not within the purview of the military budget at this time, I have consistently opposed all NASA (National Aeronautics and Space Administration) budget appropriations for the development of any weapons programs in space, including nuclear, laser, particle beam, and other space-age war-fighting concepts called for in the president's speech of March 23, 1983.

As indicated earlier, I have opposed the development of the MX missile since it was first proposed to the Congress back in 1977. With its Mark 12-A warhead and precision guidance systems, it is the most powerful of the "counterforce," first-strike, weapons ever developed. But, as I have argued countless times in the past, its real intended purpose is not deterrence but a preemptive first-strike against hardened Soviet nuclear missile silos. The administration and its like-minded supporters in the Congress have been back every session in the last six years with requests for additional funding for this deadly Trojan horse. In every instance but one they have succeeded thus far in continuing the development of the MX—another testimonial to the triumph of invincible ignorance over rational restraint.

At the present time the Pershing II missile is, in my judgment, the single most dangerous weapon in our nuclear arsenal because of its time-urgent, hard-target features. With a 200-kiloton warhead (approximately fifteen times the destructive capacity of the atomic bomb that obliterated Hiroshima), I anticipate a MIRV (multiple warhead) capacity and a range of 1,800 kilometers (over 1,000 miles). The Pershing II has the capacity to strike Soviet missile sites and command and communication centers deep within heartland Russia. In the wake of the 1983 national election results in West Germany, it seems almost inevitable that the Pershing IIs will be deployed there later this year—unless there is a significant breakthrough in the impasse that has characterized the intermediate nuclear force negotiations at Geneva thus far.

If the Pershing II missiles are deployed as planned, it will mean that the United States has put a potential first-strike weapon within six to eight minutes launch-arrival time on the Soviet Union. In 1962 President John F. Kennedy brought the world to the brink of nuclear war with his unequivocal demand for the immediate removal of Soviet nuclear missiles from Cuba. The deployment of the Pershing II missiles places the Soviet leadership in the same position that John F. Kennedy confronted during the Cuban Missile Crisis. Soviet officials have directly addressed this analogy and have hinted at the possibility of repositioning Soviet missiles back in Cuba. If that were to occur, it would represent a quantum step toward the likelihood of a nuclear holocaust.

In deploying the Pershing IIs, the United States is dramatically escalating the stakes of the nuclear arms race. It is virtually forcing the Soviets to move to a launch-on-warning strategy, thus pulling the nuclear tripwire ever tighter. In addition, it will make West Germany, and by extension, all of Western Europe, an instant hostage to U.S. nuclear war fighting strategies. Is this a valid price to pay for a weapons system that will do nothing to increase our real national security or deterrence capacity? The answer should be obvious to any person of reasoned and reasonable judgment.

For many of these same reasons I also proposed the elimination of the Trident II (D-5) submarine-launched missile program. It is a much more destructive weapon than its Trident I predecessor and provides another leg of our nuclear triad with a potential first-strike weapon. Since our nuclear submarine force is still virtually invulnerable to any Soviet anti-submarine warfare system at this time, the unnecessary Trident II missiles will be potentially even more destabilizing when fully developed and deployed. The entire program must be terminated.

The development of various Cruise missile technologies is an ominous landmark in the history of nuclear weapons verifiability. Because of their size, mobile-launch capacity, and their alleged ability to escape radar detection, they present major problems for any effective arms control efforts. Even more frightening is the prospect that this technology will soon be available to other nations in the nuclear club, thus further increasing the danger for theater nuclear war not only in Europe but also in the Middle East, southern Africa, the Indian subcontinent, and possibly even South America. Although the air-launched Cruise missiles (ALCM) can be verified to a certain extent by counting the airborne delivery systems available, they still represent a major long-term threat to regional and world peace. At this juncture, I would terminate all development of ground- and sea-launched Cruise missile programs, while deferring a decision on air-launched Cruise missiles until other strategic weapons issues have been resolved or until the development of Stealth technology forces a new assessment of the entire air-launched Cruise missile program.

In addition, I also propose the elimination of other weapons and communications systems directly associated with the further escalation of the U.S. nuclear arsenal. These include the NAVSTAR satellite (global positioning system) that will be the cornerstone of any U.S. space weapons program, the new Trident submarines, the ballistic missile defense program (BMD), the B-1B bomber program, the C³I (command, control, communications, and intelligence network) program, and the neutron weapon programs, especially those designed for use in 155mm howitzers and 8-inch guns. They add nothing to our real security but soak up huge amounts of unnecessary expenditures. The classic example in this regard is the B-1B bomber, as Gordon Adams and others pointed out so effectively in their testimony. The B-1B bomber is a political weapon that is already obsolete. The idea of a penetrating manned bomber being an effective weapon in the air war of the 1990s has as much validity as the tomahawk did against the Gatling gun in an earlier era of history.

Conventional Force Considerations

Few people are aware that the research, development, production, and deployment of our current and proposed nuclear arsenal constitute less than 25 percent of the Pentagon budget. The remainder is spent on conventional forces, personnel costs, and maintenance and overhead of *thousands* of U.S. military bases scattered in every corner of the globe. It is from this area that the major budget reductions must be derived, but this can be achieved only in the context of a major reassessment of our foreign policy goals and objectives.

The renowned German military theoretician, Karl Von Clausewitz, once wrote that "[w]ar is the extension of diplomacy by other means."

If one is to subscribe to the military's reverence for von Clausewitz, then it is necessary to note that he also advocated the development of a war machine designed to implement the foreign policy goals of the nation-state. By this definition, if one is committed to the foreign policy goals of the Reagan administration, then even their military budget proposals are much too inadequate for the global militarization containment policy they espouse. The policies advocated in the Weinberger posture statement for fiscal year 1984 are incapable of budgetary fulfillment, even if one were to accept Paul Nitze's argument in NSC-68 that the United States should be prepared to devote as much as *20 percent* of its annual gross national product (GNP) to the war machine in the vain pursuit of the global militarization of American foreign policy.

As Professor Franklyn Holzman indicated in his testimony, both the CIA and Pentagon analysts, and their Soviet counterparts as well, are using distorted sets of figures in their computations of the other side's military spending to justify further increases for their own side. Some would argue that this is the deliberate intention of the Reaganite policy planners—to force the Russians into a military spending race of such proportions that Soviet society would collapse from the internal overload on its national economy, resulting in further repression by the Soviet leadership and/or subsequent revolution by the masses in Soviet society.

It is this kind of "crackpot realism" that is the hallmark of this administration. While obsessed with the determination to inflict as much punishment as possible on all aspects of Soviet society, they have absolutely no appreciation of, or sensitivity to, the suffering and privation being inflicted on millions of Americans, mainly among the middle and lower income groups, who are being forced to subsidize the disproportionate financial burden of this military build-up. The American public must be made aware that there are constructive alternative foreign policy options to those presently being pursued—options that will enhance the cause of world peace, while substantially reducing the financial and human costs to the American taxpayer.

A foreign policy dedicated to the principles of nonintervention and international cooperation would commit this nation to allowing other nations the right to determine their destiny, rather than having it dictated to them by "gunboat diplomacy," "Yankee imperialism," or "gringo" intervention through covert or overt military activity. It would be a long-term commitment to the concept that there are always at least two sides to every diplomatic relationship—and it would mark an end to the one-dimensional, paternalistic domination that has characterized too many U.S. alliance treaties in the Cold War era.

If Secretary Weinberger is to be taken at his word—that one of the essential principles of our foreign policy should be to foster "self-determination throughout the world"—then he should apply that precept to a U.S. policy implementation of strict nonintervention, either militarily or through the covert operations of the CIA in the civil war in El Salvador. Similarly, this administration should terminate all U.S. efforts to destabilize existing governments in Nicaragua, Cuba, Grenada, Angola, and other areas of the Third World where the U.S. government's principal policy emphasis is on programs of malicious mischief, in the effort to "create an international order supportive of the interests of the United States." It should come as no surprise that the Reagan-Weinberger verbal commitment to "self-determination" specifically *excludes* the struggle of the Black majority in South Africa to gain control of their own lives through an end to the vicious apartheid government there—a government that this administration diplomatically defends and militarily supports.

A foreign policy of nonintervention and international cooperation also necessitates a serious reassessment and restructing of the entire American alliance system, both multilateral and bilateral, in an interdependent and integrated context. Accordingly, any new alliance system that might evolve from this policy reassessment should be based on mutual self-interest and mutual benefit for *all* signatory parties to such treaties. The era of *Pax Americana* is over. The United States can no longer control the world, but we can destroy it—if this administration, like some of its predecessors, persists in the pursuit of reckless policies designed to intimidate and exploit those who would be our allies, while simultaneously threatening annihilation of those who would choose to be, or are periodically chosen to be, our adversaries.

A rational military policy demands that substantive and substantial budget cuts must be made in conventional force structures and personnel systems. To do so requires a fundamental reassessment of the American role in the world as it applies to the NATO alliance system, the termination of Third World interventionism, and reduced military force projections in the Mediterranean, the Pacific and Indian Oceans, and the Caribbean Basin. In making these reassessments, it must be constantly kept in mind that, in any conventional force confrontation between the superpowers or their major alliance surrogates, both sides would soon be faced with the prospect of escalating the conflict to theater nuclear exchanges, which, in turn, would inevitably escalate to an all-out strategic nuclear exchange.

With respect to conventional forces, the principal purpose of the military budget is to amass arms and manpower to project an image of strength throughout the world against those who would be our adversaries and, ostensibly, to protect those who are deemed allies, formally or informally. Forces are related to missions, and missions are related to treaty commitments and supposed geopolitical strategic and economic considerations.

But one must ask—in the nuclear age—does this image of strength conform to the realities of power, or are there ulterior motives in stationing more than a half-million American military personnel in more than ninety nations around the world? Are American military personnel stationed in most of those countries to defend against a foreign foe—or to preserve an incumbent regime in power against the will of its own people?

The principal fiscal outlay for our present military alliance system is for continued U.S. participation in the NATO alliance. Because of overlapping force structures and missions, it is difficult to pinpoint the exact annual expenditures for maintaining and preserving the dominant U.S. role in the NATO alliance. A conservative estimate would place the figure somewhere between 35 to 45 percent of the total annual U.S. military budget, but some would argue that this figure should be 50 percent or more.

Some basic questions need to be posed concerning these expenditures. For example, how much should we spend to maintain the NATO alliance, even in its current configuration? Is the current level of funding enough, too much, or too little, and why? If the NATO alliance is that vital to "Free World" security, why are the other nations in NATO bearing a disproportionately lower share of the fiscal burden than the United States? Is it because their perceptions of the threat from the Soviet Union and/or the Warsaw Pact alliance system are significantly different from ours? If our perceptions are more valid, then they should be paying more; if their analysis is more correct, then we need a constructive downward revision in weapons and personnel deployment throughout western Europe.

The U.S. military budget allocation for NATO is predicated on the prospect of a prolonged land war in Europe. In my judgment, on a scale of 1 to 10, the possibility of a conventional land war erupting in Europe in the nuclear age is between 0 and 1. The stakes are too high—and the cost in human suffering and physical devastation would be too enormous—for either side to consider initiating such utter madness.

Given this set of perceptions and analyses, there is no rational reason in the nuclear age for the maintenance of such a large standing Army —unless one intends to use it to escalate military intervention in Third World countries, or to serve as a permanent public employment jobs program. Our alternative military budget proposes a systematic minimal annual reduction of our land forces in 5 percent increments, so that the number of Army divisions would be reduced from sixteen to thirteen by fiscal year 1988. The eventual goal would be to arrive at a permanent Army force structure of six land divisions and two airborne divisions, a more than adequate force to maintain the profile of real power necessary to defend proper national security interests or to respond to an immediate, limited crisis.

To arrive at this troop reduction level it is also necessary to reassess the nature and extent of our military commitments in Asia. At present, the United States has the equivalent of two full Army divisions stationed in South Korea, and the 3rd Marine Division, stationed on Okinawa. There are also major naval and air bases located throughout the western Pacific, including Japan, the Philippines, and Taiwan. There are other considerations involved in our participation in the ANZUS Pact with Australia and New Zealand.

It is estimated that these Pacific area force commitments require a yearly expenditure of $40 billion. Is this the price we want to pay—or must pay—to retain in power the corrupt dictatorships in South Korea and the Philippines, so long as they profess the proper amount of anti-Communist enthusiasm for the policy of global containment? Surely the proper defense of valid American interests in those regions can be achieved at cheaper cost, and with allies more committed to regional cooperation and their own common defense, than to the perpetuation of petty, corrupt dictatorships that are an insult to real American values of personal freedom and a commitment to human rights. Employing the same analysis, the number of Marine Corps divisions could be reduced from three to two, without any loss of real power in our force projections abroad. The retention of these two Marine divisions, in addition to the two airborne divisions mentioned above, makes the need for a Rapid Deployment Force totally unnecessary. The RDF is nothing more than an administration fig leaf for the development of an elite strike force designed primarily for intervention against Third World countries, where an influx of 30,000 troops could achieve quick results against an outgunned and outmanned indigenous government or guerrilla force in a civil war. To contemplate using a projected RDF in a Persian Gulf or other Middle East crisis is lunacy. The closer the geographical intervention to the Soviet Union, or to its perceived vital national interests, the greater would be the Soviet response, thus further escalating the stakes of superpower confrontation.

Another major consideration in the conventional force structure is the future mission, size, and deployment of the surface Navy. As the recent struggle in the Malvinas (Falkland) Islands between Great Britain and Argentina clearly indicated, surface vessels are becoming increasingly vulnerable to attack and destruction by precision-guided missile systems, whether launched from the air, the surface, or underwater. If older generation missiles such as the French-produced Exocet and others could wreak such havoc in such a short space of time, then imagine what devastation could be inflicted on the U.S. surface fleet by the new generations of missile systems.

During a 1982 inspection visit to the headquarters of the U.S. Atlantic Fleet in Norfolk, Virginia, I questioned the Admiral in command at length about the increasing vulnerability of the U.S. surface fleet to missile attack. When I asked him what would be the survival expectancy rate of a nuclear or conventional aircraft carrier in a conflict with the Soviet Union, he replied without hesitation: "Less than ten minutes!"

If this is the considered judgment of the professionals manning these ships, then why is this administration committed to a massive expansion of the surface Navy, from approximately 400 vessels to 640? The fantasies of the Secretary of the Navy notwithstanding, the surface fleet force configurations should not be designed for major naval engagements with their Soviet naval counterparts. World War I conclusively demonstrated the limitations of the "Dreadnought" battleships, and World War II demonstrated the vulnerability of aircraft carriers and other capital ships to air attack, as evidenced by the battles of the Coral Sea, Midway, Saipan, and Leyte Gulf. Why construct more ocean-going dinosaurs in an age of air- and space-weapons technology? The illogic of the situation should be apparent to all.

If the surface fleet cannot be used effectively in a showdown situation with the Soviet Union, then for what legitimate purpose is this massive force being created? Its size alone is out of all proportion to true U.S. security needs and force projections around the world—unless one is committed to a long-term policy of military intervention in Third World countries. In my judgment, a surface fleet significantly less than half the size of the proposed 640 ship configuration is more than adequate to preserve valid U.S. national security interests anywhere and everywhere around the globe.

At the present time, the Navy is still committed to the nuclear carrier battle group program as the centerpiece of its surface fleet force projection. But every individual carrier planned and produced means a quantum jump in the number of additional support vessels and systems required, such as missile cruisers, destroyer escort screens, attack submarines, supply and electronic surveillance vessels, carrier tactical aircraft and helicopters, and additional land-based support systems, ranging from drydock repair facilities to land-based support aircraft and missile systems. At the present time, the cost estimate for maintaining a nuclear carrier battle group ranges from $11 to $18 billion per year, contingent on whose cost-analysis figures are used. When the Navy proposes to buy just one or two more carriers, by extension they are setting in motion a chain of events that will increase the military budget by hundreds of billions of dollars.

Conversely, the centerpiece of our alternative budget proposal for the surface fleet is a direct challenge to the carrier battle group mindset and the budgetary consequences that result. At the present time there are thirteen carrier battle groups in place or in production. The administration proposes an increase to fifteen carrier battle groups by the end of the decade, with a forward deployment of five or six carrier battle groups at all times. Our alternative would eliminate the two new carrier battle groups entirely and begin a phased reduction to ten battle groups over the next five years. Even greater reductions will be undertaken after that time, as new advances in technology further demonstrate the increased irrelevancy of the carrier battle group concept as a superpower force projection. As a direct result of the above, it then becomes possible to eliminate the entire CG-47 Aegis missile cruiser program, the DDG-51 destroyer program, the SSN attack submarine program, and attack helicopter programs, such as the SH-60B. The budgetary, resource, and personnel savings effected by these proposals will reduce the federal budget deficit by additional billions in future years.

If one accepts these substantive alterations in U.S. military force projections on land, sea, and in the air, then it is possible to eliminate, or reduce substantially, unnecessary, obsolete, or redundant conventional weapons systems. Another option is an extended effort to have our allies mass-produce conventional weapons that are cheaper or that function more efficiently and that can be easily incorporated into U.S. ordnance and supply procurement considerations. The first target for total elimination is all components of the chemical and biological warfare program. Heinous, inhumane weapons such as these have no place in the planning, much less the storage-use arsenals of any nation that defines itself as a humane society. Obsolete or unnecessary weapons systems proposed for elimination include the aforementioned B-1B bomber, the M-1 Abrams tank (the German Leopard tank performs better in most functions and at far cheaper cost), the AH-64 attack helicopters, the Patriot and Tomahawk missile programs, and the DIVAD air defense gun.

In eliminating the Rapid Deployment Force, it is then possible to eliminate such budget items as the LHD-1 and LSD-41 landing craft, additional C-5A and KC-135 aircraft, and other elements designed to support U.S. interventionary forces in Third World countries and reduce our munitions inventory from a ninety-day to a forty-five-day supply. At the same time, it also provides for substantial reductions in overall tactical aircraft strength. This would include the elimination of the F-15 and F-18 fighter programs, and significant reductions in the F-14 fighter and AV-8B light attack aircraft programs. Perhaps most important, the elimination or reduction of these weapons systems would make them unavailable for escalating arms sales and transfers to Third World nations, thereby reducing the danger of national or regional instability for all parties concerned.

The reductions in force structure projections would then make possible further budget cuts in the area of personnel, the number and size of U.S. military installations, especially those overseas, and operations and maintenance overhead costs. The weapons and force structure reductions proposed above would result in a minimum 15 percent overall reduction in military personnel, the major portion of which would be in the Army and the Navy.

The savings would be enormous, not only in terms of current and future compensation costs but also in long-term pension payouts and cost-of-living-adjustment increases (COLAs). However, it ought to be noted here that I have always supported, and will continue to support, adequate pay and compensation benefits for active-duty personnel in all branches of the military and superior on-the-job training programs for them so that they can maximize their skills and be encouraged to make a long-term commitment to an active-duty military career.

A thorough study and review of the entire range of U.S. military bases around the world should be undertaken to determine which are least vital, or totally unnecessary, to our real national security needs, now and in the future. As chair of the House Armed Services Subcommittee on Military Installations and Facilities, I have already begun this effort, but it is a time-consuming and difficult process that will demand serious analysis and, in some instances, painful choices. The criteria for any decision must be the question of real national security needs and a concern for the survival and welfare of local economies and the individual human beings directly affected by these decisions.

The reductions in overhead and maintenance costs, when combined with defense contract bidding and procurement practices, constitute the major areas for savings in the stifling of waste, fraud, and abuse. In a celebrated article in the December 1981 issue of *The Atlantic Monthly* magazine, Budget Director David Stockman confessed to reporter William Greider that the administration's Pentagon budget proposal "was just a bunch of numbers written on a piece of paper." Regarding cost overruns and the like, he admitted: "Hell, I think there's a kind of swamp of $10 [billion] to $20 [billion] to $30 *billion* worth of waste that can be ferreted out if you really push hard." One wishes that the OMB watch-dogs had searched as diligently for evidence of waste, fraud, and abuse in the labyrinth of the Pentagon budget as they did in the investigation of alleged abuses in the federal food stamp program.

Since they did not, we propose that a tightly organized, tight-fisted scientific and comptroller oversight responsibility be established, either within the General Accounting Office (GAO) or in some other independent agency. Their sole function will be to investigate, approve, and monitor every Pentagon contract, from original bid through procurement to production and deployment, to eliminate or reduce cost overruns and duplication of effort and to guarantee thorough advance testing of all systems under a variety of terrain, construction, weather, and magnetic field conditions. Only then can we begin to curb the abuses inherent in the "iron triangle," which Gordon Adams discussed at length in his testimony and in the book that bears that title.

Then there is the issue of civil defense. The interview that journalist Robert Scheer conducted with T.K. Jones, the former Boeing Aircraft official who is the point-man for the Reagan administration's conceptual and programmatic approach to civil defense, should be read by every concerned citizen because no synopsis could do intellectual justice to the insanity of the arguments propounded there. That sustained flight into fantasy, complete with shovels, doors, and a requisite amount of dirt, then ought to be measured against the crushing weight of scientific evidence presented in the testimony of Dr. H. Jack Geiger and Dr. Jeremy Stone earlier in this book in order to determine who has a greater grasp of reality and the total devastation implicit in any nuclear attack.

If that is not enough, then we have the first-hand evidence every business day of the week, in virtually every major metropolitan area of the country, that it takes hours each day just to evacuate a portion of the work force to their homes in the suburbs. With Soviet nuclear weapons scarcely thirty minutes away from impact on virtually every metropolitan area of the United States, no one is safe, no matter how near or distant the shelter. And, as Dr. Geiger commented, the medical consequences of nuclear war would be such that the living and the dying will truly envy the dead in the aftermath of a nuclear attack. To spend a single cent for civil defense, beyond that absolutely necessary to respond to natural disasters such as fire, flood, drought, earthquake, volcanic eruptions, toxic waste, pollution hazards, large industrial accidents, and the like, is criminal.

Proposals For Economic Conversion

Finally, our alternative military budget is the only military budget proposal that has ever specifically incorporated economic conversion legislative proposals to effect an innovative and constructive transition to a peace economy rather than the continued maintenance of a permanent war economy. Previous efforts in this regard in recent years, such as those offered by former Senator George McGovern of South Dakota and Representative Parren Mitchell of Maryland, were contingent on projected cuts in the military budget. Since the military budgets continuously increased, rather than decreased, their proposals were repeatedly stifled in committee or were attached as amendment riders to other legislation that had little hope of final passage in that form.

Our proposal is based on two fundamental philosophical and political propositions. First, I am committed to the belief that every American is entitled to a job. This ought to be a basic human right in this nation. Second, I believe that, once a decision is made in the interest of national security that might adversely affect people or the economy at the local level, the federal government has a moral obligation to do everything possible to ease their economic, social, and psychic burdens by providing economic conversion assistance funds, high-level job training programs for conversion employment opportunities, monetary assistance, and health-care services to families and individuals during this transition period, if they cannot secure immediate employment.

On the political level, we must relieve politicians of the pyschic burden of electoral survival in this respect. We must wean them away from the reflex tendency to vote for defense budgets mainly because it means jobs for their home states or districts. We need to educate them to the stark realities outlined in the testimony by Seymour Melman, Marion Anderson, William Winpisinger, Gordon Adams and others— viz., that the perpetuation of the permanent war economy is truly looting the means of production in our society and costing this nation literally millions of productive jobs every year, and that it is allowed to continue through congressional subservience to administration demands and the fear of ballot box revenge.

Our conversion legislation would provide a minimum of $45 billion over the next five years for the specific purpose of economic conversion assistance and job-training programs for those geographical and employment areas most affected by the reductions in the Pentagon budget described above. The initial grants and training programs would go to those areas and workers who have been displaced because of the projected cuts in weapons systems programs, and then proceed to other sectors of the defense economy that will be similarly affected by these altered policy and budget priorities. It is estimated that this proposal would provide for a minimum of 300,000 new jobs in the first year of the conversion process and that the number of new jobs would increase by ever greater amounts in succeeding years.

In the period since I first introduced this legislation in 1982, I have made a concerted effort to meet with union leaders and representatives and with local officials in the communities to be most affected by the changes outlined above. I have tried to communicate my sense of concern and urgency about this matter, and have solicited their views on a wide range of issues affecting these complex problems. Much has been done already—but much more work needs to be done in this area to make conversion legislation proposals even more effective and to build a broad-based national constituency of support for these proposals. That is the challenge we face—and those are the problems we must resolve if we are to endure as a free society in the effort to make a safer world for ourselves and for our children.

A Call to Action

In his testimony during the Ad Hoc Hearings on the Full Implications of the Military Budget, Philip Berrigan, warned prophetically:

> What a crushing bit of nihilism it would be if the human family passed from life to extinction legally [through recourse to government-sanctioned nuclear war]. So, Americans must resist. Our souls depend on it, and the lives of everyone depend on our resistance . . . . Americans must lead in the resistance to nuclear weapons, even as we led in their fashioning, their production and their deployment.

With these words Philip Berrigan has defined the moral imperative for all Americans of conscience and, by extension, for the global community of conscience as well. The nuclear arms race is *the* fundamental global moral issue of our time. We must put an end to militarism as a way of life in American society if we are to have any hope of constructively contributing to a better world, one based on human dignity, personal freedom, and economic justice for all in the global community.

The planet Earth is our vehicle for traveling through space, time, and life. Regardless of how we choose to define ourselves—by race, sex, religion, national origin, or political ideology—it is our common home. Each one of us has a vested interest in its survival—but we also have a profound personal, political, and moral obligation to ensure its survival.

This global concern must transcend national, geographical and ideological boundaries to embrace common denominators of collective human concern for, and action on behalf of, the preservation and promotion of the general welfare of all humanity. There must be a collective, cohesive, *global people's effort* to "lead the leaders" of the superpowers to the negotiation table with constructive proposals designed to halt and then reverse the madness of the arms race, both nuclear and conventional.

The United States must assume the leadership role in this crusade for peace and sanity and away from the madness of death and destruction. However, in my judgment, the growth of opposition to the escalation of the nuclear arms in the United States has been due in large measure to the floodtide of opposition on the part of millions of concerned West Europeans against the projected deployment of the Pershing II and Cruise missiles in Europe. The antinuclear demonstrations, there and in the United States, have all expressed a sense of common outrage at the criminal arrogance of both superpowers in jeopardizing world peace in such a manner.

In the United States, the core constituency of antinuclear concern now includes new allies, ranging from large numbers of bishops in the Catholic Church speaking out against the immorality of nuclear war, to the widespread citizen effort to promote the cause of a mutually verifiable nuclear weapons freeze. They have been successful in eight of the nine states and the District of Columbia, where the issue has been on the ballot, and they have also been successful in forcing the Congress to deal with the matter in each of its last two sessions.

In the Republican-controlled Senate, the so-called Hatfield-Kennedy resolution was swept aside in favor of the Jackson-Warner proposal, one that is little more than a guarantee of continued nuclear arms escalation until some point of mythical parity is achieved with the Soviets. In the House, the so-called Markey-Bingham resolution was narrowly defeated last year by a margin of two votes, but a modified version of that proposal passed the House in 1983. That version will never be passed by the Senate, at least until the Republican majority and their hawkish Democratic allies are transformed into a minority.

In all honesty, it must be admitted that even if it were passed in its pristine form, any constructive congressional nuclear freeze resolution would not be binding on this administration or any other. In essence, it is little more than an expression of public concern about a critical issue. What worries me is the possibility that the nuclear freeze movement and its supporters might be content to rest on the laurels of public citizen concern rather than concerted action to *force the adminstration and Congress* to halt and reverse the arms race, both nuclear and conventional.

What is needed for the future is a monumental commitment to international solidarity on the part of concerned human beings around the globe, working in a collective and constructive fashion to terminate the nuclear arms race before it terminates the human race. What is needed is a common dedication to global education and consciousness-raising efforts on this vital issue of human survival. *What is most needed is direct citizen involvement, first to educate ourselves and then others, to the real peril and, more important, to the reality that constructive alternatives are available.*

This book and the Dellums Alternative Military Budget have been a concerted, continuing effort to expand the parameters of public awareness and debate on the need for alternative ways of looking at the world and our role in it, diplomatically, militarily, and politically. They are initial chapters in the emerging struggle between the forces of sanity and the forces of madness, in terms of who will control humanity's destiny. For our part, this struggle will continue because, as I said on the House Floor at the conclusion of the debate on the alternative military budget in 1982: "We will be back again and again and again —until we right the wrongs in this madness."

EPILOGUE ...

In April of 1967 Dr. Martin Luther King, Jr. came to the Berkeley campus of the University of California to speak out against the criminal consequences of the insane American adventurism in Indochina on American society at large. I was in the audience that day as a graduate school alumnus and as a person who had just been elected to the Berkeley City Council.

The memory of that day will live within me until the day I die. I felt Dr. King challenged me as an individual to respond to the crisis at hand by making a commitment to change society through constructive alternatives to the madness surrounding us. As he put it then: "We have flown the air like birds and swum the sea like fishes, but we have not learned the simple act of walking the earth like brothers." He then talked about the dichotomy of leadership in America—those who lead by following the popular prejudices of the moment—and those who, like himself, sought to mold a new consensus by offering new visions and new alternatives. It was those visions he described, and those constructive alternatives he proposed, that have been the twin foundations for my own educational growth on the global issues of war and peace and for an ever-increasing commitment to the goals and dreams for which he lived and died.

Twenty years after the march on Washington, the legacy of Martin Luther King, Jr., is still an unfulfilled dream. During a lifetime that was all too brief—only thirty-nine years—he was cursed, reviled, and spat upon, beaten, jailed, and stabbed, denounced as an extremist by the lords of the media, and as a "nigger" and a "traitor" in the highest councils of government. Finally, in an attempt to slay the dream they slew The Dreamer.

It is for us, the living, to make certain that his dream never dies. It is for us, the living, to pick up the fallen torch of equality and justice, peace and personal freedom, and go forward, as he said, to "make of this old world a new world" so that we and our children can truly live out the words of the Civil Rights anthem: "We Shall Live in Peace Some Day."

SUGGESTIONS FOR FURTHER READING

IN RECENT YEARS the number of published works about the Cold War and various aspects of the arms race has proliferated almost beyond verifiability. This bibliography provides selective suggestions for those readers interested in a more detailed examination and analysis of the major topics discussed in this book. It is not intended to be all-inclusive.

The principal focus is on those general works that are considered landmarks or that offer constructive intellectual and analytical challenges to the perceived conventional wisdom on a particular subject area. It also includes some recent monographs dealing with new developments in weapons systems and space technology. Those books that have been published in one or more paperback editions are denoted with an asterisk (*) at the end of each citation.

In some instances specific memoir accounts have been included. They often offer valuable insights on critical issues and policy decisions. For example, the memoirs of Dean Acheson, Walt W. Rostow, and George F. Kennan are fundamental to a more complete understanding of the competing policy philosophies in the early years of the Cold War, many of which prevail today. Similarly, the quasi-official memoir accounts of the Kennedy administration by Arthur Schlesinger, Jr., and Theodore Sorensen present useful analyses on the escalation of the nuclear arms race, civil defense, the Cuban Missile Crisis of 1962, Third World intervention, and other topics of continuing importance. Henry Kissinger's two memoir volumes document the limits of his knowledge about, and awareness of, the full implications of the complexities and intricacies of nuclear arms escalation, especially in the areas of MIRVing and verifiability.

OFFICIAL RECORDS AND DOCUMENTS

THE PUBLIC DOCUMENTS most relevant to the various aspects of the military budget can be found in the following:

Office of Management and Budget *The Budget of the United States Government for Fiscal Year 1984.* Published annually, with appropriate appendices and special analyses, it provides a detailed view of the inner recesses of the federal bureaucracy at every level of operation.

Public Papers of the Presidents of the United States. This useful compendium of formal speeches, statements, press conferences, and the like, on national and international issues is published chronologically in annual volumes, by presidential administration, and in a weekly version as *Weekly Compilation of Presidential Documents.*

U.S. Arms Control and Disarmament Agency (ACDA) *World Military Expenditures and Arms Transfers.* An annual report on the status of nuclear and conventional arms.

U.S. Department of Defense *Annual Report to the Congress* by the Secretary of Defense. Sometimes referred to as the DoD Posture Statement for a given fiscal year.

U.S. Department of State *Bulletin.* This first-hand reference for issues relating to foreign policy, arms control and other national security issues is published monthly.

U.S. Joint Chiefs of Staff *United States Military Posture for Fiscal Year 1984.* The Annual Report to the President and the Congress by the incumbent Chairman of the Joint Chiefs of Staff of the U. S. Armed Forces.

In addition, there are periodic reports published by a number of government agencies that relate directly to national security, military policy, and spending, including the Departments of State and Defense, the Office of Management and Budget (OMB), the Arms Control and Disarmament Agency (ACDA), the Federal Emergency Management Administration (FEMA), the Atomic Energy Commission (AEC), the Department of Energy (DOE), and the National Aeronautics and Space Administration (NASA).

At the congressional level, one ought to be aware of the committee *Reports* and *Hearings* of the Senate and House of Representatives relating to foreign affairs, armed services, the budget and appropriations. The *Congressional Record* contains the edited text of floor debates and record votes on all relevant legislative issues. The Congressional Budget Office (CBO), the General Accounting Office (GAO), and the Congressional Research Service (CRS) also publish valuable studies relating to national security and military policy issues, weapons systems, personnel problems, and other cost and policy considerations.

MILITARY POLICY AND WEAPONS SURVEYS

The list of quasi-official and scholarly periodic publications on these topics has also grown rapidly in recent years. The more important ones include:

Arms Control Today, published by the Arms Control Association in Washington, D.C.

The Brookings Studies in Defense Policy, published by The Brookings Institution in Washington, D.C.

The Defense Monitor, published ten times per year by the Center for Defense Information in Washington, D.C.

The Federal Budget and Social Reconstruction, a series of critical analyses of the federal budget and its implications for military and social spending programs published periodically by The Institute for Policy Studies in Washington, D.C.

Jane's All the World's Aircraft, Fighting Ships, and *Weapons Systems,* published annually in London, with various American editions.

The Military Balance and *Strategic Survey* (annual), *Survival* (bimonthly), and *Adelphi Papers* (periodic), published by the International Institute for Strategic Studies (IISS) in London.

SANE, located in Washington, D.C., publishes a monthly newsletter entitled SANE *World* and periodic legislative analyses of military matters entitled SANE *Action.*

World Armaments and Disarmament: SIPRI Yearbook, published annually in Europe and the United States by the Stockholm International Peace Research Institute (SIPRI).

OTHER RELEVANT PERIODICALS

The following periodicals contain much of the relevant, updated information and analyses related to various aspects of national security and the military budget:

Air University Review
Armed Forces Journal
Army
Aviation Week and Space Technology
Bulletin of the Atomic Scientists
Canadian Defence Quarterly
Contemporary Review
democracy
Electronic Warfare/Defense Electronics
Foreign Affairs
Foreign Policy
Health Physics
Inquiry
International Affairs
International Defense Review
International Security
Journal of Civil Defense
Journal of Conflict Resolution
Military Electronics and Countermeasures
Military Review
The Nation
National Journal
National Review
Naval War College Review
The New Republic
Nuclear Times
Physics Today
The PSR (Physicians for Social Responsibility) Newsletter
The Progressive
Scientific American
Soviet Studies
Strategic Review
World Issues
World Politics

BOOKS

AN IN-DEPTH UNDERSTANDING of the American role in the conduct of international and national security affairs must be predicated on a knowledge of recent U.S. domestic and diplomatic history. William E. Leuchtenburg's *A Troubled Feast: American Society since 1945* (Boston: Little, Brown and Company, 1979)* is a useful starting point for the conventional wisdom perspective, but many of his interpretations are challenged in Lawrence S. Wittner's *Cold War America: From Hiroshima to Watergate* (New York: Holt, Rinehart and Winston, 1978)* and Howard Zinn's *Postwar America: 1945-1971* (Indianapolis: The Bobbs-Merrill Co., Inc., 1973).*

In the realm of foreign policy, Jules Davids's *America and the World of Our Time* (New York: Random House, Inc., 3d ed., 1970) is an honest overview of twentieth century U.S. foreign policy. A more recent consensus centrist interpretation is Robert Dallek's *The American Style of Foreign Policy: Cultural Politics and Foreign Affairs* (New York: Alfred A. Knopf, 1983). A critical revisionist overview is provided in Lloyd C. Gardner's *Imperial America: American Foreign Policy since 1898* (New York: Harcourt Brace Jovanovich, 1976).*

The most sustained critique of recent American foreign policy can be found in Walter LaFeber's *America, Russia and the Cold War, 1945-1980* (New York: John Wiley & Sons, 1980).* William Appleman Williams's *Empire as a Way of Life: An Essay on the Causes and Character of America's Present Predicament Along with a Few Thoughts about an Alternative* (New York: Oxford University Press, 1980)* offers some challenging insights into viewing America's role in the world from a very different perspective. Those interested in postrevisionist accounts should consult John Lewis Gaddis's *Russia, The Soviet Union and The*

United States: An Interpretive History (New York: John Wiley & Sons, Inc., 1978)* and two books by Adam B. Ulam: *The Rivals: America and Russia since World War II* (New York: The Viking Press, 1971)* and *Dangerous Relations: The Soviet Union in World Politics, 1970-1982* (New York: Oxford University Press, 1983).

For a better understanding of America's military past, the reader ought to consult Russell F. Weigley's *The American Way of War: A History of United States Military Strategy and Policy* (New York: The Macmillan Publishing Co., Inc., 1973)* and T. Harry Williams's *The History of American Wars* (New York: Alfred A. Knopf, 1981). The evolution of the national security state mentality can be better understood through a careful reading of two books by a National Security academic/bureaucrat, Samuel P. Huntington. See *The Soldier and the State: The Theory and Politics of Civil-Military Relations* (Cambridge: Harvard University Press, 1957)* and *The Common Defense* (New York: Columbia University Press, 1961).*

In addition to the books mentioned above and in the chapter introductions, the following are all useful references for further information and analysis.

A. Foreign Policy and National Security Considerations

Acheson, Dean. *Present at the Creation: My Years in the State Department.* New York: W.W. Norton & Company, 1969.

Barnet, Richard J. *The Alliance: America, Europe and Japan.* New York: Simon and Schuster, 1983.

———. *Roots of War.* New York: Atheneum, 1972.*

Brzezinski, Zbigniew. *Power and Principle: Memoirs of the National Security Adviser, 1977-1981.* New York: Farrar . Straus . Giroux, 1983.

Carter, Jimmy. *Keeping Faith: Memoirs of a President.* New York: Bantam Books, 1982.

Divine, Robert A. *Second Chance: The Triumph of Internationalism in America during World War II.* New York: Atheneum, 1967.*

Donovan, John C. *The Cold Warriors: A Policy-Making Elite.* Lexington, Mass.: D.C. Heath and Company, 1974.*

Franck, Thomas M., and Edwin Weisband. *Foreign Policy by Congress.* New York: Oxford University Press, 1979.

Hersh, Seymour M. *The Price of Power: Kissinger in The Nixon White House.* New York: Summit Books, 1983.

Kissinger, Henry A. *White House Years.* Boston: Little, Brown and Company, 1979.

———. *Years of Upheaval.* Boston: Little, Brown and Company, 1982.

Kolko, Gabriel. *The Roots of American Foreign Policy: An Analysis of Power and Purpose.* Boston: Beacon Press, 1969.*

Morgenthau, Hans J. *Politics among Nations: The Struggle for Power and Peace.* New York: Alfred A. Knopf, 5th ed., 1978.

Morris, Roger. *Haig: The General's Progress.* New York: Playboy Press, 1982.

———. *Uncertain Greatness: Henry Kissinger and American Foreign Policy.* New York: Harper & Row, 1977.

Rostow, Walt W. *The Diffusion of Power: An Essay in Recent History.* New York: The Macmillan Company, 1972.

_____. *The United States in the World Arena: An Essay in Recent History.* New York: Harper & Brothers, 1960.

Schlesinger, Arthur M., Jr. *The Vital Center: The Politics of Freedom.* Boston: Houghton Mifflin Company, 1949, 1962.*

_____. *A Thousand Days: John F. Kennedy in the White House.* Boston: Houghton Mifflin Company, 1965.*

_____. *Robert F. Kennedy and His Times.* Boston: Houghton Mifflin Company, 1978.*

Schurmann, Franz. *The Logic of World Power: An Inquiry into the Origin, Currents and Contradictions of World Politics.* New York: Pantheon Books, 1974.

Sorensen, Theodore. *Kennedy.* New York: Harper & Row, 1965.*

Steel, Ronald. *Walter Lippmann and the American Century.* Boston: Little, Brown and Company, 1980.*

Szulc, Tad. *The Illusion of Peace: Foreign Policy in the Nixon Years.* New York: The Viking Press, 1978.

Tucker, Robert W. *Nation or Empire: The Debate over American Foreign Policy.* Baltimore: The Johns Hopkins University Press, 1968.*

Vance, Cyrus. *Hard Choices: Critical Years in America's Foreign Policy.* New York: Simon and Schuster, 1983.

B. Superpower Confrontation: United States v. U.S.S.R.

Allison, Graham T. *Essence of Decision: Explaining the Cuban Missile Crisis.* Boston: Little, Brown and Company, 1971.*

Barnet, Richard J., and Marcus G. Raskin. *After Twenty Years: Alternatives to the Cold War in Europe.* New York: Random House, Inc., 1965.*

Bialer, Seweryn. *Stalin's Successors: Leadership, Stability & Change in The Soviet Union.* Cambridge: Cambridge University Press, 1980.*

_____, ed. *The Domestic Context of Soviet Foreign Policy.* Boulder, Colo.: Westview Press, 1980.*

Chomsky, Noam. *Towards a New Cold War: Essays on the Current Crisis and How We Got There.* New York: Pantheon Books, 1982.*

Clemens, Diane Shaver. *Yalta.* New York: Oxford University Press, 1970.*

Cox, Arthur Macy. *Russian Roulette: The Superpower Game.* New York: Times Books, 1982.

Dinerstein, Herbert S. *The Making of a Missile Crisis: October 1962.* Baltimore: The Johns Hopkins University Press, 1976.*

Dulles, John Foster. *War or Peace.* New York: The Macmillan Company, 1950.

Gaddis, John Lewis. *Strategies of Containment: A Critical Appraisal of Postwar American National Security Policy.* New York: Oxford University Press, 1982.*

_____. *The United States and the Origins of the Cold War, 1941-1947.* New York: Columbia University Press, 1972.*

Gardner, Lloyd C. *Architects of Illusion: Men and Ideas in American Foreign Policy, 1941-1949.* Chicago: Quadrangle Books, 1970.

Halliday, Fred. *The Origins of the Second Cold War.* New York: Schocken Books, 1983.*

Hammond, Thomas T., ed. *The Anatomy of Communist Takeovers.* New Haven: Yale University Press, 1977.

Herring, George C., Jr. *Aid to Russia, 1941-1946: Strategy, Diplomacy and the Origins of the Cold War.* New York: Columbia University Press, 1973.

Hoffmann, Stanley. *Dead Ends: American Foreign Policy in the New Cold War.* Cambridge, Mass.: Ballinger Publishing Company, 1983.

Kennan, George, F. *Memoirs, 1925-1950.* Boston: Little, Brown and Company, 1967.*

———. *Memoirs, 1950-1963.* Boston: Little, Brown and Company, 1972.*

Kuklick, Bruce. *American Policy and the Division of Germany: The Clash with Russia over Reparations.* Ithaca: Cornell University Press, 1972.

Kuniholm, Bruce Robellet. *The Origins of the Cold War in the Near East: Great Power Conflict and Diplomacy in Iran, Turkey and Greece.* Princeton: Princeton University Press, 1980.

Lenczowski, John. *Soviet Perceptions of U.S. Foreign Policy: A Study of Ideology, Power and Consensus.* Ithaca: Cornell University Press, 1982.

Mastny, Vojtech. *Russia's Road to the Cold War: Diplomacy, Warfare and the Politics of Communism, 1941-1945.* New York: Columbia University Press, 1979.*

Paterson, Thomas G. *Soviet-American Confrontation: Postwar Reconstruction and the Origins of the Cold War.* Baltimore: The Johns Hopkins University Press, 1973.*

Sivachev, Nikolai V., and Yakovlev, Nikolai. *Russia and the United States.* Translated by Olga Adler Titelbaum. Chicago: The University of Chicago Press, 1979.*

Ulam, Adam B. *Expansion and Coexistence: The History of Soviet Foreign Policy, 1917-1967.* New York: Frederick A. Praeger, 1968.*

Wolfe, Thomas. *Soviet Power in Europe, 1945-1970.* Baltimore: The Johns Hopkins University Press, 1970.

Yergin, Daniel. *Shattered Peace: The Origins of The Cold War and the National Security State.* Boston: Houghton Mifflin Company, 1977.*

C. The United States and the Third World

Ambrose, Stephen E., and Richard H. Immerman. *Ike's Spies: Eisenhower and the Espionage Establishment.* Garden City, New York: Doubleday & Company, Inc., 1981.

Arnson, Cynthia. *El Salvador: A Revolution Confronts the United States.* Washington, D.C.: The Institute for Policy Studies, 1982*

Baldwin, Frank, ed. *Without Parallel: The American-Korean Relationship since 1945.* New York: Pantheon Books, 1974.*

Baloyra, Enrique. *El Salvador in Transition.* Chapel Hill: The University of North Carolina Press, 1983.*

Barnet, Richard J. *Intervention and Revolution: The United States in the Third World.* New York: The World Publishing Company, 1968.*

Barnet, Richard J., and Ronald E. Muller. *Global Reach: The Power of the Multi-National Corporations.* New York: Simon and Schuster, 1974.*

Barnet, Richard J., Marcus G. Raskin, and Ralph Stavins. *Washington Plans an Aggressive War.* New York: Random House, Inc., 1971.*

Berman, Larry. *Planning a Tragedy: The Americanization of the War in Vietnam.* New York: W.W. Norton & Company, Inc., 1982.

Crahan, Margaret, ed. *Human Rights and Basic Needs in The Americas.* Washington, D.C.: Georgetown University Press, 1982.*

Dinges, John, and Saul Landau. *Assassination on Embassy Row.* New York: Pantheon Books, 1980.*

Foreign Policy Study Foundation. *South Africa: Time Running Out. The Report of the Study Commission on U.S. Policy Toward Southern Africa.* Berkeley: University of California Press, 1981.*

Fredrickson, George M. *White Supremacy: A Comparative Study in American and South African History.* New York: Oxford University Press, 1981.

Gervasi, Tom. *Arsenal of Democracy: American Weapons Available for Export.* New York: Grove Press, 1978.*

Gittings, John. *The World and China: 1922-1972.* New York: Harper & Row, 1974.

Green, David. *The Containment of Latin America: A History of the Myths and Realities of the Good Neighbor Policy.* Chicago: Quadrangle Books, 1971.

Hammond, Thomas T. *Red Star over Afghanistan: The Communist Coup, The Soviet Invasion and Their Consequences.* Boulder, Colo.: Westview Press, 1983.*

Harrington, Michael. *The Vast Majority: A Journey to the World's Poor.* New York: Simon and Schuster, 1977.*

Harrison, James Pinckney. *The Endless War: Fifty Years of Struggle in Vietnam.* New York: The Free Press, 1982.

Herring, George C., Jr. *America's Longest War: The United States and Vietnam, 1950-1975.* New York: John Wiley & Sons, 1979.*

Iriye, Akira. *The Cold War in Asia: A Historical Introduction.* Englewood Cliffs, New Jersey: Prentice-Hall, Inc., 1974.*

Iriye, Akira, and Yonosuke Nagai, eds. *The Origins of the Cold War in Asia.* New York: Columbia University Press, 1977.

Kennan, George F. *The Cloud of Danger: Current Realities of American Foreign Policy.* Boston: Little, Brown and Company, 1977.

Kinzer, Stephen, and Stephen Schlesinger. *Bitter Fruit: The Untold Story of the American Coup in Guatemala.* New York: Doubleday & Company, Inc., 1982.

Kirkpatrick, Jeane J. *Dictatorships and Double Standards: Rationalism and Reason in Politics.* New York: Simon and Schuster, 1982.

Klare, Michael T. *War without End: American Planning for the Next Vietnams.* New York: Alfred A. Knopf, 1972.*

LaFeber, Walter. *The Panama Canal: The Crisis in Historical Perspective.* New York: Oxford University Press, 1978, 1979.*

———. *Inevitable Revolutions: The United States in Central America.* New York: W.W. Norton & Company, Inc., 1983.

Lansdale, Edward Geary. *In the Midst of Wars: An American's Mission to Southeast Asia.* New York: Harper & Row, 1972.

Lappé, Frances Moore, Joseph Collins, and David Kinley. *Aid as Obstacle: Twenty Questions about Our Foreign Aid and the Hungry.* San Francisco: Institute for Food and Development Policy, 1980.*

Lernoux, Penny. *Cry of the People: United States Involvement in the Rise of Fascism, Torture and Murder and the Persecution of the Catholic Church in Latin America.* Garden City, New York: Doubleday & Company, Inc., 1980.*

Lewy, Guenter. *America in Vietnam.* New York: Oxford University Press, 1978.*

Louis, William Roger. *Imperialism at Bay: The United States and the Decolonization of the British Empire, 1941-1945.* New York: Oxford University Press, 1978.

Phillips, David Atlee. *The Night Watch.* New York: Atheneum, 1977.

Pierre, Andrew J. *The Global Politics of Arms Sales.* Princeton: Princeton University Press, 1982.*

Selden, Mark, ed. *Remaking Asia: Essays on the American Uses of Power.* New York: Pantheon Books, 1974.*

Selden, Mark, and Edward Friedman, eds. *America's Asia: Dissenting Essays on Asian-American Relations.* New York: Pantheon Books, 1971.*

Shawcross, William. *Sideshow: Kissinger, Nixon and the Destruction of Cambodia.* New York: Simon and Schuster, 1979.*

Stockwell, John. *In Search of Enemies: A C.I.A. Story.* New York: W.W. Norton & Company, Inc., 1978.

Thomson, James C., Peter W. Stanley, and John Curtis Perry. *Sentimental Imperialists: The American Experience in East Asia.* New York: Harper & Row, 1981.*

Tucker, Robert W. *The Inequality of Nations.* New York: Basic Books, Inc., 1977.*

Wolpert, Stanley. *Roots of Confrontation in South Asia: Afghanistan, Pakistan, India and the Superpowers.* New York: Oxford University Press, 1982.

D. Nuclear War: Strategy, Weapons, and the Search for Arms Control

The books listed below document a distinct but accurate disproportion in writings about nuclear war strategies and weapons, *vis-à-vis* serious investigations on the subject of arms control, either nuclear or conventional. In many respects this also reflects the distorted national security priorities of both superpowers during the entire era of the Cold War.

Aldridge, Robert C. *First Strike: The Pentagon's Strategy for Nuclear War.* Boston: South End Press, 1983.*

Bader, William F. *The United States and the Spread of Nuclear Weapons.* New York: Pegasus, 1968.

Baker, David. *The Shape of Wars to Come.* New York: Stein and Day, 1982.

Bechhoefer, Bernhard G. *Postwar Negotiations for Arms Control.* Washington, D.C.: The Brookings Institution, 1961.

Berman, Robert P., and John C. Baker. *Soviet Strategic Forces: Requirements and Responses.* Washington, D.C.: The Brookings Institution, 1982.*

Betts, Richard K., ed. *Cruise Missiles: Technology, Strategy, Politics.* Washington, D.C.: The Brookings Institution, 1981.*

Blackett, P.M.S. *Studies of War: Nuclear and Conventional.* New York: Hill and Wang, 1962.

Brennan, Donald, ed. *Arms Control, Disarmament and National Security.* New York: George Braziller, 1961.

Brodie, Bernard. *War and Politics.* New York: The Macmillan Company, 1973.*

———, ed. *The Absolute Weapon: Atomic Power and World Order.* New York: Arno Press, 1977.

Brodie, Bernard, and Fawn M. Brodie. *From Crossbow to H-Bomb.* Bloomington: Indiana University Press, 1973.*

Canan, James. *War in Space.* New York: Harper & Row, 1982.

Clark, Ian. *Limited Nuclear War: Political Theory and War Conventions.* Princeton: Princeton University Press, 1982.

Clemens, Walter C., Jr. *The Arms Race and Sino-Soviet Relations.* Stanford, Calif.: The Hoover Institute on War, Revolution and Peace, 1968.

Cohen, Sam. *The Truth about the Neutron Bomb: The Inventor of the Bomb Speaks Out.* New York: William Morrow and Company, Inc., 1983.

Divine, Robert A. *Blowing on The Wind: the Nuclear Test Ban Debate, 1954-1960.* New York: Oxford University Press, 1978.

Dunn, Lewis A. *Controlling the Bomb: Nuclear Proliferation in the 1980s.* New Haven: Yale University Press, 1982.*

Dunnigan, James F. *How to Make War: A Comprehensive Guide to Modern Warfare.* New York: William Morrow and Company, 1982.*

Edwards, John. *Superweapon: The Making of MX.* New York: W.W. Norton & Company, Inc., 1982.

Egorov, Pavel Timofeevich, et al. *Civil Defense: A Soviet View.* Washington, D.C.: U.S. Government Printing Office, 1976.*

Ford, Daniel. *The Cult of the Atom: The Secret Papers of the Atomic Energy Commission.* New York: Simon and Schuster, 1982.

Freedman, Lawrence. *U.S. Intelligence and the Soviet Strategic Threat.* London: The Macmillan Company, 1977.

————. *The Evolution of Nuclear Strategy.* New York: St. Martin's Press, 1983.*

George, Alexander L., and Richard Smoke. *Deterrence in American Foreign Policy: Theory and Practice.* New York: Columbia University Press, 1974.*

George, Alexander L., David K. Hall, and William E. Simons. *The Limits of Coercive Diplomacy.* Boston: Little, Brown and Company, 1971.

Gilpin, Robert. *American Scientists and Nuclear Weapons Policy.* Princeton: Princeton University Press, 1962.

Glasstone, Samuel, and Philip J. Dolan, eds. *The Effects of Nuclear Weapons.* Washington, D.C.: U.S. Department of Defense, 1977.*

Goldman, Ralph M. *Arms Control and Peacekeeping: Feeling Safe in This World.* New York: Random House, Inc., 1982*

Gouré, Leon. *War Survival in Soviet Strategy: U.S.S.R. Civil Defense.* Coral Gables, Florida: University of Miami Press, 1976.*

Greenwood, Ted. *Making the MIRV: A Study of Defense Decision Making.* Cambridge, Mass.: Ballinger Publishing Company, 1975.

Harris, Robert, and Jeremy Paxman. *A Higher Form of Killing: The Secret Story of Chemical and Biological Warfare.* New York: Hill and Wang, 1982.

The Harvard Nuclear Study Group: Albert Carnesale, Paul Doty, Stanley Hoffmann, Samuel P. Huntington, Joseph S. Nye, Jr., and Scott D. Sagan. *Living With Nuclear Weapons.* Cambridge: Harvard University Press, 1983.*

Herken, Gregg. *The Winning Weapon: The Atomic Bomb in the Cold War, 1945-1950.* New York: Alfred A. Knopf, 1980.*

Holloway, David. *The Soviet Union and the Arms Race.* New Haven: Yale University Press, 1983.

Kahan, Jerome H. *Security in the Nuclear Age.* Washington, D.C.: The Brookings Institution, 1975.*

Kahn, Herman. *On Escalation: Metaphors and Scenarios.* New York: Frederick A. Praeger, 1965.

————. *On Thermonuclear War.* Princeton: Princeton University Press, 1961.

Kaldor, Mary. *The Baroque Arsenal.* New York: Hill and Wang, 1982.*

Kaldor, Mary, and Dan Smith, eds. *Disarming Europe.* London: The Merlin Press, 1982.*

Kaplan, Fred. *The Wizards of Armageddon: Strategists of the Nuclear Age.* New York: Simon and Schuster, 1983.

Karas, Thomas. *The New High Ground: Strategies and Weapons of Space-Age War.* New York: Simon and Schuster, 1983.

Kelleher, Catherine McArdle. *Germany and the Politics of Nuclear Weapons.* New York: Columbia University Press, 1975.

Kennan, George F. *The Nuclear Delusion: Soviet-American Relations in the Atomic Age.* New York: Pantheon Books, 1982.

Kerr, Thomas J. *Civil Defense in the U.S.: Bandaid for a Holocaust?* Boulder, Colo.: Westview Press, 1983.

Kissinger, Henry A. *Nuclear Weapons and Foreign Policy.* New York: Harper & Brothers, 1957.*

Legault, Albert, and George Lindsey. *The Dynamics of Nuclear Balance.* Ithaca: Cornell University Press, revised edition, 1976.

Lieberman, Joseph I. *The Scorpion and the Tarantula: The Struggle to Control Atomic Weapons.* Boston: Houghton Mifflin Company, 1970.

Lockwood, Jonathan Samuel. *The Soviet View of U.S. Strategic Doctrine: Implications for Decision Making.* New Brunswick, New Jersey: Transaction Books, 1983.

Mandelbaum, Michael. *The Nuclear Question: The United States and Nuclear Weapons, 1946-1976.* Cambridge: Cambridge University Press, 1979.*

_____. *The Nuclear Revolution: International Politics before and after Hiroshima.* Cambridge: Cambridge University Press, 1981.*

Markey, Edward J., and Douglas C. Waller. *Nuclear Peril: The Politics of Proliferation.* Cambridge, Mass.: Ballinger Publishing Company, 1982.

Morgan, Patrick M. *Deterrence: A Conceptual Analysis.* Beverly Hills, Calif.: Sage Publications, 1977.*

Morland, Howard. *The Secret That Exploded.* New York: Random House, Inc., 1981.

Moulton, Harland. *From Superiority to Parity: The United States and the Strategic Arms Race, 1961–1971.* Westport, Conn.: Greenwood Press, 1972.

Myrdal, Alva. *The Game of Disarmament: How the United States and Russia Run the Arms Race.* New York: Pantheon Books, 1982.*

Newhouse, John. *Cold Dawn: The Story of SALT.* New York: Holt, Rinehart and Winston, 1973.

O'Heffernan, Patrick, Amory B. Lovins, and L. Hunter Lovins. *The First World Nuclear War.* New York: William Morrow and Company, 1983.

Osgood, Robert E. *Limited War Revisited: Challenge to American Strategy.* Boulder, Colorado: Westview Press, 1979.

The Palme Commission: The Independent Commission on Disarmament and Security Issues. *Common Security: A Blueprint for Survival.* New York: Simon and Schuster, 1982.*

Panofsky, Wolfgang K. *Arms Control and SALT II.* Seattle: University of Washington Press, 1979.*

Polmar, Norman, and Thomas B. Allen. *Rickover.* New York: Simon and Schuster, 1981.

Pringle, Peter, and James Spigelman. *The Nuclear Barons.* New York: Holt, Rinehart and Winston, 1981.*

Pringle, Peter, and William Arkin. *SIOP: The Secret U.S. Plans for Nuclear War.* New York: W.W. Norton & Company, Inc., 1983.

Rathjens, George W., Abram Chayes, and J.P. Ruina. *Nuclear Arms Control Agreements: Process and Impact.* Washington, D.C.: Carnegie Endowment for International Peace, 1974.

Roberts, Chalmers M. *The Nuclear Years: The Arms Race and Arms Control, 1945-1970.* New York: Praeger Publishers, 1970.

Scheer, Robert, et al. *With Enough Shovels: Reagan, Bush and Nuclear War*. New York: Random House, Inc., 1982.*

Scoville, Herbert, Jr. *MX: Prescription for Disaster*. Cambridge: M.I.T. Press, 1981.*

Seaborg, Glenn T. *Kennedy, Khrushchev and The Test Ban*. Berkeley: University of California Press, 1982.*

Sherwin, Martin J. *A World Destroyed: The Atomic Bomb and the Grand Alliance*. New York: Alfred A. Knopf, 1975.*

Smith, Gerald. Doubletalk: The Story of the First Strategic Arms Limitation Talks. New York: Doubleday & Company, Inc., 1980.

Snyder, Glenn. *Deterrence and Defense: Toward a Theory of National Security*. Princeton: Princeton University Press, 1961.

Spanier, John W., and Joseph L. Nogee. *The Politics of Disarmament: A Study in Soviet-American Gamesmanship*. New York: Frederick A. Praeger, 1962.

Talbott, Strobe. *Endgame: The Inside Story of SALT II*. New York: Harper & Row, 1979, 1980.*

Tsipsis, Kosta, et al. *The Future of the Sea-Based Deterrent*. Cambridge: M.I.T. Press, 1974.*

Willrich, Mason, and John B. Rhinelander, eds. *SALT: The Moscow Agreements and Beyond*. New York: The Free Press, 1974.*

Wohlstetter, Albert, et al. *Swords from Plowshares: The Military Potential of Civilian Nuclear Energy*. Chicago: The University of Chicago Press, 1979.*

Wolfe, Thomas W. *The SALT Experience*. Cambridge, Mass.: Ballinger Publishing Company, 1979.

York, Herbert F. *The Advisors: Oppenheimer, Teller and the Superbomb*. San Francisco: W.H. Freeman and Company, 1976.

Yoshpe, Harry B. *Our Missing Shield: The U.S. Civil Defense Program in Historical Perspective*. Washington, D.C.: Federal Emergency Management Agency, 1981.*

Zuckerman, Solly. *Nuclear Illusion and Reality*. New York: The Viking Press, 1982.

E. What Constitutes Adequate Defense?

Aliano, Richard. *American Defense Policy from Eisenhower to Kennedy: The Politics of Changing Military Requirements*. Athens: Ohio University Press, 1975.*

Baskir, Lawrence M., and William A. Strauss. *Chance and Circumstance: The Draft, the War and the Vietnam Generation*. New York: Alfred A. Knopf, 1978.*

Borklund, Carl W. *Men of the Pentagon: From Forrestal to McNamara*. New York: Frederick Praeger, 1966.

Breyer, Siegfried and Norman Polmar. *Guide to the Soviet Navy*. Annapolis, Md.: U.S. Naval Institute Press, 1977.

Brown, Harold. *Thinking about National Security: Defense and Foreign Policy in a Dangerous World*. Boulder, Colo.: Westview Press, 1983.

Caraley, Demetrios. *The Politics of Military Unification: A Study of Conflict and the Policy Process*. New York: Columbia University Press, 1966.

Clausewitz, Karl von. *On War*. Edited and translated by Michael Howard and Peter Paret. Princeton: Princeton University Press, 1976.*

Cockburn, Andrew. *The Threat: Inside the Soviet Military Machine*. New York: Random House, Inc., 1983.

Collins, John M. *U.S. Defense Planning: A Critique*. Boulder, Colo.: Westview Press, Inc., 1982.*

Colton, Timothy J. *Commissars, Commanders and Civilian Authority: The Structure of Soviet Military Politics*. Cambridge: Harvard University Press, 1979.

Coulam, Robert. *The Illusions of Choice: Robert S. McNamara, the F-111 and the Problem of Weapons Acquisition Reform*. Princeton: Princeton University Press, 1971.

Davis, Vincent. *The Admirals' Lobby*. Chapel Hill: The University of North Carolina Press, 1967.

_____. *Postwar Defense Policy and the U.S. Navy, 1943-1946*. Chapel Hill: The University of North Carolina Press, 1966.

Donovan, Col. James A., U.S.M.C., Ret., ed. *U.S. Military Force-1980: An Evaluation by the Staff of the Center for Defense Information*. Washington: The Center for Defense Information, 1980.*

Enthoven, Alain, and K. Wayne Smith. *How Much Is Enough? Shaping the Defense Program, 1961-1969*. New York: Harper & Row, 1971.

Etzold, Thomas H. *Defense or Delusion? America's Military in the 1980s*. New York: Harper & Row, 1982.

Fallows, James. *National Defense*. New York: Random House, Inc., 1981.*

Fulbright, J. William. *The Pentagon Propaganda Machine*. New York: Liveright Publishing Corporation, 1970.

Halperin, Morton H. *Defense Strategies for the Seventies*. Boston: Little, Brown and Company, 1971.

Janowitz, Morris. *The Professional Soldier: A Social & Political Portrait*. New York: The Free Press, 1960.*

_____. *Sociology and the Military Establishment*. Beverly Hills, Calif.: Sage Publications, 1974.*

Jordan, Amos A., and William J. Taylor, Jr., et al. *American National Security: Policy and Process*. Baltimore: The Johns Hopkins University Press, 1981.*

Kanter, Arnold. *Defense Politics: A Budgetary Perspective*. Chicago: The University of Chicago Press, 1979.

Knorr, Klaus, ed. *Historical Dimensions of National Security Policy*. Lawrence: The University of Kansas Press, 1976.*

Kolodziej, Edward. *The Uncommon Defense and Congress, 1945-1963*. Columbus: Ohio State University Press, 1966.

Lee, William T. *The Estimation of Soviet Defense Expenditures, 1955-1975: An Unconventional Approach*. New York: Praeger Publishers, 1977.

Newhouse, John. *U.S. Troops in Europe*. Washington, D.C.: The Brookings Institution, 1971.

O'Connor, Raymond G., ed. *American Defense Policy in Perspective: From Colonial Times to the Present Day*. New York: John Wiley & Sons, 1965.*

O'Sullivan, John, and Alan M. Meckler, eds. *The Draft and Its Enemies: A Documentary History*. Urbana: University of Illinois Press, 1974.

Reichart, John F., and Steven R. Sturm, eds. *American Defense Policy*. Baltimore: The Johns Hopkins University Press, 5th ed., 1982.

Ropp, Theodore. *War in the Modern World*. Durham: Duke University Press, 1958.

Schilling, Warner R., Paul Y. Hammond, and Glenn H. Snyder. *Strategy, Politics and Defense Budgets*. New York: Columbia University Press, 1962.

Sherry, Michael S. *Preparing for the Next War: American Plans for Postwar Defense, 1941-1945*. New Haven: Yale University Press, 1977.

Smith, Perry McCoy. *The Air Force Plans for Peace, 1941-1945*. Baltimore: The Johns Hopkins University Press, 1970.

Sokolovskiy, V.D. *Soviet Military Strategy*. Translated and edited by Harriet Fast Scott. New York: Crane, Russak and Company, 3d ed. 1975.*

Suvorov, Viktor. *Inside the Soviet Army*. New York: The Macmillan Company, Inc., 1982.

Trewhitt, Henry. *McNamara: His Ordeal at the Pentagon*. New York: Harper & Row, 1971.

Vagts, Alfred. *A History of Militarism: Civilian and Military*. New York: The Free Press, 1959.*

Yarmolinsky, Adam, and Gregory D. Foster. *Paradoxes of Power: The Military Establishment in the Eighties*. Bloomington: Indiana University Press, 1983.

F. The Socioeconomic Implications of the Military Budget

Ackerman, Frank. *Reaganomics: Rhetoric v. Reality*. Boston: South End Press, 1982.*

Bluestone, Barry and Bennett Harrison. *The Deindustrialization of America: Plant Closings, Community Abandonment and the Dismantling of Basic Industry*. New York: Basic Books, Inc., 1982.

Blum, John Morton. *V Was for Victory: Politics and American Culture during World War II*. New York: Harcourt Brace Jovanovich, 1976.*

Bowles, Samuel, and Herbert Gintis. *Schooling in Capitalist America: Educational Reform and the Contradictions of Economic Life*. New York: Basic Books, Inc., 1976.*

Bowles, Samuel, David M. Gordon, and Thomas E. Weisskopf. *Beyond The Waste Land: A Democratic Alternative To Economic Decline*. Garden City, New York: Anchor Press/Doubleday, 1983.

Calleo, David. *The Imperious Economy*. Cambridge: Harvard University Press, 1982.

Calleo, David, and Benjamin M. Rowland. *America and the World Political Economy: Atlantic Dreams and National Realities*. Bloomington: Indiana University Press, 1973.*

Clark, Wilson, and Jake Page. *Energy, Vulnerability and War: Alternatives for America*. New York: W.W. Norton & Company, Inc., 1981.*

Eckes, Alfred E., Jr. *A Search for Solvency: Bretton Woods and the International Monetary System, 1941-1971*. Austin: University of Texas Press, 1975.

Gansler, Jacques S. *The Defense Industry*. Cambridge: M.I.T. Press, 1980.*

Goldman, Marshall I. *U.S.S.R. in Crisis: The Failure of an Economic System*. New York: W.W. Norton & Company, Inc., 1983.

Greider, William. *The Education of David Stockman and Other Americans*. New York: E.P. Dutton, 1982.*

Harrington, Michael. *Toward a Democratic Left: A Radical Program for a New Majority*. New York: The Macmillan Company, 1968.*

_____. *Decade of Decision: The Crisis of the American System*. New York: Simon and Schuster, 1980.*

Hayden, Tom. *The American Future: New Visions beyond Old Frontiers*. Boston: South End Press, 1981.*

Kaldor, Mary. *European Defense Industries: National and International Implications*. Brighton, England: Institute for the Study of International Organization, 1972.*

_____. *The Disintegrating West*. New York: Hill and Wang, 1978.*

Klose, Kevin. *Hammer and Sickle*. New York: W.W. Norton & Company, 1983.

Leader, Stefan, and Shelah, et al. *What Kind of Guns Are They Buying for Your Butter?* New York: William M. Morrow Company, 1983.

Lekachman, Robert. *Greed Is Not Enough: Reaganomics.* New York: Pantheon Books, 1982.*

———. *Economists at Bay: Why the Experts Will Never Solve Your Problems.* New York: McGraw-Hill Book Company, 1976.

Melman, Seymour. *The Permanent War Economy.* New York: Simon and Schuster, 1976.*

———. *Pentagon Capitalism: The Management of the New Imperialism.* New York: McGraw-Hill Book Company, 1970.*

Patterson, James T. *America's Struggle against Poverty, 1900-1980.* Cambridge: Harvard University Press, 1981.

Piven, Frances Fox, and Richard A. Cloward. *The New Class War.* New York: Pantheon Books, 1982.*

———. *Regulating the Poor: The Functions of Public Welfare.* New York: Pantheon Books, 1971.*

———. *The Politics of Turmoil: Essays on Poverty, Race and the Urban Class.* New York: Pantheon Books, 1974.*

Polenberg, Richard. *War and Society: The United States, 1941-1945.* Philadelphia: J.B. Lippincott Company, 1972.*

———. *One Nation Divisible: Class, Race and Ethnicity in the United States Since 1938.* New York: The Viking Press, 1980.*

Sexton, Patricia Cayo, and Brendan Sexton. *Blue Collars and Hard Hats: the Working Class and The Future of American Politics.* New York: Random House, Inc., 1971.*

Steinfels, Peter. *The Neo-Conservatives: The Men Who Are Changing America's Politics.* New York: Simon and Schuster, 1979.*

Stevens, Robert Warren. *Vain Hopes, Grim Realities: the Economic Consequences of The Vietnam War.* New York: New Viewpoints, 1976.

Thurow, Lester C. *The Zero-Sum Society: Distribution & the Possibilities for Economic Change.* New York: Basic Books, Inc., 1980.*

———. *Dangerous Currents: The State of Economics.* New York: Random House, Inc., 1983.

Tsongas, Paul. *The Road from Here: Liberalism and Realities in the 1980s.* New York: Alfred A. Knopf, 1981.*

Wolfe, Alan. *America's Impasse: The Rise and Fall of the Politics of Growth.* New York: Pantheon Books, 1981.*

Yergin, Daniel and Martin Hillenbrand, eds. *Global Insecurity: A Strategy for Energy and Economic Renewal.* Boston: Houghton Mifflin Company, 1982.*

G. The Moral Implications of the Military Budget: Citizen Responsibility v. Government Intimidation

To date, there has been no overview history of the peace movements in America, especially those in recent times, but some of the better episodic histories are listed below. A useful list of many of the major peace and anti-militarist groups currently active in the United States can be found in the book published by Senators Edward M. Kennedy and Mark O. Hatfield: *Freeze! How You Can Prevent Nuclear War* (New York: Bantam Books, 1982).* The religious press in recent years has begun to take an active interest in the fundamental issue of war and peace in the nuclear age. The coverage in such religious periodicals as *The National Catholic Reporter, Sojourners,* and *Christianity and Crisis* has been substantial.

The occupational hazard of dedicated, persevering citizen activism on behalf of peace and human dignity has often been one of personal persecution or political prosecution. There has always been the justified concern, sometimes matched by reality, that the government will respond in a repressive fashion, in order to preserve the position of those who would dictate our destiny rather than allow the democratic process to be the true determinant of our future history. An important introduction to the government's repressive role can be found in Frank J. Donner's *The Age of Surveillance: The Aims and Methods of America's Political Intelligence System* (New York: Alfred A. Knopf, 1980).* Two outstanding recent biographies that superbly document the perils faced by those who struggle for peace and nonviolent social change are: Nick Salvatore, *Eugene V. Debs: Citizen and Socialist* (Urbana: University of Illinois Press, 1982) and Stephen B. Oates, *Let The Trumpet Sound: The Life of Martin Luther King, Jr.* (New York: Harper & Row, 1982).

In addition to the works cited above, and those mentioned earlier in the book, the reader might also consult the following for further information and insights:

Bamford, James. *The Puzzle Palace: A Report on America's Most Secret Agency.* Boston: Houghton Mifflin Company, 1982.

Beer, Francis A. *Peace against War: The Ecology of International Violence.* San Francisco: W.H. Freeman and Company, 1981.*

Berrigan, Daniel. *Ten Commandments for the Long Haul.* Nashville, Tenn.: Abingdon, 1981.

Berrigan, Philip. *A Punishment for Peace.* New York: The Macmillan Company, 1969.

_____. *Widen the Prison Gates: Writings from Jails, April 1970 - December 1972.* New York: Simon and Schuster, 1973.

Brock, Peter. *Pacifism in the United States: From the Colonial Era to the First World War.* Princeton: Princeton University Press, 1968.

Caldicott, Helen. *Nuclear Madness.* New York: Bantam Books, 1981.*

Chatfield, Charles. *For Peace and Justice: Pacifism in America, 1914-1941.* Knoxville: The University of Tennessee Press, 1971.

_____, ed. *Peace Movements in America.* New York: Schocken Books, 1973.*

Clecak, Peter. *America's Quest for the Ideal Self: Dissent and Fulfillment in the 60s and 70s.* New York: Oxford University Press, 1983.

Chevian, Eric, M.D., et al. (for the International Physicians for the Prevention of Nuclear War). *Last Aid: The Medical Dimensions of Nuclear War.* San Francisco: W.H. Freeman and Company, 1982.*

Committee for the Compilation of Materials on Damage Caused by the Atomic Bombs in Hiroshima and Nagasaki: The Physical, Medical and Social Effects of the Bombings. Translated by Eisei Ishikawa and David L. Swain. New York: Basic Books, Inc., 1981.*

Dolbeare, Kenneth M., and Patricia Dolbeare, with Jane Hadley. *American Ideologies: The Competing Political Beliefs of the 1970s.* Chicago: Markham/Rand McNally Publishing Company, 2d ed. 1973.*

Freeman, Leslie J. *Nuclear Witnesses: Insiders Speak Out*. New York: W.W. Norton & Company, Inc., 1981.*

Frei, Daniel. *Risks of Unintentional Nuclear War*. London: Allanheld, Osmun, 1983.*

Gofman, John W. *Radiation and Human Health*. San Francisco: Sierra Club Books, 1981.

Goldstein, Robert Justin. *Political Repression in Modern America: 1870 to the Present*. Cambridge, Mass.: Schenkman Publishing Co., 1978.*

Halperin, Morton H., Jerry J. Berman, Robert L. Borosage, and Christine M. Marwick. *The Lawless State: the Crimes of The U.S. Intelligence Agencies*. New York: Penguin Books, 1976.*

Hilgartner, Stephen, Richard C. Bell, and Rory O'Connor. *Nukespeak: The Selling of Nuclear Technology in America*. San Francisco: Sierra Club Books, 1982.

Kaku, Michio, and Jennifer Trainer, eds. *Nuclear Power: Both Sides. The Best Arguments for and against the Most Controversial Technology*. New York: W.W. Norton & Company, 1982.

Katz, Arthur M. *Life after Nuclear War: The Economic and Social Impacts of Nuclear Attacks on the United States*. Cambridge, Mass.: Ballinger Publishing Company, 1982.*

Lifton, Robert J. *Death in Life: The Survivors of Hiroshima*. New York: Random House, Inc., 1967.*

_____. *Home from the War. Vietnam Veterans: Neither Victims Nor Executioners*. New York: Simon and Schuster, 1974.*

Lifton, Robert J., and Richard Falk. *Indefensible Weapons: the Political and Psychological Case against Nuclearism*. New York: Basic Books, Inc., 1982.*

Marks, John. *The Search for the "Manchurian Candidate": The C.I.A. and Mind Control*. New York: Times Books, 1979.*

Merton, Thomas. *The Nonviolent Alternative*. Edited and with an Introduction by Gordon C. Zahn. New York: Farrar . Straus . Giroux, 1980.

Miller, William D. *Dorothy Day: A Biography*. New York: Harper & Row, 1982.

Minnion, John and Philip Bolsevar, eds. (for the Campaign for Nuclear Disarmament). *The CND Story*. London: Allison and Beasley, 1983.*

Molander, Roger (for Ground Zero Project). *Nuclear War: What's in It for You?* New York: Pocket Books, 1982.*

_____. *What about the Russians—and Nuclear War?* New York: Pocket Books, 1983.*

Powers, Thomas. *The Man Who Kept the Secrets: Richard Helms & the C.I.A.*. New York: Alfred A. Knopf, 1979.*

_____. *Thinking about the Next War*. New York: Alfred A. Knopf, 1982.

Schell, Jonathan. *The Fate of the Earth*. New York: Alfred A. Knopf, 1982.*

Shapiro, Fred C. *Radwaste*. New York: Random House, Inc., 1981.

Shatz, Marshall S. *Soviet Dissent in Historical Perspective*. Cambridge: Cambridge University Press, 1981.

Solomon, Norman, and Harvey Wasserman. *Killing Our Own: The Disaster of America's Experience with Atomic Radiation*. New York: Delacorte, 1982.

Sullivan, William C., with Bill Brown. *The Bureau: My Thirty Years with Hoover's F.B.I.* New York: W.W. Norton & Company, 1979.*

Theoharis, Athan G. *Spying on Americans: Political Surveillance from Hoover to the Huston Plan*. Philadelphia: Temple University Press, 1978.

Thompson, Edward P. *Beyond the Cold War: A New Approach to the Arms Race and Nuclear Annihilation*. New York: Pantheon Books, 1982.*

Thompson, Edward P., and Dan Smith, eds. *Protest and Survive*. New York: Monthly Review Press, 1981.*

Ungar, Sanford J. *F.B.I.* Boston: Little, Brown and Company, 1976.*

Wallis, Jim. *Waging Peace: A Handbook for the Struggle to Abolish Nuclear Weapons*. New York: Harper & Row, 1982.*

Walzer, Michael. *Just and Unjust Wars: A Moral Argument with Historical Illustrations*. New York: Basic Books, Inc., 1977.*

_____. *Obligations: Essays on Disobedience, War and Citizenship*. Cambridge: Harvard University Press, 1982.*

Wise, David. *The American Police State: The Government against the People*. New York: Random House, Inc., 1976.*

Wittner, Lawrence S. *Rebels against War: The American Peace Movement, 1941-1960*. New York: Columbia University Press, 1969.

Zinn, Howard. *The Politics of History*. Boston: Beacon Press, 1970.

_____. *Disobedience and Democracy: Nine Fallacies on Law and Order*. New York: Random House, Inc., 1968.*

INDEX

ABOUT THE AUTHORS

CONGRESSMAN RONALD V. DELLUMS represents the 8th Congressional District of California. A veteran of the U.S. Marine Corps, he earned a B.A. degree from San Francisco State College and a M.S.W. degree from the University of California at Berkeley. He is currently a senior Member of the House Armed Services Committee, and is Chair of its Subcommittee on Military Installations and Facilities. He was the first Member of Congress to call for termination of all funding for the MX Missile in 1977, and the Pershing II Missile in 1979. He was an advisor to President Jimmy Carter on the decision to abandon the B-1 Bomber in 1977, and was an original co-sponsor of the Nuclear Freeze resolution in the U.S. House of Representatives.

H. LEE HALTERMAN earned his B.A. in Political Science from the University of California at Berkeley, and his Juris Doctor degree from its Boalt Hall School of Law. A member of the bars of the State of California and the U.S. District Court for the Northern District of California, he served as a legal officer (intern) at the International Commission of Justice in Geneva, Switzerland. He has worked for Congressman Dellums since Dellums' first campaign for Congress in 1970.

R. H. (MAX) MILLER is a U.S. Army overseas veteran and former Peace Corps training instructor. He taught at the university level for fourteen years, specializing in U.S. Diplomatic History and National Security affairs. He has written and lectured extensively in the United States and Europe about the Cold War era, the nuclear arms race, Third World interventionism and contemporary politics. He has worked for Congressman Dellums since 1979.

DATE DUE

DEMCO 38-296

Please remember that this is a library book,
and that it belongs only temporarily to each
person who uses it. Be considerate. Do
not write in this, or any, library book.